Pornography
And
Censorship

Pornography And Censorship

edited by David Copp
and Susan Wendell

 Prometheus Books

700 East Amherst St. Buffalo, New York 14215

Then we must not only compel our poets, on pain of expulsion, to make their poetry the express image of noble character; we must also supervise craftsmen of every kind and forbid them to leave the stamp of baseness, licence, meanness, unseemliness, on painting and sculpture, or building, or any other work of their hands; and anyone who cannot obey shall not practice his art in our commonwealth. We would not have our Guardians grow up among representations of moral deformity, as in some foul pasture where, day after day, feeding on every poisonous weed they would, little by little, gather insensibly a mass of corruption in their very souls.

Plato, Republic *401 b (Cornford translation)*

. . . the only purpose for which power can be rightfully exercised over any member of a civilized community, against his will, is to prevent harm to others.

John Stuart Mill, On Liberty

Pornography is the undiluted essence of antifemale propaganda.

Susan Brownmiller, Against Our Will: Men, Women and Rape

. . . there is today in America substantial and growing disagreement regarding many questions of sexual and personal morality, . . . In this context, pornography can be seen as the unique medium of a vision of sexuality, a "pornotopia"—a view of sensual delight in the erotic celebration of the body, a concept of easy freedom without consequences, a fantasy of timelessly repetitive indulgence.

David A. J. Richards, The Moral Criticism of Law

New Concepts in Human Sexuality

Vern L. Bullough, Series Editor

Published 1983 by Prometheus Books
700 East Amherst Street, Buffalo, NY 14215

Library of Congress Catalog Number: 83-61031
ISBN 0-87975-181-9 (Cloth)
ISBN 0-87975-182-7 (Paper)

Published in the United States of America

Contents

PART THREE: JUDICIAL ESSAYS

PREFACE

Pornography may seem an odd topic for a book edited by two philosophers. The topic interests us because of the philosophical issues to which it is related, and because of the questions that have recently been raised about pornography, especially by the women's movement and the so-called "moral majority." However, the book is interdisciplinary, and the reader will find that it offers useful and important information as well as non-technical philosophical discussions.

The purpose of this anthology is to facilitate rational and informed debate on the topic of pornography and censorship. The book is unusual in bringing together empirical studies by social scientists, conceptual studies by philosophers, and judicial essays. This reflects our conviction that wise decision making on public issues requires at least the elements of empirical knowledge, philosophical clarity, and an understanding of the difficulties of formulating principles that apply in acceptable ways to specific situations.

Pornography has long been thought to raise ethical or moral issues, and proposals to censor it raise obvious issues of social policy. These are the main issues addressed in the philosophical essays collected in Part One. The essays are by contemporary philosophers in the Anglo-American tradition, and the issues are approached from a number of theoretical points of view. It is worth mentioning, though, that the essays are secular; those whose thoughts on the morality of pornography are based on a theological position, or on faith, will not find their underlying viewpoints discussed here. It is also worth mentioning that there are no examples here of the large polemical literature on pornography. But those who wish their views to be based on reasons and, in particular, on reasons that do not presuppose any particular theology, will appreciate these essays. It is not possible to think deeply about the moral and social policy issues of pornography and censorship without considering basic questions which are philosophical in nature.

Many of the important questions that arise in connection with the moral and social policy issues are empirical, rather than conceptual or philosophical. Part Two contains essays by social scientists that address the most central of these questions, viz., whether the wide availability of pornography, or of some kinds of pornography, has harmful consequences. Everyone will see this question as bearing on the moral and social policy issues of pornography and censorship. Some may see it as the pivotal question, the question whose answer will determine the proper position on the moral and social policy issues. Yet, despite its centrality, and despite the fact that Part Two includes some of the best and most recent work on the topic, the question cannot yet be given a definitive answer. The interpretation of the empirical results is itself a problem, and raises methodological issues that are themselves philosophical in nature. These methodological issues are addressed in the introductory essay and in several of the articles.

If academia sometimes provides a grindstone for social policy, the judiciary is one of the cutting edges. The essays in Part Three are selections from judicial decisions in three countries. Some are from landmark decisions. But they were chosen less for their legal significance than for their argumentative qualities and for the theoretical issues they raise. Social policy is sometimes formulated, and more often applied, by the courts. These essays illustrate how this process can work, while at the same time they approach the philosophical issues in the context of specific legal problems.

This anthology represents a small selection from a large body of writing that bears on pornography and censorship either directly or indirectly. We believe we have collected here some of the best of the most recent articles. Classic works on free speech and the enforcement of morality are well known and readily available. We draw the reader's attention to John Stuart Mill's *On Liberty*, and the recent famous debate between Lord Patrick Devlin, writing in *The Enforcement of Morals*, and H. L. A. Hart, writing in *Law, Liberty and Morality*.

The idea for this book originated in the fall of 1979 with a conference on pornography which was sponsored by the Philosophy Department and the office of Continuing Studies at the editors' university. We would like to thank those who helped and advised at that time, and especially Margit Nance and Ehor Boyanowsky. Since that time we have incurred many additional debts of gratitude. Raymond Bradley urged us to take seriously the idea of preparing this anthology; Bernard Williams gave us very welcome advice and help; Lorenne Clark was kind enough to tailor her essay to the book; Steven L. Mitchell, college division editor of Prometheus, had many helpful suggestions. Much tedious work was done for us by Moira Gutteridge, Bonnelle Strickling, Merrily Allanson, and Kalen Wild. Finally, our preparation of the book was enlivened by flaming discussions with spouses and friends, especially Susan Lagacé, Bob Hadley, and Bonnelle Strickling.

David Copp and Susan Wendell

David Copp

Pornography and Censorship: An Introductory Essay

Should pornography and obscenity be controlled in society, and, if so, what kind of control is desirable? This issue deeply concerns and excites the passions of people in many countries. Of course, many would think pornography to be one of the least pressing of the issues that face us in the late twentieth century. Indeed, some regard pornography as raising only trivial issues in itself, and as becoming important only as other people inflate its importance to the point where they are prepared to interfere with fundamental democratic freedoms. Nevertheless, many regard pornography as an affront to the dignity and self-respect of half of the human species, if not as creating the risk of serious harm to women through its effects on its users. Still others consider pornography to be an evil in itself, regardless of its possible effects on others, and think that its widespread use is symptomatic of a crisis of values in Western society. Anyone could perhaps agree at the outset that pornography is of interest and importance, if only because each of the various positions regarding it is held with such conviction, and because the issue of whether and how to control pornography is connected with fundamental issues such as the desirable scope of the rights of free speech and freedom of choice.

It is difficult to make a wise decision regarding the control of pornography, for the debate tends to be distorted by impassioned rhetoric and misinformation. A wise decision would require at least empirical information and philosophical clarity. In this respect, the issue of whether and how to control pornography merely illustrates a general fact about wise decision making on matters of public policy: a wise decision combines political and ethical principles and factual information. Philosophy can help us to assess proposed principles and to assess the bearing of various factual claims on the social issues. Empirical investigation can help us assess these claims. But neither philosophical reflection nor empirical investigation is alone sufficient.

This introduction discusses the interplay between the empirical and the philosophical issues. It reviews some of the ethical and political principles that provide the logical link between factual claims and conclusions about the control of pornography. Finally, it aims to clarify some of the central concepts and to make a modest contribution to the assessment of various positions.

1. PORNOGRAPHY AND OBSCENITY

A sensible discussion of the issue of pornography and censorship obviously depends on our having either a shared conception of pornography or, at least, a clear understanding of our differences. Consider, for instance, the empirical question whether the free availability of pornography in society would have harmful consequences. This question could not be answered without specifying what will be counted as pornography. Moreover, the account of pornography used to answer this question will affect the bearing the answer has on the public policy issue that concerns us. That is, if we who pose the public policy issue have a conception of pornography different from that employed by researchers who are attempting to answer the empirical question, their answers may be misleading. Also, philosophical positions about the issue of pornography and censorship may be misleading in the context of the popular debate if the philosophical and popular conceptions of pornography differ.

Conceptions of pornography do in fact differ quite widely. And even when *conceptions* of pornography are similar, there are differences in what things are *counted* as pornographic. It could happen that two people share a single *conception* of pornography as, say, sexually explicit depictions that violate the proper canons of modesty; yet, because of different beliefs about the canons of modesty, they differ on whether a particular depiction is pornographic. In short, two kinds of disagreement occur: there are differences about the conception on the one hand; and there are differences about the "extension" of the concept on the other hand, differences that may occur between people even if they share a conception. These two kinds of disagreement cause confusion and, in fact, may make it misleading to describe the debate as a debate about pornography. The latter description may suggest, perhaps falsely, that one specifiable kind of phenomenon is the sole subject of the debate.

However, insofar as it is true that one kind of phenomenon is a shared subject of debate, it is clear that that phenomenon consists of at least depictions of sexual organs and behavior. The word "pornography" was originally used in English to refer to descriptions of the lives, manners, etc., of prostitutes and their patrons. It now refers to obscene or unchaste depictions in literature, art, and so on.[1] It is true that depictions can be obscene without having to do with sex. For instance, depictions of human excremental functions are often regarded as obscene because they are offensive to modesty; but the etymology of the word "pornography" suggests that its primary use should be to refer to obscene depictions of *sexual* organs or behavior. We need the qualification that the depictions be *obscene* because we do not regard depictions in medical or sociological studies of sexual organs or behavior as pornographic; nor are they obscene. Accordingly, in this introduction I will take pornography to consist in obscene depictions of sexual organs or behavior.

It should be clear that poems, novels, plays, movies, photographs, and staged acts can all be, or include, depictions of sexual subjects. Most people would regard as pornographic explicit depictions of violent sadomasochistic sex and explicit depictions of certain of the more recherché sex acts. The mere exposure of human mammary and genital organs would less generally be regarded as obscene. Then again, certain novels that once were generally found obscene, such as *Lady Chatterley's Lover* or *Ulysses*, are probably less widely considered so today. One person's "pornographic passage" may be another person's "realistic depiction of an important part of life."

One conclusion that might mistakenly be drawn from such disagreements would be that porngoraphy is "in the eye of the beholder," that pornography relative to a given person consists of sexual depictions that *offend* that person. Of course, people are often deeply offended and affronted by depictions they regard as pornographic. It may even be that we would not think of anything as pornographic if we believed that no one is *ever* offended by a sexual depiction. However, some people may be quite detached about what they regard as pornographic; it need not cause one shocked sensibility, embarrassment, or feelings of anger, disgust, or what have you. The possibility of having this kind of detached attitude suggests that a belief rather than an emotional reaction is central to one's decision that a given sexual depiction is obscene, and hence pornographic. The belief would be that there are standards or canons that delineate what may not properly or appropriately be depicted, as well as the manner of appropriate depiction. I will call these "canons of propriety" or of "appropriateness," leaving open for the moment many questions about their nature and justification. Different people might accept different standards in relation to sexual depictions.

of modesty; others would regard much of the allegedly pornographic as merely erotic. The difference would be neither merely a difference in aesthetic reaction, nor merely a difference in emotional reaction, though both of these could be involved. The central difference would lie in what is believed to be the *correct* standard of propriety or of appropriateness in relation to sexual depictions.

I am proposing first that pornography consists in obscene sexual depictions, and second, that the obscenity of a sexual depiction is determined in relation to a canon or standard of propriety or appropriateness that governs sexual depictions. The claim, for example that *lysses* is pornographic would imply that *Ulysses* contains obscene sexual depictions. This would imply in turn that the sexual depictions contained in *Ulysses* violate a standard of appropriateness governing sexual depictions.

The standards of propriety relevant to the concept of pornography govern the *sexual* nature of what is depicted. Depictions may be obscene for other reasons. For instance, gluttony is arguably obscene, as would be an explicit portrayal of gluttony.[2] Nevertheless, even if it were obscene, a depiction of gluttony would not be pornographic properly speaking. It would not be pornographic even if it also portrayed sexual behavior, provided that the latter aspect of it were within the bounds of appropriateness. In this way, sexual depictions may be obscene without being pornographic. The obscenity of a sexual depiction, if the depiction is indeed pornographic, depends upon the sexual nature of what it depicts.

It will be worthwhile to consider briefly other accounts of the concepts of pornography and obscenity. We will shortly see a need to qualify my proposal. I have already considered in passing the notion that obscenity is a matter of causing offense. I agree that, if one regards a sexual depiction as obscene, it typically will cause one offense. But it may not. Even if it does, one presumably would think that one is *justified* in taking offense *because* the depiction is obscene and pornographic, not that the depiction's being obscene depends on one's being offended. One would not think that if one became *desensitized* to the muck, such that one's feelings were no longer offended, then it would no longer be obscene and no longer be pornographic! My proposal attempts to explain why a depiction's being pornographic would justify a person in being offended. In my view, one's offense would be justified or appropriate precisely because a pornographic depiction, being obscene, would violate a standard of propriety.

The British Committee on Obscenity and Pornography, a committee chaired by the philosopher Bernard Williams, argued for a different position in its recent report.[3] The committee held that a pornographic representation combines two features:

> it has a certain function or intention, to arouse its audience sexually, and also a certain content, explicit representations of sexual material (organs, postures,

activity, etc.). A work has to have both this function and this content to be a piece of pornography.

Here is a conception of pornography different from what I recommend. Ann Garry and Joel Feinberg propose similar characterizations in their papers for this volume. My disagreements with characterizations of this kind are threefold. However, a preliminary problem arises because of the difficulty of the notion of a function or intention of a representation or depiction. In order to discuss the committee's recommendation, I will assume that the intention "of a representation" is simply the intention of the person who made it, and that the "function" of a represenation is its usual effect. On this interpretation, I have three differences with the committee. In the first place, a depiction can be pornographic even if it has neither the intention nor the function of arousing its audience sexually. There can be pornography that is unintentional. A pornographer may naively think that he is within the bounds of propriety, and may intend merely to describe a love affair. Nevertheless, unacceptable explicitness may make his work pornographic. Nor need his work actually arouse its audience; instead it may provoke embarassed laughter. In fact, most people may find some of the most offensive material they woudl regard as pornographic not to be sexually arousing at all. In the second place, I do not think that *explicit* sexual content is *conceptually* necessary. Prudish people do not contradict themselves in regarding as pornographic works that they would agree are not explicitly sexual, works that are merely suggestive, or that contain certain kinds of sexual metaphor. Of course, they may thereby show themselves to have somewhat exaggerated and unrealistic beliefs about standards of propriety. If so, then the mistake they make would consist in accepting implausible standards of propriety, not in failing to grasp the concept of pornography. Finally, as the committee itself would recognize, a work may possess the above pair of characteristics without being pornographic. For example, clinical aids to arousal, and much that is merely erotic, may possess both the relevant function and the relevant content. However, representations of these kinds are not pornographic if they remain within the bounds of appropriate standards of propriety.

Some would claim that the pornographic consists in depictions of violence. I think that this is a misleading use of the term "pornographic," a use that departs too far from etymology. However, certain depictions of violence may be thought *obscene* in that, like certain sexual depictions, they may be thought to transgress appropriate standards of propriety. Hence, speaking metaphorically, we can recognize the possibility of a so-called "pornography" of violence, analogous in some ways to the pornography of sex. Nevertheless, I do not find the metaphor illuminating.

My co-editor Susan Wendell uses the phrase "coercive pornography" in her paper for this volume. On her usage, depictions of "unjustified physical coercion of human beings" will, with some exceptions, count as "pornographic," even if the depictions are not *sexual* depictions. Expressions of opinion "recommending or condoning" either unjustified physical coercion or sexual acts between adults and children also will count as "pornographic." This will be so even if the expressions of opinion are not, and do not include, *depictions* or *representations* of the acts recommended or condoned. Both of these features of Wendell's usage depart from the term's usual meaning. The reader needs to notice that Wendell uses the phrase "coercive pornography" as a kind of technical term, and that it is not used literally.

It is a feature of the account I am recommending that a judgment that a work is pornographic implies a normative judgment to the effect that the work itself, or perhaps that the work in its usual context, violates the standards of appropriateness that govern the depiction of sexual matters. In particular, I think it is implied that the work violates *ethical* standards of appropriateness. However, I do not need to insist on this. Some might conceive of pornography as a violation of an esthetic standard or of a standard of etiquette, rather than as a violation of some moral standard. I can agree that there is a conception of a pornography of the unesthetic as well as a conception of a pornography of immorality. I do insist, however, that the latter conception be taken seriously. Those who are most affronted, offended, and rendered indignant by pornography do not conceive of the offending sexual depiction merely as esthetically displeasing. They conceive of the offending material as somehow immoral. Some see the popularity of certain forms of explicit sexual material as indicating a crisis in the values of our Western societies, as signaling the loss of certain sexual virtues. E. J. Mishan is concerned for the "moral tone" of society and writes of the need for "moral improvements."[4] D. H. Lawrence says that one can recognize "genuine pornography" by the unpardonable insult it offers to sex and the human spirit. It makes human nudity and sex "ugly, cheap, nasty and degraded."[5] Others see certain types of explicit sexual material as dehumanizing women or as undermining respect for women. Susan Brownmiller asserts that "pornography is the undiluted essence of antifemale propaganda."[6] It appears to me that these writers mean that pornography violates certain moral standards, so I think that the moral conception is important and indeed central to the debate. On this conception, pornography consists in sexual depictions that trangress ethical canons of appropriateness or propriety.

On the moral conception, if there were *no* ethical standards governing sexual depictions, then nothing would be *truly* pornography. Consider a person who thought that no depiction could be improper simply because it is a sexual depiction, or because of its sexual content, or because of the manner in which it depicted a sexual matter, or because of the context of its display or use: a person who thought there could be "nothing wrong" in a sexual depiction per se.

I think such a person would not want to call a sexual depiction "porno-graphic." Such a person would mentally put "scare-quotes" around the word, if he used it at all, to indicate that he was using it to refer to what is standardly *believed* to be pornographic. I concede, of course, that there is such a scare-quotes use of "pornography" that corresponds to what I will call the "neutral conception." One who is skeptical about standards of propriety would tend to employ the word to refer to sexual depictions that are *standardly* or *typically believed* in a certain reference group to violate standards of propriety or appropriateness.

It should be evident from this discussion that there is room for a good deal of confusion in the debate about pornography. Consider the question about the harmfulness of pornography. Given the disagreement about which depictions are in fact pornographic, if any, it would perhaps be best to interpret this question in light of the neutral conception of pornography, that is, to read the question as if "pornography" were being employed in the scare-quotes use. I think that this is how Berl Kutchinsky's work should be understood. However, some researchers employ different criteria. For instance, in some cases the effects of "erotic" or sexually arousing material are studied, and in others sexually explicit material is taken to be porno-graphic.[7] Kutchinsky's work has been criticized on the apparent ground that the material whose effects it studies is not "truly pornographic."[8] But the question of what is truly pornographic raises questions that are not simply empirical.

The reader must take caution in studying the essays included in this book. Different authors have different conceptions of pornography or count different materials as pornographic. The reader has the task of sorting out the differences.

2. THE PORNOGRAPHIC AND THE TRULY PORNOGRAPHIC

Discussions of pornography often vacillate between the moral conception and the neutral conception of pornography. Asked to list the most famous of the English pornographic novels, we might include *Ulysses* and *Lady Chatterley's Lover*. But when asked whether *Ulysses* is pornographic, we might well balk, holding that nothing is wrong with its depictions of sexual matters, that it is not "truly pornographic." Here we would have shifted from the neutral conception to the moral conception. The question whether pornography ought to be censored or controlled in society can be under-stood in light of either of these conceptions.

Understood in light of the neutral conception, the question would be whether items that are standardly taken to be pornographic within a given society ought to be controlled in some way. This is often the most sensible way to understand the question when it arises in public debate. Citizens' groups sometimes challenge certain books, plays, or what have you, on the ground that they are pornographic. They then typically seek to ban the accused items: certain books from school curricula, certain plays from municipal halls, etc.[9] Such issues may be approached from two directions. The question could be asked whether the item alleged to be pornographic is indeed pornographic; however, I suspect that this approach would not be fruitful in most instances. It would usually be more fruitful to consider directly what grounds there are for banning the item in question, leaving aside the question whether it is pornographic. Often, the mooted reasons for banning the item will not turn essentially on whether the item violates plausible standards of propriety for sexual depictions; other issues will be raised, such as the alleged harmfulness of exposing children to sexual depictions of certain kinds.

However, the question whether pornography should be censored may be asked quite abstractly and generally. In this case, it would be appropriate to understand the question in light of the moral conception of pornography. Understood in this light, the question would be whether to censor items that violate plausible standards of propriety for sexual depictions, and answering the question would require determining what would be plausible standards of propriety. Arguments in support of proposed standards could be of two kinds. Consequentialist arguments would be based on claims alleging bad effects of certain kinds of sexual depictions, or alleging good effects of accepting or recognizing a given standard of propriety. Nonconsequentialist arguments would be based perhaps on claims alleging objectionable intrinsic features of certain kinds of sexual depiction. The problem of determining what would be plausible standards of propriety is approached in different ways in four essays included in this collection.

The Williams Committee suggests that pornography by its nature involves a violation of the appropriate line between public and private. Pornography makes certain private acts public. The suggestion seems to be that the standards of propriety governing sexual depictions derive from standards of privacy that govern sexual acts themselves.[10]

Susan Wendell takes a radical position in her "Pornography and Freedom of Expression." If read in light of the moral conception of pornography, she claims in effect that nothing is properly or truly pornographic. She holds that the important issues raised by pornography are not concerned with its sexual content, that nothing is immoral in virtue of its being sexual, and that this has implications for our treatment of sexual representations. Wendell does advocate restrictions on the distribution of certain kinds of depiction of sexual acts between adults and children, and of acts of unjustified physical coercion; but the relevant factor here is not that the acts depicted are sexual, but that they are coercive. Accordingly, I think it best to understand Wendell as holding that there are no plausible moral standards governing sexual depictions per se, although there are moral standards governing depictions of *coercive* acts, both sexual and nonsexual.

Lorenne Clark may also be read in light of the moral conception of pornography, and, so read, she seems to argue that the truly pornographic consists of depictions of humiliating or oppressive sexual situations. Pornography is wrong, she tells us, because it portrays the use of sexuality "as an instrument of active oppression." It depicts women "in humiliating, degrading and violently abusive situations," and "it frequently depicts them willingly, even avidly, suffering and inviting such treatment." It would be a mistake to reply to these claims that some pornography lacks these features, and that some pornography, such as male homosexual pornography, does not feature women. She would agree that some so-called "pornography" lacks these features. Her claim, as I understand it, is that the standards of propriety for sexual depictions condemn depictions of people in humiliating or abusive sexual situations, and depictions of the use of sex as an instrument of oppression. Only such depictions are genuinely pornographic.

"Pornography and Respect for Women," by Ann Garry, considers whether one can object to pornography on moral grounds. That is, it considers whether one can object on moral grounds to items that, as she says, are the worst and least artistic material, the kind that almost everyone would agree is pornographic. Garry is specifically interested in whether such "pornography" shows, expresses, or commends behavior or attitudes that exploit or degrade people. If it does, she is interested in whether this shows such material to be morally objectionable. Her answer to these questions is affirmative, given present conditions, but she finds it not impossible for there to be nondegrading and morally acceptable "pornography." Garry's view can easily be rephrased in a way that would cater to the conception of pornography I recommended above. I read her view as follows: There could be nonobjectionable erotica. However, the items now almost universally regarded as pornographic are truly pornographic. Given the nature of the audience for sexually explicit material, these items express and commend exploitative and degrading behavior and attitudes.

It can be seen that Garry and Clark are in rough agreement. There is an important difference, however. For Clark, a sexual depiction is pornographic basically when the sexual behavior it depicts is objectionable. For Garry, however, a sexual depiction is pornographic especially when, in addition, it *condones* or *expresses* objectionable behavior or attitudes *by* depicting what it depicts in the way it does. Wendell also is concerned that depictions may recommend or condone objectionable behavior. This very interesting idea challenges us to provide an account of the sense in which a depiction can condone or recommend behavior or attitudes, or can express an attitude. The idea that pornography is a species of hate propaganda is obviously related to Garry's idea, for propaganda promotes certain ideas or attitudes. On the other hand, this idea of why pornography is immoral confronts proposals to *censor* or *control* pornography with objections based on the right to freedom of expression. I will return to this matter presently.

The central point here is that proper navigation through the pornography debate can be aided if the distinction between the moral and the neutral conceptions of pornography is kept in mind.

3. LEGAL CRITERIA OF OBSCENITY

The law in this area typicallv treats of obscenity, rather than of pornography. Obscenity is a broader concept, so the law may treat of obscenity in order not to be restricted to *sexual* obscenity. At any rate, criteria of obscenity used by the law are not intended to be definitive of either the concept of obscenity or the concept of pornography. In statutory law, or in case law, criteria of obscenity are part of the delineation of an offense. Typically, their purpose is to create an offense. In United States constitutional law, the purpose is to delineate the legislative competency of the states in relation to obscenity law. In no case, however, would it be germane to criticize the legal criteria for failing to capture the prelegal conception of obscenity.

Excerpts are printed from a number of judicial judgments regarding obscenity and censorship. The cases are from three different but historically related legal systems, the British, Canadian, and American. Included is an excerpt from a classic English case, Chief Justice Cockburn's reasoning in the 1868 case, *R. v. Hicklin*.[11] Cockburn proposed a definition of obscenity that became the definitive test in English law. He said the test of obscenity is "whether the tendency of the matter charged as obscenity is to deprave and corrupt those whose minds are open to such immoral influences, and into whose hands a publication of this sort may fall." With some modifications, this definition was adopted into statutory law with the Obscene Publications Act, 1959, and remains a test of obscenity in English law today.[12] The "Hicklin test," or the "deprave and corrupt test," as Cockburn's definition is sometimes called, has had a great influence on Anglo-American legal systems.[13] It was the basis of obscenity law in Canada until the Criminal Code was amended in 1959.[14] It was also applied commonly by American courts until the 1957 *Roth* decision by the United States Supreme Court.[15]

Obscenity is defined for Canadian law in section 159(8) of the Criminal Code.[16] In various sections the code defines a number of offenses regarding "obscene things," including publishing, circulating, selling, exposing to public view, and using the mails for the purpose of transmitting an obscene thing. It provides that publications found to be obscene may be forfeited to the state. For all of these sections, the definition of obscenity, at least as it pertains to publications, is stated as follows:

> any publication, a dominant characteristic of which is the undue exploitation of sex, or of sex and any one or more of the following subjects, namely, crime, horror, cruelty and violence, shall be deemed to be obscene.

The test of undue exploitation under this definition is whether the book is tolerable under national "community standards," that is, roughly, whether the "average person" would object to the publication's being seen or read by those who so desire.[17] In some sections of the code, the operative words are "indecent," "immoral," or "scurrilous," as well as "obscene."[18] The *Pink Triangle Press* case, which is included in this volume, hinges on judicial interpretation of these words.[19] This case illustrates the use of obscenity law to interfere with the press, the journal in this instance being the newspaper of a homosexual community.

One would expect freedom of the press to be more protected in the United States than in most other countries because of the First Amendment to the Constitution.[20] The First Amendment states in part that "Congress shall make no law . . . abridging the freedom of speech, or of the press," and the due process clause of the Fourteenth Amendment has been the basis for extending this provision to the states.[21] The key question for American obscenity law therefore became whether the prohibition on laws abridging freedom of speech and of the press extends to "obscene" publications. *Roth* held that "obscene" materials are not protected,[22] and that "obscenity" may be regulated. Subsequent cases modified the criterion of obscenity that was stated in *Roth*. Currently, the leading case is *Miller* v. *California*.[23] The key passage reads as follows:

> As a result, we now confine the permissible scope of such regulation to works which depict or describe sexual conduct. . . .
>
> The basic guidelines for the trier of fact must be (a) whether "the average person, applying contemporary community standards" would find that the work, taken as a whole, appeals to the prurient interest, . . . (b) whether the work depicts or describes, in a patently offensive way, sexual conduct specifically defined by the applicable state law; and (c) whether the work, taken as a whole, lacks serious literary, artistic, political, or scientific value.[24]

The development of United States obscenity law is discussed in detail in Joel Feinberg's "Pornography and the Criminal Law." We can see that in *Miller* the subject matter of permitted regulation has been narrowed from obscenity in general, as defined by the Hicklin test, to obscene sexual depictions, as defined by the applicable laws.

4. CENSORSHIP

The various legal criteria of obscenity define the type of material whose censorship, regulation, or control is envisaged under the corresponding legal system. The issue addressed in this book is what, if anything, would *justify* a state in censoring, regulating, or otherwise controlling obscenity or pornography. What types of obscene material would a state be justified in regulating, if any, and on what basis?

Anything truly pornographic violates a moral standard of propriety. Some would think this a sufficient reason in itself for the state to place controls on the availability of pornography. It should also be noted that, presumably, anything generally regarded as pornographic in a society violates a standard of propriety that is generally shared in that society. Some would think that *this* is a significant reason in itself for the state to place controls.

Viscount Simonds subscribed to the second view in *Shaw* v. *Director of Public Prosecutions*, an English case that is excerpted in Part Three. Simonds cited with approval the view that the courts have the superintendency of offenses *contra bonos mores*. He asserted that there is in the courts "a residual power to enforce the supreme and fundamental purpose of the law, to conserve not only the safety and order, but also the moral welfare of the state."[25] This is, of course, a controversial claim. I do not mean to question its plausibility as a claim about the power of the English courts.[26] My point is that it is controversial as a claim about the *proper* function or purpose of the law. What reason do we have for believing that it would be proper to use the law to conserve the "good morals" of the people?

In a famous 1959 lecture, Lord Patrick Devlin argued that society is justified in using the law to enforce its moral code.[27] He claimed that "what makes a society of any sort is community of ideas," including community of moral ideas. Moreover, key aspects of a society's common morality are "built into the house in which we live and could not be removed without bringing it down."[28] That is, he seemed to say, the preservation of the moral code shared in a society is essential to that society's existence.[29] True, some changes in a society's morality are compatible with the continued existence of the society, but certain changes, or sufficiently extensive changes, would destroy the society. Similarly, sufficiently extensive changes in the rules of a game would mean that one game had disappeared and another had taken its place.[30] In addition to all of this, Devlin held that a society is justified in taking those measures that will help to preserve its existence, and that the legal enforcement of a moral code will help to preserve the currency of the code in a population.[31] Given these claims, he concluded that a society is justified in using the law to enforce its moral code. Such enforcement will tend to strengthen the currency of the moral code accepted by the society and, in this way, will help to preserve the society.

Devlin's position has been vigorously attacked by a number of writers.[32] Many critics argue that he is mistaken to think that the preservation of a society's moral code is logically necessary for the preservation of that society. There is a need to distinguish between changes that would merely alter a society's characteristics, and changes that would destroy a society. A society might well continue to exist even if the moral code generally accepted by its members underwent a drastic change. For instance, it is possible that a society's morality should so change, and the society become sufficiently decadent, that it does not recognize its own decadence. This possibility illustrates the fact that a society might continue to exist even if its morality underwent a significant change. Many critics also agree that a government is not morally justified in taking *whatever* measures will help to preserve society from change, even from change in its accepted moral code. Many would agree that there are quite general moral limits to justified government interventions in society. If so, certain measures that could be taken to preserve a society's moral code or certain features of its code would be unjustified even if the code itself were unobjectionable.

These considerations suggest that certain conditions must be shown to hold in order to justify morally a proposal to use the legal system to preserve or to strengthen a feature of the socially accepted morality. First, it must be shown that the currency or prevalence of the feature in question, a moral canon, attitude, or trait of character, *needs* preserving or strengthening, and that it *merits* preserving or strengthening. Second, it must be shown that the use of the legal system in the manner proposed would contribute to preserving or strengthening the relevant feature. Third, it must be shown that the proposed use of the legal system for the purpose at hand would not violate any moral limits to legitimate government interventions in society. At least these three things would have to be shown in order to justify such uses of the legal system.

We must consider whether these conditions can be shown to hold with regard to the use of the legal system to control the availability of pornography: Do certain canons of propriety, moral attitudes, or moral virtues currently maintained in society need and merit support? Could they be supported by appropriate legal controls on the availability of pornography? Would such controls violate moral limits on legitimate uses of the legal system?

Some hold that the government should always act with the objective of maximizing the general welfare. On this position, legislative action to control the availability of pornography would be justified if and only if it would contribute to the general welfare. A corollary presumably would be that there is no moral presumption in favor of individual liberty, and that there is no moral limitation on the use of the legal system to pursue the general welfare. However, this view is rejected by most of the philosophers

phers whose articles are collected in .this book. They essentially take for granted in these articles that we do value liberty, and that the value of liberty is the source of certain moral limits on government action to control pornography.

In the first place, there is the idea that John Stuart Mill expressed in *On Liberty*: "That the only purpose for which power can be rightfully exercised over any member of a civilized community, against his will, is to prevent harm to others."[33] This principle—often called the "harm principle"[34]— requires examination. First, we might sensibly think that there can be cases of justified paternalism, yet this seems to conflict with the harm principle. Second, the relevant notion of harm needs to be explained. For instance, Mill does not want to allow that a person is harmed merely by being offended by the behavior of another.[35] But we need a notion of harm that enables us to draw a principled distinction between what Mill calls "definite damage" or "perceptible hurt" and what he calls "merely constructive injury."[36] Finally, in the case of pornography, we need to determine what evidence there is that the availability of pornography yields definite damage to innocent third parties, that is, to parties other than the producers and consumers of pornography. I will explore some of the issues raised by the harm principle in sections six and seven of this introduction.

In the second place, there is the idea that a moral right to freedom of expression exists, and that this right imposes a moral barrier on government action to control the availability of pornography. This idea also requires examination: how would one support the claim that such a right exists, and closely related to this, how would one define the notion of *expression* to explain what this right entails? Finally, in connection with the pornography issue per se, is pornography a kind of expression protected by the right to freedom of expression? I will turn to some of these issues in the next section.

Both of these principles, the harm principle and the principle invoking the right of free expression, place limits on a government's pursuit of the general welfare. It might be argued that these limits themselves contribute in the long run to the general welfare; in fact, I think this is how Mill would have argued.[37] Nevertheless, a commitment to these principles does seem to represent an acceptance that promotion of the general welfare cannot directly justify all legislation.

5. FREEDOM OF EXPRESSION

A right to freedom of expression is a corollary of the harm principle. In particular, it follows from the harm principle that interference with a person's freedom to express his ideas, attitudes, or what have you, could only be justified if such interference were necessary to prevent harm to others. In this section I will consider whether a principle of freedom of expression might be justified on grounds independent of the harm principle. The key question for our present purposes is whether there is an argument for freedom of expression that would support freedom to express whatever is expressed by pornography.

Mill does have arguments independent of the harm principle, but they are arguments for a freedom of *thought* and *discussion,* or a freedom to express one's *opinion.*[38] His arguments proceed from the value of truth and the idea that silencing an opinion can only undermine the truth. The opinion silenced might itself be the truth, or part of the truth; even if it is not the truth, received opinions need to be challenged by competing views in order not to be accepted merely as prejudices, and in order that their meaning not be "lost or enfeebled."[39] Hence, there ought to be freedom to express one's opinions. Another line of argument is based on the idea that freedom of speech is essential for the preservation of democratic decision procedures.[40] What these lines of argument support is a narrow freedom of expression, a freedom to express *opinions.*

The question that arises, therefore, is whether government restrictions on the availability of pornography, or on what would typically be regarded as pornography, would constitute restrictions on the expression of opinions. Of course, an unscrupulous government might present a law as intended to control pornography, and then use it to control the expression of dissenting political views. However, our question is whether the control of pornography would *ipso facto* constitute a control on the expression of opinions. Do obscene sexual depictions, or sexual depictions typically regarded as obscene, express opinions?

Some of our authors consider this issue. If the truly pornographic is antifemale propaganda, or if it condones or recommends objectionable behavior, then it presumably implicitly expresses opinions. If it expresses opinions, and we believe in a right to express one's opinions, then pornography must be protected by this right.

It might be said that the truly pornographic recommends or condones violent or exploitative behavior and that the right to express one's opinions does not extend to a right to advocate violence. However, this position is debatable. Even if there were an advocacy of violence in anything that was truly pornographic, it is not obvious that advocacy of violence is unprotected by the right to free speech. Mill holds that the *instigation* of violence is unprotected, but that the mere *advocacy* of it is protected, provided that there is no *probable* connection to *acts* of violence.[41] So it may be that if some pornography expresses opinions, it should be given a kind of protection not given to other kinds of pornography. T. M. Scanlon seems to reach this conclusion in his paper for this volume, "Freedom of Expression and Categories of Expression."

However, it is surely doubtful that much that is *typically* regarded as pornography expresses any opinions at all. It is also debatable that obscene sexual depictions per se express any opinions. Of course, in some cases opinions may be expressed in conjunction with pornography, or expressed in a way that is pornographic. Also, a person's production or consumption of pornography may be *evidence* that the person has certain opinions. However, the idea that obscene sexual depictions per se *express* certain opinions, and, in particular, that they condone or advocate certain behavior, or are antifemale propaganda, needs both elucidation and defense. This issue is discussed by Clark and Garry.

As we saw, protected speech has been a central issue in American obscenity trials. In essence, the position taken by the American courts in these cases has been that laws placing restrictions on a narrowly defined class of obscene sexual depictions do not abridge freedom of speech. The Williams Committee reached a similar conclusion. The committee held, in discussing its own reasons for advocating restrictions, that

> it is important for the rationale for restricting pornographic publications that it is not for advocating any opinion that the restriction is proposed, and that the upset that they cause to the public is not a reaction to opinions which are found unacceptable.

Even if some pornographic publications do advocate opinions, their restriction under the committee's recommendations would be "because the form of its advocacy was offensive, apart from what was being advocated."[42]

Susan Wendell argues to the contrary that it would be legitimate to restrict the freedom to express certain opinions partly on the ground that people would be upset by the open expression of *those opinions*. She holds that it would be legitimate to place restrictions on expressions of opinion recommending or condoning unjustified physical coercion, or sexual acts between adults and children. This would be legitimate because the expression of the relevant kind of opinion would cause people to experience fear, anxiety, and loss of self-esteem, and the opinions recommend or condone the relevant kind of unjustified coercion. In her view, the legitimacy of the recommended restrictions is grounded partly in the reaction people would have to the expression of certain opinions, and partly in the contnet of those opinions.

The American Bill of Rights is similar to other manifestos of rights in being apparently concerned mainly with freedom to express opinions. The French Declaration of the Rights of Man and of Citizens asserts that "every citizen may speak, write, and publish freely";[43] the United Nations' Universal Declaration of Human Rights asserts that "Everyone has the right to freedom of opinion and expression," and that this right includes freedom to "hold opinions" and to "seek, receive and impart information and ideas";[44] the new Canadian Charter of Rights and Freedoms seeks to accord to everyone a "freedom of thought, belief, opinion, and expression, including freedom of the press and other media of communication."[45] However, insofar as these documents refer to an unqualified freedom of expression, or to an unqualified freedom of the press, they may be thought to have envisaged protection for the freedom to express or to publish *anything*. It is not at all obvious that the envisaged freedom was restricted to the expression of opinion.

In "Freedom of Expression and Categories of Expression," T. M. Scanlon urges that the right to freedom of expression not be construed narrowly as concerning freedom merely to express opinions. As well as opinions, one may be said to express ideas, attitudes, desires, mores, emotions, esthetic appreciation, fantasies, a sense of humor, and so on. Construed widely, freedom of expression would imply a freedom to express any of these things, and anything else that can be expressed. On a wide construal, even pornography that does not express opinions would enjoy protection, for all pornography presumably expresses something, whether it be a fantasy, an attitude, or any of the other things that pornography is commonly said to express.

Scanlon holds that the right of freedom of expression is of instrumental value. It protects our interests as participants, in "being able to call something to the attention of a wide audience," and our interests as an audience, in having "expression available to [us] should [we] want to attend to it."[46] That is, the right to freedom of expression is of value, not only because it protects our interests when we wish to call something to someone's attention, but also because it protects our interest in having access to expression. To say that freedom of expression is a right, Scanlon asserts, is to say that "limits on the power of governments to regulate expression are necessary to protect [these] central interests . . . and . . . that such limits are not incompatible with a healthy society and a stable political order."[47] The question therefore arises whether an absence of restrictions on pornography is compatible with a "healthy society" and with political stability.

It is important to realize that if Scanlon is correct, then in order to justify restricting expression, even in the case of pornography, one would have to show a risk of very serious harms. In particular, one would have to show that an absence of restrictions on pornography would risk harm to the health of society or to the stability of the political order. Alternatively, one would have to argue that the interests of those who enjoy pornography, and the interests of those who produce it, are less significant than the interests at stake in the case of other forms of expression, such as the expression of political views or esthetic attitudes. That is, one would have to argue that the audience and participant interests in the case of pornography are importantly different from those at stake in the case of other forms of expression. The latter strategy seems the more plausible. However, as Scanlon points out, some of the most interesting arguments against pornography undermine the plausibility of this strategy by alleging a basic similarity between the aims and potential effects of political speech and of pornography. These arguments maintain that pornography is objectionable because it can "contribute to undesirable changes in our attitudes toward sex [or toward women] and in our sexual mores,"[48] or because it advocates or condones objectionable attitudes or behavior. Arguments of this sort are put forward in this volume by Clark and Garry, at least with respect to what they regard as pornographic. Fred Berger disputes similar claims regarding what is typically regarded as pornographic.[49] For Scanlon, the important point is that if we take these arguments seriously, "it is difficult to construct a principled argument for restriction that is consistent with our policy toward other forms of expression. . . ."[50]

6. HARMS AND LIBERALISM

According to the harm principle, government restrictions on the availability of pornography are justified only if its availability creates a risk of harm to third parties. The more serious the risk, the more stringent would be the justified restriction. The weaker the evidence that harm may result, or the less serious the harm that is likely, the less stringent the justified restriction. For instance, Fred Berger contends, in "Pornography, Sex and Censorship," that to justify a program of *censorship*, "we should require a strong showing of likely harms which are far from remote."[51] Berger suggests that if we value freedom, then to justify a program of restriction, it would not be enough to show that the expected losses to the users and producers of pornography are counterbalanced by the expected benefits to others. It would not be enough simply to show a marginal gain in the expected general welfare.

Harms can be controversial in at least two ways. First, it can be controversial whether something would be harmful if it were to occur. Of course, some harms are uncontroversial, such as detrimental effects on one's health, or coercive interferences with one's liberty. However, other alleged harms are more controversial, and the controversy is ethical or normative. It may even be that the concept of harm cannot be understood independently of normative notions. For instance, on the one hand, some religious leaders have seen pornography as contributing to changes in people's attitudes toward love, sex, and the family, and as contributing to a weakening of the virtues of sexual modesty and temperance. Many would see these supposed effects of pornography as harmful. However, others would see these as improvements, as allowing a liberation of people from overly constraining moralistic attitudes toward sex. On the other hand, some have held that the free availability of pornography creates and perpetuates undesirable attitudes, and especially, leaving aside child pornography and homosexual pornography, undesirable attitudes toward women. A normative assumption lies behind the assessment of these kinds of alleged effects either as harmful or as not harmful. There is a problem here for the application of the harm principle. How should we take into account the fact that reasonable people can disagree on normative grounds about the harmfulness of something?

I think that Lorenne Clark attacks the harm principle partly because she objects to the normative assumptions that she thinks have usually underlain the assessment of harms. She claims that certain important kinds of harm are traditionally not taken into account in the application of the principle. The fundamental problem here seems to be to find an account of harm that makes the harm principle plausible.

There is a second way in which harms may be controversial. It can be debated whether something that would be harmful if it did occur, is likely to occur, or does occur, as a result of some policy. If we value liberty, we must have sound evidence that someone faces a substantial risk of suffering harm before we can be justified in interfering with another person's freedom. The risk must not be merely speculative, and the probability of harm must not be negligible.

Special considerations arise in the case of children. We do, of course, need to take into account harms that may be suffered by children if there is no restriction on selling them pornography, or on using them in its production. We have parental duties toward children, and so we may rightly be more reluctant to allow children to be exposed to risks than we are to allow adults to be exposed to risks of similar magnitude. Consequently, we may be prepared to restrict certain freedoms in order to protect children from risk of harm, even if the nature of and evidence for the risk would not justify similar restrictions designed to protect adults.

It has been argued that the harm principle is too strong in demanding a demonstration of *harm*. Lorenne Clark suggests that it may be legitimate to restrict liberty in order to provide resources and opportunities necessary for social equality, even if the restrictions are not necessary to prevent harm. Joel Feinberg suggests that restrictions on liberty may be justified, not only to prevent harm to others, but also to prevent offensive nuisances to others.

Much of the debate about pornography is empirical in nature. Potential harms are identified, and the question is raised whether, in the absence of restrictions, pornography would actually cause these harms. For example, on the one hand, it can hardly be doubted that the unrestricted marketing of pornography would result in some people unwillingly being confronted with material that they find shocking and offensive. This harm seems both relatively uncontroversial and remediable. Harms of this kind are discussed in Feinberg's paper, and a policy for dealing with them is proposed in the selection from the *Williams Report* that is reprinted in this book. However, on the other hand, some views discussed in this book about additional harmful effects of the widespread availability of pornography are quite speculative. Part Two contains articles that present evidence relevant to the issue of whether there are some possibly unexpected harmful effects. Nevertheless, empirical research has had little bearing on some of the more interesting speculations. Scanlon and Berger consider whether the availability of pornography contributes to changes in our attitudes and mores, a possibility that concerns Clark. There is little argument and no direct evidence that would establish the direction of the causal connection, or even whether there is one. Research in the last decade bears only indirectly on the issue and must be interpreted with some caution.

7. EMPIRICAL RESEARCH

The key question posed by researchers has been whether the availability of pornography contributes to acts of violence, especially to violence directed against women. The evidence is from three types of source:[52] anecdotal evidence consisting of reports of incidents in which a connection between pornography and criminal or coercive behavior has been claimed; experimental evidence consisting of reports of experiments into people's responses, aggressive or otherwise, after exposure to pornographic material; and finally, statistical evidence consisting of analyses of variations in crime statistics as compared with variations in the availability of pornography. Examples of these types of report are found in Part Two.

Diana Russell's paper reports the results of a survey in which women were asked whether they had ever been upset by a person's trying to get them to do what that person had seen in pornography. The results bear careful scrutiny even if the testimony Russell received was entirely honest. She points out that the testimony does not constitute clear evidence of the nature of the link between pornography and interest in sexual experimentation. Would this interest have arisen independently of the pornography? Did this interest lead people to the pornography, or did the pornography stimulate this interest? Did the idea for a particular experiment originate in the pornography, or did the pornography give people a sense that the idea could be broached? The full story would no doubt be complex, so one must question the significance of Russell's results.[53]

Experimental findings are no less difficult to interpret. For obvious ethical and practical reasons, experiments cannot be designed to produce situations in which one person will actually harm another person. In the experiments reported here, situations are contrived in which the subjects are meant to believe that they can harm another person, and often that they are permitted to do so. Differences are then noted between the behavior of subjects who have been exposed by the experimenter to "pornographic" material and subjects who have been exposed to "neutral" material. The results are highly suggestive. Nevertheless, they must be read with caution.

In the first place, a general reservation attaches to all experiments of this kind. The Williams Committee asserted that

> correlation experiments in artificial conditions are regarded by many competent critics as an unilluminating and unreliable way of investigating complex behavior, even in many other species, let alone in human beings.[54]

In the second place, although these experiments are suggestive, they are studies of people's reactions in contrived and artificial situations; in most of them, people are invited to, or given an apparent opportunity to, exhibit aggressive behavior. Permission is often implied. Typically, subjects will first be angered or not angered by a confederate of the experimenter, then exposed to a stimulus of one of several degrees of eroticism or of violence, and finally ostensibly provided with an opportunity to hurt the confederate with an electric shock. The aggression machine used appears to, but does not actually, deliver a shock to the apparent victim.[55] Some of the experimental situations are more subtle in the way in which they are contrived to elicit aggression, and attempt to avoid suggesting to the subject that aggression is permitted.[56] One report printed below is of a study of sexual arousal, rather than of aggression.[57] Nevertheless, all of the experimental situations are obviously contrived, and this undermines the plausibility of drawing inferences about behavior in nonexperimental situations. Mosher and Katz note this problem and remark studies of this kind have "the disadvantage of trying to generalize from a specific controlled situation to other life situations."[58]

As a related problem, the experimental subjects are not chosen at random from the general population. In these studies, they are college students enrolled in an introductory course. Participation in the study usually gives them some credit toward meeting their course requirements. The subjects are not a random sample from even the university population. An experimenter's interest in studying pornography might become known on a campus and affect his course enrolments. His students' knowledge of the methodology of psychology experiments, and their knowledge that these particular experiments involve deception, might affect their responses in the experimental situation. In addition, results achieved using youthful subjects might not be generalizable. In a review of the literature for the Williams Committee, Stephen Brodie asserted that

> The most reasonable interpretation of the considerable quantity of research results so far available would suggest that some people—particularly young people—may be inclined both to actual aggressiveness . . . and to a preference

for entertainment dealing with aggressive themes, for reasons which probably originate with the development of personality and character; but that watching violent action on the screen is unlikely in itself to impel ordinary viewers to behave in ways they would otherwise not have done.[59]

Despite these concerns, the research often leads people to draw inferences to real-life situations. Donnerstein and Berkowitz seem to think that their study, and other similar ones, shows that scenes of violence in the mass media cause a heightening of the audience's aggressive inclinations.[60] Donnerstein also holds that experimental results have shown that media depictions of both an erotic and aggressive nature account in part for the incidence of rape and other sexual assaults.[61]

However, the central difficulty with the experimental studies is that although we may be tempted to draw inferences or to generalize to real-life situations, we do not know how reliable these inferences would be. Ultimately, the issue remains an empirical one. In order to support the reliability of the kind of inference sometimes drawn from the experimental studies, further research would have to establish whether the experimental results are borne out by studies conducted outside of the laboratory. The experimental studies cannot by themselves provide sufficient evidence to warrant the kind of inference that is sometimes drawn from results achieved in experimental situations.

The third type of research consists of statistical evidence, in particular, analyses of variations in the statistics of sex crimes as compared with changes in the availability of pornography. The *Williams Report* suggests that if the experimental research has the significance for situations outside of the laboratory that is often ascribed to it, then sound statistical research should bear this out.[62]

The paper by Berl Kutchinsky, "The Effect of Easy Availability of Pornography on the Incidence of Sex Crimes: The Danish Experience," reports changes in the incidence of sex crimes in Denmark following the liberalization of the Danish obscenity laws. In 1967, the general prohibition on obscene books was lifted, and in 1969, most prohibitions on obscene pictorial publications were lifted. There still remains a number of obscenity offenses, such as selling obscene pictures or objects to persons under sixteen years of age;[63] however, after these changes in the law, pornography of all sorts became readily available in Denmark. Kutchinsky analyzed Danish statistics of sexually related crimes both before and after the liberalization.

Kutchinsky is very careful to take into account many standard problems in the analysis of crime statistics. Nevertheless, his work has been widely criticized.

The most basic and well-known problem with studies of the correlation between two variables, such as, in this case, rates of sex crimes and the availability of pornography, is that the existence of a correlation does not establish a causal connection between the variables. A correlation between increasing rates of sex crimes and increasing availability of pornography could be explained in many other ways than by assuming that availability is causally responsible for increasing sex crimes. Instead, both trends might have a common cause in some other unknown factor. Also, if rates of non-sexual crimes are also increasing, presumably there are factors influencing crime rates in general that are unconnected with pornography. The explanation of changes in crime rates in general, and of rates of sex crime in particular, is no doubt quite complex, and a correlation between the two variables in question here would be weak evidence on which to base the claim of a causal connection.

Nevertheless, Kutchinsky's research mainly suggests a *lack* of correlation between rates of sex crimes and the availability of pornography. It tends to undercut claims that there is a causal connection. Kutchinsky notes the chief exception to be a dramatic *decrease* in the incidence of indecent assaults on young children in the period immediately following the liberalization of Danish obscenity law. Kutchinsky suggests that this decrease in the incidence of child molestation is explained by the sudden increase in the availability of pornography. Although quite cognizant of the hazards of drawing inferences from correlation studies like this, the Williams Committee concluded that the decrease in child molestation,

> in consequence of the careful studies undertaken by Dr. Kutchinsky, cannot readily be explained by any other likely factor. While Dr. Kutchinsky's explanation cannot be conclusive, we have to admit that it is plausible.[64]

In addition to the basic problem about inferences from correlation to causation, work like Kutchinsky's faces several other problems. First, the number of sexual offenses reported to the police is no doubt less than the number that actually occur. Many offenses are unreported, and, what is worse, the proportion of the total number of offenses that are reported may fluctuate over time. Hence, trends in reported offenses may not accurately track trends in the total number of actual offenses. Second, it is difficult to obtain an accurate measure of the quantity and kind of pornography that is actually available. Third, it is not clear what kinds of pornography are most pertinent to correlation studies. The laboratory research suggests that different results might be expected in studies of different kinds of pornography. There may be a direct correlation between the incidence of violent sexual offenses and the availability of violent or aggressive pornography. On the other hand, there may be no significant correlation at all between the incidence of sexual offenses in general and the availability of erotica. If so, correlation studies that do not distinguish finely enough between different kinds of pornography and different kinds of offence may fail to reveal important correlations.[65] The reader must pay close attention to Kutchinsky's work in order to determine whether problems such as these are adequately guarded against.

A great deal of caution is appropriate in evaluating the empirical research in this field. Very little can be said to have been securely established, and this raises an additional issue. Decisions about the censorship or regulation of pornography must be made in a condition of uncertainty about whether the availability of pornography.has any significant harmful effects. Uncertainty suggests caution, but a great deal may hinge on whether the status quo, or an ideal situation of government noninterference, is taken to be the benchmark for change. One who places a high value on individual liberty will surely want to argue that the burden of proof is on those who would regulate. On the other hand, where children's access to pornography is concerned, many would prefer the status quo. Unfortunately, philosophers have paid little systematic attention to the ethical problem of making decisions under conditions of uncertainty.

8. POLICY OPTIONS

If one desires that some form of regulation of pornography is desirable, there is a wide range of policy options. Some options interfere very little with the availability of pornography, simply restricting its sale to certain locations and to persons above a given age. Other options, of course, are highly restrictive, and the law in many jurisdictions accords powers of outright censorship.

A central issue here is whether one can formulate a policy that selects just those types of pornography that one desires to regulate. There is a danger that regulation will spill over and affect other types of publication. Proposals and policies must ultimately be written into a statute, and it may be difficult to regulate exactly the right kind of publication through a statute. Of couuse, the judgment of judges, juries, or panels of experts must be relied upon at some point. However, a statute ought to provide guidance in clear language, and the concepts and valuus involved in the area of pornography are vague, slippery, and controversial. One may find it useful to review the *Pink Triangle Press* case in this connection. The case concerns a newspaper called "The Body Politic" that, in one issue, discussed and apparently condoned pedophilia. The judge's written opinion in this case includes selections from the newspaper that are reprinted in Part Three. One would do well to test a proposal for regulating pornography against this issue of "The Body Politic." Would "The Body Politic" have been affected by the proposal, and should it have been restricted?

I do not here advocate any particular resolution to the debate. It is presumably clear that I lean strongly in the direction of opposing any but minimal regulation. However, my objective in this introduction has been to navigate through the multitude of philosophical, empirical, and legal questions raised by the pornography issue. I hope that this introduction helps the reader to see how these questions are interrelated.[66]

NOTES

1. *The Shorter Oxford English Dictionary*, 1973.

2. I am indebted to D. D. Todd for this example.

3. *Report of the Committee on Obscenity and Pornography*, Bernard Williams, Chairman (London: Her Majesty's Stationery Office, 1979), paragraphs 8.2-8.7. Hereafter cited as the *Williams Report*. Chapters seven and eight are reprinted in this volume.

4. E. J. Mishan, "Making the World Safe for Pornography" in *Making the World Safe for Pornography and Other Intellectual Fashions* (London: Alcove Press, 1973), pp. 107-150, esp. pp. 117-125.

5. D. H. Lawrence, "Pornography and Obscenity" in his *Phoenix* (New York: Viking, 1972), pp. 174-5. I owe this reference to Dennis Bevington.

6. Susan Brownmiller, *Against Our Will: Men, Women and Rape* (New York: Simon and Schuster, 1975), p. 394. See Lorenne Clark, "Liberalism and Pornography," in this volume, and see the discussion in Ann Garry, "Pornography and Respect for Women," also in this volume. I would suppose that child pornography and homosexual pornography would somehow be factored into Brownmiller's view.

7. Compare the criteria used in the various articles in Part Two of this volume. Diana Russell's study concerns what her *subjects* take to be pornographic.

8. By some speakers at the 1979 Simon Fraser University conference on pornography.

9. Events of this kind will be familiar to many readers. See William French, "The Good Book versus good books," *The Globe and Mail* (Toronto, Canada), June 14, 1979. French describes a town meeting in Clinton, Ontario, at which was debated a proposal to remove three novels from the high school curriculum: Margaret Laurence's *The Diviners*, J. D. Salinger's *Catcher in the Rye*, and John Steinbeck's *Of Mice and Men*. I owe the reference to the Book and Periodical Development Council pamphlet, *Censorship: Stopping the Book Banners*.

10. See *Williams Report*, in Part One, paragraphs 7.4-7.7. Cicero introduces a notion of propriety or decorum in connection with the line between public and private. See Cicero, *De Officiis*, translated by Walter Miller (Cambridge, Mass.: Harvard University Press, 1913), Book I, sections xxviii and xxxv, pp. 101-3, 129-31. I owe this reference to Moira Gutteridge.

11. (1868) L. R. 3 Q.B. 360.

12. The present English law is explained in the *Williams Report*, chapter two and Appendix 1.

13. *Williams Report*, Appendix 4.

14. R. G. Fox, "Obscenity," *Alberta Law Review*, volume 12, 1974, pp. 172-235.

15. 354 U.S. 476 (1957). See Joel Feinberg's discussion in "Pornography and the Criminal Law," in Part One, and Judge Frank's discussion in *United States* v. *Roth* 237 F. 2d 796 (2d cir., 1956), in Part Three.

16. R.S.C. 1970, Chap. C-34. See generally sections 159, 160, 161, 163, 164, 165.

17. See Fox, "Obscenity"; *R.* v. *Prairie Schooner News Ltd., and Powers* (1970), 1 C.C.C. (2d) 251, 75 W.W.R. 585 (Man. C.A.); and *R.* v. *The MacMillan Co. of Canada Ltd.* (1976), 31 C.C.C. (2d) 286, 72 D.L.R. (3d) 33 (Ont. Co. Ct.). See also *Martin's Annual Criminal Code* (Agincourt, Ont.: Canada Law Book).

18. Sections 163 and 164.

19. *R.* v. *Pink Triangle Press et al.* (1979) 45 C.C.C. (2d) 385 (Ont. P.C.).

20. See Robert P. Davidow and Michael O'Boyle, "Obscenity Laws in England and the United States: A Comparative Analysis," *Nebraska Law Review*, vol. 56 (1977), pp. 249–287.

21. "Obscenity Laws in England and United States," fn. 6.

22. *Roth* v. *United States* 354 U.S. 476 (1957).

23. 413 U.S. 15 (1973). See the excerpts printed in Part Three.

24. 413 U.S. at 29. See pg. 360 in this volume.

25. (1961) 2 All E. R. 446, at 452. See p. 330 in this volume.

26. The decision in *Shaw* has been confirmed, for instance, in *Knuller* v. *Director of Public Prosecutions* (1972) 2 All E.R. 898.

27. Patrick Devlin, *The Enforcement of Morals* (Oxford: Oxford University Press, 1965), pp. 9–13.

28. *Enforcement of Morals*, p. 9.

29. *Enforcement of Morals*, p. 13.

30. *Enforcement of Morals*, p. 13, fn. 1.

31. *Enforcement of Morals*, p. 11.

32. Most notably by H. L. A. Hart in *Law, Liberty and Morality* (Oxford: Oxford University Press, 1963). The literature prompted by the Hart-Devlin debate is enormous.

33. John Stuart Mill, *On Liberty* (Indianapolis: Bobbs-Merrill, 1956), Chapter I, p. 13.

34. It is widely discussed in the literature. See, for instance, Joel Feinberg, *Social Philosophy* (Englewood Cliffs, N.J.: Prentice-Hall, 1973), Chapters 2 and 3.

35. *On Liberty*, Chapter IV, pp. 103–113.

36. *On Liberty*, p. 100.

37. See David Lyons, "Human Rights and the General Welfare," *Philosophy and Public Affairs* 6 (1977), pp. 113–129.

38. *On Liberty*, Chapter II.

39. *On Liberty*, p. 64.

40. See Peter Singer, *Democracy and Disobedience* (Oxford: Oxford University Press, 1974), pp. 64–67.

41. *Democracy and Disobedience*, p. 20, fn. 1. In this connection, see Judge Frank's discussion of the "clear and present danger test" in *United States* v. *Roth* 237 F. 2d 796 (2d cir., 1956), in Part Three.

42. *Williams Report*, paragraph 7.17, in this volume.

43. Article XI, see A. I. Melden, *Human Rights* (Belmont, Cal.: Wadsworth, 1970), p. 141.

44. Article 19, see Melden, *Human Rights*, p. 146.

45. Section 2(b). The Charter is Part I of the Constitution Act, 1982. Section 33(1) provides that Parliament or a legislature may override Section 2 by including in a piece of legislation an explicit statement that the legislation shall operate notwithstanding a provision included in Section 2.

46. See pp. 141, 143 in this volume.

47. See p. 153 in this volume.

48. See p. 158 in this volume.

49. Fred E. Berger, "Pornography, Sex and Censorship," in Part One.

50. See p. 163 in this volume.

51. See p. 100 in this volume.

52. In this categorization, and in much of my analysis, I follow the *Williams Report*, chapter six, especially paragraph 6.3.

53. See the *Williams Report*, paragraph 6.15.

54. *Williams Report*, paragraph 6.14.

55. For an example of a study of this kind, see the paper in this volume by Edward Don-

nerstein and Leonard Berkowitz. See also the summary of experiments in Donnerstein, "Pornography and Violence Against Women: Experimental Studies."

56. See the study by Dolf Zillman et al., in this volume.

57. See the study by Neil Malamuth and James Check, in this volume.

58. Donald L. Mosher and Harvey Katz, "Pornographic Films, Male Verbal Aggression Against Women, and Guilt," in United States, *Technical Report of the Commission on Obscenity and Pornography*, vol. 8 (Washington, D.C.: Government Printing Office, 1970), p. 372.

59. *Williams Report*, paragraph 6.18.

60. See p. 254 in this volume.

61. See p. 230 in this volume.

62. *Williams Report*, paragraph 6.4.

63. *Williams Report*, Appendix 3, pp. 100–110.

64. *Williams Report*, paragraph 6.55.

65. *Williams Report*, paragraphs 6.24–6.29.

66. I would like to thank Susan Wendell, D. D. Todd, Peter Horban, Steven Davis, and Dennis Bevington for helpful comments and suggestions.

PART ONE:
PHILOSOPHICAL ESSAYS

Lorenne M. G. Clark

Liberalism and Pornography

Since at least the mid-nineteenth century, the fight for women's rights has largely been fought under the banner of liberalism. The ethical principles of people like John Stuart Mill formed the moral justification for these struggles, and many of these individuals were themselves committed to the cause of women's equality.[1] Thus, the cause of women's liberation has much thanks to give both to the theory and to its proponents. But it is, I believe, time to take another look at the moral underpinnings we have until now accepted, though I am by no means suggesting that utilitarianism, or more popular versions of liberal, or libertarian ethics, have been the only moral touchstones upon which the demand for sexual equality has rested. This has been fed by other moralities as well, notably that deriving from the work of Marx and Engels. But at least insofar as both of these moral systems acknowledged that the historical position of women had been an oppressed and exploited one, it was possible to present a united front on many issues, particularly those most clearly related to the achievement of legal and social reform. Most of these fights were publicly defended on liberal principles, and the most famous one, the fight for the right to vote, certainly was.

A version of this article appeared under the title "Sexual Equality and the Problem of an Adequate Moral Theory" in Mary Kathryn Shirley and Rachel Emma Vigier, editors, *In Search of the Feminist Perspective: The Changing Potency of Women. Resources for Feminist Research Special Publication #5*, Toronto (Spring 1979). Reprinted by permission of the author and *Resources for Feminist Research.*

The reason for this is clear. The central value of liberalism is the freedom, or liberty, of the individual. Thus, demands by women for greater participation in public life were straightforward demands for greater liberty. The demands made in the name of sexual equality were, first, to establish that women ought to be entitled to the same rights as men, and, second, to ensure that these rights could be practically and effectively exercised. But there is a central difficulty with liberalism in this respect. The central value of liberalism is freedom, or what has been termed more specifically "negative liberty."[2] "Negative" liberty or freedom is the freedom to do or get what you want unimpeded by interference from others. It is contrasted with "positive" liberty, which entails not only that other persons refrain from interference, but that the person with the freedom in fact has the means or ability to get what he or she wants. Thus one is free in the negative sense when one is not prohibited or prevented from entering a restaurant to obtain a meal even if one lacks the money to pay for it. One is free in the positive sense only if one has both the means to get what is wanted and is not prevented from using those means to get what he or she wants. Negative freedom can be seen therefore to consist merely in the *absence of restraint.* Thus, while liberals could accept that it was wrong to prevent women from voting, they have more difficulty accepting that effective exercise of the right to reproductive autonomy necessitates providing publicly financed clinics for the provision of safe, cheap abortion. Achieving the right to vote was a good cause for liberal support, because all that it required was the removal of a legal impediment which would result in greater liberty. But fights which necessitate not the removal of legal restraints, but the creation of legal duties on others in order to give persons the means needed to do what they want, are not good causes on which to seek liberal support, because these necessarily involve a reduction in negative liberty. Reproductive autonomy requires not only the removal of legal restraints on one's ability to get an abortion but providing the means whereby women who cannot afford expensive medical and hospital care can nonetheless obtain an abortion if they want one. But providing safe, publicly financed clinics to perform abortions regardless of the woman's ability to pay places restraints on doctors and hospitals as to whom they can choose to treat, and on the government's choices as to which social service programmes it will support. Thus, promoting reproductive autonomy as a positive as well as a negative freedom reduces the negative freedoms that some persons and legal bodies currently enjoy. It places restraints on their freedom of choice and therefore infringes their negative freedom.

Since a central tenet of liberalism is that one can be said to be free, or to have a right to something merely from the fact that there is no statute or other legal limitation which prohibits the doing of the thing in question, the absence of a prohibition is itself enough to generate the idea that one has a right. Legally speaking, the right that one has is what is properly termed a "privilege" or "liberty" right,[3] and does not entail that anything or anyone has a correlative duty to do anything, or provide anything, which would facilitate one in actually getting that to which the right entitled one. A "privilege" or "liberty" right is a right which arises from the absence of restraint, like one's right to use a public park or to vote. It entails simply that one has no duty to refrain from doing the thing in question. But it also entails that no one else is under a duty to see that we do or get the thing we are not duty-bound to refrain from. Thus, if the right we have is a privilege right, we can do it if we want to, since we are under no duty not to do it; but if we lack the means to do it, no one has an obligation to see that we can do it, our lack of resources notwithstanding. Rights of this sort are contrasted with "claim" rights, rights which arise out of the fact that others have a duty to see that we get that to which we are said to have the right, things such as the right to an education up to at least a certain minimum age or standard. Claim rights do not therefore depend for their effective exercise on our having the means to utilize them. They are things to which we are entitled regardless of our other resources. Thus, if a right is a claim, this entails that someone or something necessarily has a duty with respect to providing us with the thing, or the means to the thing, in question, whereas if the right is a privilege, no such correlative obligation exists on others.

As is obvious, there are more impediments to human endeavor than legal impediments, and there is more to having rights than simply not being prohibited from doing something, at least if the having of rights is to mean anything to those who do not have the other means needed to get what they want. In the face of pre-existing social inequality, the effective exercise of rights can be assured only by creating a legal *claim*-right which *does* entail obligations on the part of someone or something else to provide the thing, or the means to the thing, guaranteed by the right. Thus, mere privilege rights must be *converted into claim rights* if those who have the rights are to be ensured the effective exercise of their rights. They can only get what the right gives them if someone else has an obligation to provide them with it, independent of the recipient's ability to pay and things of that sort. But the conversion of privileges into claims involves creating obligations on others. And the creation of legal obligations on others is one of the most important ways of limiting a person's ability to do what he or she wants. Thus, the establishment of claim rights is itself an *infringement* of liberty, or negative freedom, since it makes it mandatory to do what it was before permissible either to do or not to do. The history of social reform is largely the history of first establishing that some previously disenfranchised group ought to have rights that have already been accorded to others, then removing legal or other social and institutional impediments to their getting what they want, and then fighting further to have these privileges converted into claims. But this involves liberalism in a fundamental contradiction, because it means that, during the third stage, the libertarian has to argue for the *limitation* of the freedom of some in the name of promoting greater equality among all those nominally said to be in possession of the right. On the face of it, utilitarianism has no difficulty with this, since its principle is that it is best to do whatever promotes the greatest happiness of the greatest number, where each individual counts as one. But utilitarianism thus parts company with the central tenet of liberalism in those cases in which the greater positive liberty of all demands diminished negative liberty for some. Worse, it is powerless as a moral tool in just those cases in which the loss to some is evenly balanced by the gains to others, because it does not have a principle of justice independent of the principle of utility which would justify such a redistribution even in cases where the original distribution occurs within a domain characterized by inequality. While the promoters of utilitarianism, and many of their followers, have been dedicated social reformers, there are some aspects of our continuing historical reality which they either take for granted, or about which they are at any rate unaware or unaffected by the fact, that the application of their principles within these contexts perpetrates, and indeed reinforces, fundamental inequalities.

The fundamental question we have to ask is: Is the moral theory of liberalism consistent with equality? If it is, then we must be able to show how the mistakes it has made can be explained without throwing out the theory, and hence, how it must be revised in order to prevent similar errors from occurring in future. And if it isn't, then it is time we turned our attention to looking for or developing moral alternatives which are.

One of the fundamental principles endorsed by a liberal ethic is that there must be some areas of one's life in which one has the freedom to do what one wants, free from interference by others. It has been argued that there simply are some areas of life which are none of the law's business. For those familiar with the Wolfenden Report on Homosexuality in England, and the subsequent debate that this started both within and outside academic circles, this phrase, "none of the law's business," will have a familiar ring. Philosophically, this is reflected in debates about which areas of one's life should be essentially characterized by negative freedom, the ability to act free of the restraints and scrutiny of others. Legally, it is reflected in debates about privacy, about the areas of one's life into which others should be legally prohibited from interfering.[4] Among the areas often said to be protected by a right to privacy are those parts of a person's life designated as "personal," his or her home and family, or interpersonal, particularly emotional and sexual, life. Other areas dealt with in the same way are freedom of speech and of the press. The right to use pornography relates to both these broad areas and has been justified both because it is personal, related solely to one's individual private sexual proclivities and preferences, and because it has to do with freedom of the press, or more broadly speaking, freedom of information, the right to read and to see what one wants and to the need to promote a wide divergence in the range of available materials.

There is virtually no one who would want to say that we should have no negative liberty or no privacy, but the debate still rages as to which areas of one's life should be guaranteed as areas of negative liberty through the creation of a legal right to privacy. The difficulty is that no one has found a satisfactory method of drawing the boundaries between the private and other areas of life. In the past, the boundary was thought to be a *natural* one, based on the traditional distinction between the public and the private. The private just *was* "the private," and, as such, should be guaranteed as an area of negative liberty and fully protected by means of a legally enforceable right to privacy. This was one of the bases of the argument in the Wolfenden Report. Here it was alleged that sexual relations between consenting adults are simply none of the law's business. It was further argued that such behavior should justifiably be left to the absolute discretion of individuals, because it has effects on no one other than the participants. This was the rationale provided by John Stuart Mill in "On Liberty," which was reiterated and defended by Herbert Hart in *Law, Liberty, and Morality*.[5] The best defence of this liberal tenet is the view developed by Mill that the law is justified in prohibiting actions if and only if doing them results in the inability of others to exercise rights of a similar kind. The underlying view is that rights should be distributed equally, which entails that no one can have rights the exercise of which would prevent others from exercising similar rights. The difficulty is that liberals have all too often assumed that the area of life traditionally thought to be "private," and hence immune from regulation and control, conforms to the rules Mill laid down as to what should be left as an area of negative freedom.

But as is now abundantly clear, it is indefensible to draw the legal boundary between public and private on the basis of the historical division between these spheres of human activity. Privacy functioned historically to protect those who were privileged to begin with. Privacy was a consequence of the ownership of private property and, hence, a commodity purchased with property. It has been a privilege accorded those of wealth and high social status. More important from a feminist perspective, it protected not only the dominant economic class in the Marxist sense, but the dominant sex-class as well. The traditionally "private" was the sphere of the personal, home and hearth. And that area was the area within which women and children were forms of private property under the exclusive ownership and control of males. As the person in whom the absolute personality of the family vested, male heads of households had virtually absolute rights over their wives and children. The family, clearly, was not and is not a partnership of equals. There is no mutuality in the marital relation, and the rights and duties are decidedly one-sided.

Of course it is not the concept of privacy which is responsible for this state of affairs. But in drawing the boundary between the historically private and public, for the purpose of entrenching a legal right to privacy in the area of the traditionally private, it certainly functioned to condone and encourage the abusive and unjustified practices which were possible within this unequal relation. As is now clear, the family has been characterized by a great deal of physical violence. The legitimate basis of authority in the family is physical coercion, and it is and has been regularly relied on to secure to the male head of the house the attitudes and behaviors he wants. Women, much less children, had no right to protest such behavior but were expected to suffer it, willingly or otherwise. Thus, the last place feminists want to see a right to privacy is in the family. What possible sense can be made of the notion of being a *consenting adult* when one is in a relation in which one has no right to say no? Clearly, if we want privacy at all, where we do not want it is in the home, at least as that has been institutionalized historically.

The area of life most in need of regulation and control in the interest of creating more liberty and equality for women is the area of the traditionally private and personal. Greater liberty and equality for women can be purchased only at the cost of less liberty, and a loss of status, for men. To the extent that women are given more rights within marriage, men are less able to do as they please. What was before permissible would now be either mandatory, as, for example, in making it a duty for men to share in housework and child-care; or prohibited, as for example in allowing a charge of rape between spouses. Within terms of the basic principle, such changes are justified. The past operation of the law has permitted many forms of behavior which in fact caused physical and other direct and tangible harms to others, and which certainly prevented the effective exercise of like rights on the part of others. On the principle of like liberties for all, marriage must be turned into a relation of mutuality, and the relationships within it must be subject to regulation and control.

Why, then, has the demand for privacy centered so exclusively on preserving the traditional domain of male privilege? And why do the staunchest defenders of that view fail to see that in invoking these principles within a domain characterized by fundamental sexual inequality they are in fact both reinforcing that inequality and sanctioning its worst abuses? At the very least, adherents of the liberal ethic must acknowledge that there is no *natural* basis for deciding on what is private and what public for the purpose of entrenching a legal right to privacy, and that the traditional area of the private is the area most in need of loss of privacy in the name of promoting greater positive liberty and greater equality. How this fares on a purely utilitarian principle is of course problematic, for since men and women each make up roughly half the population, we cannot be sure that the benefits to women will in fact outweigh the losses to men.

Equality cannot flourish without limiting the privileges some already have in both the private and the public spheres, because the inequalities of the present system were a product of the unequal attribution of rights in the first instance; thus greater equality and liberty for those least advantaged under the present system necessitates placing restrictions on the privilege rights of those who are presently most advantaged. And since this must be done by creating obligations either to do or to forbear actions previously permitted, it can be accomplished only at the expense of negative liberty. While the principles of the liberal ethic itself do not require the historical division between public and private, it has certainly been presupposed in liberal thinking about these issues. Recognition of the extent to which this has played a role must lead to a reappraisal of what it is that people should be at liberty to do, and it must find a basis for this which does not rest on traditional views of the different spheres of life, and the different roles of the sexes.

What is needed, at base, is a reappraisal of what is *harmful*. That, too, has historically been defined in terms of what the dominant sex and the dominant economic class find "harmful." An analysis of rape law demonstrates that point as well as anything could. Physically coerced sexual intercourse has been regarded as constituting a redressable harm if and only if the female victim was a dependent female living under either parental or matrimonial control, and in possession of those qualities which made her desirable as a piece of sexual reproductive property available for the exclusive use of a present or future husband, and only if the perpetrator was someone other than the victim's lawful husband.[6] Physically coerced intercourse between husband and wife was not regarded as harmful, much less as redressable. It was regarded as "normal," a privilege of the head of the household, the bearer of the legal personality of the family unit; it was a hallmark of the essential legal relation of husband and wife, which was a species of the master-servant relationship in which the wife had the status of a chattel. The right that husbands had with respect to access to their wives' sexuality and reproductivity was a claim right, since wives had a legal duty to honor the conjugal demands of their husbands. It goes without saying that no similar right was accorded to wives and no similar duty devolved on husbands. Husbands also had a privilege right with respect to the use of physical coercion in pursuance of their exercise of their claim right to sexual access, since they had no legal duty to refrain from its use in this context (or indeed in others, since this was sanctioned as legitimate "discipline"). Thus, the structure of marriage with respect to sexuality and reproductivity represents a clear violation of Mill's approach to the private, since it accords rights to some which prohibit the exercise of like rights by others. Despite that, liberals have persistently seen the family as the paradigm of the private and have seen attempts to rectify its injustices and abuses as unwarranted infringements of liberty. The strength of Mill's position is that it does *not* depend on drawing a boundary between the public and the private and indeed lays down principles which can themselves be invoked to justify enforcing the same principles within the traditionally private as well as within the traditionally public sphere.

But liberals have been unwilling to apply these principles in evaluating the matrimonial relationship in particular, and sexual relations between men and women in general. Their unwillingness to see that male privileges relating to access to female sexuality and to being able to use physical coercion to effect this is a fundamental inequality, a violation of women's rights and clear harm to women, can only reflect their unwillingness to give up their advantaged position. It is this same unwillingness to acknowledge that men have been advantaged in what they have been legally permitted to do in their sexual relationships with women which makes them intransigent about the pornography issue, because pornography stands as a living testament to men's ability to use physical coercion within the sexual context. And they can rely on liberalism's central commitment to negative liberty in opposing feminist views on this and related issues precisely because rectifying the fundamental injustices which have historically characterized male-female sexual relations necessarily infringes negative liberties, both by creating obligations to refrain which previously did not exist and by abolishing previously existing privilege rights. While the basic principles Mill enunciated certainly do not commit liberals to continuing to uphold this inequality, it remains to be seen whether or not liberalism can survive and transcend the limitations of its own historical perspective. In so far as it must renounce much of its accepted thinking about what sorts of actions individuals ought to be free to do, and must recognize that negative liberty must at least temporarily take a back seat to the promotion of equality, I cannot say I am hopeful about the outcome. But the ethics of liberalism will not do as the moral framework for the achievement of sexual equality unless it can meet this challenge.

But it is clear from a consideration of the issue of pornography that so far at least the ethic of liberalism has been unable to rethink its concept of harm in a way which is consistent with sexual equality. Feminists and civil libertarians are now at complete loggerheads over this issue. The trend among feminists is clear. More and more of them are coming to see pornography as a species of hate literature.[7] Hate literature seeks to make one dislike and despise the people depicted, to make those persons seem inferior and unworthy of our respect. It seeks to set them apart and to show them as relevantly different from "us" in a way which justifies "us" in treating them differently, or it shows them as deserving to be treated badly because they have no respect for "us" or "our" values. What it must do to succeed is enforce a radical sense of their difference, their non-identity, with "us," a difference which is either utterly distasteful to "us," or one utterly opposed to "our" shared goals and values. It may also revel in their misery in an attempt to encourage feelings of wishing to contribute to that misery by doing things to them we would not think of doing to those we perceive to be relevantly similar to ourselves. So too with pornography. To achieve its impact, it relies on depicting women in humiliating, degrading, and violently abusive situations. To make matters worse, it frequently depicts them willingly, even avidly, suffering and inviting such treatment. As is obvious to even the naivest of eyes, such re-creations of heterosexual behavior and relationships feed traditional male phantasies about both themselves and women, and glorify the traditional advantages men have enjoyed in relation to exploitation of female sexuality.

Pornography is a method of socialization; it is the tangible, palpable embodiment of the imposition of the dominant sexual system which is a part of the dominant sex-class system. It is a vivid depiction of how to deploy male sexuality in just the way that will achieve maximum effect in maintaining the *status quo*. Pornography would be neither desired nor tolerated within any system other than one which sprang from the differential attribution of rights of ownership in which women and children are forms of sexual property, and in which they must either like it or quite literally lump it. It is a morality which stresses female passivity and submissiveness, and it encourages the actualization of such states through active aggression and violence. Pornography has very little to do with sex, certainly with any conception of egalitarian sexual relations between the sexes, but it has everything to do with showing how to use sexuality as an instrument of active oppression, and that is why it is wrong. Some allege that it also feeds female phantasies about themselves and men, but that is certainly being questioned, at least in so far as it can be said that there is any hard empirical data to support it.

That there should be no laws prohibiting the manufacture, sale, and distribution of pornography has traditionally and increasingly been defended as a freedom of speech, and freedom of press, issue. It is alleged that the reading or viewing of such material does not cause any harm, or that if it does, it is harm only to those who willingly consent to it. The premise that it doesn't cause harm is defended by arguing that it relates only to the phantasy level and does not translate itself into interpersonal behavior. And it goes further than this to argue that, indeed, it provides a healthy outlet, a cathartic effect, for those who might otherwise be tempted to act out their phantasies. Those who oppose pornography, particularly those who advocate its prohibition, are treated as Victorian prudes with sexual hangups. Women who object to it are seen as up-tight, unliberated, and just not "with it," sexually speaking.

The general principle underlying the liberal view is of course that expressed by Mill in "On Liberty," who argued against any form of censorship on the ground that it was only through the free flow of information that the true and the false could be separated. Prohibitions against the dissemination of any form of information function to preserve the *status quo* and to prevent the development of a critically reflective morality which is itself necessary to pave the way for needed social change. The principle has much to be said for it. But that cannot change the fact that when it is uncritically made to apply within a domain characterized by inequality and by frankly abusive behavior, a domain which is fundamentally shaped by a framework of social relations and institutions which makes all sexual relationships between men and women fundamentally coercive in nature,[8] it is bound to produce results which will be unacceptable because harmful to those who are in the preexisting inferior position and who stand to be most affected by the attitudes and beliefs, as well as the practices, of those who use it.

The liberal argument has been that such material isn't harmful at all, and certainly cannot be seen as harmful because it functions merely to inflame male sexual desire. What is the harm if all it does is give a guy a bit of a rush? And it is right here that we must begin our critique. Surely we must acknowledge at least two things. First, it is not "normal" to get one's rushes from just nything. Secondly, if one gets desirable reactions from things which create a clear and substantial risk to others, then one can justifiably be prohibited from getting them that way. Persons who get their sexual stimulation from watching the atrocities perpetrated against the Jews during the holocaust are not regarded as "normal," and rightly so. Furthermore, we do not feel that we are infringing any legitimate rights of others in preventing them access to material designed to provide sexual stimulation by this means. And the reasons for that are at least two-fold. First, as history has made all too clear, actions of this particular species do not remain at the level of mere phantasy. They have been acted out on the grand scale, so grand as to make any rational and reflective person aware that the possibility of a correlation between thought and action is at least strong enough to justify the imposition of prohibitions against material of this sort. Second, it stems from recognizing that even if the actual actions themselves are not acted out, the attitudes and beliefs of the persons enjoying it reflect attitudes toward the objects of the actions which are bad in themselves and which are bound to produce practical effects in real life, if only to be expressed in bigoted and racist attitudes. All of the same arguments apply to material which depicts black people in degrading, humiliating, and abusive circumstances. Such material is, in itself, an affront to the dignity of the objects depicted, not least because they *are* being depicted purely as objects, dehumanized and depersonalized instruments for the satisfaction of someone else's perverted tastes.

The same case can be made with respect to heterosexual pornography.[9] As Camille Le Grand puts it, "pornography teaches society to view women as less than human. It is this view which keeps women as victims."[10] The typical way in which women are depicted in pornography certainly reflects a view of them as inferior to men, as inherently masochistic, and as primarily of value as instruments for the satisfaction of male lust. That is, in itself, offensive to women, and is a straightforward objective affront to their dignity as equal persons. So on that ground alone, pornography ought to be prohibited, just as we prohibit material depicting other social groups in such a fashion.

Of course, we could hardly argue within the parameters of our present culture that it is abnormal for males to react as they do to pornography. It is, unfortunately, all too normal, at least where we have any notion of statistical normality in mind. But neither is it unusual for rape victims to feel shamed, humiliated, and degraded by being raped; this is "normal" in the culture, but from any more rational perspective, it certainly is not "normal" in any normative sense. Much of recent efforts around the issue of rape have been designed specifically to change the perspective which rape victims have on that experience. Rape victims can come to see the assaultive behavior perpetrated against them as legitimizing the anger which is appropriate to the nature of the attack. In short, it is possible both to identify the specific effects of socialization within a male supremacist and sexually coercive society, and to offset these effects with appropriate reconceptualization of the event. Women can come to identify the masochism and victimization into which they have been socialized, and can then act both to counteract it, and to be sublimely angry at a culture which socialized them into that mode. So, too, it should be possible for men to identify the sadism and attitudes of sexual aggressivity into which they are socialized and so act both to counteract them, and to be angry at a social system that produced that response. In short, *it is not a mark of personal depravity or immorality to be aroused by such material.* Given the cultural pattern of which it is a manifestation, that is not at all surprising. Indeed, it is just what we would expect. But what must be recognized is that it *is* a socialized response, and that it is a response about which men as well as women should be both concerned and angry. And certainly, once its cultural roots are exposed, it is a response which should not be seen as needing or justifying the sale and distribution of the material which elicited it. Women must object to pornography because it both reflects and reinforces the patterns of socialization appropriate to a system based on the unequal status of the sexes, in which women are consistently regarded and treated as the inferiors, and the sexual property, of men. The socialization it brings about is *in itself* a limitation of the autonomy of women. Men ought to object to it for the same reason, and they ought to recognize that the socialization it brings about in terms of their self-images and internalized standards of conduct is also undesirable, given any commitment to the notion of sexual equality.

To the extent that men are able to internalize the conviction that women and men are equal persons, and that men are not justified in using physical coercion to force women into sexual servitude, they must recognize that the pleasurable responses they get from pornography are inappropriate to that conviction and are destructive to their ability to form self-images consistent with it. But that does not entail that they are in any sense to blame for those responses: they had as little choice about that as they did about their names. But we have, then, given strong arguments in support of the view that the eliciting of a pleasurable response is not in itself any reason to condone the sale and distribution of pornography, and that a proper understanding of the nature and causes of that response gives men as well as women solid grounds for objecting to the material which occasioned it. I believe that many more men would be able to understand and accept the feminist perspective on pornography if they could come to realize that they are not responsible for their sexual responses to it given the pattern of socialization which exists to mould us all into a set of social relations which institutionalizes male aggression and female passivity.

Thus, pornography is harmful, both to women and to men, because it encourages men to combat feelings of inadequacy and low self-esteem by being aggressive and sadistic and women to feel shamed and humiliated just for being women. It encourages just that radical difference between men and women which allows men to see women as deserving of treatment they would refrain from subjecting someone to whom they perceived to be like themselves. To the extent that it also encourages women to combat insecurity and low self-esteem by becoming passive and masochistic, it presents even clearer dangers to them than it does to men, since it creates the conditions for their own victimization, but the damage it does to men who do not identify themselves as aggressive and superior to women cannot be underestimated either. However, that does not end the argument with defenders of liberalism, because their argument then moves on to the assertion that the harm to women is not direct enough to justify the legal prohibition of pornography. Frankly, I think that the argument that pornography is intrinsically offensive to the dignity of women ought to carry the day, but in the interests of completeness I want to go on to consider the other arguments that are brought to pornography's defence.

Apart from this notion of being intrinsically offensive and an infringement of the rights of women, it will be argued that even if pornography is harmful to the user, it does not lead to direct harm to women, because the phantasies it supports remain phantasies, and it in fact prevents direct harm to women through its cathartic effect. I may say at the outset that I'm not at all impressed with either of these arguments. So far as the first is concerned, there is plenty of hard evidence available which supports the contention that role modeling has a powerful effect on human behavior. Studies of wife and child abuse consistently attest to the fact that there is a strong correlation between those who are abusers and those who come from family situations which were themselves abusive. The battered child becomes the battering parent; the son who witnessed his father battering his mother, and who was himself battered, becomes a battering husband.[11] Also, the evidence about the effect of violence depicted on television on the behavior of children also points strongly in this direction.[12] People tend to act out and operationalize the behavior that they see typically acted out around them. And surely that is hardly surprising. It is what has kept civilization going. If we weren't able to perpetuate the patterns of behavior developed through cultural organization we wouldn't have come very far. So far as I know, however, there is no hard data to support the catharsis theory. It is a theory espoused by those who are looking for a rationale, though doubtless it has its roots in their awareness that they read pornography but don't rape and brutalize women. But raping and brutalizing women isn't the only harm that can be perpetrated against women. But so far there is little empirical support offered for the view that pornography feeds only the phantasy. Most psychiatric literature dealing with the "perversions" asserts that some people remain content with the phantasy while others do not.[13] But no one knows what differentiates the one who does actualize it from the one who doesn't. If this argument is going to be effective, it must be empirically demonstrated that this is so, and surely we cannot predict until the data is in that those who don't so outnumber those who do that we should, in the interests of an open society, tolerate the risk that some will. And since we are all imprisoned by the cultural stereotypes and the patterns of socialization appropriate to a society based on the sexual coercion of one sex by the other, how can those who do read it assert with certainty that they do not cause harm to women? They are hardly the best judges. As rape makes clear again, there is nowhere greater difference in perception than there is in the confusion surrounding rape and seduction. The men believe they are merely seducing, but the women perceive it as rape. And who is to judge? Certainly it is unfair to permit only those who are the perpetrators of such behavior to have a say in its interpretation.

While the liberal principle behind opposition to censorship is based on a recognition that desirable social change requires public access to information which challenges the beliefs and practices of the *status quo*, what it does not acknowledge is that information which supports the *status quo* through providing role models which advocate the use or threat of coercion as a technique of social control directed at a clearly identifiable group depicted as inferior, subordinate, and subhuman, works against the interest both of desirable social change and of the members of the subgroup so identified. This has been clearly acknowledged in the case of violently anti-semitic and other forms of racist literature. The same principles apply with respect to violently anti-female literature, and the same conclusion should follow. But this cannot come about until it is recognized and acknowledged that the dissemination of such material is itself a harm to the members of the group involved. It remains to be seen whether liberalism can accomplish this, but until it does, we cannot hope for its support on this issue.

In refusing to count as "harms" actions and practices which serve the interest of the dominant sex by reinforcing the patterns and effects of modes of socialization which support a sexist system, it renders itself incapable of changing that system and of promoting greater equality and positive liberty for women. Liberalism serves the interest of the dominant sex and the dominant class, though it contains within itself the potential for promoting greater equality and greater positive liberty for all. It can realize this potential, however, only by reconceptualizing harm in a way consistent with sex and class equality, and by recognizing that negative liberty must take second place to the promotion of equality, at least until we have achieved a framework of enforceable rules which guarantees equality within both the public and the private spheres.

When no one is allowed to do what is harmful to others, and/or what prevents them from effectively exercising liberty rights to autonomy and equality consistent with the equal attribution and effective exercise of like rights on the part of others, then we will have achieved a state in which liberty is concrete, and not a chimera which upholds the liberty of some at the expense of inequality to the rest. As women we are members of the disadvantaged sex. We are thus acting contrary to the interests of our sex in accepting any position which does not place the achievement of legally enforceable sexual equality at the forefront of its programme, particularly in relation to sexual and reproductive relations between the sexes.

That entails that we have to challenge traditional concepts of harm, and of liberty as the absence of restraint. We have been successful in removing many of the legal restraints which made both equality and liberty impossible, and that was the stage at which the ethics of liberalism served our purpose well. But unless it can extend its own principles into the sphere of interpersonal relations between the sexes, it not only cannot be relied on to serve our interests but must be confronted as adverse to those interests. The achievement of real rather than merely possible equality and liberty now depends on placing effective, enforceable restraints on those who have in the past enjoyed advantages which made both our equality and our liberty impossible. Liberalism may be prepared to scrap its reliance on the traditional division into public and private, and it may be prepared to acknowledge that the negative liberty and the privilege rights which men have traditionally been accorded, and which legitimize the use of physical coercion in their sexual and reproductive relations with women, constitute a harm and an infringement of the rights of women to reproductive and sexual autonomy and to protection from physical assault. Unless it is so prepared, we can expect little support from liberals on the issue of pornography or any other issues which reflect that basic and fundamental inequality between the sexes.

NOTES

1. This is, of course, true of John Stuart Mill himself, as is clear from his essay, "The Subjection of Women," written in 1860 and first published in 1869.

2. After the distinction between "negative" and "positive" liberty made current by Isaiah Berlin in "Two Concepts of Liberty," in *Four Essays on Liberty*, O.U.P., London, 1969.

3. I am relying here on the distinctions first made by W. N. Hohfeld, *Fundamental Legal Conceptions*, Yale U.P., 1932.

4. A more detailed account of the relationship between these philosophical and legal debates, as well as a discussion of the complexity of the legal issue of privacy itself, is found in Clark, Lorenne M. G., "Privacy, Property, Freedom, and the Family," *Philosophical Law*, (Ed.) R. Bronaugh, Greenwood Press, Conn., and London, U.K., 1978, and *Towards a Feminist Political Theory*, University of Toronto Press, Toronto, forthcoming.

5. Hart, H. L. A., *Law, Liberty, and Morality*, O.U.P., London, 1963. This was Hart's answer to the objections raised by Lord Devlin to the recommendations and theory expressed in the Wolfenden Report. Devlin's position on this and other related matters is found in Devlin, Lord Patrick, *The Enforcement of Morals*, O.U.P., London, 1965.

6. For a discussion of the way in which the historical evolution and conception of rape law functioned to maintain the sexual *status quo*, and indeed continues to produce just the results we should expect to find with respect to the treatment and handling of rape cases within the criminal justice system, see Clark, Lorenne M. G., and Lewis, Debra J., *Rape: The Price of Coercive Sexuality*, Canadian Women's Educational Press, Toronto, 1977.

7. Among the articles that spring readily to mind are Morgan, Robin, "Theory and Practice: Pornography and Rape," *Going Too Far*, Random House, N.Y., 1977, Ch. IV, pp. 163-69; Russell, Diana, "Pornography: A Feminist Perspective," unpublished paper; Brownmiller, Susan, *Against Our Will*, Simon & Schuster, N.Y., 1975, pp. 394-6; and Shear, Marie, "Free Meat Talks Back," *J. of Communication*, Vol. 26, No. 1, Winter, 1976, pp. 38-9.

8. Clark and Lewis, *Rape: The Price of Coercive Sexuality*, *op. cit.*, Chs. 7 and 8 in particular.

9. Indeed, it is true of male homosexual pornography as well. But in the interest of not legislating in the interest of others, I am not advocating that we should prohibit this species of pornography. If men object to it, as in my view they should, whether homo- or heterosexual, it is up to them to express their opposition. Certainly I do not wish to infringe the rights homosexuals have to look at what they like, even though I cannot say with certainty that I am not adversely affected by it.

10. Quoted in Russell, Diana, "Pornography: A Feminist Perspective," *op. cit.*, p. 7, no reference given.

11. See, for example, Martin, Del, *Battered Wives*, Glide Publications, San Francisco, 1976, pp. 22-3; Pizzey, Erin, *Scream Quietly or the Neighbours Will Hear*, Penguin Books, England, 1974, Ch. 4; Van Stolk, Mary, *The Battered Child in Canada*, McClelland & Stewart, Toronto, 1972, pp. 23-7.

12. Bandura, A., Ross, D., and Ross, S. A., "Transmission of Aggression Through Imitation of Aggressive Models," *J. Abnormal and Social Psychology*, 63, No. 3, 575-82.

13. Kraft-Ebbing, Richard von, *Psychopathia Sexualis*, 11th ed. rev. and enlarged, Stuttgard, 1901, pp. 94-5; Freud, S., *Introductory Lectures on Psycho-Analysis*, Standard Edition, 16:306.

Ann Garry

Pornography and Respect for Women

Pornography, like rape, is a male invention, designed to dehumanize women, to reduce the female to an object of sexual access, not to free sensuality from moralistic or parental inhibition. . . . Pornography is the undiluted essence of anti-female propaganda.

> Susan Brownmiller, *Against Our Will: Men, Women and Rape*[1]

It is often asserted that a distinguishing characteristic of sexually explicit material is the degrading and demeaning portrayal of the role and status of the human female. It has been argued that erotic materials describe the female as a mere sexual object to be exploited and manipulated sexually. . . . A recent survey shows that 41 percent of American males and 46 percent of the females believe that "sexual materials lead people to lose respect for women." . . . Recent experiments suggest that such fears are probably unwarranted.

> Presidential Commission on Obscenity and Pornography[2]

The kind of apparent conflict illustrated in these passages is easy to find in one's own thinking as well. For example, I have been inclined to think that pornography is innocuous and to dismiss "moral" arguments for censoring it because many such arguments rest on an assumption I do not share—that sex is an evil to be controlled. At the same time I believe that it is wrong to

This article first appeared in *Social Theory and Practice*, 4 (Summer 1978). It is reprinted here as it appears in Sharon Bishop and Marjorie Weinzweig, eds., *Philosophy and Women*, Wadsworth (1979). Reprinted by permission of the author.

exploit or degrade human beings, particularly women and others who are especially susceptible. So if pornography degrades human beings, then even if I would oppose its censorship I surely cannot find it morally innocuous.

In an attempt to resolve this apparent conflict I discuss three questions: does pornography degrade (or exploit or dehumanize) human beings? If so, does it degrade women in ways or to an extent that it does not degrade men? If so, must pornography degrade women, as Brownmiller thinks, or could genuinely innocuous, nonsexist pornography exist? Although much current pornography does degrade women, I will argue that it is possible to have nondegrading, nonsexist pornography. However, this possibility rests on our making certain fundamental changes in our conceptions of sex and sex roles.

I

First, some preliminary remarks: Many people now avoid using 'pornography' as a descriptive term and reserve 'obscenity' for use in legal contexts. Because 'pornography' is thought to be a judgmental word, it is replaced by 'explicit sexual material,' 'sexually oriented materials,' 'erotica,' and so on.[3] I use 'pornography' to label those explicit sexual materials intended to arouse the reader or viewer sexually. I seriously doubt whether there is a clearly defined class of cases that fits my characterization of pornography. This does not bother me, for I am interested here in obvious cases that would be uncontroversially pornographic—the worst, least artistic kind. The pornography I discuss is that which, taken as a whole, lacks "serious literary, artistic, political, or scientific merit."[4] I often use pornographic films as examples because they generate more concern today than do books or magazines.

What interests me is not whether pornography should be censored but whether one can object to it on moral grounds. The only moral ground I consider is whether pornography degrades people; obviously, other possible grounds exist, but I find this one to be the most plausible.[5] Of the many kinds of degradation and exploitation possible in the production of pornography, I focus only on the content of the pornographic work. I exclude from this discussion (i) the ways in which pornographic film makers might exploit people in making a film, distributing it, and charging too much to see it; (ii) the likelihood that actors, actresses, or technicians will be exploited, underpaid, or made to lose self-respect or self-esteem; and (iii) the exploitation and degradation surrounding the prostitution and crime that often accompany urban centers of pornography.[6] I want to determine whether pornography shows (expresses) and commends behavior or attitudes that exploit or degrade people. For example, if a pornographic film conveys that raping a woman is acceptable, then the content is degrading to women and might be called morally objectionable. Morally objectionable content is not peculiar to pornography; it can also be found in nonpornographic books, films, advertisements, and so on. The question is whether morally objectionable content is necessary to pornography.

II

At the beginning of this paper, I quoted part of a passage in which the Presidential Commission on Obscenity and Pornography tried to allay our fears that pornography will lead people to lose respect for women. Here is the full passage:

> It is often assumed that a distinguishing characteristic of sexually explicit material is the degrading and demeaning portrayal of the role and status of the human female. It has been argued that erotic materials describe the female as a mere sexual object to be exploited and manipulated sexually.
>
> One presumed consequence of such portrayals is that erotica transmits an inaccurate and uninformed conception of sexuality, and that the viewer or user will (a) develop a calloused and manipulative orientation toward women and (b) engage in behavior in which affection and sexuality are not well integrated. A recent survey shows that 41% of American males and 46% of the females believe that "sexual materials lead people to lose respect for women" (Abelson, et al. 1970). Recent experiments (Mosher 1970a, b; Mosher and Katz 1970) suggest that such fears are probably unwarranted.[7]

The argument to which the Commission addresses itself begins with the assumption that pornography presents a degrading portrayal of women as sex objects. If users of pornography adopt the view that women are sex objects (or already believe it and allow pornography to reinforce their beliefs), they will develop an attitude of callousness and lack of respect for women and will be more likely to treat women as sex objects to be manipulated and exploited. In this argument the moral objection to be brought against pornography lies in the objectionable character of the acquired attitudes and the increased likelihood of objectionable behavior—treating women as mere sex objects to be exploited rather than as persons to be respected.

A second moral argument, which does not interest the Commission, is that pornography is morally objectionable because it exemplifies and recommends behavior that violates the moral principle to respect persons. This argument contains no reference to immoral consequences; there need be no increased likelihood of behavior degrading to women. Pornography itself treats women not as whole persons but as mere sex objects "to be exploited and manipulated sexually." Such treatment is a "degrading and demeaning portrayal of the role and status" (and humanity) of women.

I will explain and discuss the first argument here and the second argument in Part III of this paper. The first argument depends on an empirical premise—that viewing pornography leads to an increase in "sex calloused" attitudes and behavior.[8] My discussion of this premise consists of four parts: (1) examples of some who accept the premise (Susan Brownmiller and the Supreme Court); (2) evidence presented for its denial by Donald Mosher for the Presidential Commission; (3) a critical examination of Mosher's studies; and (4) a concluding argument that, regardless of who (Mosher or Brownmiller) is correct, moral grounds exist for objecting to pornography.

1

Although I know of no social scientist whose data support the position that pornography leads to an increase in sex calloused behavior and attitudes, this view has popular support. For example, the Presidential Commission survey cited above finds it supported by 41 percent of American males and 46 percent of the females. In addition, passages from both Susan Brownmiller and the United States Supreme Court illustrate a similar but more inclusive view: that use of pornography leads to sex callousness or lack of respect for women (or something worse) and that we do not need social scientists to confirm or deny it.

The following passage from Brownmiller forms part of her support for the position that liberals should rethink their position on pornography because pornography is anti-female propaganda:

> The majority report of the President's Commission on Obscenity and Pornography tried to pooh-pooh the opinion of law enforcement agencies around the country that claimed their own concrete experience with offenders who were caught with the stuff led them to conclude that pornographic material is a causative factor in crimes of sexual violence. The commission maintained that it was not possible at this time to scientifically prove or disprove such a connection.
>
> But does one need scientific methodology in order to conclude that the anti-female propaganda that permeates our nation's cultural output promotes a climate in which acts of sexual hostility directed against women are not only tolerated but ideologically encouraged?[9]

In at least two 1973 opinions, the Supreme Court tried to speak to the relevance of empirical data. They considered antisocial acts in general, without any thought that "sex calloused" behavior would be particularly antisocial. In *Kaplan* v. *California*, the Court said:

> A state could reasonably regard the "hard-core" conduct described by *Suite 69* as capable of encouraging or causing anti-social behavior, especially in its impact on young people. States need not wait until behavioral experts or educators can provide empirical data before enacting controls of commerce in obscene materials unprotected by the First Amendment or by a constitutional right to privacy. We have noted the power of a legislative body to enact such regulatory law on the basis of unprovable assumptions.[10]

From *Paris Adult Theatre I* v. *Slaton:*

> But, it is argued, there is no scientific data which conclusively demonstrates that exposure to obscene materials adversely affects men and women or their society. It is urged on behalf of the petitioner that, absent such a demonstration, any kind of state regulation is "impermissible." We reject this argument. . . . Although there is no conclusive proof of a connection between antisocial behavior and obscene material, the legislature of Georgia could quite reasonably determine that such a connection does or might exist.[11]

The disturbing feature of these passages is not the truth of the view that pornography leads to sex callousness but that the Court and Brownmiller seem to have succumbed to the temptation to disregard empirical data when the data fail to meet the authors' expectations. My intention in citing these passages is not to examine them but to remind the reader of how influential this kind of viewpoint is. For convenience I call it "Brownmiller's view"— the position that pornography provides a model for male sex calloused behavior and has a numbing effect on the rest of us so that we tolerate sex calloused behavior more readily.

2

Donald L. Mosher has put forward evidence to deny that use of pornography leads to sex callousness or lack of respect for women.[12] In a study for the Presidential Commission, Mosher found that "sexually arousing pornographic films did not trigger sexual behavior even in the [sex calloused] college males whose attitudes toward women were more conducive to sexual exploitation" (p. 306), and that sex calloused attitudes toward women decreased after the viewers saw pornographic films.

Mosher developed the operative concept of "sex callousness" in one study for the Commission,[13] then used the concept as part of a more comprehensive study of the effects of pornography.[14] In the second study Mosher rated his 194 unmarried undergraduate male subjects for "sex callousness." Men who have sex calloused attitudes approve of and engage in "the use of physical aggression and exploitative tactics such as falsely professing love, getting their dates drunk, or showing pornography to their dates as a means of gaining coitus" (pp. 305–6). Men rated high in sex callousness believe that sex is for fun, believe that love and sex are separate (p. 306), and agree to statements such as "Promise a woman anything, but give her your ———," "When a woman gets uppity, it's time to ——— her," and "——— teasers should be raped" (p. 314, expletives deleted in report). Mosher suggests that this attitude is part of the "*Macho* syndrome" (p. 323).

The highly sex calloused men rated the two pornographic films they saw as more enjoyable and arousing, and less offensive or disgusting than did other subjects; but, like all of the subjects, these men did not increase their sexual activity. Mosher found no increase in "frequencies of masturbation, heterosexual petting, oral-genital sex, or coitus" in the twenty-four hours after the subjects saw the two films.[15] He did not indicate whether a change occurred in the proportion of exploitative sexual behavior to nonexploitative sexual behavior.

In addition, the data from all the male subjects indicated a *decrease* in their sex calloused attitudes. The sharpest decrease occurred in the twenty-four hours after they saw the films. Two weeks later, their level of sex callousness was still lower than before they viewed the films. Although Mosher used several "equivalent" tests to measure callousness and did not explain the differences among them, the test I saw (*Form B*) was presumably typical. It measured the extent to which the subjects agreed or disagreed with the statements such as "———teasers should be raped."

Mosher's explanation for the decrease in sex calloused attitudes is, in his own words, "speculative." Sex callousness is an expression of "exaggerated masculine style" that occurs during a period of male development ("ideally followed by an integration of love with exploitative sex" [pp. 322–23]). During this period, men, especially young men without occupational success, use the "macho" conquest mentality to reassure themselves of their masculinity. Mosher thinks that seeing a pornographic film in the company of only men satisfies the need for macho behavior—the same need that is satisfied by exploiting women, endorsing calloused attitudes, telling "dirty" jokes, or boasting about one's sexual prowess. Thus the immediate need to affirm the sex calloused statements about women decreases once the men have seen the pornographic films (pp. 322–33, 306–7).

3

For Mosher pornography is an outlet for the expression of calloused attitudes—not, as for Brownmiller, a model for calloused behavior. Some of the limitations of Mosher's study are clear to him; others apparently are not. My comments on his study fall into three categories: the limitations of his design and method, difficulties with his conclusions about sexual behavior, and difficulties with his conclusions about calloused attitudes. I am not raising general methodological issues; for example, I do not ask what measures were used to prevent a subject's (or experimenter's) civil libertarian beliefs from influencing a subject's tendency to show less calloused attitudes after seeing the films.

Limitations of Design and Method (i) Mosher's was a very short-term study: His last questions were asked of subjects two weeks after they saw the pornographic films. But since pornography is supposed to provide only a temporary outlet, this limitation may not be crucial. (ii) Mosher believes that, given the standard of commercial pornography, the films he showed displayed more than the usual amount of affection and less than the usual amount of exploitative, "kinky," or exclusively male-oriented appeal. (iii) His test was designed only to measure the most readily testable, gross ways of talking callously about, and acting callously toward, women. Women, especially recently, have become aware of many more and less subtle ways in which men can express hostility and contempt for them. An obvious example is a man who would deny that "most women are cunts at heart" but would gladly talk about women as "chicks" or "foxes" to be captured, conquered, and toyed with. In short, many more men than Mosher thinks might well fall into the "sex calloused" class; and the questions asked of all the men should have included tests for more subtle forms of callousness.

Conclusions About Sexual Behavior One of the most problematic parts of Mosher's study is that he did not test whether exploitative sexual behavior increased after the films were viewed; he tested only whether *any* sexual behavior increased and whether the endorsement of statements expressing calloused attitudes increased. One learns only that no increase occurred in the sexual behavior of the subjects (both calloused and not so calloused). One wants to know how the sex calloused men treated their partners after they saw the films; the frequency of sex, increased or not, implies nothing about the quality of their treatment of their female partners. It is not enough for Mosher to tell us that a decrease occurred in endorsing statements expressing calloused attitudes. Mosher himself points out the gap between verbal behavior in the laboratory and behavior in real-life situations with one's chosen partners.[16]

Conclusions About Calloused Attitudes (i) The most serious difficulty is one that Mosher recognizes: There was no control for the possibility that the men's level of sex callousness was unusually high in the beginning as a result of their anticipation of seeing pornographic films. (ii) Nor was there a control for the declining "shock value" of the statements expressing calloused attitudes. (iii) No precise indication of the relative decreases in sex calloused attitudes for the high- and low-callousness groups was given. Mosher states the differences for high- and low-guilt groups and has told us that highly calloused men tend to feel less guilt than other men;[17] however, one wants to know more precisely what the different effects were, particularly on the high-callousness group. (iv) Mosher realizes that his explanation for the decrease in calloused attitudes is still speculative. If seeing pornography with a group of men provides an outlet for callousness, there should be a control group of subjects seeing pornography while isolated from others. There should also be a control group experience not involving pornography at all. For example, subjects in such a group could watch a film about a Nazi concentration camp or about the first American presidents.

4

Although I am obviously critical of Mosher's work, let us suspend for a moment our critical judgment about his data and their interpretation. Even if the experience of seeing pornographic movies with other undergraduate men provides an opportunity to let out a small amount of male contempt and hostility toward women, very little follows from this for social policy or moral judgments. No sensible person would maintain that a temporary outlet is an adequate substitute for getting to the root of a problem. Given the existence of a large reservoir of male contempt and hostility toward women, and given that our society is still filled with pressures to "affirm one's manhood" at the expense of women, there is little reason to suppose a "cathartic" effect to be very significant here. Much of the research on the effects of pornography indicates that *any* effect it has—positive or negative—is short lived. At best pornography might divert or delay a man from expressing his callousness in an even more blatantly objectionable manner.

One could make the point in moral terms as follows: Sex calloused attitudes and behavior are morally objectionable; if expressing one's sex calloused attitudes lessens them temporarily, they are still morally objectionable if they persevere at some level. The most that one could say for pornography is that expressing callousness by enjoying pornography in a male group is a lesser evil than, for example, rape or obnoxiously "putting down" a woman in person. This is saying very little on behalf of pornography; it is still morally objectionable.

If pornography is morally objectionable even if Mosher is correct, then given the two alternatives posed, it is surely morally objectionable. For Brownmiller's alternative, remember, was that pornography provides a model for sex calloused behavior and has a numbing effect on many of us so that we more readily tolerate this behavior. This view, much more obviously than Mosher's, implies that pornography is morally objectionable.[18]

Before leaving Mosher and Brownmiller, let me point out that their views are not wholly incompatible. They disagree about pornography's function as an outlet or a model, of course, but Mosher's data (as he interprets their significance) are compatible with the numbing effect of pornography. Pornography may have numbed all of us (previously sex calloused or not) to the objectionable character of exploitative sex; the fact that the sex calloused men were numbed does not imply that they will feel the need to endorse calloused attitudes just after expressing their callousness in other ways. Further, Mosher's data have no bearing at all on the numbing influence on women; certainly Brownmiller means for her claim to apply to women too.

One final point remains to be considered. The Presidential Commission assumes a connection between sex callousness and the lack (or loss) of respect for women; for it appealed to Mosher's data about sex callousness to show that pornography probably will not lead people to lose respect for women.[19] But look at the results of replacing Mosher's talk about sex calloused attitudes with talk about respect for women: One would conclude that seeing pornography (with a group of men) leads to an increase in respect for women. The explanation would be that men who tend toward low respect for women can use pornography as a way of expressing their low respect. They then feel no need to endorse statements exemplifying their low respect because they have just expressed it. "Therefore" pornography provides the opportunity for their respect for women to increase. The last idea is bothersome. To think of viewing and enjoying pornography as a way of expressing lack of respect, and at the same time as a way of expressing or increasing respect, seems very strange. This is not to say that such a feat is impossible. Given our complex psychological make-up, we might be able to express both respect and lack of respect at the same time in different ways: it might also be possible to express disrespect that leads to respect (e.g., if shame at feeling disrespect leads to a temporary increase in respect). But one would need far more information about what actually happens before agreeing that any of these possibilities seems very plausible. It is necessary to spell out both the possible connections and suitable explanations for each. Without much more information, one would not want to base either favorable moral judgments about pornography or social policy on the possibility that pornography can lead to more respect for women.

Although much more remains to be said about the connection between pornography and respect for women, I will defer discussion of it to Part III of this paper. For now, let us note that even if the Presidential Commission appropriately allayed our fears about being molested on street corners by users of pornography, it would not have been warranted in placating us with the view that pornography is morally acceptable. It is fortunate that it did not try.

III

The second argument I will consider is that pornography is morally objectionable, not because it leads people to show disrespect for women, but because pornography itself exemplifies and recommends behavior that violates the moral principle to respect persons. The content of pornography is what one objects to. It treats women as mere sex objects "to be exploited and manipulated" and degrades the role and status of women. In order to evaluate this argument, I will first clarify what it would mean for pornography itself to treat someone as a sex object in a degrading manner. I will then deal with three issues central to the discussion of pornography and respect for women: how "losing respect" for a woman is connected with treating her as a sex object; what is wrong with treating someone as a sex object; and why it is worse to treat women rather than men as sex objects. I will argue that the current content of pornography sometimes violates the moral principle to respect persons. Then, in Part IV of this paper, I will suggest that pornography need not violate this principle if certain fundamental changes were to occur in attitudes about sex.

To many people, including Brownmiller and some other feminists, it appears to be an obvious truth that pornography treats people, especially women, as sex objects in a degrading manner. And if we omit 'in a degrading manner,' the statement seems hard to dispute: How could pornography *not* treat people as sex objects?

First, is it permissible to say that either the content of pornography or pornography itself degrades people or treats people as sex objects? It is not difficult to find examples of degrading content in which women are treated as sex objects. Some pornographic films convey the message that all women really want to be raped, that their resisting struggle is not to be believed. By portraying women in this manner, the content of the movie degrades women. Degrading women is morally objectionable. While seeing the movie need not cause anyone to imitate the behavior shown, we can call the content degrading to women because of the character of the behavior and attitudes it recommends. The same kind of point can be made about films (or books or TV commercials) with other kinds of degrading, thus morally objectionable, content—for example, racist messages.[20]

The next step in the argument is to infer that, because the content or message of pornography is morally objectionable, we can call pornography itself morally objectionable. Support for this step can be found in an analogy. If a person takes every opportunity to recommend that men rape women, we would think not only that his recommendation is immoral but that he is immoral too. In the case of pornography, the objection to making an inference from recommended behavior to the person who recommends is that we ascribe predicates such as 'immoral' differently to people than to films or books. A film vehicle for an objectionable message is still an object independent of its message, its director, its producer, those who act in it, and those who respond to it. Hence one cannot make an unsupported inference from "the content of the film is morally objectionable" to "the film is morally objectionable." Because the central points in this paper do not depend on whether pornography itself (in addition to its content) is morally objectionable, I will not try to support this inference. (The question about the relation of content to the work itself is, of course, extremely interesting; but in part because I cannot decide which side of the argument is more persuasive, I will pass.[21]) Certainly one appropriate way to evaluate pornography is in terms of the moral features of its content. If a pornographic film exemplifies and recommends morally objectionable attitudes or behavior, then its content is morally objectionable.

Let us now turn to the first of our three questions about respect and sex objects: What is the connection between losing respect for a woman and treating her as a sex object? Some people who have lived through the era in which women were taught to worry about men "losing respect" for them if they engaged in sex in inappropriate circumstances find it troublesome (or at least amusing) that feminists—supposedly "liberated" women—are outraged at being treated as sex objects, either by pornography or in any other way. The apparent alignment between feminists and traditionally "proper" women need not surprise us when we look at it more closely.

The "respect" that men have traditionally believed they have for women—hence a respect they can lose—is not a general respect for persons as autonomous beings; nor is it respect that is earned because of one's personal merits or achievements. It is respect that is an outgrowth of the "double standard." Women are to be respected because they are more pure, delicate, and fragile than men, have more refined sensibilities, and so on. Because some women clearly do not have these qualities, thus do not deserve respect, women must be divided into two groups—the good ones on the pedestal and the bad ones who have fallen from it. One's mother, grandmother, Sunday School teacher, and usually one's wife are "good" women. The appropriate behavior by which to express respect for good women would be, for example, not swearing or telling dirty jokes in front of them, giving them seats on buses, and other "chivalrous" acts. This kind of "respect" for good women is the same sort that adolescent boys in the back seats of cars used to "promise" not to lose. Note that men define, display, and lose this kind of respect. If women lose respect for women, it is not typically a loss of respect for (other) women as a class but a loss of self-respect.

It has now become commonplace to acknowledge that, although a place on the pedestal might have advantages over a place in the "gutter" beneath it, a place on the pedestal is not at all equal to the place occupied by other people (i.e., men). "Respect" for those on the pedestal was not respect for whole, full-fledged people but for a special class of inferior beings.

If a person makes two traditioanl assumptions—that (at least some) sex is dirty and that women fall into two classes, good and bad—it is easy to see how that person might thing that pornography could lead people to lose respect for women or that pornography is itself disrespectful to women.[22] Pornography describes or shows women engaging in activities inappropriate for good women to engage in—or at least inappropriate for them to be seen by strangers engaging in. If one sees these women as symbolic representatives of all women, then all women fall from grace with these women. This fall is possible, I believe, because the traditional "respect" that men have had for women is not genuine, wholehearted respect for full-fledged human beings but half-hearted respect for lesser beings, some of whom they feel the need to glorify and purify.[23] It is easy to fall from a pedestal. Can we imagine 41 percent of men and 46 percent of women answering "yes" to the question, "Do movies showing men engaging in violent acts lead people to lose respect for men?"?

Two interesting asymmetries appear. The first is that losing respect for men as a class (men with power, typically Anglo men) is more difficult than losing respect for women or ethnic minorities as a class. Anglo men whose behavior warrants disrespect are more likely to be seen as exceptional cases than are women or minorities (whose "transgressions" may be far less serious). Think of the following: women are temptresses; Blacks cheat the welfare system; Italians are gangsters; but the men of the Nixon administration are exceptions—Anglo men as a class did not lose respect because of Watergate and related scandals.

The second asymmetry concerns the active and passive roles of the sexes. Men are seen in the active role. If men lose respect for women because of something "evil" done by women (such as appearing in pornography), the fear is that men will then do harm to women—not the women will do harm to men. Whereas if women lose respect for male politicians because of Watergate, the fear is still that male politicians will do harm, not that women will do harm to male politicians. This asymmetry might be a result of one way in which our society thinks of sex as bad—as harm that men do to women (or to the person playing a female role, as in homosexual rape). Robert Baker calls attention to this point in " 'Pricks' and 'Chicks': A Plea for 'Persons'."[24] Our slang words for sexual intercourse—'fuck,' 'screw,' or older words such as 'take' or 'have'—not only can mean harm but have traditionally taken a male subject and a female object. The active male screws (harms) the passive female. A "bad" woman only tempts men to hurt her further.

It is easy to understand why one's proper grandmother would not want men to see pornography or lose respect for women. But feminists reject these "proper" assumptions: good and bad classes of women do not exist; and sex is not dirty (though many people believe it is). Why then are feminists angry at the treatment of women as sex objects, and why are some feminists opposed to pornography?

The answer is that feminists as well as proper grandparents are concerned with respect. However, there are differences. A feminist's distinction between treating a woman as a full-fledged person and treating her as merely a sex object does not correspond to the good-bad woman distinction. In the latter distinction, "good" and "bad" are properties applicable to groups of women. In the feminist view, all women are full-fledged people—some, however, are treated as sex objects and perhaps think of themselves as sex objects. A further difference is that, although "bad" women correspond to those thought to deserve treatment as sex objects, good women have not corresponded to full-fledged people; only men have been full-fledged people. Given the feminist's distinction, she has no difficulty whatever in saying that pornography treats women as sex objects, not as full-fledged people. She can morally object to pornography or anything else that treats women as sex objects.

One might wonder whether any objection to treatment as a sex object implies that the person objecting still believes, deep down, that sex is dirty. I don't think so. Several other possibilities emerge. First, even if I believe intellectually and emotionally that sex is healthy, I might object to being treated *only* as a sex object. In the same spirit, I would object to being treated *only* as a maker of chocolate chip cookies or *only* as a tennis partner, because only one of my talents is being valued. Second, perhaps I feel that sex is healthy, but it is apparent to me that you think sex is dirty; so I don't want you to treat me as a sex object. Third, being treated as any kind of object, not just a sex object, is unappealing. I would rather be a partner (sexual or otherwise) than an object. Fourth, and more plausible than the first three possibilities, is Robert Baker's view mentioned above. Both (i) our traditional double standard of sexual behavior for men and women and (ii) the linguistic evidence that we connect the concept of sex with the concept of harm point to what is wrong with treating women as sex objects. As I said earlier, 'fuck' and 'screw,' in their traditional uses, have taken a male subject, a female object, and have had at least two meanings: harm and have sexual intercourse with. (In addition, a prick is a man who harms people ruthlessly; and a motherfucker is so low that he would do something very harmful to his own dear mother.)[25] Because in our culture we connect sex with harm that men do to women, and because we think of the female role in sex as that of harmed object, we can see that to treat a woman as a sex object is automatically to treat her as less than fully human. To say this does not imply that no healthy sexual relationships exist; nor does it say anything about individual men's conscious intentions to degrade women by desiring them sexually (though no doubt some men have these intentions). It is merely to make a point about the concepts embodied in our language.

Psychoanalytic support for the connection between sex and harm comes from Robert J. Stoller. Stoller thinks that sexual excitement is linked with a wish to harm someone (and with at least a whisper of hostility). The key process of sexual excitement can be seen as dehumanization (fetishization) in fantasy of the desired person. He speculates that this is true in some degree of everyone, both men and women, with "normal" or "perverted" activities and fantasies.[26]

Thinking of sex objects as harmed objects enables us to explain some of the first three reasons why one wouldn't want to be treated as a sex object: (1) I may object to being treated only as a tennis partner, but being a tennis partner is not connected in our culture with being a harmed object; and (2) I may not think that sex is dirty and that I would be a harmed object; I may not know what your view is; but what bothers me is that this is the view embodied in our language and culture.

Awareness of the connection between sex and harm helps explain other interesting points. Women are angry about being treated as sex objects in situations or roles in which they do not intend to be regarded in that manner —for example, while serving on a committee or attending a discussion. It is not merely that a sexual role is inappropriate for the circumstances, it is thought to be a less fully human role than the one in which they intended to function.

Finally, the sex-harm connection makes clear why it is worse to treat women as sex objects than to treat men as sex objects, and why some men have had difficulty understanding women's anger about the matter. It is more difficult for heterosexual men than for women to assume the role of "harmed object" in sex; for men have the self-concept of sexual agents, not of passive objects. This is also related to my earlier point concerning the difference in the solidity of respect for men and for women; respect for women is more fragile. Despite exceptions, it is generally harder for people to degrade men, either sexually or nonsexually, than to degrade women. Men and women have grown up with different patterns of self-respect and expectations regarding the extent to which they deserve and will receive respect or degradation. The man who doesn't understand why women do not want to be treated as sex objects (because he'd sure like to be) would not think of himself as being harmed by that treatment; a woman might.[27] Pornography, probably more than any other contemporary institution, succeeds in treating men as sex objects.

Having seen that the connection between sex and harm helps explain both what is wrong with treating someone as a sex object and why it is worse to treat a woman in this way, I want to use the sex-harm connection to try to resolve a dispute about pornography and women. Brownmiller's view, remember, was that pornography is "the undiluted essence of anti-female propaganda" whose purpose is to degrade women.[28] Some people object to Brownmiller's view by saying that, since pornography treats both men and women as sex objects for the purpose of arousing the viewer, it is neither sexist, anti-female, nor designed to degrade women; it just happens that degrading of women arouses some men. How can this dispute be resolved?

Suppose we were to rate the content of all pornography from most morally objectionable to least morally objectionable. Among the most objectionable would be the most degrading—for example, "snuff" films and movies which recommend that men rape women, molest children and puppies, and treat nonmasochists very sadistically.

Next we would find a large amount of material (probably most pornography) not quite so blatantly offensive. With this material it is relevant to use the analysis of sex objects given above. As long as sex is connected with harm done to women, it will be very difficult not to see pornography as degrading to women. We can agree with Brownmiller's opponent that pornography treats men as sex objects, too, but we maintain that this is only pseudoequality: such treatment is still more degrading to women.[29]

In addition, pornography often exemplifies the active/passive, harmer/harmed object roles in a very obvious way. Because pornography today is male-oriented and is supposed to make a profit, the content is designed to appeal to male fantasies. Judging from the content of the most popular legally available pornography, male fantasies still run along the lines of stereotypical sex roles—and, if Stoller is right, include elements of hostility. In much pornography the women's purpose is to cater to male desires, to service the man or men. Her own pleasure is rarely emphasized for its own sake; she is merely allowed a little heavy breathing, perhaps in order to show her dependence on the great male "lover" who produces her pleasure. In addition, women are clearly made into passive objects in still photographs showing only close-ups of their genitals. Even in movies marketed to appeal to heterosexual couples, such as *Behind the Green Door*, the woman is passive and undemanding (and in this case kidnapped and hypnotized as well). Although many kinds of specialty magazines and films are gauged for different sexual tastes, very little contemporary pornography goes against traditional sex roles. There is certainly no significant attempt to replace the harmer/harmed distinction with anything more positive and healthy. In some stag movies, of course, men are treated sadistically by women; but this is an attempt to turn the tables on degradation, not a positive improvement.

What would cases toward the least objectionable end of the spectrum be like? They would be increasingly less degrading and sexist. The genuinely nonobjectionable cases would be nonsexist and nondegrading; but commercial examples do not readily spring to mind.[30] The question is: Does or could any pornography have nonsexist, nondegrading content?

IV

I want to start with the easier question: Is it possible for pornography to have nonsexist, morally acceptable content? Then I will consider whether any pornography of this sort currently exists.

Imagine the following situation, which exists only rarely today: Two fairly conventional people who love each other enjoy playing tennis and bridge together, cooking good food together, and having sex together. In all these activities they are free from hang-ups, guilt, and tendencies to dominate or objectify each other. These two people like to watch tennis matches and old romantic movies on TV, like to watch Julia Child cook, like to read the bridge column in the newspaper, and like to watch pornographic movies. Imagine further that this couple is not at all uncommon in society and that nonsexist pornography is as common as this kind of nonsexist sexual relationship. This situation sounds fine and healthy to me. I see no reason to think that an interest in pornography would disappear in these circumstances.[31] People seem to enjoy watching others experience or do (especially do well) what they enjoy experiencing, doing, or wish they could do themselves. We do not morally object to people watching tennis on TV; why would we object to these hypothetical people watching pornography?

Can we go from the situation today to the situation just imagined? In much current pornography, people are treated in morally objectionable ways. In the scene just imagined, however, pornography would be nonsexist, nondegrading, morally acceptable. The key to making the change is to break the connection between sex and harm. If Stoller is right, this task may be impossible without changing the scenarios of our sexual lives—scenarios that we have been writing since early childhood. (Stoller does not indicate whether he thinks it possible for adults to rewrite their scenarios or for social change to bring about the possibility of new scenarios in future generations.) But even if we believe that people can change their sexual scenarios, the sex-harm connection is deeply entrenched and has widespread implications. What is needed is a thorough change in people's deep-seated attitudes and feelings about sex roles in sex (sexual roles). Although I cannot even sketch a general outline of such changes here, changes in pornography should be part of a comprehensive program. Television, children's educational material, and nonpornographic movies and novels may be far better avenues for attempting to change attitudes; but one does not want to take the chance that pornography is working against one.

What can be done about pornography in particular? If one wanted to work within the current institutions, one's attempt to use pornography as a tool for the education of male pornography audiences would have to be fairly subtle at first; nonsexist pornography must become familiar enough to sell and be watched. One should realize too that any positive educational value that nonsexist pornography might have may well be as short-lived as most of the effects of pornography. But given these limitations, what could one do?

Two kinds of films must be considered. First is the short film with no plot or character development, just depicted sexual activity in which nonsexist pornography would treat men and women as equal sex partners.[32] The man would not control the circumstances in which the partners had sex or the choice of positions or acts; the woman's preference would be counted equally. There would be no suggestion of a power play or conquest on the man's part, no suggestion that "she likes it when I hurt her." Sexual intercourse would not be portrayed as primarily for the purpose of male ejaculation—his orgasm is not "the best part" of the movie. In addition, both the man and woman would express their enjoyment; the man need not be cool and detached.

The film with a plot provides even more opportunity for nonsexist education. Today's pornography often portrays the female characters as playthings even when not engaging in sexual activity. Nonsexist pornography could show women and men in roles equally valued by society, and sex equality would amount to more than possession of equally functional genitalia. Characters would customarily treat each other with respect and consideration, with no attempt to treat men or women brutally or thoughtlessly. The local Pussycat Theater showed a film written and directed by a woman (*The Passions of Carol*), which exhibited a few of the features just mentioned. The main female character in it was the editor of a magazine parody of *Viva*. The fact that some of the characters treated each other very nicely, warmly, and tenderly did not detract from the pornographic features of the movie. This should not surprise us, for even in traditional male-oriented films, lesbian scenes usually exhibit tenderness and kindness.

Plots for nonsexist films could include women in traditionally male jobs (e.g., long-distance truckdriver) or in positions usually held in respect by pornography audiences. For example, a high-ranking female Army officer, treated with respect by men and women alike, could be shown not only in various sexual encounters with other people but also carrying out her job in a humane manner.[33] Or perhaps the main character could be a female urologist. She could interact with nurses and other medical person-nel, diagnose illnesses brilliantly, and treat patients with great sympathy as well as have sex with them. When the Army officer or the urologist engage in sexual activities, they will treat their partners and be treated by them in some of the considerate ways described above.

In the circumstances we imagined at the beginning of Part IV of this paper, our nonsexist films could be appreciated in the proper spirit. Under these conditions the content of our new pornography would clearly be non-sexist and morally acceptable. But would the content of such a film be morally acceptable if shown to a typical pornography audience today? It might seem strange for us to change our moral evaluation of the content on the basis of a different audience, but an audience today is likely to see the "respected" urologist and Army officer as playthings or unusual prostitutes —even if our intention in showing the film is to counteract this view. The ef-fect is that, although the content of the film seems morally acceptable and our intention in showing it is morally flawless, women are still degraded.[34] The fact that audience attitude is so important makes one wary of giving wholehearted approval to any pornography seen today.

The fact that good intentions and content are insufficient does not imply that one's efforts toward change would be entirely in vain. Of course, I could not deny that anyone who tries to change an institution from within faces serious difficulties. This is particularly evident when one is trying to change both pornography and a whole set of related attitudes, feelings, and institutions concerning sex and sex roles. But in conjunction with other at-tempts to change this set of attitudes, it seems preferable to try to change pornography instead of closing one's eyes in the hope that it will go away. For I suspect that pornography is here to stay.[35]

NOTES

1. (New York: Simon and Schuster, 1975), p. 394.
2. *The Report of the Commission on Obscenity and Pornography* (Washington, D.C., 1970), p. 201. Hereinafter, *Report*.
3. *Report*, p. 3, n. 4; and p. 149.
4. Roth v. United States, 354 U.S. 476, 489 (1957).
5. To degrade someone in this situation is to lower her/his rank or status in humanity. This is morally objectionable because it is incompatible with showing respect for a person. Some of the other moral grounds for objecting to pornography have been considered by the Supreme Court: Pornography invades our privacy and hurts the moral tone of the community. See Paris Adult Theatre I v. Slaton, 413 U.S. 49 (1973). Even less plausible than the Court's position is to say that pornography is immoral because it depicts sex, depicts an immoral kind of sex, or caters to voyeuristic tendencies. I believe that even if moral objections to pornogra-phy exist, one must preclude any simple inference from "pornography is immoral" to "por-nography should be censored" because of other important values and principles such as freedom of expression and self-determination.
6. See Gail Sheehy, *Hustling* (New York: Dell, 1971) for a good discussion of prostitu-

tion, crime, and pornography.

7. *Report*, p. 201. References cited can be found in notes 12, 13, 14, and 22, below.

8. 'Sex callousness' is a term used by Donald Mosher in the studies to be discussed here. See notes 12 and 13 below. Although the concept of sex callousness will be explained later, the core of the meaning is obvious: To be a sex calloused male is to have attitudes toward women (e.g., lack of respect) conducive to exploiting them sexually.

9. Brownmiller, *Against Our Will*, p. 395.

10. 413 U.S. 115, 120 (1973).

11. 413 U.S. 49, 60-61.

12. "Psychological Reactions to Pornographic Films," *Technical Report of the Commission on Obscenity and Pornography,* vol. 8 (Washington, D.C., 1970), pp. 255-312. Hereinafter, *Tech. Report*, often cited by page number only in body of text.

13. "Sex Callousness toward Women," *Tech. Report*, vol. 8, pp. 313-25.

14. "Psychological Reactions to Pornographic Films." See note 12. Both of Mosher's experiments used the same questions to test "sex callousness"; I treat the experiments together, citing only page numbers in the body of the text. As far as I know, no other social scientists are working on the relationship between pornography and sex callousness toward women. Mosher made another study with Harvey Katz that is on even less secure ground. They asked undergraduate males to "aggress verbally" at female student assistants before and after seeing a pornographic film. No increase in verbal aggression occurred after they saw the film. The authors seem to be aware of many limitations of this study; particularly relevant here are the facts that only verbal aggression was tested and that the film did not show violent or aggressive behavior. "Pornographic Films, Male Verbal Aggression Against Women, and Guilt," *Tech. Report*, vol. 8, pp. 357-77.

15. *Tech. Report*, vol. 8, p. 255. In his "Conclusions" section, Mosher qualifies the claim that no increase occurred in sexual behavior for sex calloused males. He says that they "reported no increased heterosexual behavior" (p. 310).

16. "Pornograhic Films, Male Verbal Aggression Against Women, and Guilt," *Tech. Report*, vol. 8, pp. 372-73.

17. *Tech. Report*, vol. 8, p. 274. The low-guilt subjects showed a rebound in sex callousness two weeks after seeing the films; however, the level of callousness still did not reach the prefilm level.

18. Of course, pornography might have no effect at all. If this were true, some other basis must be found before calling it morally objectionable.

19. *Report*, p. 201.

20. Two further points need to be mentioned here. Sharon Bishop pointed out to me one reason why we might object to either a racist or rapist mentality in film: it might be difficult for a Black or a woman not to identify with the degraded person. A second point concerns different uses of the phrase 'treats women as sex objects.' A film treats a subject—the meaninglessness of contemporary life, women as sex objects, and so on—and this use of 'treats' is unproblematic. But one should not suppose that this is the same use of 'treats women as sex objects' that is found in the sentence 'David treats women as sex objects'; David is not treating the *subject* of women as sex objects.

21. In order to help one determine which position one feels inclined to take, consider the following statment: It is morally objectionable to write, make, sell, act in, use, and enjoy pornography, in addition, the content of pornography is immoral; however, pornography itself is not morally objectionable. If this statement seems extemely problematic, then one might well be satisfied with the claim that pornography is degrading because its content is.

22. The traditional meaning of "lose respect for women" was evidently the one assumed in the Abelson survey cited by the Presidential Commission. No explanation of its meaning is given in the report of the study. See H. Abelson et al., "National Survey of Public Attitudes Toward and Experience With Erotic Materials," *Tech. Report*, vol. 6, pp. 1-137.

23. Many feminists point this out. One of the most accessible references is Shulamith Firestone, *The Dialectic of Sex: The Case for the Feminist Revolution* (New York: Bantam, 1970), especially pp. 128-32.

24. In Richard Wasserstrom, ed., *Today's Moral Problems* (New York: Macmillan, 1975), pp. 152-71; see pp. 167-71. Also in Robert Baker and Frederick Elliston, eds., *Philosophy and Sex* (Buffalo, N.Y.: Prometheus Books, 1975).

25. Baker, in Wasserstrom, *Today's Moral Problems*, pp. 168-169.

26. "Sexual Excitement," *Archives of General Psychiatry* 33 (1976), 899-909, especially p. 903. The extent to which Stoller sees men and women in different positions with respect to harm and hostility is not clear. He often treats men and women alike, but in *Perversion: The Erotic Form of Hatred* (New York: Pantheon, 1975), pp. 89-91, he calls attention to differences between men and women especially regarding their responses to pornography and lack of understanding by men of women's sexuality. Given that Stoller finds hostility to be an essential element in male-oriented pornography, and given that women have not responded readily to such pornography, one can speculate about the possibilities for women's sexuality: their hostility might follow a different scenario; they might not be as hostile, and so on.

27. Men seem to be developing more sensitivity to being treated as sex objects. Many homosexual men have long understood the problem. As women become more sexually aggressive, some heterosexual men I know are beginning to feel treated as sex objects. A man can feel that he is not being taken seriously if a woman looks lustfully at him while he is holding forth about the French judicial system or the failure of liberal politics. Some of his most important talents are not being properly valued.

28. Brownmiller, *Against Our Will*, p. 394.

29. I don't agree with Brownmiller that the purpose of pornography is to dehumanize women; rather it is to arouse the audience. The differences between our views can be explained, in part, by the points from which we begin. She is writing about rape; her views about pornography grow out of her views about rape. I begin by thinking of pornography as merely depicted sexual activity, though I am well aware of the male hostility and contempt for women that it often expresses. That pornography degrades women and excites men is an illustration of this contempt.

30. Virginia Wright Wexman uses the film *Group Marriage* (Stephanie Rothman, 1973) as an example of "more enlightened erotica." Wexman also asks the following questions in an attempt to point out sexism in pornographic films:

Does it [the film] portray rape as pleasurable to women? Does it consistently show females nude but present men fully clothed? Does it present women as childlike creatures whose sexual interests must be guided by knowing experienced men? Does it show sexually aggressive women as castrating viragos? Does it pretend that sex is exclusively the prerogative of women under twenty-five? Does it focus on the physical aspects of lovemaking rather than the emotional ones? Does it portray women as purely sexual beings? ("Sexism of X-rated Films," *Chicago Sun-Times*, 28 March 1976.)

31. One might think, as does Stoller, that since pornography today depends on hostility, voyeurism, and sado-masochism (*Perversion*, p. 87), that sexually healthy people would not enjoy it. Two points should be noticed here, however: (1) Stoller need not think that pornography will disappear because hostility is an element of sexual excitement generally; and (2) voyeurism, when it invades no one's privacy, need not be seen as immoral; so although enjoyment of pornography might not be an expression of sexual health, it need not be immoral either.

32. If it is a lesbian or male homosexual film, no one would play a caricatured male or female role. The reader has probably noticed that I have limited my discussion to heterosexual pornography, but there are many interesting analogies to be drawn with male homosexual pornography. Very little lesbian pornography exists, though lesbian scenes are commonly found in male-oriented pornography.

33. One should note that behavior of this kind is still considered unacceptable by the military. A female officer resigned from the U.S. Navy recently rather than be court-martialed for having sex with several enlisted men whom she met in a class on interpersonal relations.

34. The content may seem morally acceptable only if one disregards such questions as, "Should a doctor have sex with her patients during office hours?" More important is the propriety of evaluating content wholly apart from the attitudes and reactions of the audience; one might not find it strange to say that one film has morally unacceptable content when shown tonight at the Pussycat Theater but acceptable content when shown tomorrow at a feminist conference.

35. Three "final" points must be made:

1. I have not seriously considered censorship as an alternative course of action. Both Brownmiller and Sheehy are not averse to it. But as I suggested in note 5, other principles seem too valuable to sacrifice when other options are available. In addition, before justifying censorship on moral grounds one would want to compare pornography to other possible offensive material: advertising using sex and racial stereotypes, violence in TV and films, and so on.

2. If my nonsexist pornography succeeded in having much "educational value," it might no longer be pornography according to my definition. This possibility seems too remote to worry me, however.

3. In discussing the audience for nonsexist pornography, I have focused on the male audience. But there is no reason why pornography could not educate and appeal to women as well.

Earlier versions of this paper have been discussed at a meeting of the Society for Women in Philosophy at Stanford University, California State University, Los Angeles, Claremont Graduate School, Western Area Meeting of Women in Psychology, UCLA Political Philosophy Discussion Group, and California State University, Fullerton Annual Philosophy Symposium. Among the many people who made helpful comments were Alan Garfinkel, Jackie Thomason, and Fred Berger. This paper grew out of "Pornography, Sex Roles, and Morality," presented as a responding paper to Fred Berger's "Strictly Peeking: Some Views on Pornography, Sex, and Censorship" in a Philosophy and Public Affairs Symposium at the American Philosophical Association, Pacific Division Meeting, March 1975.

Fred R. Berger

Pornography, Sex, and Censorship

An observer of American attitudes toward pornography faces a bewildering duality: on the one hand, we buy and read and view more of it than just about anyone else, while, on the other hand, we seek to suppress it as hard as anybody else. I presume that these facts do not merely reflect a judgment of social utilities, namely, that the best balance of goods is achieved by having it available, but under conditions of prohibition![1] I believe, in fact, that this state of things reflects aspects of our attitudes toward sex, and much of the current controversy has tended to obscure this fact, and to ignore important issues concerning sex and freedom to which the pornography issue points.

There is an important reason why the pornography controversy in the American context has tended to be narrowly focused. Our First Amendment prohibits government from abridging freedom of speech and press. Whatever interpretation is to be given that amendment, it is, in fact, stated in absolutist terms, and carries no mention or definition of obscenity or pornography. This difficulty is exacerbated by the fact that in the common-law background of our legal system, there is very little litigation which established clear legal definitions and doctrines. Obscenity convictions in the form we know seem very much an invention of the 1800s, and the late

---

Reprinted from *Social Theory and Practice*, Vol. 4, No. 2 (1977), by permission of *Social Theory and Practice* and the author.

1800s at that.[2] Moreover, in our experience with obscenity litigation, we have discovered that an enormous array of serious, even important, literature and art has fallen to the censor's axe. Thus, liberals and conservatives alike have feared that the removal of pornography from the protections of the First Amendment can endanger materials the Constitution surely ought to protect. This has given the constitutional issue great urgency.

The upshot has been that much of the debate has centered on the question of definition, and, moreover, that question has been pursued with legal needs in mind.

In this paper, I want to put aside the First Amendment to ask if there are any justifiable grounds for rejecting the arguments offered for the censorship of pornography independent of First Amendment considerations. Moreover, I shall be concerned with the *censorship* of pornography, not its *regulation*. The regulation of speech often has the same effect as censorship, and that is an important danger; nevertheless, censorship and regulation differ radically in intention, and that is an important difference.[3] I should also indicate that I shall suppose that those who favor censorship (I shall refer to them as "the censors") are not *generally* in favor of censorship, and would not prohibit what they regard as "true" art or literature.

Moreover, to lend further clarity to my discussion I shall propose a definition which is useful for the purposes of this paper, and which picks out most of what is usually regarded as pornographic, and that is all I claim for it. I define pornography as art or literature which explicitly depicts sexual activity or arousal in a manner having little or no artistic or literary value.[4] (I am assuming that scientific and medical texts are a kind of literature, with appropriate criteria of acceptability.)

The definition does, I believe, make pornography a relatively objective classification, insofar as there are clear cases on both sides of the divide, and there are relatively standard literary and artistic criteria by which to judge disputed cases.[5] In this respect, I am somewhat sympathetic to the conservatives who chide those liberals who claim they are not able to recognize standard cases of pornography as such.[6]

1. OBJECTIONS TO PORNOGRAPHY: CONFLICTING VIEWS ON SEX

Generally speaking, there are three forms of argument employed by the conservatives in favor of censorship. First, they simply hold that pornography itself is immoral or evil, irrespective of ill-consequences which may flow from it.[7] Second, they sometimes assert that, irrespective of its morality, a practice which most people in a community find abhorrent and disgusting may be rightfully suppressed. Finally, they sometimes contend that pornography promotes or leads to certain kinds of socially harmful attitudes and/or behavior.

In this paper, I wish to concentrate on this last form of argument. The proponents of the first kind of claim cannot, for the most part, meet Ronald Dworkin's challenge to specify some recognizable sense of morality according to which their claims are true.[8] Though I am aware of one form of this argument which I think *can* meet that challenge, it is dealt with obliquely in my responses to the other claims. The second form of argument has been widely debated in the literature, and I have little to add to that debate.[9] The arguments do not turn on the nature of pornography as such, and, moreover, it is fairly clear that in contemporary America there is not an overwhelming abhorrence of pornography as such.[10] The last form of argument has been given new life, however, by claims based on analyses of pornographic materials as such. These new conservative arguments differ in important ways from the traditional views of the censors, and their arguments have been extremely influential. Each of the articles I shall discuss has been widely referred to; each has been reprinted a number of times, and all but one are cited in support of recent decisions in the courts.[11]

The traditional form of the claim can be labeled the "incitement to rape" theory. It holds that pornography arouses sexual desire, which seeks an outlet, often in antisocial forms such as rape. It is this version of the claim we are most familiar with, and the evidence which is available tends to refute it.[12] I shall have more to say about it later.

The conservative views I want to take up hold that the harms from pornography are somewhat long-range. These commentators maintain that the modes of sex depicted in pornography, and the manner of depiction, will result in altering our basic attitudes toward sex and to one another, so that in the end a climate of antisocial behavior will result. I have isolated four instances of such arguments in the literature of pornography.

The first claim I shall take up is put forth in an essay by George Steiner, entitled "Night Words," which has provoked considerable comment.[13] Though Steiner expressed disapproval of censorship because it is "stupid" and cannot work, his views have been taken as an argument supporting censorship. Steiner holds that pornography constitutes an invasion of privacy:

> Sexual relations are, or should be, one of the citadels of privacy, the night place where we must be allowed to gather the splintered, harried elements of our consciousness to some kind of inviolate order and repose. It is in sexual experience that a human being alone, and two human beings in that attempt at total communication which is also communion, can discover the unique bent of their identity. There we may find ourselves through imperfect striving and repeated failure, the words, the gestures, the mental images which set the blood to racing. In that dark and wonder ever renewed both the fumblings and the light must be our own.

The new pornographers subvert this last, vital privacy; they do our imagining for us. They take away the words that were of the night and shout them over the rooftops, making them hollow. The images of our love-making, the stammerings we resort to in intimacy come prepackaged. . . . Natural selection tells of limbs and functions which atrophy through lack of use; the power to feel, to experience and realize the precarious uniqueness of each other's being, can also wither in a society.[14]

The second claim against pornography is made by Irving Kristol, in an article arguing for censorship. Kristol claims that pornography depersonalizes sex, reducing it to animal activity and thus debases it; that it essentially involves only the readers' or viewers' sexual arousal, and thus promotes an infantile sexuality which is dangerous to society:

The basic psychological fact about pornography and obscenity is that it appeals to and provokes a kind of sexual regression. The sexual pleasure one gets from pornography and obscenity is autoerotic and infantile; put bluntly, it is a masturbatory exercise of the imagination, when it is not masturbation pure and simple. . . . Infantile sexuality is not only a permanent temptation for the adolescent or even the adult—it can quite easily become a permanent, self-reinforcing neurosis. It is because of an awareness of this possibility of regression toward the infantile condition, a regression which is always open to us, that all the codes of sexual conduct ever devised by the human race take such a dim view of autoerotic activities and try to discourage autoerotic fantasies. Masturbation is indeed a perfectly natural autoerotic activity. . . . And it is precisely because it is so perfectly natural that it can be so dangerous to the mature or maturing person, if it is not controlled or sublimated in some way.[15]

The danger is borne out, he thinks, in *Portnoy's Complaint*. Portnoy's sexuality is fixed in an infantile mode (he is a prolific and inventive masturbator), and he is incapable of an adult sexual relationship with a woman. The final consequences are quite dire, as Kristol concludes: "What is at stake is civilization and humanity, nothing less. The idea that 'everything is permitted,' as Nietzsche put it, rests on the premise of nihilism and has nihilistic implications."[16]

Professor Walter Berns, writing in the magazine *The Public Interest*, maintains that pornography breaks down the feelings of shame we associate with sex. This shame, he holds, is not merely a dictate of our society, it is natural in that it protects love, and promotes the self-restraint which is requisite for a democratic polity:

Whereas sexual attraction brings man and woman together seeking a unity that culminates in the living being they together create, the voyeur maintains a distance; and because he maintains a distance he looks at, he does not communicate; and because he looks at he objectifies, he makes an object of that which it is natural to join; objectifying, he is incapable of uniting and is therefore incapable of love. The need to conceal voyeurism—the concealing shame—is corollary of the protective shame, the shame that impels lovers to search for privacy and for an experience protected from the profane and the eyes of the stranger. . . . Shame, both concealing and protective, protects lovers and therefore love.[17]

The upshot, as we might have suspected, is catastrophe. Under the banner of "the forgotten argument," Berns writes:

To live together requires rules and a governing of the passions, and those who are without shame will be unruly and unreliable; having lost the ability to restrain themselves by observing the rules they collectively give themselves, they will have to be ruled by others. Tyranny is the natural and inevitable mode of government for the shameless and the self-indulgent who have carried liberty beyond any restraint, natural and conventional.[18]

Finally, Professor Ernest van den Haag, in a series of articles, has argued for censorship on the grounds that pornography encourages "the pure libidinal principle," which leads to loss of empathy with others, and encourages violence and antisocial acts:

By de-individualizing and dehumanizing sexual acts, which thus become impersonal, pornography reduces or removes the empathy and the mutual identification which restrain us from treating each other merely as objects or means. This empathy is an individual barrier to nonconsensual acts, such as rape, torture, and assaultive crimes in general. . . .

By reducing life to varieties of sex, pornography invites us to regress to a premoral world, to return to, and to spin out, preadolescent fantasies—fantasies which reject reality and the burdens of individualism, of restraint, of tension, of conflict, of regarding others as more than objects of commitment, of thought, of consideration, and of love. These are the burdens which become heavy and hard to avoid in adolescence. By rejecting them, at least in fantasy, a return to the pure libidinal pleasure principle is achieved. And once launched by pornography, fantasy may regress to ever more infantile fears and wishes: people, altogether dehumanized, may be tortured, mutilated, and literally devoured.[19]

My response to these claims has two parts. First, I shall try to show that they reflect certain attitudes toward sex that are rejected by many, and that pornography will be judged differently by people with different attitudes toward sex. Second, I shall try to show why the gruesome results these writers foresee as the consequences of the state's failure to suppress dirty books and art are *not* likely consequences. Pornographic materials, *by their nature*, I shall contend, are an unlikely source or means of altering and influencing our basic attitudes toward one another.

Let us begin by noting certain features of pornography on which the conservative claims seem to hinge. First of all, by virtue of its lack of finesse, pornography is stark; it tends to remove those nuances of warmth and feeling which a more delicate approach is more apt to preserve. Second, there is some tendency of much pornography to assault our sensibilities and sense of the private, to estrange us somewhat. This is not difficult to understand, and it is not simply a result of our culture's attitudes toward sex. Sex, quite naturally, is associated with the notion of privacy because in sex we are in a vulnerable state, both emotionally and physically—we are very much in the control of our feelings and sensations, less aware of environmental factors, very much involved in and attending to our state of feeling and present activity.[20] Such vulnerability is the mark of private states—states on which we do not want others to intrude. This is reflected also in our attitudes toward grief and dying. Moreover, because we *want* to be totally taken with the activity itself, we do not usually want others present. So, we can concede that there is some truth to the conservative analyses of the nature of pornography.

These conservative arguments, however, involve and presuppose views on sex that many people reject. I think it is important to make these more explicit. Steiner, as we have seen, regards sex as a source of "inviolate order and repose," in which a sense of our identity is achieved by virtue of the private words, gestures, mental images which are shared with loved ones. (I envisage a hushed atmosphere.) For Van den Haag, sex, or mature sex, properly involves the burdens of "conflict, commitment, thought, consideration and love." And Kristol has distinguished mere "animal coupling" from making love, labeling the former "debased." Professor Berns's views about the nature of sex are, perhaps, clarified in a footnote:

> It is easy to prove that shamefulness is not the only principle governing the question of what may properly be presented on the stage; shamefulness would not, for example, govern the case of a scene showing the copulating of a married couple who love each other very much. That is not intrinsically shameful —on the contrary—yet it ought not to be shown. The principle here is, I think, an aesthetic one; such a scene is dramatically weak because the response of the audience would be characterized by prurience and not by a sympathy with what the scene is intended to portray, a beautiful love.[21]

The trouble with these views is that they see sex as normal or proper only within the context of deep commitment, shared responsibility, loving concern, and as involving restraint and repression of pure pleasure. Indeed, Professor Berns's footnote not only carries the suggestion that anything but married love is shameful, but also could be uncharitably interpreted as holding that "a beautiful love" is something which holds between disembodied souls, and in no way involves sexual communion, or the sharing of physical joy and pleasure. It seems to him that if we got some sense of the pleasure the couple take in one another physically, some hint of the physical forms of their communications and sense of mutuality, that this would somehow detract from our sympathy with their "beautiful love."

Now, many in our society reject these analyses of sex, either totally or partially. I want to sketch two possible views so that we might have a sense of the wider context of attitudes within which the pornography problem should be discussed. As many liberals share the conservative attitudes toward sex and many political conservatives do not, I shall label the views I discuss as "radical" and "radical-liberal," with no further political significance to be attached to them.

The radical maintains that the entire facade of sexual attitudes in contemporary society represent sham, hypocrisy, and unnecessary forms of social control. Sexual relations are governed by the notions of duty, shame, guilt. As such, there can be no honest sexuality, since mediating all sexual relations are feelings and associations which have nothing to do with our feelings *for* one another, and, often, little to do really with our sexual natures. The conservative picture of shared communication, in an aura of intimate connection, expressive of tender love, concern, commitment which are involved in mature (preferably married) sex, is an idealized, romanticized, unreal (perhaps even infantile) depiction of what really happens in sex. The fact is that most sex is routinized, dull, unfulfilling, a source of neurosis, precisely because its practice is governed by the restraints the conservatives insist on. Those constraints dictate with *whom* one has sex, *when* one has sex, how *often* one has sex, *where* one has sex, and so on. Moreover, the web of shame and guilt which is spun around sex tends to destroy its enjoyment, and thus to stunt our sexual natures—our capacity for joy and pleasure through sex. The result is a society which is highly neurotic in its attitudes toward and practice of sex—all of which interferes with honest communication and self-realization.

The radical solution to this perceived situation is to treat sex *as* a physical act, unencumbered with romanticized notions of love. Human sex just *is* a form of animal coupling, and to make more of it is to invite dishonesty and neurosis.

It seems to me that it is *this* sort of attitude which the conservative most fears. Though the conservative claims that such an attitude will result in devaluing humans, it is not clear why. He seems to infer that because the radical is willing to treat others as sources of pleasure, without the necessity of emotional commitment, he therefore perceives them as mere *instruments* of pleasure. This, of course, does not follow, either logically or as a matter of probability. Nor have I ever met a conservative who thought that correspondingly, if people are permitted to make profits from others in business dealings, they will come to view them as mere sources of profits. The point is that it is absurd to suppose that one who no longer thinks of *sex* in terms of shame and guilt must lose the sense of shame and guilt at harming others, either through sex, or in other ways.

I do not wish to dwell on the radical position, however, because there is a more widespread view which I have labeled the "radical-liberal" view which I wish to consider. This conception accepts a large part of the radical critique, in particular the notion that guilt and shame, duty and commitment, are not necessary to fully human sex. The radical-liberal agrees that much of our ordinary sexual relations are marred by the inhibitions these impose. He or she need not, however, reject sex as an element in loving relationships, and he or she may well insist that love does engender special commitments and concern with which sex is properly entangled. But, the radical-liberal does not reject physical sex for its own sake as something debased or wicked, or shorn of human qualities. Indeed, he or she may insist that greater concern with the physical aspects of sexuality is needed to break down those emotional connections with sex which stand as barriers to its enjoyment, and as barrier to free open communication with others, and to one's development of a sense of one's sexual identity—a development in terms of one's own needs, desires, and life-style.

The intensity of such needs on the part of many people is, I believe, well-depicted in Erica Jong's contemporary novel, *Fear of Flying*. In the book, her heroine expresses her reaction to the attitude that a woman's identity is to be found in her relationship with a man. Female solitude is perceived as un-American and selfish. Thus, women live waiting to be half of something else, rather than being simply themselves. These American attitudes are perceived as inhibitions to the woman's self-discovery. The heroine describes her reaction:

> My response to all this was not (not yet) to have an affair and not (not yet) to hit the open road, but to evolve my fantasy of the Zipless Fuck. The zipless fuck was more than a fuck. It was a platonic ideal. Zipless because when you came together zippers fell away like rose petals, underwear blew off in one breath like dandelion fluff. Tongues intertwined and turned liquid. Your whole soul flowed out through your tongue and into the mouth of your lover.
>
> For the true, ultimate zipless A-1 fuck, it was necessary that you never get to know the man very well. I had noticed, for example, how all my infatuations dissolved as soon as I really became friends with a man, became sympathetic to his problems, listened to him *kvetch* about his wife, or ex-wives, his mother, his children. After that I would like him, perhaps even love him—but without passion. And it was passion that I wanted.[22]

She thus concludes that brevity and anonymity are requisite to the perfect zipless fuck. Finally, after describing a sample fantasy, she says:

> The incident has all the swift compression of a dream and is seemingly free of all remorse and guilt; because there is no talk of her late husband or of his fiancee; because there is no rationalizing; because there is no talk at *all*. The zipless fuck is absolutely pure. It is free of ulterior motives. There is no power

game. The man is not "taking" and the woman is not "giving." No one is attempting to cuckold a husband or humilate a wife. No one is trying to prove anything or get anything out of anyone. The zipless fuck is the purest thing there is. And it is rarer than the unicorn.[23]

Whatever one may interpret as the book's final evaluation of the Zipless Fuck, it is clear that the fantasy is a response to the need for a different attitude toward sex.

The point is that to many people, the conservative's picture of sex, and the sorts of social relations in which he imbeds it, has served to starve them of the unique development of their personalities, or an aspect of it. The antidote they see is a freer, more open attitude toward sex, removed from what they regard as a mystique of duty and guilt and shame.

People with the attitudes of the radical-liberal, or who see themselves as impeded in their full self-realization by the traditional views on sex, may well find pornography something of no consequence, or may even find it beneficial—a means of removing from their own psyches the associations which inhibit their sexual natures. The plain fact is that pornography is used for this effect by various therapists, who have thereby aided people to more fulfilled lives for themselves, and happier, healthier relations with loved ones.[24]

Will such a concern with physical pleasure result in nonattachment, in antihuman feelings, in the loss of loving relationships? It is at least as plausible that just the opposite is the probable result, that by virtue of lessened anxiety and guilt over sex, an important source of human communion will be enhanced. In a Kinsey-type sex survey sponsored by *Playboy*, there was demonstrated a greatly heightened freedom in sex in America, and a greater emphasis on physical enjoyment, but this has not resulted in a significant lessening of the importance accorded to emotional ties.[25] Greater concern with pleasure has been used to *enhance* those relationships. Thus, it is no accident that among the millions who have lined up to see *Deep Throat, Behind the Green Door,* and *The Devil in Miss Jones,* have been a great many loving, married couples. Indeed, that there has come to be a body of "popular pornography"—porno for the millions—holds out some small hope that our culture will eventually develop a truly erotic artistic tradition, as explicitness becomes more natural, and tastes demand more of the productions.

We have seen that the conservative position presupposes attitudes toward sex which many reject, and that the alternative attitudes are consistent both with the acceptance of pornography and the values of care and concern for others. Let us turn now to the specific points the conservatives make concerning alleged harms.

2. THE RESPONSE TO CONSERVATIVE OBJECTIONS

I want to consider first the argument concerning privacy. It was Steiner's claim that pornography takes the "words of the night," and "by shouting them over the rooftops," robs us of the ability to use them or find them in private—sex becomes a matter in the public domain. Moreover, by dehumanizing the individual, people are treated as in concentration camps. As Steiner expressed it, subsequent to the original publication of his essay: "Both pornography and totalitarianism seem to me to set up power relations which must necessarily violate privacy."[26]

If there is any plausibility to the first part of these claims, it must derive entirely from the metaphor of shouting the sacred night words over the rooftops. Were anyone to do such a thing with night words, day words, winter words, and so on, we would have a legitimate gripe concerning our privacy. But in what *way* is the voluntary perusal or viewing of pornography an invasion of privacy? His point *seems* to be that the constant consumption by the public of explicit sexual materials will come to make sex something "pre-packaged" for us, so that we will not discover how to do it ourselves, in our own ways. This is extraordinarily implausible, and if it were true, would constitute a reason for banning all literature dealing with human feelings and emotions, and ways of relating to one another. The evidence is that greater sexual explicitness is utilized as a means for people to have greater awareness of their sexuality and its possibilities, and to assimilate the experiences of others into their own lifestyles. The capacity to do this is *part* of what is involved in our being the unique individuals we are. At any rate, people who *want* the stimulation of erotic materials, who feel freer in expressing themselves through the influence of sexy art, who do not *want* an environment in which sex cannot be appreciated through explicit literature and art, will hardly be impressed with the manner in which the censor protects *their* privacy.

I want now to turn to Kristol's view that pornography is autoerotic, hence, infantile, and thus promotes a sexual regression which is a danger to civilization itself. The danger which this supposed form of infantilism poses is that it would destroy the capacity for an integral feature of mature relations (and ultimately civilized relations) if "not controlled or sublimated in some way."

Now the ultimate ground for censorship which the argument poses really has only secondary connections with the charges of autoeroticism and infantilism. Lots of things are "self-pleasuring" without being thought infantile or dangerous on that account. Consider the pleasures of the gourmet, or wine afficionado, or devotees of Turkish baths.

Kristol believes that masturbation, and pornography which is its mental form, has an appeal to us as adults, and this is dangerous. Because it *is so* attractive, it is liable to draw us away from real love, and this is why it must be headed off at the pass. The charge of infantilism, then, is only Kristol's way of making us feel bad about masturbating. By virtue of his claiming to know the rationale underlying "all the codes of sexual conduct ever devised by the human race," we are made to feel beyond the pale of civilized adult society. The argument turns, really, on the supposed dangers of an *overly* autoeroticized society, which he thinks the legalization of pornography will help produce.

In criticizing pornography on these grounds, Kristol has surely overshot his mark; for, there is nothing more masturbatory than masturbation itself. If Kristol is right, then his concern with pornography is too tepid a treatment of the danger. What the argument would show is that we must stamp out masturbation itself!

Moreover, Kristol is mistaken if he thinks that censorship of pornography will make one whit of difference to the incidence of masturbation. This is because the masturbatory imagination is perfectly limitless; it does not *need* explicit sexual stimuli. Deprived of that, it can make do with virtually anything—the impassioned kisses of film lovers, a well-filled female's sweater, or male's crotch,[27] even, we are told, a neatly displayed ankle or bare shoulder. The enormity of the problem Kristol faces is shown in the revelation of the *Playboy* survey that: "a large majority of men and women in every age group say that while they masturbate, they fantasize about having intercourse with persons they love."[28] The implications for the censor are staggering!

There are two further reasons why reasonable people will not take Kristol's view seriously. First, he underestimates the human capacity to assimilate varieties of sexual experience. People can enjoy pornography and intercourse without giving up one or the other.[29] Second, his entire argument grossly undervalues the appeal and attraction to us of the very thing he wants to preserve—mature sexual love which is fulfilling, rewarding, and integrated into the course of a loving relationship. Pornography may be in some sense autoerotic; it can be pleasant to be sexually stimulated. But it is rarely its own source of ultimate satisfaction; it usually stimulates to acquire further satisfactions. Indeed, this is presupposed by some of the conservative arguments. But there is no reason to assume that such satisfaction will be sought exclusively through masturbation, when a healthy sex relation is available with a loved one. I have *never* heard anyone, male or female, complain that their love life had been ruined by their partner's turn to masturbation as a result of an excess of pornography. On the other hand, I have heard couples rave about sex had after viewing pornographic films.

Still, there does seem to be a lingering problem which the conservatives will regard as not adequately dealt with in anything said thus far. They think that literature and art *can* influence people's attitudes and beliefs, and also their behavior, and they cannot understand why the liberal, who believes this to be true in other cases, is unwilling to admit this with respect to pornography. Now, I believe the liberal *can* admit the possibility of a causal role for pornography with respect to people's attitudes and behavior. Such an admission does not, however, establish a case for censorship.

It would be quite extraordinary if literary and visual materials which are capable of arousing normal men and women did not also have some tendency to arouse people already predisposed to harmful conduct, and especially people with an unstable psychological makeup. It is believable, even apart from any evidence, that such people might act from the fantasies such stimuli generate.

When the conservative is reasonable, however, he recognizes that the stimulation and consequent influence of pornography is a function not merely of the nature of the stimulus, but also of the person's background, upbringing, cultural environment, and his own genetic and personality structure and predisposition[30] Put *this* way, the conservative has a somewhat plausible claim that pornography can sometimes be implicated as having some causal role in the etiology of social harms.

Put in its most reasonable form, however, the claim makes quite *un*reasonable the censorship of pornography. There are two primary reasons for this: (1) Pornography is not distinguishable from other materials in producing *direct* harms of this kind; it may, in fact, exert a counter-influence to other materials which are more likely to have these effects. (2) The *indirect* harms—those produced through the influence of altered attitudes and beliefs, are highly unlikely, and not of a kind a society which values freedom will allow to become the basis of suppression without strong evidence of probable causal connections. It will seek to counter such remote influences with noncoercive means.

Let us turn to the first point—that other materials which no one would dream of suppressing are as likely to produce harms. Earl Finbar Murphy, writing in the *Wayne Law Review*, has given some graphic illustrations. He begins by pointing out that "everything, every idea, is capable of being obscene if the personality perceiving it so apprehends it." He continues:

> It is for this reason that books, pictures, charades, ritual, the spoken word, *can* and *do* lead directly to conduct harmful to the self indulging in it and to others. Heinrich Pommerenke, who was a rapist, abuser, and mass slayer of women in Germany, was prompted to his series of ghastly deeds by Cecil B. DeMille's *The Ten Commandments*. During the scene of the Jewish women dancing about the Golden Calf, all the doubts of his life came clear: women were the source of the world's trouble and it was his mission to both punish them for this and to execute them. Leaving the theater, he slew his first victim in a park nearby. John George Haigh, the British vampire who sucked his victims' blood through soda straws and dissolved their drained bodies in acid baths, first had his murder-inciting dreams and vampire-longings from watching the "voluptuous" procedure of—an Anglican High Church Service!

The prohibition and effective suppression of what the average consensus would regard as pornographic would not have reached these two. Haigh, who drank his own urine as well as others' blood, was educated to regard "all forms of pleasure as sinful, and the reading of newspapers undesirable." Pommerenke found any reference to sex in a film, however oblique, made him feel so tense inside that, "I had to do something to a woman." Albert Fish, who has been called the most perverse case known to psychiatry, decided he had a mission to castrate small boys and offer them as human sacrifices to God as a result of reading the Old Testament. Each of these had the common quality of being beyond the reach of the conventionally pornographic. They had altered the range of the erotically stimulating, and each illustrates how impossible it is to predict what will precipitate or form psycho-neurotic conduct. . . . The scope of pornography, so far from being in any way uniform, is as wide as the peculiarities of the human psyche.[31]

These are extreme cases, but they do represent a pattern on the part of people disposed to deviant behavior, as is borne out by studies of the personalities and backgrounds of sex offenders. In their book, *Pornography and Sexual Deviance*, Michael J. Goldstein and Harold S. Kant report:

A problem that arises in studying reactions to pornography among sex offenders is that they appear to generate their own pornography from nonsexual stimuli. . . . The sex offenders deduced a significantly greater number of sexual activities from the drawings (children playing near a tree, figure petting a dog, and three people standing unrelated to each other) than did the nonsex offenders. They also were more prone to incorporate recently viewed sexual pictures into a series of gradually more explicit drawings. These results imply that the sex offender is highly receptive to sexual stimuli, and reads sexual meanings into images that would be devoid of erotic connotations for the normal person. Certainly, this finding was borne out by our study of institutionalized pedophiles (child molesters), who found the familiar suntan lotion ad showing a young child, with buttocks exposed to reveal his sunburn as a dog pulls at his bathing suit, to be one of the most erotic stimuli they had encountered.[32]

Indeed, their studies seem to yield the conclusion that pornography itself does not tend to produce antisocial behavior, and that, at least in the case of rapists, other materials are more likely to do so:

We must consider that sex offenders are highly receptive to suggestions of sexual behavior congruent with their previously formed desires and will interpret the material at hand to fit their needs. It is true, however, that while few, if any, sex offenders suggest that erotica played a role in the commission of sex crimes, stimuli expressing brutality, with or without concomitant sexual behavior, were often mentioned as disturbing, by rapists in particular. This raise the question of whether the stimulus most likely to release sexual behavior is one representing sexuality, or one representing aggression.[33]

In summarizing the evidence they gathered, and which is supported by other studies, they conclude that pornography does not seem to be a significant factor in the behavior of sex offenders. Moreover, there is some evidence that "for rapists, exposure to erotica portraying 'normal' heterosexual relations can serve to ward off antisocial sexual impulses."[34]

The point is that if we take the conservative's "harm" claim in its most plausible form, we must conclude that while pornography *can* play a causal role of this type, the evidence is that many other ordinary visual and literary depictions are more likely to do so. If we take seriously the claim that having this kind of causal role is sufficient for a case for censorship, then we must do a much greater housecleaning of our media offerings than we had imagined. The problem is that while we know where to begin—with unalloyed portrayals of violence, we can hardly know where to end.

A further serious difficulty for the conservative "harm" argument arises when we ask just what *kinds* of backgrounds and attitudes *do* predispose to the unwanted behavior. The studies of Kant and Goldstein are of help here, especially with respect to rapists:

> The rapists, who found it very difficult to talk about sex, said there was little nudity in their homes while they were growing up and that sex was never discussed. Only 18 percent of the rapists said their parents had caught them with erotic materials; in those instances the parents had become angry and had punished them. (In the control group, 37 percent reported that their parents know they read erotic materials, but only 7 percent reported being punished. Most said their parents had been indifferent, and some said their parents had explained the materials to them—an occurrence not reported by any other group.)[35]
>
> For the *rapists*, the data suggest very repressive family backgrounds regarding sexuality.[36]

Moreover: "It appears that all our noncontrol groups, no matter what their ages, education, or occupations, share one common characteristic: they had little exposure to erotica when they were adolescents."[37]

These results at the very least carry the suggestion that the very attitudes toward sex which motivate the censor are part of the background and psychological formation of the personality patterns of sex offenders— backgrounds which include the repression of sexual feelings, repression of exposure to explicit sexual stimuli, an overly developed sense of shame and guilt related to sex. As we have seen, some of the censors advocate *just* this sort of model for all of society, wherein suppression of pornography is just *one* way of safeguarding society. It may well be that they are in the paradoxical position of isolating a possible evil of great extent, and then recommending and fostering a response which will help produce that very evil.[38]

There is, however, a more profound reason why the admission of a possible causal role for pornography in affecting attitudes and behavior need not support the conservative view, and why the traditional liberal may well have been right in not taking pornography seriously.

To begin with, I believe we have granted the conservatives too much in admitting that pornography depersonalizes sex. While there is a measure of truth in this claim, it is not literally true. By concentrating on physical aspects of sex, pornography does, somewhat, abstract from the web of feelings, emotions, and needs which are usually attendant on sexual experience in ordinary life. Nonetheless, people are not depicted as mere machines or animals. Indeed, where there is explicit pornographic purpose—the arousal of the reader or viewer—the end could not be accomplished were it not real fleshy people depicted. In addition, pornography almost always does have *some* human context within which sex takes place—a meeting in a bar, the bridegroom carrying his bride over the threshold, the window washer observing the inhabitant of an apartment. A study of pornography will reveal certain set patterns of such contexts; there is, indeed, a sort of orthodoxy among pornographers. And, there is an obvious reason: pornography springs from and caters to sexual fantasies. This also explains why so little context is needed; the observer quickly identifies with the scene, and is able to elaborate it in his or her own mind to whatever extent he or she wishes or feels the need. That pornography is intimately tied to fantasy—*peopled* fantasy—also accounts for one of its worst features—its tendency to treat women in conventional male chauvinist ways. Pornography, as a matter of sociological fact, has been produced by and for men with such sexual attitudes.

There are further grounds for holding that pornography does not, by its nature, dehumanize sex in the feared ways. It usually depicts people as enjoying physical activity, that is, as mutually experiencing *pleasure*. Typical pornography displays sex as something people take fun in and enjoy. There is usually little doubt the persons involved are *liking* it. All of the censors we have discussed treat *Fanny Hill* as pornographic, but it is obvious to anyone who has read the book that it absolutely resists the claim that the characters are not portrayed as real people with the usual hopes and fears, who desire not to be harmed, and desire a measure of respect as persons. The book concentrates on sex and sexual enjoyment, and *that* is why it is taken as pornographic.[39] Even sadistic pornography, it should be noted, depicts people as having enjoyment; and, it is usually sado-*masochistic* pleasures which are portrayed, with a resultant equalizing of the distribution of pleasure (if not of pain). In this respect, most pornography does not portray humans as *mere* instruments of whatever ends we have. And, in this respect, pornography does not express or evoke the genuinely immoral attitudes which a great deal of our movie, television, and literary materials cater to and reinforce.[40]

Indeed, much of what is found in the media *is* immoral in that it is expressive of, caters to, and fosters attitudes which *are* morally objectionable.

People are treated as expendable units by international spies for whom *any-thing* is permitted in the name of national security; the typical laundry soap commercial treats women as idiotic house slaves; situation comedy typically portrays fathers as moronic bunglers who, nonetheless, rightfully rule their homes as dictators (albeit, benevolent ones); the various detective programs cater to the aggressive, dominating, *macho* image of male sexuality which is endemic within large portions of American society. Pornography cannot get off the hook merely by pointing out that it depicts *people*. On the other hand, most of it does not reflect or cater to attitudes as objectionable as one now finds dominating the output of television alone. And, where it does, it is not a result of the fact it is pornographic, but, rather, that it reflects conventional views widely expressed in other forms.[41]

There remains a final point to be made about the influence of pornography on attitudes. Pornography, when it does attract us, affect us, appeal to us, has a limited, narrowly focused appeal—to our sexual appetite. Such appeal tends toward short-lived enjoyments, rather than any far-reaching effects on the personality.[42] This is why pornography has essentially entertainment and recreational use and attraction; it is taken seriously by almost no one but the censors. It shows us people having sex, and that is it; we must do the rest. Serious literature and art, however, appeal to the whole person —to the entire range of his sensibilities, desires, needs, attitude patterns and beliefs and is thus far more likely to affect our ultimate behavior patterns. Even the limited reaction of sexual arousal is often better achieved through artistic technique. The conservatives deny this, but it is difficult to see on what grounds. Both in the essays of Van den Haag and Walter Berns, there is the claim that aesthetic value would detract from the purely sexual appeal of a work.[43] I can only suppose that they think all people are possessed with, and exercise, the aesthetic sensibilities of literary and art critics, and thus readily separate out and analyze devices of technique in the experiencing of a work. This assuredly is not the case. Moreover, it is hardly plausible that artistic technique should enhance and further every *other* objective of an artist, and *not* be an accessory to the end of evoking sexual arousal. Real artistic value is unobtrusive in this respect.

Of course, television pap may well influence attitudes without having significant artistic value, merely by its sheer preponderance on the airwaves. But it is not *this* sort of role we need envisage for pornography liberated from censorship. Moreover, it is not clear its influence would be worse than that of other materials which now hog the channels.

It seems to me, however, that we have yet to make the most important response to the conservative's claims. For, up to now, we have treated the issue as if it were merely a matter of weighing up possible harms from pornography against possible benefits, and the likelihood of the occurrence of the harms. Unfortunately, this is the form the debate usually takes, when it is not strictly concerned with the First Amendment. But, something important is lost if we think the issue resolves into these questions. The more important issue turns on the fact that a great many people *like* and *enjoy* pornography, and *want* it as part of their lives, either for its enjoyment, or for more serious psychological purposes. This fact means that censorship is an interference with the freedom and self-determination of a great many people, and it is on this ground that the conservative harm argument must ultimately be rejected. For a society which accepts freedom and self-determination as centrally significant values cannot allow interferences with freedom on such grounds as these.

To give a satisfactory argument for these claims would require another paper. Moreover, I believe (with certain reservations) this has been adequately done in Mill's *On Liberty*. As the conservatives do not regard *that* as enunciating a clear, defensible body of doctrine,[44] I cannot hope to present an entirely convincing argument here. I want at the very least, however, to outline a minimal set of claims which I think bear on the issue, and which can provide ground for further debate.

The idea of a self-determining individual involves a person developing his or her own mode of life according to the person's own needs, desires, personality, and perceptions of reality. This conception has at least three features: (1) the person's desires are (so far as possible) expressions of his or her own nature—not imposed from without; (2) the manner of the development of his or her character and the pattern of the person's life, are, in large measure, a resultant of his or her own judgment, choice, and personal experience; and (3) the person's unique capacities and potentialities have been developed, or at least tried out.[45] Now, *if* one regards this as a valuable manner of living, and freedom as of value, *both* because it is intrinsic to treating others *as* self-determining agents, *and* because it is requisite for the realization of self-determination, then I think one will accept the following propositions concerning freedom:

1. The burden of producing convincing reasons and evidence is always on the person who would interfere with people's freedom and lifestyles.

2. The person who would interfere with freedom must show that the activity interfered with is likely to harm others or intefere with their rights as individuals.[46]

3. Those who would deny freedom must show that the harm or interference threatened is one from which others have a superior right to protection.

Though these propositions are subject to considerable interpretation, it seems to me that one who accepts them will, at the least, recognize that the burden of proof is not symmetric either in structure or degree. The person who would deny freedom shoulders the burden, and, moreover, he or she does not succeed merely by showing *some* harms are likely to result. Accepting freedom and self-determination as central values entails accepting some risks, in order to *be* free. We do *not* presuppose that freedom will always produce good. And, insofar as the alleged harms are indirect and remote, we are committed to employing noncoercive means to combat them. Of course, we need not interpret this in a suicidal way—allowing interference only when the harm is inevitably upon us. But, at the least, we should require a strong showing of likely harms which are far from remote, and this is a burden which the censors of pornography *cannot* meet. Indeed, on this score, the conservative arguments are *many* times *weaker* than ones which can be made concerning many other kinds of communications, and such activities as hunting for sport, automobile racing, boxing and so on.[47] If anyone wants a display of the extent to which our society allows recreation to instigate socially harmful attitudes and feelings, all he or she need do is sit in the stands during a hotly contested high school football or basketball game. And, of course these feelings quite often spill over into antisocial behavior.

Though I have defended pornography from criticism based on its content or nature, I have certainly not shown that it is always unobjectionable. Insofar as it arises in a social context entirely infused with male sexism, much of it reflects the worst aspects of our society's approved conceptions of sexual relations. Too often, the scenes depicted involve male violence and aggression toward women, male dominance over women, and females as sexual servants. Moreover, there are aspects of the commercial institutions which purvey it in the market which are quite objectionable. My argument has been that this is not necessary to pornography as such; where it is true, this reflects social and sexual attitudes already fostered by other social forces. Moreover, I have maintained that by virtue of a feature which does seem to characterize pornography—its break with certain inhibiting conceptions of sexuality, pornography may well play a role in people determining for themselves the life-style which most suits them. A society which values self-determination will interfere with it only under circumstances which the censors of pornography cannot show to hold.

Of course, I have said almost nothing about the nature of the specific freedoms we incorporate in our notion of freedom of speech. It may well be that that set of rights imposes even stricter obligations on those who would suppress forms of its exercise.

NOTES

A somewhat shorter version of this paper was presented at the meeting of the Society for Philosophy and Public Affairs, held in conjunction with the Pacific Division meetings of the American Philosophical Association, March 28, 1975, in San Diego. Professor Ann Garry delivered a commentary on the paper, for which I am grateful; in several places I have utilized points she made. I also wish to thank Susan Denning for her extremely diligent and helpful research assistance.

1. This proposition is argued for by one advocate of censorship. See Irving Kristol, "Pornography, Obscenity, and the Case for Censorship," *New York Times Magazine* (March 28, 1971): 23.

2. There are a number of brief summaries available of the development of the common-law approach to obscenity. See *The Report of the Commission on Obscenity and Pornography* (New York: Bantam, 1970), 348-54; Michael J. Goldstein and Harold S. Kant, *Pornography and Sexual Deviance* (Berkeley: University of California Press, 1973), 154-56; and an untitled essay by Charles Rembar in *Censorship: For and Against*, ed. Harold H. Hart (New York: Hart Publishing Co., 1971), 198-227. Apparently, the leading case prior to the 18th century involved Sir Charles Sedley, who, with some friends, had become drunk in a tavern, appeared naked on a balcony overlooking Covent Gardens, and shouted profanities at the crowd which gathered below; then he urinated upon, and threw bottles of urine on, the bystanders.

3. Regulation of speech is one of the most pressing problems for free speech in our contemporary, mass society, in which the control of the media is in relatively few hands, primarily concerned with the use of that media to produce profits. Moreover, the spectre of nonlegal controls, which Mill feared, is very much with us. It is surprising that so little attention has been given to the issue of the principles properly governing regulation. An indication of various forms of control utilized by government for the suppression of pornography is found by studying the development of censorship in the United States. See James C. N. Paul and Murray L. Schwartz, *Federal Censorship: Obscenity in the Mail* (New York: The Free Press, 1961).

4. I regard it as a serious drawback of the definition that it rules out by *fiat*, the claim that pornography *can* be, in and of itself, significant literature. This claim is convincingly argued for by Susan Sontag in her essay "The Pornographic Imagination," reprinted in *Perspectives on Pornography*, ed. Douglas A. Hughes (New York: St. Martin's Press, 1970), 131-69; also in her book *Styles of Radical Will* (New York: Farrar, Straus & Giroux, 1966). The argument for a broader, more inclusive definition is made convincingly by Morse Peckham in *Art and Pornography* (New York: Basic Books, 1969), chapter 1. Anyone with a serious interest in the subject of pornography will find this a most important work.

5. It is also clear that the definition would be a disaster in the legal context, since there is so great an area of *disagreement*. Moreover, there is a tremendous danger of a secondary form of censorship, in which literary critics come to watch closely how they criticize a work lest the critique be used by the censors. That this in fact has happened is testified to in an eye-opening note by the English critic Horace Judson, in *Encounter* 30 (March 1968): 57-60. To his dismay, a critical review he wrote of Selby's *Last Exit to Brooklyn* was read into the record and used in banning that book in England.

6. See, for example, Ernest van den Haag, writing in *Censorship: For and Against*, 158. Also, in "Is Pornography a Cause of Crime?" *Encounter* 29 (December 1967): 54.

7. I believe that the minority report of the Presidential Commission on Obscenity and Pornography reduces to such a view, when it is not concerned specifically with possible harms. See, for example, the rationale given on 498-500 of the report, for their legislative recommendations. Sense can be made of these passages *only* on the assumption the commissioners believe pornography is itself immoral. I might also note that if one looks up "pornography" in the *Readers' Guide*, he is advised "See immoral literature and pictures."

8. Ronald Dworkin, "Lord Devlin and the Enforcement of Morals," *Yale Law Journal* 75 (1966): 986-1005; reprinted in *Morality and the Law*, ed. Richard Wasserstrom (Belmont, Calif.: Wadsworth, 1971), 55-72.

9. For starters, one might review the essays in Wasserstrom, *Morality and the Law*.

10. In surveys done for the Presidential Commission, it was found that a (slim) majority of adults would not object to the availability of pornography if it could be shown it is not harmful. While hardly a declaration of adoration for pornography, this is not a demonstration of utter, overwhelming intolerance for it, either.

11. See, for example, Paris Adult Theatre I v. Slaton, 431 U.S. 49 (1973).

12. Report of the Commission on Obscenity, 26–32, in which the effects are summarized. Also, Goldstein and Kant, *Pornography and Sexual Deviance*, 139–53.

13. George Steiner, "Night Words: High Pornography and Human Privacy," in *Perspectives on Pornography*, 96–108.

14. Ibid., 106–07.

15. Kristol, "Pornography, Obscenity and the Case for Censorship," 113.

16. Ibid.

17. Walter Berns, "Pornography vs. Democracy: The Case for Censorship," *The Public Interest* 22 (Winter 1971): 12.

18. Ibid., 13. Berns cites Washington, Jefferson, and Lincoln as holding that democracy requires citizens of good character and self-restraint, and he seems to think that somehow this is a "forgotten argument" against pornography.

19. Van den Haag, in *Censorship: For and Against*, 146–48.

20. The extent to which feelings of vulnerability can be involved in sex is testified to by the kinds of fears which can inhibit orgasmic response. In her book reporting on techniques she has used with non- or preorgasmic women, Dr. Lonnie Garfield Barbach reports that among the factors which inhibit these women from having orgasm is the fear of appearing ugly, of their partners being repulsed by them, of losing control, fainting, or screaming. See Lonnie Garfield Barbach, *For Yourself: The Fulfillment of Female Sexuality* (Garden City, NJ: Doubleday, 1975), 11–12.

21. Berns, "Pornography vs. Democracy," 12.

22. Erica Jong, *Fear of Flying* (New York: Signet, 1973), 11.

23. Ibid., 14.

24. In *For Yourself*, Dr. Lonnie Garfield Barbach recommends the use of pornography for preorgasmic women seeking increased sexual responsiveness and fulfillment. See *For Yourself*, 75, 77, 85, 86. Dr. Wardell B. Pomeroy, one of Kinsey's collaborators, wrote *Playboy* in reaction to a 1973 Supreme Court ruling on pornography:

As a pychotherapist and marriage counselor, I sometimes recommend various erotic films, books and pictures to my patients. Many of them report that erotica helps them to free them of their inhibitions and, thus, helps them function better with their spouses. Now they will have more difficulty in seeing and reading such seriously valuable material, and I am afraid I must enlarge my own library for their perusal. *Playboy* 20 (October 1973): 57.

25. This point is made at length in the report. One example: "Despite the extensive changes that the liberation has made in the feelings that most Americans have about their own bodies, about the legitimacy of maximizing sexual pleasure and about the acceptability and normality of a wide variety of techniques of foreplay and coitus, sexual liberation has not replaced the liberal-romantic concept of sex with the recreational one. The latter attitude toward sex now coexists with the former in our society, and in many a person's feeling, but the former remains the dominant ideal." *Playboy* 20 (October 1973): 204.

26. Steiner, "Night Words," in *Perspectives*, 97.

27. That women look at, and are excited by, the bulges in men's trousers is given ample testimony in Nancy Friday's book on women's sexual fantasies. See *My Secret Garden* (New York: Pocket Book, 1974), the section entitled "Women Do Look," 214–22.

28. *Playboy*, 202.

29. See, for example, *Report of the Commission on Obscenity*, 28–29; also, Goldstein and Kant, *Pornography and Sexual Deviance*, 30.

30. Van den Haag seems to recognize this point. See "Is Pornography a Cause of Crime?" in *Encounter*, 53.

31. Earl Finbar Murphy, "The Value of Pornography," *Wayne Law Review* (1964): 668–69.

32. Goldstein and Kant, *Pornography and Sexual Deviance*, 31.

33. Ibid., 108–09.

34. Ibid., 152.

35. Ibid., 143.

36. Ibid., 145.

37. Ibid., 147.

38. To compound the paradox, if being a remote cause of harms is a prima facie ground for censoring literature, then we have some evidence that the conservative arguments ought to be censored. This is *not* a view I advocate.

39. I do not appeal to its conventional format—girl meets boy, girl loses boy, girl reunites with boy in marriage.

40. Professor Van den Haag holds that pornography "nearly always leads to sadistic pornography." It is not clear what this means; moreover, his argument is that this results *because* pornography dehumanizes sex. Since we have grounds for doubting this, we have grounds for doubting the alleged result. Also, since I am denying that pornography significantly dehumanizes sex, I am implicitly rejecting a further conservative argument I have not taken up, namely, that pornography is itself expressive of immoral attitudes irrespective of any further harmful effects. Since some liberals seem to be willing to silence Nazis or racists on such grounds, some conservatives think this argument will appeal to such liberals. I believe that both Kristol and Van den Haag maintain this view. See also Richard Kuh, *Foolish Figleaves?* (New York: Macmillan, 1967), 280ff. A position of this sort is maintained by Susan Brownmiller in her book *Against Our Will: Men, Women and Rape* (New York: Simon and Schuster, 1975), 201. Brownmiller regards pornography as an invention designed to humiliate women. I have not responded to her arguments as she gives none. Moreover, she employs a curious "double standard." She gives great weight to law enforcement officials' opinions about pornography, but would hardly be willing to take these same persons' views on rape at face value.

41. In this paragraph I have attempted to bring to bear on the argument some points made by Professor Ann Garry, in her commentary on the paper at the meeting of the Society for Philosophy and Public Affairs in San Diego, March 18, 1975.

42. *Report of the Commission on Obscenity*, 28; and Goldstein and Kant, *Pornography and Sexual Deviance*, 151.

43. Berns, in *The Public Interest*, 12 footnote, and Van den Haag, in *Perspectives*, 129.

44. See, for example, Gertrude Himmelfarb's recent critical account of Mill, *On Liberty and Liberalism: The Case of John Stuart Mill* (New York: Alfred A. Knopf, 1974). It appears to me that she has not really understood Mill. Ronald Dworkin has picked out some of the most glaring of her errors in his review in *The New York Review of Books* 21 (October 31, 1974): 21.

45. I believe this is Mill's conception. See also Sharon Hill's essay, "Self-Determination and Autonomy," in *Today's Moral Problems,* ed. Richard Wasserstrom (New York: Macmillan, 1975), 171–86.

46. I want to note three points here. First, this view of freedom permits interferences for *moral* reasons; it does *not* insist on the moral neutrality of the law. It does, however, focus on the *kinds* of moral reasons allowed to count as grounds for the denial of freedom. Second, it does not rule out special legal recognition of modes of living which are central to the culture, for example, monogamous marriage. This will have indirect effects on freedom which a liberal theory would have to recognize and deal with, but it need not rule out such recognition out of hand. In addition, the notion of "harm" could be taken to include conduct or practices which are both intrusive on public consciousness, and offensive. This could provide a basis for *regulating* the sale and distribution of pornography, even if *prohibition* is not justified. Important discussion of the principles underlying the treatment of offensiveness in the law is to be found in an article by Joel Feinberg, "Harmless Immoralities and Offensive Nuisances," in *Issues in Law and Morality*, ed. Norman Care and Thomas Trelogan (Cleveland: Case Western Reserve University, 1973). Michael Bayles's commentary on that paper, also found in the same volume, is very useful. Third, valuing self-determination may entail a limited paternalism in circum-

stances where noninterference cannot possibly further autonomy. That it is at least possible for noninterference to promote self-determination seems to have been conceived by Mill as a presupposition for applications of his principle of liberty. This helps explain some of his "applications" at the end of the essay. Just how to incorporate limited paternalism in a liberal theory is a thorny issue. The pornography issue, however, does not appear to significantly involve that issue. A useful treatment of paternalism is in Gerald Dworkin, "Paternalism," in *Morality and the Law*, 107–26.

47. So far as I can judge, the most telling "evidence" the conservatives have thus far come up with is: (a) *some* reasonable criticisms of the studies which have been done, and the interpretations which have been given them; and (b) a few, isolated, contrary studies (which are, coincidentally, open to similar or stronger objections). See especially the criticism of Victor B. Cline in the minority report of the Presidential Commission on Obscenity and Pornography, 463–89. While I do not think the conservatives need produce ironclad scientific data demonstrating their claims, we surely cannot allow the suppression of freedom when the reasons offered are poor, and the weight of available evidence is heavily *against* those claims. The minority report (it may be Dr. Cline writing in this instance—it is unclear) asserts that the "burden of proof" is on the one who would change current law. This is an indefensible imprimatur of existing law as such; and it is absolutely inconsistent with the recognition of freedom and self-determination as important moral values. The mere *existence* of law cannot be allowed as a ground for its continued existence, if freedom is to have anything but secondary importance.

Joel Feinberg

Pornography and the Criminal Law

When the possession, use, or display of sexually explicit materials is prohibited by law, and violations are punished by fine or imprisonment, many
thousands of persons are prevented from doing what they would otherwise
freely choose to do. Such forceful interference in private affairs seems
morally outrageous, unless, of course, it is supported by special justifying
reasons. In the absence of appropriate reasons, the coercive use of governmental power, based ultimately on guns and clubs, is merely arbitrary and
as such is always morally illegitimate. Criminal prohibitions, of course, are
sometimes backed by appropriate reasons, and when that is the case, they
are not morally illicit uses of force but rather reasonable regulations of our
social activities.

What then are "appropriate reasons" for criminal prohibitions? Surely
the need to prevent harm or injury to persons other than the one interfered
with is one kind of legitimate reason. Some actions, however, while harmless in themselves, are great nuisances to those who are affected by them,
and the law from time immemorial has provided remedies, some civil and
some criminal, for actions in this category. So a second kind of legitimate
reason for prohibiting conduct is the need to protect others from certain

This article is reprinted from the *University of Pittsburgh Law Review*, Vol. 40, No. 4 (Summer, 1979), by permission of the *University of Pittsburgh Law Review* and the author. This
essay will be the basis of a chapter in Professor Feinberg's forthcoming book, *The Moral
Limits of the Criminal Law*, to be published by Oxford University Press, New York, in 1983.

sorts of offensive, irritating, or inconveniencing experiences. Extreme nuisances can actually reach the threshold of harm, as when noises from the house next door prevent a student from studying at all on the evening before an examination, or when an obstructed road causes a person to be late for an important appointment. But we are not very happy with nuisances even when they do not harm our interests, but only cause irritations to our senses, or inconvenient detours from our normal course. The offending conduct produces unpleasant or uncomfortable experiences—affronts to sense or sensibility, disgust, shock, shame, embarrassment, annoyance, boredom, anger, or humiliation—from which one cannot escape without unreasonable inconvenience or even harm.

We demand protection from nuisances when we think of ourselves as *trapped* by them, and we think it unfair that we should pay the cost in inconvenience that is required to escape them. In extreme cases, the offending conduct commandeers our attention from the outside, forcing us to relinquish control of our inner states, and drop what we were doing in order to cope, when it is greatly inconvenient to do so. That is why laws prohibiting nuisances are sometimes said to protect our interest in "privacy."

What distinguishes the "liberal position" on this question is the insistence that the need to prevent harm to others and the need to prevent offensive nuisances to others between them exhaust all the types of reasons which may appropriately support criminal prohibitions. Insofar as a criminal statute is unsupported by reasons of either of these two kinds, it tends to be arbitrary and hence morally illicit. In this respect certain commonly proffered reasons are no better than no reasons at all. The need to protect either the interests or the character of the actor himself from his own folly, does not, according to the liberal, confer moral legitimacy on a criminal statute, nor does the need to prevent inherently sinful or immoral conduct as such. Liberalism so construed does not purport to be a guide to useful public policy for the utilitarian legislator, nor does it claim to provide a key to the interpretation of the American, or any other, constitution. (It is entirely possible that the moral restrictions liberalism would place on legislative discretion are not always socially useful, and also that the Constitution itself allows some morally illegitimate statutes to remain as valid laws.) Instead liberalism purports to indicate to the legislator where the moral limits to government coercion are located.

Let me state from the outset that I am a committed liberal, in this sense, on the question of the legal regulation of pornography. Like the late Herbert Packer, I believe that pornography, at its worst, is not so much a menace as a nuisance, and that the moral right of legislatures to restrict it derives from, and is limited by, the same principles that morally entitle the state to command owners of howling dogs to stop their racket, to punish owners of fertilizing plants for letting odors escape over a whole town, to prohibit indecent exposure and public defecation, and so on. It is absurd to punish nuisances as severely as harmful or injurious conduct, however, and unless certain well-understood conditions are satisfied, it may be illegitimate to punish a given nuisance at all. For that reason it may be useful, before looking at the pornography problem, to examine the restrictions recognized by legislatures and courts on the proper regulation of harmless but offensive nuisances.

I.

The most interesting aspect of the law of nuisance is its version of the unavoidable legal balancing act. Both legislatures, when they formulate statutes that define public nuisances, and courts, when they adjudicate conflicts between neighboring landowners in "private nuisance" cases, must weigh opposing considerations. Establishing that one person's conduct is or would be a nuisance to someone else is by no means sufficient to warrant legal interference. First one must compare carefully the magnitude of the nuisance to the one against the reasonableness of the conduct of the other, and the necessity "that all may get on together."[1] William Prosser, describing the various factors that weigh on one side of the scale, tells us that the magnitude of the nuisance (or "seriousness of the inconvenience") to the plaintiff in a private nuisance action depends upon (1) the extent, duration, and character of the interference, (2) the social value of the use the plaintiff makes of his land, and (3) the extent to which the plaintiff can, without undue burden or hardship, avoid the offense by taking precautions against it.[2] These three factors yield the weight to be assigned to the seriousness of the inconvenience. They must be weighed against the reasonableness of the defendant's conduct, which is determined by (1) "the social value of its ultimate purpose, (2) the motive of the defendant [in particular its character as innocent or spiteful], and (3) whether the defendant by taking reasonable steps can avoid or reduce the inconvenience to the plaintiff without undue burden or inconvenience to himself."[3] Finally Prosser would have us throw on to the scale the interests of the "public at large," in particular its interest in "the nature of the locality" where the nuisance occurred—to "what paramount use it is already devoted"—and given that background, "the suitability of the use made of the land by both plaintiff and defendant."[4] In sum, the more extended, durable, and severe the inconvenience to the plaintiff, and the greater the social value of the land uses interfered with, then the greater is the magnitude of the nuisance, while the greater the ease with which the plaintiff can avoid the nuisance, the smaller its magnitude. Similarly, the greater the social value of the defendant's conduct[5] and the freer his motives of spite toward the plaintiff, the more reasonable is his conduct, despite its inconvenience to the plaintiff, while the easier it is for him to achieve his goals by means that do not inconvenience the plaintiff, the less reasonable is his offending conduct. Finally, the prevalent character of the neighborhood weighs heavily, so that a householder who takes up residence in a manufacturing district cannot complain, as a plaintiff in a private nuisance suit, of the noise, dust, or vibration, whereas the same amount of disturbance caused by a factory in a primarily residential district, will be declared a nuisance to the landowners in its vicinity.

If, as I recommend, we think of pornographic exhibitions and publications as nuisances which may properly be controlled by the law under certain very strict conditions, we shall have to posit a similar set of conflicting considerations to be weighed carefully, not only by juries in private tort suits, but also by legislatures in their deliberations over the wording of criminal statutes designed to prohibit and punish pornography. Let me suggest that legislators who are impressed by the model of "public nuisance" should weigh, in the case of each main category and context of pornography, the seriousness of the offense caused to unwilling witnesses against the reasonableness of the offender's conduct. The magnitude of the offensiveness would be determined by (1) the intensity and durability of the repugnance the material produces, and the extent to which repugnance could be anticipated to be the general reaction of strangers to the conduct displayed or represented (conduct offensive only to persons with an abnormal susceptibility to offense would not count as *very* offensive), (2) the ease with which unwilling witnesses can avoid the offensive displays, and (3) whether or not the witnesses have willingly assumed the risk of being offended either through curiosity or the anticipation of pleasure. (The maxim *volenti non fit injuria* applies to offense as well as to harm.) We can refer to these norms, in order, as "the extent of offense standard" (with its "exclusion of abnormal susceptibility corollary"), "the reasonable avoidability standard," and "the *volenti* standard."

These factors would be weighed as a group against the reasonableness of the pornographers' conduct as determined by (1) its personal importance to the exhibitors themselves and its social value generally, remembering always the enormous social utility of unhampered expression (in those cases where expression is involved), (2) the availability of alternative times and places where the conduct in question would cause less offense, (3) the extent if any to which the offense is caused by spiteful motives. In addition, the legislature would examine the prior established character of various neighborhoods, and consider establishing licensed zones in areas where the conduct in question is known to be already prevalent, so that people inclined to be offended are not likely to stumble on it to their surprise.

A legislature, of course, does not concern itself with judging specific actions and specific offended states after they have occurred. Rather its eyes are to the future, and it must weigh against one another, or authorize courts to weigh against one another, generalized *types* of conduct and offense. In hard cases this balancing procedure can be very complex and uncertain, but there are some cases that fall clearly within one or another standard in such a way as to leave no doubt how they must be decided. Thus, the *volenti* standard, for example, preempts all the others when it clearly applies. Film exhibitors cannot reasonably be charged with criminally offensive conduct when they have seen to it that the only people who witness their films are those adults who voluntarily purchased tickets to do so, knowing full well what sort of film they were about to see. One cannot be *wrongfully* offended by that to which one fully consents. Similarly, bans on *books* must fail to be morally legitimate in view of the ease with which offense at printed passages can be avoided. Since potential readers are not "captive audiences," here the reasonable avoidability standard is preemptive. So also do inoffensively expressed political or theological opinions fail to qualify as "criminal nuisances," by virtue of their personal and social importance as "free expression." On the other hand, purely spiteful motives in the offender can be a preemptive consideration weighting the balance scale decisively on the side of unreasonableness.

In some cases, no one standard is preemptive, but nevertheless all applicable standards pull together towards one inevitable decision. The public eating of excrement (coprophagia) fully and unambiguously satisfies the extent of offense standard. One doesn't have to be abnormally squeamish to be offended by the very sight of it. If it is done (say) on a public bus, it definitely fails to win the support of the reasonable avoidability and *volenti* standards, which is to say that it causes intense disgust to captive observers. Hence, by *all* the relevant criteria, it is seriously offensive. By all the criteria for weighing reasonableness, public coprophagia does poorly too. It cannot be very important to the neurotic person who does it (not as important, for example, as earning a living, or eating fresh food); it has a definitely limited social utility; it is not the expression in language of an opinion, nor does it fall into a recognized genre of aesthetic expression; and it could as well be done in private. Hence it is both seriously offensive and unredeemed by independent "reasonableness." It would not of course be called "pornography," but its criminal proscription under another name would be morally legitimate in principle, even though in practice it might be unwise, uneconomical, or unnecessary.

II.

One final preliminary matter: to what are we referring when we use the terms "pornographic" and "obscene"? There is no more unfortunate mistake in the discussion of obscenity than simply to identify that concept, either in meaning or in scope of designation, with pornography.[6] To call something obscene, in the standard uses of that term, is to condemn that thing as blatantly disgusting, for the word "obscene," like the word "funny," is used to claim that a given response (in this case disgust, in the other amusement) is likely to be the general one and/or to endorse that response as appropriate.[7] The corresponding term "pornographic," on the other hand, is purely descriptive, referring to sexually explicit writing and pictures designed entirely and plausibly to induce sexual excitement in the reader or observer. To use the terms "obscene" and "pornographic" interchangeably, then, as if they referred to precisely the same things, is to beg the essentially controversial question of whether any or all (or only) pornographic materials really are obscene. Surely, to those thousands of persons who delight in pornographic books, pictures, and films, the objects of their attachment do not seem disgusting or obscene. If these materials are nevertheless "truly obscene," they are not so merely by virtue of the definitions of the terms "obscene" and "pornography," but rather by virtue of their blatant violation of some relevant standards, and to establish their obscenity requires serious argument and persuasion. In short, whether any given acknowledged bit of pornography is *really* obscene is a logically open question to be settled by argument, not by definitional fiat.

The United States Supreme Court has committed itself to a different usage. In searching for definitions and tests of what it calls "obscenity," it has clearly had on its collective mind only pornography: not expressive oaths and intensifiers, not abusive curses and epithets, not profanity, (usually) not scatology, nor any other impolite language for which the term "obscene" is a conventional label; not objects disgusting to the senses, or non-sexual conduct and materials that offend the higher sensibilities; but *only* verbal, pictorial, and dramatic materials and exhibitions *designed effectively to be instruments of erotic arousal.* "Obscene" came to *mean* "pornographic" in the Court's parlance. Justice Harlan quite explicitly underwrote this usage in *Cohen* v. *California* in 1971.[8] Paul Robert Cohen had been convicted in a county court of disturbing the peace by wearing a jacket emblazoned on its back with the words "Fuck the draft." When the Supreme Court considered his appeal, Harlan wrote:

> This is not . . . an obscenity case. Whatever else may be necessary to give rise to the State's broader power to prohibit obscene expression, such expression must be, in some significant way, erotic. It cannot plausibly be maintained that this vulgar allusion to the Selective Service System would conjure up such psychic stimulation in anyone likely to be confronted with Cohen's crudely defaced jacket.[9]

Whatever the word "obscene" might mean to the world at large, within the chambers of the Supreme Court,[10] it has a narrow meaning indeed. Nothing can be "obscene" in the Court's primary usage unless it tends to cause erotic states in the mind of the beholder, and anything that does tend to produce that kind of "psychic stimulation" is a likely candidate for the obscenity label whether or not the induced states are offensive to the person who has them or to anyone else who may be aware of them. As we shall see, the court has occasionally departed from this narrow usage when it labels quite anti-erotic materials "obscene" because of the extreme and universal disgust they produce. On these occasions the Court has recalled its liberal function to protect unwilling audiences from offensive nuisances. But on many other occasions the Court has spoken as if "prurient interest," offensive or not, is its real enemy, as if its tests of obscenity were intended to prevent and punish inherently evil mental states (invoking the illiberal principle of "legal moralism") or else to "protect" adults from the corruption of their own characters even when that corruption is produced by their own voluntary conduct and threatens neither harm nor offense to others (invoking a moralistic version of "legal paternalism").[11] The simple liberal approach would have been to ascribe to the word "obscene" the same meaning in the law that it has in ordinary usage, namely "blatantly disgusting," and to interpret anti-obscenity laws as having the traditional liberal function of preventing offensive nuisances, subject of course to the usual balancing tests. Instead the court chose to *mean* by "obscene," "lust-inducing," and to attribute to antiobscenity statutes the quite illiberal functions of preventing sexy states of mind as an end in itself, and protecting autonomous adult citizens from moral corruption. I shall suggest that these two related mistakes—that of misdefining "obscene," and that of endorsing as constitutional the principles of moralism and paternalism—have led the Court to its present uncomfortable impasse in the law of obscenity.

III.

Although this is not an essay in American constitutional law, it will be interesting to cast a quick glance at some extraordinary recent decisions of the Supreme Court about the permissibility of pornography, and in particular the various judicial formulae the Court has produced for dealing with the problem. Even a hasty survey will reveal, I think, that the Court has moved back and forth among our various legitimizing principles, applying now a liberal offense principle mediated by balancing tests and later a thinly disguised moralism, here flirting with paternalism, there sniffing for subtle public harms, and never quite distinguishing with any clarity among them. Moral philosophers, of course, have different objectives from courts of law. My purpose is to determine which governmental restrictions and suppressions are morally legitimate; the Supreme Court aims to establish which restrictions are permitted by the Constitution, especially the First Amendment. (Still a third kind of concern, to be sharply distinguished from both of the others, is that of federal and state legislators who must decide which restrictions from among those that are consistent both with the Constitution and with principles of moral legitimacy it would be good public policy to write into law.) Despite these different concerns, it should be possible to interpret each crucial formula in various leading court decisions in the terms of our own recommended liberal standards (derived in part from nuisance law), and to criticize the deviations. Where the Court's standards depart from our own, we can conclude either that the Court has misread the Constitution or that the Constitution itself fails to satisfy our ideal prescriptions. We need not opt for one of these verdicts or the other, since this is not an essay in philosophical jurisprudence. A "legal positivist" no doubt would argue that the Constitution, for better or worse, is the law of the land, and that if it falls short of our moral ideals we should work for its amendment. A "natural law" theorist, on the other hand, would insist that all valid moral ideals are tacitly incorporated by the Constitution, so that any interpretation that ascribes to it moral ideals of an inferior or defective kind must be mistaken. Fortunately, my limited purposes in this paper enable me to evade this vexatious jurisprudential issue.

When one approaches the problem of obscenity from within a First Amendment framework, the distinction between action and expression is vitally important. Offensive conduct, as such, poses no particular constitutional problem. American legislatures are perfectly free to employ the offense principle as mediated by the standards we have recommended in prohibiting loud, raucous conduct, brazenly indecent conduct, public nudity, lewdness, offensive solicitation, and the like. But when the only "conduct" involved is the expression of some proposition, attitude, or feeling in speech or writing, or of whatever it is that gets "expressed" in art, music, drama, or film, then restrictive legislation would seem to contravene the explicit guarantees of the First Amendment. And when the "conduct" in question is the mere possession of protected symbolic or expressive materials like books, pictures, tapes, or films, or the distribution or exhibition of such materials to willing recipients or observers, then its prohibition would also seem to violate the First Amendment's strictures since it would render dangerous the creation of such materials and have a "chilling effect" on the spontaneity and freedom of expression generally. Moreover, expression is rarely valued or valuable in itself but only as part of the process of communication, and that process requires an audience. It follows that to deprive a symbol-user of his willing audience is to interfere with his "expression," and that is precisely what the First Amendment forbids. The problem that presents itself to the Supreme Court then is this: how, if at all, can statutes that forbid and punish offensive obscenity be reconciled with the First Amendment's "free speech" and "free press" guarantees when the offensiveness of the prohibited conduct resides in spoken or printed words, in pictures, plays, or films?

Until the 1950s, the United States Supreme Court had never taken a clear stand on the question of whether "obscene" (i.e. "sexy," "lust-inducing," "erotic," etc.) materials and actions are protected by the First Amendment's ban on statutes that "abridge the freedom of speech, or the press." By that time, both the federal government and virtually every state had enacted criminal statutes prohibiting obscenity, and more and more convictions were being appealed on the ground that these statutes were unconstitutional as violating freedom of expression. At the time the Court first decided to hear some of these appeals it might have appeared (as it does now to our privileged hindsight) that there were two broad alternative courses open to it:

(i) It could hold that explicitly erotic materials, or the act of distributing or exhibiting them, do qualify as "speech" or expression, and hence for protection under the First Amendment. In that case, obscene expressions, like every other use of "speech," cannot be banned because of their expressive content (the proposition, opinion, feeling, or attitude that they express) but at most, only because of the manner in which they are expressed in the circumstances. Just as speech that is ordinarily free might be punishable if it is defamatory or fraudulent, or if it is solicitation, or incitement to crime, so obscene speech, while ordinarily free, might be prohibited if in its circumstances it is a public nuisance or falls under some other recognized heading of exception. Under this alternative, the exceptive headings that include defamation, fraud, and the like, do *not* include "obscenity" (in the Supreme Court's sense) as such.

Even if the Court took this first course it could allow that statutes prohibiting obscenity might nevertheless be constitutional if they are drawn with sufficient care. Statutes might, for example, prohibit public showings of obscene matter on the grounds that such materials are extremely offensive, but in that case, one would think that the Constitution would require satisfaction of something like our proposed balancing tests for the offense principle. That is to say that even admittedly "obscene" (that is, erotic) material cannot be prohibited if the offense is only moderate or sporadic, or if it is reasonably avoidable, or if its risk is voluntarily assumed, etc. One could easily imagine what a constitutional statute controlling pornography (sexual "obscenity") would be like. Only patently offensive exhibitions to captive audiences in public places or to children would be prohibited. In short, on this first alternative course, either there would be no statutes prohibiting "obscenity," or else the statutes would all be of the kind that control public nuisances and are legitimized by a properly mediated offense principle.

A model for this first interpretation of the constitutional status of obscenity can be found in the long sequence of Supreme Court decisions interpreting the "free exercise of religion" clause of the First Amendment.[12] Normally, any conduct that is an essential part of what is recognizably a

religious service or observance, or is required by a moral rule of a recognizably religious sect, is protected. Nevertheless, such conduct can be punished
if it should happen to satisfy the definition of a crime, such as ritual human
sacrifice, or incitement to crime in a sermon read from the pulpit. Given
that the First Amendment explicitly recognizes the distinctively important
value of religious freedom, we can infer that there is a proportionately
greater burden on those who would criminalize any conduct that is part of a
religious observance. The more important a part of the religious observance
is the conduct in question, the more important must be the "state's
interest" (i.e., the harm, offense, or other evil for the aversion of which the
prohibition is necessary). Thus, balancing tests of the sort we have found in
nuisance law and then built into the offense principle are an essential element in the application of the First Amendment to statutes that restrict
religious liberty.[13]

(ii) The Court could hold, alternatively, that purely pornographic
materials do not qualify as speech or artistic expression, that in terms of the
values enshrined in the First Amendment, they are utterly without worth or
significance. This is by no means a wildly implausible or "illiberal" alternative. It would be more implausible to interpret most works of pornography
as expressions of "ideas," and while the line between erotic realism in
drama or literature, on the one hand, and pure pornography on the other, is
obscure, at least the clear cases of pornography are easily distinguishable
from any kind of expressive art. So-called "filthy pictures" and hard-core
pornographic "tales" are simply devices meant to titillate the sex organs *via*
the mediation of symbols. They are designed exclusively to perform that
function and are valued by their users only insofar as they succeed in that
limited aim. For the pure cases (if only they could always be identified!) it
would be as absurd to think of them as speech or art as it would to think of
"French ticklers," and other mechanical devices made solely to stimulate
erotic feelings, in the same fashion.

This second alternative course for the Court then would be to deny
pornography the protection of the First Amendment on the ground that it is
not "speech" in the requisite sense. It does not follow, however, that pornography is not protected by any part of the Constitution just because it is
not protected by the First Amendment; nor would it follow from the fact
that it stands beyond the scope of the whole Constitution that it is morally
legitimate to prohibit it unconditionally. If legislatures are free to bar individuals from wholly private and harmless indulgences just on the ground
that they are "obscene" (sexually stimulating), then the exercise of that
legislative freedom in many cases will lead to an invasion of the "privacy"
of individuals, or (avoiding that troublesome word) of their liberty to control their own sexual experiences in any way they like short of harming or
offending others. Unqualified prohibition of pornography may well be in
this way a violation of individual rights even though, *ex hypothesi*, it does

not violate First Amendment rights.

Faced with this morally repugnant consequence, the Supreme Court following this second alternative might respond in either of two ways. It could look, if it were so disposed, elsewhere in the Constitution for an implicit right that is violated by the prohibition of private, consented to, harmless conduct in so basic a department of human experience as sexuality. In *Griswold* v. *Connecticut*,[14] for example, the Court discovered in the interstices of the First, Fourth, Fifth, Ninth, and Fourteenth Amendments a hitherto unnoticed "right to privacy," which would perhaps be less misleadingly described as a right to personal *autonomy* in self-regarding and peculiarly intimate affairs. In *Griswold* the right to privacy was invoked to defend the sanctity of the marriage bed against laws that would prohibit the use of contraceptives. The same right was extended to unmarried persons in *Eisenstadt* v. *Baird*,[15] and to the viewing of pornographic films in one's own home in *Stanley* v. *Georgia*.[16] Once more the same right was invoked in *Roe* v. *Wade*[17] to strike down statutes that would deny to women the opportunity to have abortions and thus violate their "privacy," that is, their autonomy in respect to what is done to their own bodies. It may be stretching things a bit to use one label, "the right to privacy," for such a diversity of rights, except to indicate that there is a realm (or a number of realms) of human conduct that are simply nobody's business except that of the actors, and a fortiori are beyond the legitimate attention of the criminal law. Graham Hughes was encouraged by the trend of the Supreme Court "privacy" decisions to speak cautiously of "the maturing constitutional freedom to engage in discreet sexual stimulation or gratification."[18] What provides coherence to those motley decisions as a group, he suggests, "must be that there is something special about erotic activity that entitles a person to protection from the law unless the activity is being offensively thrust before members of the public."[19]

The second possible approach of the Court, if it were to exclude pornography from the scope of the First Amendment, would be to conclude that there is no protection to be found anywhere in the Constitution for "obscene materials" even when they are used discreetly and restricted to adults. In that case, a judge might personally regret that the properly mediated offense principle is not written into the Constitution and urge legislatures to initiate the amendment process. Or he might advocate that those antiobscenity statutes that can be legitimized only by paternalistic or moralistic principles be modified or repealed. But as a justice sworn to uphold the Constitution as he understands it, he would not be free arbitrarily to strike down the offending statutes, odiously unfair though they may be.

The two generic alternative courses sketched above will not always be as distinct as they first appear, for they will overlap in mixed cases of pornography-cum-art-or-opinion, and in instances of erotic materials that are borderline-expressive. One would think that the chief need of the Court in these cases would be not for a criterion of "obscenity" but for a criterion of "protectible expression," for where such expression is present *and* there is no captive audience or children involved, then it doesn't matter how lurid, tawdry, provocative, or unseemly the expression is; it cannot be proscribed. The point is not that explicit sexiness per se is prohibitable if only we can learn how to recognize and define it; but rather that expression per se is not prohibitable (except where it is a nuisance), so we had better learn how to recognize and define *it*.

IV.

Until the United States Supreme Court took its first close look at the problem of obscenity in 1957, the leading judicial precedent in the field was an English one. In the famous case of *Regina* v. *Hicklin*[20] Lord Cockburn formulated a test for obscenity that was "widely accepted in the American courts well into the twentieth century."[21] Between 1868 and 1957 American appellate courts commonly applied the *Hicklin* test in judging appeals of convictions under vaguely worded federal and state statutes against obscenity.[22] Lord Cockburn's words were quoted over and over again during that period: "I think the test of obscenity is this, whether the tendency of the matter charged as obscenity is to deprave and corrupt those whose minds are open to such immoral influences, and into whose hands a publication of this sort may fall."[23]

The first thing to notice about the *Hicklin* formula is that it is a test of obscenity, not a definition of the word "obscenity." Lord Cockburn apparently means by "obscenity" something like "objectional treatment of sexual materials," so his "test" tells us how to determine whether a given treatment of sex in writing or pictures is sufficiently objectionable to be banned by statutes that forbid "obscenity."

It is important to notice next that Lord Cockburn's test appeals in no way to an offense principle but rather to certain speculative harms that might be produced by exposure to erotic materials. Reading dirty books and leering at filthy pictures can "deprave and corrupt" persons who might otherwise remain innocent and pure. Virgins will become libertines and harlots; virtuous men will become rakes and lechers. Even if the skeptical view of former New York mayor Jimmy Walker is correct ("No nice girl was ever ruined by a book") and pornography does not cause virtuous people to commit sexual sins, it may yet strengthen the habit to dwell on one's sexual thoughts, and be absorbed in one's sexual fantasies short of actual conduct. That too might be a form of "corruption" or "depravity" by Victorian standards. The ultimate (and tacit) justification of the *Hicklin* test might have been derived from the harm principle, if Lord Cockburn had in mind "social harms" like the weakening of the social fabric that would come about if people generally abandoned themselves to lives of debauchery. There was no doubt an element of moralism involved too, since we can suppose that Lord Cockburn held lustful states of mind to be inherent evils whether or not they issue in harmful conduct. More likely still, the ultimate rationale is a blend of moralism and paternalism. Potential viewers of pornography need to be protected from "moral harm"; that is, harm to their characters. No matter that they voluntarily run the risk of corruption; they need to be protected from themselves. The Victorian justification for keeping pornography from adults, on this interpretation of motives, is precisely the same as our own noncontroversial rationale for keeping it away from children. Nowhere does Lord Cockburn express concern for the captive observer who might be caused offense; he is much too preoccupied with the danger to "those whose minds are open to such immoral influences" to worry about offenses to the sensibilities of those not in moral jeopardy.

There would appear to be more than a hint of the traditional British patronizing of the lower classes in Lord Cockburn's concern for those "into whose hands a publication of this sort may fall." Educated gentlemen no doubt can read pornographic books without fear of serious corruption, or corruption beyond that which motivates them in the first place, but what if the dirty book should just happen to fall into the hands of their servants, and be disseminated among ordinary workers and others (not to mention their own wives) who may be more susceptible to such influences? Perhaps Lord Cockburn's models for those "whose minds are open to such immoral influences" were alcoholics who can't hold their liquor and can't leave it alone. Perhaps he suspected that there is a similar class of "sex-addicts" who can get "hooked" on pornography and need ever greater stimulation to satisfy their growing needs, so that in the end mere pornography won't do, and illicit sexual conduct in ever greater frequency takes its place. Such would not be the normal reaction to dirty books, of course, but only the response of those unnamed susceptibles "whose minds are open to such immoral influences."

Mr. Justice Brennan, when he came to write his ground-breaking majority opinion in *Roth* v. *United States*[24] in 1957, rightly found the *Hicklin* formula (as it had come to be interpreted) objectionable on three grounds: (1) it permitted books to be judged obscene on the basis of isolated passages read out of context; (2) it allowed the obscenity of a work to be determined by its likely effects on unusually susceptible persons; (3) it posited fixed standards of propriety regardless of time, place, and circumstances.[25] These three objectionable features had made it possible for courts in Massachusetts to uphold the ban on Dreiser's *American Tragedy*,[26] Lillian Smith's *Strange Fruit*,[27] and Erskine Caldwell's *God's Little Acre*,[28] and for federal prosecutors to attempt (unsuccessfully) to ban Joyce's *Ulysses*.[29] The "isolated passage" and "culturally invariant standard" part of the *Hicklin* test now seem to be simple mistakes, but the "susceptible person" standard seems especially wrongheaded in the light of our discussion of the mediating standards for determining the gravity of a nuisance which minimizes the seriousness of offenses to abnormally susceptible individuals.[30] *Hicklin*'s concentration on the abnormally vulnerable moral character invites comparison with laws that would impose civil liability for frightening unusually skittish horses or laws that would ban the use of table salt on the grounds that some persons are allergic to it. Whatever else Brennan would put into the new test for obscenity in his *Roth* opinion, he would certainly correct the three errors of *Hicklin*, and that he did. Henceforth, he decreed, a book can be judged obscene only if "the dominant theme of the material taken as a whole"[31] is so judged; and only if it is the likely effect of the materials on "the average person" (and not the especially susceptible person) that is taken into account,[32] and only if "contemporary community standards"[33] (and not eternally fixed Victorian upper class standards) are applied to the work. The three key expressions—"dominant theme of the material taken as a whole," "average person," and "contemporary community standards"—became a fixed part of subsequent court formulations of an obscenity test, and while their vagueness did breed some mischief, they were clearly distinct improvements over *Hicklin*. Brennan had made a good start.

Unfortunately the rest of the *Roth* opinion caused a good deal of confusion, much of which remains to this day. Some of the trouble stems from the locutions "utterly without redeeming social importance" and "appealing to prurient interest," which are of course the fourth and fifth famous phrases of the *Roth* opinion. It is possible that Brennan intended his statement that obscenity is utterly without redeeming social importance to be a "synthetic judgment" giving low grades to some class of objects that can be independently identified and defined. But I suspect that his statement functions more naturally in his argument as part of the stipulation of a new legal *definition* of "obscenity." The other part of the definition is constituted by the "appeal to prurient interest" clause. So interpreted, he is saying: This is what we shall henceforth *mean* by "obscene," namely "whatever is produced for the sole purpose of arousing lustful thoughts and thus has no expressive value or function that is protected by the First Amendment." Risque novels are still literature, and the First Amendment protects *all* literature. But pure pornography, whether it uses words or pictures, or both, is no kind of literature or art at all, good or bad, but rather some quite different kind of thing, properly classifiable with chemical aphrodisiacs and mechanical sex aids rather than with poems, plays, and the like. Radical opinions advocating more sexual liberty are expressions of opinion about sexual titillation, and, as such, they too are protected, even if they should happen themselves to be intended to titillate. "Mixed cases" of art-cum-pornography (if there are any such cases when one judges "dominant themes" of "whole works") are also to be treated as protectible expression.

When you add "no value" to "small value" you get a diluted value, but even diluted values must be protected.

This interpretation finds some support in a subsequent paragraph of the *Roth* opinion where what looks like a formal definition of "obscenity" is presented: "Obscene material is material which deals with sex [genus] in a manner appealing to prurient interest [difference]."[34] In other words, pornography. The generic part of the definition makes clear that it is the realm of the erotic only which is on the Court's mind; the phrase "appealing to prurient interest" serves to rule out various non-pornographic ways of portraying sex, "for example, in art, literature and scientific works."[35] The whole definition says simply that legal obscenity is pornography; then the "utterly without importance" clause adds "and nothing but pornography." The complete definition thus identifies legal obscenity, in effect, with *pure* pornography.

What remains vague is the meaning of "appealing to." Does it mean "intended to excite such interest" or "having the function, intended or not, of exciting such interest?" Very likely, intention and probable effect are each necessary and are jointly sufficient for a work to qualify as pornography. We must embrace this interpretation if we are to handle plausibly the case of the inept pornographer who tries to earn a living selling photographs of embarrassed and heavily garbed middle-aged relatives, under the mistaken impression that they will "turn on" lustful customers. His appeal to prurience is genuine enough, just as the appeal to the mercy or charity of a hard-hearted skinflint might be genuine enough, but in neither case does it seem to be the sort of appeal that could hit its mark. The inept pornographer tried to make pornography but failed despite his evil intentions. So an "appeal," in the sense of simple intention, to the prurience of one's audience is not enough to constitute pornography. In addition the effort must be of a general character that can plausibly be expected to strike a responsive chord in . . . in whom? "In the average person in one's own contemporary community," say the earlier clauses about the "average person" and "community standards," thus filling out the definition.

If we are right about the Court's definition of "obscenity," what then is its test for determining obscenity? A chemist can tell us what he means by the word "acid" by citing a feature of the molecular structure of acids, for example that they contain hydrogen as a positive radical, or by mentioning other essential characteristics of all acids. But then when we ask him how we can go about telling an acid when we see one, he will give us answers of a different kind, theoretically less interesting, but more useful for our purposes, for example that acids are soluble in water, sour in taste, and turn litmus paper red. Similarly, a dictionary can explain the meaning of "drunk" and a physiologist can enumerate the biochemical characteristics that underlie all instances of drunkenness, but if we wish a useful and precise test of drunkenness, then we need something like a drunkometer machine and a and a metric criterion. The old *Hicklin* formula had not been meant to be a definition of "obscene," but to be more like a litmus test or drunkometer test for determining when obscenity is present. Just as the one test says that drunkenness is present when there is a certain percentage of alcohol in the blood, so the other test says that materials are obscene when they are capable of producing a certain effect on susceptible persons. Actually, the analogy is much closer to a test for determining when a substance is intoxicating than to a test for determining when a person is intoxicated. In each case what is being tested is the capacity of an object to produce effects of some measurable kind on a precisely defined class of subjects. Obviously the *Hicklin* test fails totally to do its assigned job in a satisfactory way. Does *Roth* provide a test that does any better?

Probably the best way of interpreting *Roth* is to conclude that it doesn't even attempt to supplement its definition of "obscenity" (as pornography) and its analysis of pornography (as nonexpressive) with a practical test for determining the presence of obscenity.[36] More likely the Court, both in *Roth* and its numerous *sequalia*, never even attempted to provide identifying tests of obscenity. The difficulty of doing so, in fact, filled it with collective despair, most piquantly expressed by Mr. Justice Stewart in *Jacobellis* v. *Ohio*[37] who said that he would not try to specify a criterion of "hard-core pornography," and "perhaps I could never succeed in intelligibly doing so. But I know it when I see it. . . ."[38] It may be that no litmus test of "obscenity" is needed since pure unredeemed and unsupplemented pornography is indeed accurately characterized in general descriptive formulae[39] and is easily recognized by the ordinary men and women who sit in juries. Once we have it that a given book, for example, is pornographic, the only test that is needed is whether, "taken as a whole," it is also literature or opinion, that is, protectible expression. Pure pornography is easy to recognize; what are hard to spot are the "redeeming" units or aspects of expression in such impure admixtures as artfully pornographic films and erotic realism in novels.

When all five famous phrases are combined in the *Roth* opinion, there emerges, nevertheless, a formula that bears the superficial appearance of an identifying test. It is one of the predominant confusions of the Court in those subsequent decisions in which the *Roth* formula is refined, that it is unclear whether or not the Court intended the formula to provide a practical litmus test. Indeed, Mr. Justice Brennan refers to the standard as a "substituted test" for *Hicklin* in the very sentence in which he formulates it: ". . . this test: whether to the average person, applying contemporary community standards, the dominant theme of the material taken as a whole appeals to prurient interest."[40] The central source of the confusion in this formula, however, is not its obscure status or its imprecision as a test; it does no worse, surely, than *Hicklin* on those counts. Rather the confusion stems from the fact that it is not really a "substitute" for *Hicklin* so much as a mere modification of *Hicklin*: "average person" is substituted for unusually susceptible persons, "contemporary community standards" for eternally fixed Victorian standards, "the material as a whole" for isolated passages. These substitutions suggest that the *Roth* formula shares starting points, purposes, and initial assumptions with the *Hicklin* test, but just does its common job more carefully, avoiding undesirable side-effects.

But in fact the *Hicklin* test judges that sexual materials are sufficiently objectionable to be denominated "obscene" when they are capable of producing effects of a certain kind. Those effects are taken to be so evil in themselves that even responsible adults can be protected from their own choices and not permitted to run the risk of infection. The ultimate principles appealed to are, as we have seen, moralistic and paternalistic; the idea of offensive nuisance is not used or mentioned even implicitly. Can we believe that Mr. Justice Brennan, one of the Supreme Court's staunchest liberals, really intended to incorporate moralistic paternalism as a principle of constitutional jurisprudence? Can we believe that he thought that the state has a right to protect "the average person" from morally deleterious mental states ("itches") induced in him by materials he has freely chosen precisely because he wished to experience such states, when there is no clear and present danger of public harm and no third parties to be offended? The only answer to these questions, I think, is that Mr. Justice Brennan may not quite have understood what he was saying.

His confusions come out most strikingly in his use of the phrase regarding the "average person, applying . . . standards." Standards of what? And who, exactly, applies them: the average person or later, the court? There are at least three possible answers to these questions. First of all, if *Roth* really is but a small modification of *Hicklin*, the "standards" in question are norms for determining when materials have sufficient capacity to cause corruption or depravity. (The analogous question is when a beverage has sufficient capacity to cause intoxication in the "average person.") In that case the standards are not applied *by* the average person (as suggested by Brennan's syntax) but rather by the court *to* the average person. The Court's task, according to this interpretation, is to determine whether the likely effect of the materials on the average person would be a change in his character which, according to the standards of his (our?) community, would be corrupting or depraving. In effect, the plural term "standards," on this view, refers to two distinct standards: one for determining what the causal effects of the materials on the average person would be, and one for evaluating those effects as morally corrupting. The former standard would come from the social sciences, the latter from "the contemporary community."

Still, it is hard to believe, especially in the light of the opinions in later obscenity cases, that standards of offensiveness were not lurking somewhere in the penumbra of Brennan's opinion in *Roth*. These standards too

vary from place to place, and change from time to time. On a second interpretation of *Roth* they too are among the "standards" that must be "applied." Quite apart from, or in addition to, their desirable or undesirable
effects on traits of character, would the materials be likely to *shock* the
average person? To answer this question about offensiveness, we must look
to the standards of decorum in a given historical community that are held by
its "average member" in such a way that their violation causes him shock or
disgust (quite apart from the speculative effect on his own character).

The actual wording of the *Roth* formula, however, suggests a third
interpretation, that the relevant "standards" are to guide yet another determination, namely whether the materials in question can be expected to
excite ("appeal to") the average person's lustful thoughts ("prurient interests"). These standards too vary from community to community and from
one culture to another. These standards too are in gradual constant change
within one community over extended periods of time. With changes in the
norms determining permissible conduct and dress come concomitant
changes in the customary effects of different styles of dress and deportment
on observers. Grandpa was excited even by bare ankles, dad by flesh above
the knee, grandson only by flimsy bikinis. According to this third interpretation, a court must look at a contemporary community and decide what it
takes then and there to excite the average person to a certain level of lust,
and that will depend, in part, on what the average person is accustomed to
see, to do, to experience.

Which of these three interpretations of the *Roth* formula is correct?
My conclusion is that the court simply hadn't thought these matters out,
that there is some plausibility in each interpretation, that ambiguities in
judicial language here reflect uncertainties and conflicts in judicial thought.
If the first interpretation is the correct one, then Mr. Justice Brennan, like
Lord Cockburn before him, was basically a moralistic paternalist, endorsing the propriety and constitutionality of legislative efforts to protect
citizens from harm to their own characters, quite apart from other consequences. Since it is difficult to believe that Mr. Justice Brennan, of all people, held such a view, the first interpretation is perhaps not very convincing.
On the second interpretation, the Court was applying the offense or
nuisance principle to the question of obscene materials, but—astonishingly
—without the mediating maxims that would protect the privacy of willing
consumers. The third interpretation is perhaps the one that is closest to the
Court's conscious intentions, because it understands the *Roth* formula to be
a test of when something is pornographic, hence "obscene" in the Court's
sense, quite apart from further questions about its effects on sensibility and
character. On this interpretation, as on the other two, the concept of
obscenity is a relative one, varying on this reading with the average person's
susceptibility to lustful feelings. In a way, this interpretation of the formula
makes it even more disappointing to the liberal than the others. In the

Court's view, so understood, there is no question about a legislature's right to ban lust-inducing materials, and no explanation why "obscenity" defined in this way (as pornography) and determined by these varying standards may be prohibited. The unwritten assumption apparently is that if legislatures think lustful states of mind are inherently evil (quite apart from harm of offense), that is sufficient.

V.

From the language of the majority opinion in *Roth* it would appear that the offensiveness of materials has nothing to do with the question of whether they are obscene or properly subject to legislative ban. Obscenity *means* pornography, and pure pornography without redeeming literary or scientific admixture totally lacks qualification for First Amendment protection. What then is the test of whether a given set of materials—a book or a film— is truly pornographic? Whether a court, applying prevailing community standards to the average person, finds that "the dominant theme of the materials taken as a whole appeals to prurient interests." Not a word about whether they are repulsive, abhorrent, disgusting, or shocking to anyone. Not a suggestion that the state's legal interest in their regulation might derive from their character as nuisances.

Five years later, however, in *Manual Enterprises* v. *Day*[41] the Court recalled the concept of offensiveness, and added it, as a kind of afterthought to the *Roth* formula. The Post Office Department had barred from the mails on the grounds of obscenity three magazines (*Manual, Trim,* and *Grecian Guild Pictorial*) that specialized in photographs of nude or nearly nude male models. Manual Enterprises, the publisher of all three, appealed to the Supreme Court objecting that, among other things, the publications were "body-building magazines" and therefore not obscene. Justice Harlan, the author of one of the two opinions supporting the petitioner in this case, sidestepped the question of whether the materials could be judged obscene on the grounds that they appealed to the prurient interests of the average (male) homosexual rather than the "average person" (the question of relevant audience that was finally settled in *Mishkin* v. *New York* in 1966),[42] and gave emphasis instead to the question of offensiveness: "These magazines cannot be deemed so offensive on their face as to affront current community standards of decency—a quality that we shall hereafter refer to as 'patent offensiveness' or 'indecency.' "[43] Mr. Justice Harlan then went on to spell out a "twofold concept of obscenity" according to which "patent offensiveness" and "appeal to prurient interest" are each necessary and jointly sufficient for obscenity.[44] Only one of these "distinct elements"[45] (at most) was present in the body-building magazines; hence they were not obscene, however much they may have excited homosexual lust. The presence of both elements is determined by the application of community standards: offensiveness by standards of decorum or "customary limits of candor,"[46] prurience presumably by standards of average susceptibility. "In most obscenity cases," Harlan rushed to reassure us, "the elements tend to coalesce," [47] and what obviously appeals to prurience will on that account alone be "patently offensive."

The next steps in the evolution of the *Roth* formula occurred on one strange day in 1966 when the Court handed down decisions in *Ginzburg* v. *United States*,[48] *Mishkin* v. *New York*,[49] and *A Book Named "John Cleland's Memoirs of a Woman of Pleasure"* v. *Attorney General of Massachusetts* (*"Memoirs"* v. *Massachusetts*, for short).[50] The *Mishkin* case makes the best transition from *Enterprises* v. *Day*, so I shall begin with it. This case settled the problem of relevant audience which Mr. Justice Harlan had put aside in *Enterprises*. Mishkin was appealing a conviction and a sentence of three years in jail and a $12,000 fine for violation of a New York state criminal statute prohibiting publication, possession, and distribution for sale of obscene materials. The books in question described sado-masochistic sexual acts, fetishisms, lesbianism, and male homosexuality. It was clear that the "average person"[51] would be repelled rather than aroused by such materials and that the books, therefore, made no appeal to the prurience of the "average person" at all. In a 6-3 decision, the Supreme Court upheld Mishkin's conviction anyway, and reformulated the *Roth* criteria at the same time: "Where the material is designed for and primarily disseminated to a clearly defined deviant sexual group, rather than the public at large, the prurient-appeal requirement of the *Roth* test is satisfied if the dominant theme of the material taken as a whole appeals to the prurient interest in sex of the members of that group."[52] Thus were the equal rights of sado-masochists, fetishists, and homosexuals to be free from stimulants to their own kind of lustfulness vindicated in the highest court. Apparently, "patent offensiveness" is determined by the standards of the "average person" (even when no average person is in fact offended), while the prurient interest test is applied to the special audience at which the materials are aimed.

One would think, that as a general rule, the more special the audience addressed, the greater the offensiveness as measured by the standards of the general public. The average person is more offended (shocked, disgusted) by homosexuality than by heterosexuality, more repelled by bestiality than even by human homosexuality, etc. On the other hand, as a general rule one would expect that the more special the audience addressed, the smaller the total amount of lustfulness induced. It would follow then that the more fully the offending materials satisfy the "patent offensiveness" test, the smaller the amount of prurience they actually produce in the community as a whole—at least for the more familiar sorts of sexual deviance. In a limiting case, the offensiveness might be extreme but the lust actually stimulated so minuscule as to be insignificant, in which case the materials would satisfy only one of the two necessary conditions for obscenity. Apparently, however, the Court recognizes no lower limit to the amount of prurience that must be stimulated by a book in order for it to be judged obscene. Given satisfaction of the "patent offensiveness" standard, any increase in the net amount of prurience is an evil that a legislature is entitled to prevent. Where offensiveness is extreme, then, the appeal to the prurient interest standard hardly seems necessary at all. In fact, sale or display of the offending materials might be prohibitable as nuisances anyway in that case; minimal appeal to prurience is necessary only if the prohibition is made on the grounds of "obscenity." But what importance is there in a mere name?

The addition of the "patent offensiveness" component to the *Roth* formula saves the Court from another kind of severe embarrassment that would result from the applications to certain hypothetical cases, at least, of a test for obscenity that makes no reference to offensiveness at all. Without the offensiveness component, the *Roth-Mishkin* criteria would require only that socially valueless materials appeal to the prurient interest of some audience, no matter how special or small, in order to be judged obscene. In that case, if there are seventeen people in the entire United States who achieve their sexual gratification primarily by fondling stones, then a magazine aimed directly at them which publishes lurid color photographs of rocks and pebbles would be obscene. As it is, the Court is saved from such an absurdity by Mr. Justice Harlan's afterthought of offensiveness. Since the *Mishkin* decision, a sex magazine for rock fetishists would qualify as obscene only if it published, for example, pictures of naked people rubbing up against a variety of sandstone, limestone, basalt, and marble rocks in various erotic postures suggesting abandonment to ecstasy. Then no doubt the deviant cultish magazine would be fully obscene by both the "prurient interest" standard (minimally satisfied) and the "patent offensiveness" standard, though it might yet be "redeemed" by scientifically serious articles about geology interspersed among the photographs.

United States v. *Ginzburg*,[53] decided the same day as *Mishkin*, took a wholly unexpected new path for which *Roth* had not prepared observers of the Court. That path led the Court into a thicket from which it subsequently retreated, and it led Ralph Ginzburg, to his astonishment and despair, to prison for a five-year term. Ginzburg had been convicted of violating the federal statute against obscenity by publishing among other things the magazine *Eros* and the book, *The Housewife's Handbook on Selective Promiscuity*.[54] He appealed, and the Supreme Court spent most of its time during oral argument trying to apply the newly interpreted "three pronged" *Roth* formula to the publications to determine whether they were truly obscene. To be obscene, a majority agreed, the materials must appeal to their audience's prurient interests, be patently offensive by community

standards of decorum, and be "utterly without redeeming social importance." Ginzburg's lawyers were especially concerned to argue that respectable literary and journalistic materials were intermixed with the avowedly
pornographic materials, thus establishing some redeeming social value in
the materials taken as a whole. But none of this mattered, according to the
decision which the Court dropped like a bomb shell on March 21, 1966.
Justice Brennan argued in his majority opinion that Ginzburg's publications could be found obscene because of the "leer of the sensualist" that
permeated the *advertising* for the publications.[55] If the Court had considered it solely on the basis of the *content* of the publications, he admitted,
this would have been a close and difficult case, but the emphasis of Ginzburg's advertising made all the difference.[56]

A close examination of Mr. Justice Brennan's decision reveals the
usual uncritical mixture of appeals to moralism, paternalism, and the oddly
unmediated offense principle. Mr. Justice Brennan, employing his own
Roth formula (at that time in *Memoirs* the three-pronged test),[57] must first
decide whether the materials are pornographic. Do they "appeal" to the
prurient interests of prospective readers? Well, of course they do; their own
advertising explicitly makes such an appeal.[58] The materials are "openly
advertised to appeal to the erotic interest of their customers."[59] To be sure,
in court Ginzburg's lawyers had argued that some of the articles and stories
conferred a redeeming social importance to the publications taken as a
whole, but this doubtful claim, Brennan argues, is belied by Ginzburg's
own sales pitch where his "appeal" is made. The advertising is "relevant to
determining whether social importance claimed for material in the court-
room was, in the circumstances, pretense or reality—whether it was the
basis upon which it was traded in the marketplace or a spurious claim for
litigation purposes."[60] And it must be admitted that there was not a single
mention of literary values, scientific studies, or moral-political advocacy in
Ginzburg's advertising; "[T]he purveyor's sole emphasis is on the sexually
provocative aspects of his publications. . . ."[61] This then is Brennan's first
argument: In "close cases" the advertising for publications may be used as
evidence of whether or not the materials appeal exclusively to prurient interest, that is, are purely pornographic, meaning legally obscene.[62] When in
doubt, judges should take the defendant's own words into account as
evidence of the obscene content of his publications. This last-minute ration-
alization that could not possibly have been anticipated at the time of the
criminal conduct sent poor Ginzburg to prison for five years. Subsequent
publishers of pornography took warning. Their advertisements used
euphemisms and code words like "adult books" and "erotic literature,"
but their books were as "dirty" as ever. This decision sent one man to
prison, but changed little else.

Mr. Justice Brennan's opinion did pay some homage to the offense
principle, as indeed it had to, since "patent offensiveness" was now one of

the three prongs of the revised *Roth* formula. But his words are very sparse on this subject: "The deliberate representation of petitioners' publications as erotically arousing . . . would tend to force public confrontation with the potentially offensive aspects of the work; the brazenness of such an appeal heightens the offensiveness of the publications to those who are offended by such material."[63] Perhaps these cryptic words do make a good point. An unavoidable sign in large red letters on a billboard in a crowded place that shrieks "FILTHY PICTURES FOR SALE" will be predictably offensive to anyone who would be offended by the filthy pictures themselves, and no doubt also to a great many who would not be offended by a private perusal of the advertised products. Still, the advertisement for the filthy pictures could hardly be as offensive as the filthy pictures themselves would be if *they* were on the public billboard. In comparison with the latter impropriety, the shrill advertising is a mere pecadillo. In any case, advertising can be regulated by explicit statutes that put advertisers on warning. No such statutes were violated by Ginzburg's advertisements; he was jailed, in effect, for conduct that he could not have known to be criminal.

The final argument in Brennan's opinion for the relevance of advertising to the determination of obscenity is a moralistic-paternalistic one. "EROS was created, represented, and sold solely as a claimed instrument of the sexual stimulation it would bring. Like the other publications, its pervasive treatment of sex and sexual matters rendered it available to *exploitation by those who would make a business of pandering to 'the widespread weakness for titillation by pornography.'* "[64] The latter phrase is especially revealing. It is not pornography and erotic stimulation as such that are the object of Brennan's wrath, but rather "the sordid business of pandering— 'the business of purveying textual or graphic matter openly advertised to appeal to the erotic interest of their customers.' "[65] Brennan here follows the Model Penal Code[66] in taking an "oblique approach" to the problem of obscenity. That approach is well explained by Louis B. Schwartz:

> The meretricious "appeal" of a book or picture is essentially a question of the attractiveness of the merchandise from a certain point of view: what makes it sell. Thus, the prohibition of obscenity takes on an aspect of regulation of unfair business or competitive practices. Just as merchants may be prohibited from selling their wares by appeal to the public's weakness for gambling, so they may be restrained from purveying books, movies, or other commercial exhibition by exploiting the well-nigh universal weakness for a look behind the curtain of modesty.[67]

Customers, in short, need protection from the state from enticing advertisements that "exploit their weaknesses," whether the weakness be for erotic fantasy, gambling, or whatever. (But why not then also for cigarettes, sweets, and fried foods?)

In treating the desire for titillation by pornography as a "weakness,"

Brennan seems to be making a contestable moral judgment that permits him in effect to incorporate part of the conventional sexual morality into the law. Suppose that a regular customer for pornographic materials were to deny that his need and taste is a weakness? "I don't think of the titillation I crave as a temptation to do something evil by my own standards," he might say. "Rather it is an appetite like any other, entirely innocent in my eyes. I seek it in good conscience, and find it patronizing indeed to be told that my moral sense needs correction, or that my moral resolution needs reenforcement by the law." Another user might have moral reservations. He might admit that he is sometimes ashamed of his pornographic indulgences, but deny vehemently that his moral struggles are anyone else's business. Certainly, he will say, they are not the law's business. Both of these users might admit that they have a need for erotic titillation, while denying that every need is a "weakness" that renders them incapable of governing themselves without outside help.

The reasonableness of these replies to Mr. Justice Brennan is underscored by the contrast between the taste for titillation and the genuine weakness of the alcoholic for whiskey, the drug addict for heroin, perhaps even the cigarette smoker for nicotine. An advertising sales pitch aimed directly at alcoholics encouraging them to strengthen their habit would be unfair not only to one's more scrupulous competitors in the liquor business (one of Schwartz's prime concerns)[68] but also to the poor wretches one is trying to exploit. Their addiction is a weakness in the sense that it is something they regret and try to resist themselves, something that is objectively bad for them, as they would be the first to admit. Similarly cigarette advertisements aimed directly at teenagers can fix a fatal habit on unsuspecting innocents from which many will find relief only in a painful and premature death. But these analogies fail to provide convincing models for the willing customer of pornography. The tenability of the principle of moralistic paternalism is a matter to which justice cannot be fully done here. It suffices to point out that Brennan's final argument for the relevance of advertising to determinations of obscenity tacitly invokes that principle.

We need not linger long over the last of the three obscenity cases decided by the Supreme Court in March, 1966.[69] *John Cleland's Memoirs of a Woman of Pleasure* was much more widely known by the name of its central character, *Fanny Hill*. The book, first distributed in England in 1750, was published anew in the United States in 1963. Obscenity charges were promptly brought against it by the Commonwealth of Massachusetts whose Supreme Court, in a 4-3 decision, officially declared it obscene.[70] Many expert witnesses, including distinguished professors of English and history, testified that the book was not utterly without redeeming value, although its similarity to more recent works of pure hard-core pornography was marked. The sole issue in the case according to Mr. Justice Brennan's majority opinion, was whether the book actually is obscene as determined by the *Roth* formula, and he decided that it was not.[71] The main significance of the opinion stems from Brennan's explicit endorsement of the "three pronged test"—appeal to prurient interest, patent offensiveness, and utter absence of redeeming social value—as the proper criterion of obscenity, naturally evolved from his own *Roth* formula laid down nine years earlier. That criterion came to be called "the *Memoirs* criterion," or "the Fanny Hill test" more commonly than "the *Roth* formula" in the years following.

The next landmark obscenity decision left the formula for obscenity unchanged, but was important for its judgment on another matter. *Stanley* v. *Georgia*[72] raised the issue whether mere possession in one's own home of an admittedly obscene film, where there is no attempt to sell it or distribute it further, could be grounds for prosecution. In a resounding 9-0 decision the Court emphatically denied that it could. Mr. Justice Marshall derived the right to possess obscene materials from a more general right to privacy implicitly guaranteed, he claimed, by the First and Fourteenth Amendments, and made explicit in *Griswold* v. *Connecticut*.[73] Civil libertarians applauded the result, as well they should have, but in a cooler hour many of them had some misgivings about Mr. Justice Marshall's reasoning, for the privacy Marshall invoked was not so much a personal privacy as a set of rights derived from the "sanctity of the home." The appellant, Marshall wrote, "is asserting . . . the right to satisfy his intellectual and emotional needs in the *privacy of his own home.* He is asserting the right to be free from state inquiry into the contents of *his library.* . . . If the First Amendment means anything, it means that a State has no business telling a man, sitting alone *in his own house*, what books he may read or what films he may watch."[74] But though the state has no business investigating the contents of a person's library or bedroom, there is nothing in the Marshall opinion to deny that the state has business inquiring into the contents of a person's boat or automobile, or luggage, or his pockets, briefcase, or wallet. The confines of one's home can make very narrow boundaries for the area of one's privacy.

The next important day in the history of the Supreme Court's struggle with the riddles of obscenity, and the last important day to this date, was June 21, 1973, when the Court decided both *Miller* v. *California*[75] and *Paris Adult Theatre I* v. *Slaton*.[76] By that time the membership of the Court had undergone a new change and a "conservative" majority had emerged under the leadership of Chief Justice Warren Burger. There had been a great outcry in the country against pornography and excessively "permissive" Supreme Court decisions. Chief Justice Burger and his conservative colleagues clearly wished to tighten legal controls on obscenity to help "stem the tide," but they also felt bound to honor the Court's own precedents and particularly the *Memoirs* formula. The result was a pair of 5-4 decisions in which the opinion of the Court delivered by Chief Justice Burger gave some lip service to the *Memoirs* test while modifying each of its three prongs.

Henceforth: (1) whether materials appeal to prurient interest is to be determined by the application of local community standards rather than a national standard;[77] (2) the use or display of sexually explicit materials may be deemed patently offensive even when it involves only willing adult observers in a commercial theatre (nor can the privacy of the home be equated "with a 'zone' of 'privacy' that follows a distributor or a consumer of obscene materials wherever he goes."[78] Furthermore, not all conduct directly involving "consenting adults" only has a claim to constitutional protection.[79]); (3) a finding of obscenity requires not that the materials be utterly without redeeming social value but only that they lack "serious literary, artistic, political, or scientific value."[80]

The intended consequence of this decision clearly was to permit more aggressive prosecutions of pornographers while maintaining continuity with earlier Court tests for obscenity. Recourse to a local community norm rather than a national standard for applying the "prurient interest" test permits local courts to find persons guilty for distributing materials that could not plausibly be found obscene in other, more sophisticated, jurisdictions. In denying that there is a movable zone of privacy that follows a person wherever he goes and that private transactions between consenting adults cannot be patently offensive, the Court permits local authorities to prevent the display of pornographic films in public theatres no matter how discreetly they are advertised, no matter how effectively customers are forewarned, no matter how successfully children are denied admittance. By insisting that a book with sexual themes must have serious literary, artistic, political, or scientific value if it is to qualify for the First Amendment protection, the Court allows successful prosecutions of such borderline works as *Fanny Hill* which had a certain elegance of language and an incidental interest to critics and scholars of history and sociology, although it was basically pornographic in intention. *Fanny Hill* admittedly was not *utterly* without social value, but it could hardly be said to have *serious* literary value.

Burger then did achieve his double goal. He tightened the screws on obscenity and maintained fidelity to the Court's basic *Roth-Memoirs* approach. In so doing, however, he reduced that approach to something approaching absurdity. The substitution of local community standards in effect makes it difficult to publish anywhere materials that would violate the most puritanical standards in the country. Publishers will have to screen out-of-state orders more carefully than Larry C. Flynt did when he routinely mailed a copy of his publication *Hustler* to a person who had ordered it by mail from a town in Ohio. He was subsequently tried for violation of the Ohio obscenity statutes and sentenced to 7-25 years in prison![81] How can a national publisher or film producer hope to distribute his book or film nationally when he might misjudge the "community standards" of one small town somewhere and thereby end up in jail? Publication will be commercially feasible only when the materials are unchallengeable anywhere in the country. Willard Gaylin describes these absurdities and inequities well when he writes that:

> The principle established by the Supreme Court . . . was intended to let local communities set their own standards, allowing diversity to flourish as the people of each area wished. Instead, . . . what community control does is to set the limits for nationally distributed literature and television at the level of the bluest-nosed small town critic.[82]

The Burger Court's second modification of the *Memoirs* formula is, from the moral point of view, even more absurd, for at a stroke it restricts personal privacy arbitrarily to the confines of one's home and denies constitutional recognition of the *volenti* maxim. (But of course it is always possible that it is the Constitution that is absurd, not the five-man majority of the Supreme Court.) The third "modification" is more than a mere tightening or adjustment of the *Roth* "utterly without redeeming social value" formula; it completely guts the theory of the First Amendment that Mr. Justice Brennan had employed when he formulated that clause. That people should be free to make serious efforts to produce works of art and literature, political and moral judgments, and scientific discoveries; that they should be free to innovate and experiment, to depart from or defend orthodoxies; that they should be free to fail and thus to produce bad art or to be in error, if that's what it comes to, as they themselves choose and see fit: *that* is what has "social value" and is defended by the First Amendment.

The Burger "modification" seems to limit constitutional protection to good novels and films, seriously valuable political commentaries, and importantly correct scientific reports and theories. If future courts take his words seriously, they shall have to strip protection from most novels that deal with sexual themes, since assuredly most of them, like most other novels, lack "serious literary importance." The Court's message to writers is a discouraging one: If you plan to write a novel that contains explicitly sexual scenes that an average person in a remote community would judge to be titillating or shocking, you had better make sure that it has important literary value; if it turns out to be merely mediocre on literary grounds, your publisher may end up in jail. How could anyone seriously believe that this is the way the First Amendment protects the enterprise of literature?

Mr. Justice Brennan, whose opinion in *Roth* sixteen years earlier had set the Court on the serpentine path that led to *Miller* and *Paris Adult Theatre*, lost his patience finally with that basic approach, and in a ringing dissent to *Paris Adult Theatre* urged a new beginning.[83] Chief Justice Burger's majority opinion, Brennan wrote, was not a "veering sharply away from the *Roth* concept," but rather simply a new "interpretation of *Roth*."[84] The *Paris Adult Theatre* decision, while ostensibly tougher on pornographers, nevertheless shares in equal degree the primary defects of the earlier decisions. First, Justice Brennan argued, these cases rely on essentially obscure formulas that fail to "provide adequate notice to persons who are engaged in the type of conduct that [obscenity statutes] could be thought to proscribe."[85] "The underlying principle," as Chief Justice Warren had written earlier, "is that no man shall be held criminally responsible for conduct which he could not reasonably understand to be proscribed."[86] No one now can predict how the Supreme Court is going to decide close obscenity cases, of which there are in principle an endless number, and the resulting uncertainty not only makes "bookselling . . . a hazardous profession"[87] but also "invites arbitrary and erratic enforcement of the law."[88] Secondly, it creates a chilling effect on all writing that deals candidly with sexual matters, since at any point the wavering and uncertain line that separates permissible from impermissible expression may veer suddenly and leave a writer unprotected on the wrong side of the line.[89] Finally, Brennan concluded, constant need to apply obscure formulas to materials accused of obscenity imposes a severe burden on the Supreme Court amounting to a kind of "institutional strain."[90] Brennan is therefore forced to conclude that no amount of tinkering with the *Roth-Memoirs-Paris Adult Theatre* formulas will ever lead to definitions of obscenity sufficiently clear and specific to avoid these unfortunate by-products.

How then can the Court find a new approach? Brennan suggests a strategy. "Given these inevitable side-effects of state efforts to suppress what is assumed to be *unprotected* speech, we must scrutinize with care the state interest that is asserted to justify the suppression. For in the absence of some very substantial interest in suppressing such speech, we can hardly condone the ill effects that seem to flow inevitably from the effort."[91] What is the alleged "state interest" that makes the unobtrusive and willing enjoyment of pornographic materials the state's business to control and prevent? That interest could not be the prevention of harm to persons caused by other persons, since the conduct at issue is freely consented to, and that kind of private harm is excluded by the *volenti* maxim. It cannot be the protection of children, since there is no controversy about the state's right to prevent the dissemination of obscene materials to juveniles, and the fact that the Paris Adult Theatre had effectively excluded children from its performances had been deemed irrelevant by the Georgia Supreme Court in its ruling that was upheld by the Burger majority opinion.[92] It cannot be the prevention of offensive nuisances, since the materials in Paris Adult Theatre had not been obtruded on unwilling witnesses nor advertised in luridly offensive ways. "The justification for the suppression must be found, therefore, in some independent interest in regulating the reading and viewing habits of consenting adults."[93]

The implicit rationale for such regulation is not hard to find, and it has been present all along in the background of *Roth* as well as *Hicklin*, in *Memoirs* as well as in *Paris Adult Theatre*. Even when some lip service is paid to the requirement of offensiveness, the ultimate appeal has been to the principle of *moralistic paternalism*. How else can we explain why the Court recognizes a state interest in proscribing pornography *as such*, even when privately and unobtrusively used by willing adults? Moralistic paternalism, however, is extremely difficult to reconcile with the Constitution, which the Court has interpreted in other cases to permit responsible adults to go to Hell morally in their own way provided only they don't drag others unwillingly along with them. "In *Stanley*," writes Brennan, "we rejected as 'wholly inconsistent with the philosophy of the First Amendment' the notion that there is a legitimate state concern in the 'control [of] the moral content of a person's thoughts.' "[94] Brennan concludes then that there is no legitimate state concern in preventing the enjoyment of pornography as such, but that there may be valid state interests in regulating the "manner of distribution of sexually oriented materials,"[95] these being, presumably, prevention of the corruption of children, protection of captive audiences from offense, and the preservation of neighborhoods from aesthetic decay. Brennan thus ends up precisely where years earlier he could have begun: with a concept of pornography as a potential source of public nuisance subject to control by statutes that satisfy the provisions of a properly mediated offense principle. Where pornography is not a nuisance, then it can be none of the state's business.

NOTES

1. Practically all human activities, unless carried on in a wilderness, interfere to some extent with others or involve some risk of interference, and these interferences range from mere trifling annoyances to serious harms. It is an obvious truth that each individual in a community must put up with a certain amount of annoyance, inconvenience and interference, and must take a certain amount of risk in order that all may get on together. The very existence of organized society depends upon the principle of "give and take, live and let live," and therefore the law of torts does not attempt to impose liability or shift the loss in every case where one person's conduct has some detrimental effect on another. Liability is imposed only in those cases where the harm or risk [or inconvenience or offense] to one is greater than he ought to be required to bear under the circumstances. . . . RESTATEMENT OF TORTS §822, comment j (1939).

2. W. PROSSER, HANDBOOK OF THE LAW OF TORTS 597 (4th ed. 1971).

3. *Id.* at 597-99.

4. *Id.* at 599-600.

5. "The world must have factories, smelters, oil refineries, noisy machinery, and blasting, as well as airports, even at the expense of some inconvenience to those in the vicinity, and the plaintiff may be required to accept and tolerate some not unreasonable discomfort for the general good. . . . On the other hand, a foul pond, or a vicious or noisy dog, will have little if any social value, and relatively slight annoyance from it may justify relief." *Id.* at 597-98 (footnotes omitted).

6. High on the honor roll of those who have *not* made this pernicious mistake is the late Paul Goodman, who wrote in his article *Pornography, Art, and Censorship*, reprinted in PERSPECTIVES ON PORNOGRAPHY 42-60 (D. A. Hughes ed. 1970) that "[t]he pornographic is not *ipso facto* the obscene," but rather simply that which is designed and used for the purpose of

arousing sexual desires. But—"if the stirring of desire is *defined* [emphasis added], and therefore treated, as obscene, how can a normal person's interest in sex be anything *but* shameful? This is what shame is, the blush at finding one's impulse to be unacceptable. . . . So the court [by treating pornography as *ipso facto* obscene] corrupts. It is a miserable social policy." The honor roll also includes Stanley Edgar Hyman, whose essay *In Defense of Pornography* also is reprinted in the Hughes volume; D. A. J. RICHARDS, THE MORAL CRITICISM OF LAW 63 (1977); and F. F. SCHAUER, THE LAW OF OBSCENITY 1 (1976).

7. Still another use of "obscene" is as a conventional label, without prediction or endorsement of disgust, as in the phrase "obscene epithet." Similarly one can refer to a certain class of terms as "dirty words" without expressing or predicting disapproval of those words.

8. 403 U.S. 15 (1971).

9. *Id.* at 20 (citations omitted).

10. And also in lower courts bound to follow the usage of the highest court. A recent bizarre example is the case of Connecticut v. Anonymous, 34 Conn. Supp. 575, 377 A.2d 1342 (1977), in which a high school student appealed his conviction under a statute that makes it a crime for making an "obscene gesture," in this case to the occupants of a police cruiser. That gesture, in which one extends the middle finger, is an ancient form of insult called "giving the finger." The appellate court decreed that the gesture was not obscene (not even in the sense intended in the statute) because "[t]o be obscene, the expression must be, in a significant way, erotic. . . . It can hardly be said that the finger gesture is likely to arouse sexual desire. The more likely response is anger." 377 A.2d at 1343.

11. For a more detailed statement and criticism of the illiberal principles of legal moralism and paternalism, *see* J. FEINBERG, SOCIAL PHILOSOPHY 36–54 (1973) and M. BAYLES, PRINCIPLES OF LEGISLATION 119–40 (1978).

12. *See, e.g.,* Meyer v. Nebraska, 262 U.S. 390 (1923); Cantwell v. Connecticut, 310 U.S. 296 (1940); Abington School Dist. v. Schempp, 374 U.S. 203, 253-58 (1963) (Brennan, J., concurring); *see also* P. KAUPER, RELIGION AND THE CONSTITUTION 53-57 (1964).

13. A wire service press dispatch describes a very typical occasion for interest-balancing in the application of the free exercise clause:

OAK CREEK, WIS., OCT. 23, 1977 (AP). The folks at the Parkway Apostolic Church believe in making a joyful noise unto the Lord. Some of their neighbors think it's just noise.

In fact, the neighbors were upset enough to get the Common Council in this Milwaukee suburb to make the church subject to the same ordinance that prohibits industries in residential neighborhoods from exceeding a 58-decibel limit.

"We have the only church and school in Oak Creek where voices cannot be raised above 58 decibels," said the Rev. Frank Tamel, pastor of the church. "That's discriminatory."

Admitting that "our people do sing loudly," the minister said, "There's a joyful noise that comes under the heading of worship—if you infringe on that noise, you infringe upon the First Amendment."

The church's band includes guitars, trumpets, and saxophones. There is a 50-person choir and a sound system.

Alderman Dell Nirode reported that at one nearby home it was impossible to carry on a conversation on the patio because of the noise. Most of the complaints have come during summer when windows are open.

The first provision that the church keep the noise below 58 decibels came in September 1976 when the church received permission to expand its educational facilities. Earlier this month, when the church was granted approval to build a school, the same limit was stipulated.

Four times last summer, city building inspector George Simmons made unannounced visits to the church, carrying a decibel meter. Each time he found the noise level below 58, but he said a true reading was difficult to obtain because the church service was not a constant noise source. . . .

"You have to expect some noise to come out of a church when you live next door," he said. "It's not a tomb."

While the ordinance so far has not been enforced against the church, Tamel said it might be if enough people complain about the noise level.

He also said biblical stories indicated that the gatherings held by the original Apostles weren't always quiet.

"If the Apostles had met in Oak Creek, they would have been disturbing the peace," he said.

No doubt this is a close case, but it is worth noting that the only way it differs from any other public nuisance problem is that the offending practices have a special constitutional standing, a kind of constitutionally certified social value. That would seem to imply that if 58 decibels is the highest permitted noise level for commercial-industrial activities, then the permissible level ought to be somewhat higher for activities that enjoy a First Amendment shelter. Apart from that, there is nothing special about the problem, and the unavoidable balancing tests must be applied. How central to the religion of the Apostolic Christian Church are trumpets and amplifiers? How great an inconvenience would it be to require neighbors to leave their homes for one hour on summertime Sundays, or to lower their windows? (Is the offense reasonably avoidable or is there a genuinely captive audience?) One can easily imagine similar tests for the dissemination or exhibition of pornographic materials that affront not the senses but the sensibilities of neighbors and passersby. If the offending materials have First Amendment protection as "speech" or expression, that would be a substantial weight on the side of toleration, but if their offensiveness is extreme and not reasonably avoidable, and the like, the weight on the side of prohibition could be even greater.

14. 381 U.S. 479 (1965).

15. 405 U.S. 438 (1972).

16. 394 U.S. 557 (1969).

17. 410 U.S. 113 (1973).

18. G. HUGHES, THE CONSCIENCE OF THE COURTS 56 (1975).

19. *Id.*

20. L.R. 3 Q.B. 360 (1868).

21. T. I. EMERSON, THE SYSTEM OF FREEDOM OF EXPRESSION 469 (1970).

22. *See, e.g.,* American Civil Liberties Union v. City of Chicago, 3 Ill. 2d 334, 121 N.E.2d 585 (1954); Excelsior Pictures Corp. v. Regents of the State of New York, 3 N.Y.2d 237, 144 N.E.2d 31, 165 N.Y.S.2d 42 (1957); People v. Doubleday & Co., 297 N.Y. 687, 77 N.E.2d 6 (1947), *aff'd.,* 335 U.S. 848 (1948).

23. L.R. 3 Q.B. at 371.

24. 354 U.S. 476 (1957).

25. *Id.* at 488–90.

26. Commonwealth v. Friede, 271 Mass. 318, 171 N.E. 472 (1930).

27. Commonwealth v. Isenstadt, 318 Mass. 543, 62 N.E.2d 840 (1945).

28. Attorney General v. "God's Little Acre," 326 Mass. 281, 93 N.E.2d 819 (1950).

29. United States v. One Book Called "Ulysses," 5 F. Supp. 182 (S.D.N.Y. 1933), *aff'd,* 72 F.2d 705 (2d Cir. 1934).

30. Similar standards in other cases for determining the seriousness of harms would also minimize the seriousness of harms produced by socially useful activities only to rare individuals with unusual vulnerabilities. For the use of such standards in tort cases where harm and not mere offense is involved, *see* Rogers v. Elliot, 146 Mass. 349, 15 N.E. 768 (1888) (hypersensitive individual sues bell-ringer because church bells throw him into epileptic convulsions; the suit failed). *See also* Rozell v. Northern Pac. R.R. Co., 39 N.D. 475, 167, N.W. 489 (1918) (A keg of spikes by the side of a road is not a public nuisance because it frightens an unduly

skittish horse).
31. 354 U.S. at 489.
32. *Id.*
33. *Id.*
34. *Id.* at 487.
35. *Id.*
36. Not unless the peculiar term "prurient interest" provides such a test. Some commentators might be tempted to try this approach. They could look up the word "prurient" in an etymological dictionary and learn that it derives from the Latin term that translates "to itch or long for a thing, to be lecherous." Hence, it now means "having lustful ideas or desires." But this doesn't tell us anything about the erotic states characteristically induced by pornography that we didn't already know. It hardly gives us new information that can help us identify erotic materials more accurately.
37. 378 U.S. 184, 197 (1964) (Stewart, J., concurring).
38. *Id.* at 197.
39. *See, e.g.,* D. KRONHAUSEN & P. KRONHAUSEN, PORNOGRAPHY AND THE LAW (rev. ed. 1964).
40. *Roth*, 354 U.S. at 489.
41. 370 U.S. 478 (1962).
42. 383 U.S. 502 (1966).
43. 370 U.S. at 482.
44. *Id.* at 485–86.
45. *Id.*
46. *Id.*
47. *Id.*
48. 383 U.S. 463 (1966).
49. 383 U.S. 502 (1966).
50. 383 U.S. 413 (1966).
51. I owe to Professor Barbara Levenbook the further point that the phrase "average person" may be useless in obscenity contexts. When it comes to prurient appeal, there may be only an "average man" and an "average woman."
52. 383 U.S. at 508.
53. 383 U.S. 463 (1966).
54. 224 F. Supp. 129 (E.D. Pa. 1963), *aff'd,* 338 F.2d 12 (3rd Cir. 1964), *aff'd,* 383 U.S. 463 (1966).
55. 383 U.S. at 468.
56. *Id.* at 474–75.
57. 383 U.S. at 418.
58. *Ginzburg*, 383 U.S. at 468.
59. *Id.* at 467, quoting *Roth*, 354 U.S. at 495–96 (Warren, C. J., concurring).
60. *Id.* at 470.
61. *Id.*
62. *Id.* at 475–76.
63. *Id.* at 470.
64. *Id.* at 471, quoting Schwartz, *Morals Offenses and the Model Penal Code*, 63 COLUM. L. REV. 669, 677 (1963) (emphasis added).
65. *Id.* at 467, quoting Roth v. United States, 354 U.S. 476, 495–96 (1957) (Warren, C. J., concurring).
66. MODEL PENAL CODE §207.10 (Official Draft 1962).
67. Schwartz, *Morals Offenses and the Model Penal Code*, 63 COLUM. L. REV. 669, 678 (1963).
68. *Id.* at 677–81.

69. A Book Named "John Cleland's Memoirs of a Woman of Pleasure" v. Attorney General, 383 U.S. 413 (1966).

70. 349 Mass. 69, 206 N.E.2d 403 (1965).

71. 383 U.S. at 418.

72. 394 U.S. 557 (1969).

73. *Id.* at 564–66 (discussing *Griswold*, 381 U.S. 479 (1965)).

74. 394 U.S. at 565 (emphasis added).

75. 413 U.S. 15 (1973).

76. 413 U.S. 49 (1973).

77. *Miller*, 413 U.S. at 30–34.

78. *Paris Adult Theatre I*, 413 U.S. at 66.

79. *Id.* at 68–69.

80. *Miller*, 413 U.S. at 24–26.

81. State v. Flynt, No. B-761618 (Com. Pleas Hamilton County, Ohio 1976).

82. Gaylin, *Obscenity*, Washington Post, Feb. 20, 1977, Outlook Section, at 1.

83. 413 U.S. 49, 73–74 (1973) (Brennan, J., dissenting).

84. *Id.* at 81.

85. *Id.* at 86.

86. United States v. Harriss, 347 U.S. 612, 617 (1954).

87. *Paris Adult Theatre I*, 413 U.S. at 88 (Brennan, J., dissenting), citing Ginsberg v. New York, 390 U.S. 629, 674 (1968) (Fortas, J., dissenting).

88. *Paris Adult Theatre I*, 413 U.S. at 88 (Brennan, J., dissenting).

89. *Id.* at 88–90.

90. *Id.* at 91-93.

91. *Id.* at 103.

92. 228 Ga. 343, 185 S.E.2d 768 (1971).

93. 413 U.S. at 107.

94. *Id.* at 108, quoting *Stanley*, 394 U.S. at 565, 566.

95. 413 U.S. 113.

T. M. Scanlon, Jr.

Freedom of Expression and Categories of Expression

I. INTRODUCTION

Freedom of expression, as a philosophical problem, is an instance of a more general problem about the nature and status of rights. Rights purport to place limits on what individuals or the state may do, and the sacrifices they entail are in some cases significant. Thus, for example, freedom of expression becomes controversial when expression appears to threaten important individual interests in a case like the Skokie affair, or to threaten some important national interest such as the ability to raise an army. The general problem is, if rights place limits on what can be done even for good reasons, what is the justification for these limits?

A second philosophical problem is how we decide what these limits are. Rights appear to be something we can reason about, and this reasoning process does not appear to be merely a calculation of consequences. In many cases, we seem to decide whether a given policy infringes freedom of expression simply by consulting our conception of what this right entails. And while there are areas of controversy, there is a wide range of cases in which we all seem to arrive at the same answer. But I doubt that any of us could

This article is reprinted from the *University of Pittsburgh Law Review*, Vol. 40, No. 4 (Summer, 1979), by permission of the *University of Pittsburgh Law Review* and the author.

write out a brief, non-circular definition of freedom of expression whose mechanical application to these clear cases would yield the answers on which we all agree. In what, then, does our agreement consist?

My aim in this paper is to present an account of freedom of expression that provides at least a few answers to these general questions. I will also address a more specific question about freedom of expression itself. What importance should a theory of freedom of expression assign to categories of expression such as political speech, commercial speech, libel and pornography? These categories appear to play an important role in informal thought about the subject. It seems central to the controversy about the Skokie case, for example, that the proposed ordinance threatened the ability of unpopular *political* groups to hold demonstrations.[1] I doubt whether the residents of Skokie would have been asked to pay such a high price to let some other kind of expession proceed. To take a different example, laws against false or deceptive advertising and the ban on cigarette advertising on television suggest that we are willing to accept legal regulation of the form and content of commercial advertising that we would not countenance if it were applied to other forms of expression. Why should this be so?

While I do not accept all of these judgements, I find it hard to resist the idea that different categories of expression should to some degree be treated differently in a theory of freedom of expression. On the other hand some ideas of freedom of expression seem to apply across the board, regardless of category: intervention by government to stop the publication of what it regards as a false or misleading view seems contrary to freedom of expression whether the view concerns politics, religion, sex, health, or the relative desirability of two kinds of automobile. So the question is, to what extent are there general principles of freedom of expression, and to what extent is freedom of expression category-dependent? To the degree that the latter is true, how are the relevant categories defined?

I will begin by considering the individual interests that are the basis of our special concern with expression. In section three I will consider how several theories of freedom of expression have been based on certain of these interests, and I will sketch an answer to the first two questions raised above. Finally, in sections four and five, I will discuss the place of categories of expression within the framework I have proposed and apply this to the particular categories of political speech, commercial speech, and pornography.

II. INTERESTS

What are the interests with which freedom of expression is concerned? It will be useful to separate these roughly into those interests we have in being able to speak, those interests we have in being exposed to what others have to say, and those interests we have as bystanders who are affected by expression in other ways. Since, however, I want to make it clear that "expression" as I am using it is not limited to speech, I will refer to these three groups of interests as the interests of participants, the interests of audiences, and the interests of bystanders.

A. PARTICIPANT INTERESTS

The actions to which freedom of expression applies are actions that aim to bring something to the attention of a wide audience. This intended audience need not be the widest possible audience ("the public at large"), but it must be more than one or two people. Private conversations are not, in general, a matter of freedom of expression, not because they are unimportant to us but because their protection is not the aim of this particular doctrine. (It is a matter, instead, of privacy or of personal liberty of some other sort.) But private conversations might be viewed differently if circumstances were different. For example, if telephone trees (or whispering networks) were an important way of spreading the word because we lacked newspapers and there was no way for us to gather to hear speeches, then legal restrictions on personal conversations could infringe freedom of expression as well as being destructive of personal liberty in a more general sense. What this shows, I think, is that freedom of expression is to be understood primarily in terms of the interests it aims to protect and only secondarily in terms of the class of actions whose protection is, under a given set of circumstances, an adequate way to safeguard these interests.

The most general participant interest is, then, an interest in being able to call something to the attention of a wide audience. This ability can serve a wide variety of more specific purposes. A speaker may be interested in increasing his reputation or in decreasing someone else's, in increasing the sales of his product, in promoting a way of life, in urging a change in government, or simply in amusing people or shocking them. From a social point of view, these interests are not all equally important, and the price that a society is required to pay in order to allow acts of expression of a particular kind to flourish will sometimes be a function of the value of expression of that kind.

This is one reason why it would be a mistake to look for a distinction between pure speech (or expression), which is protected by freedom of expression, and expression that is part of some larger course of action, which is not so protected. It is true that some acts of expression seem not to qualify for First Amendment protection because of the larger courses of action of which they are a part (assault, incitement). But what distinguishes these from other acts of expression is not just that they are part of larger courses of action (which is true of almost all acts of expression), but rather the character of the particular courses of action of which they form a part. Their exclusion from First Amendment protection should be seen as a special case of the more general phenomenon just mentioned: the protection to which an act of expression is entitled is in part a function of the value of the larger purposes it serves.

This cannot mean, of course, that the protection due a given act of expression depends on the actual value of the particular purposes at which it aims. It would be clearly antithetical to freedom of expression, for example, to accord greater protection to exponents of true religious doctrines than to exponents of false and misleading ones. Despite the fact that the objectives at which these two groups aim are of very different value, their acts of expression are (other things being equal) accorded equal status. This is so because the "further interest" that is at stake in the two cases is in fact the same, namely the interest we all have in being able to follow and promote our religious beliefs whatever they may be.

Here, then, is one way in which categories of expression arise. We are unwilling to bear the social costs of granting to just any expressive purpose the opportunities for expression that we would demand for those purposes to which we, personally, attach greatest importance. At the most concrete level, however, there is no agreement about the values to be attached to allowing particular acts of expression to go forward. It is just this lack of consensus, and the consequent unacceptability of allowing governments to regulate acts of expression on the basis of their perceived merits, that makes freedom of expression an important issue. In order to formulate a workable doctrine of freedom of expression, therefore, we look for something approaching a consensus on the relative importance of interests more abstractly conceived—the interest in religious expression, the interest in political expression, etc. Even this more abstract consensus is only approximate,[2] however, and never completely stable. As people's values change, or as a society becomes more diverse, consensus erodes. When this happens, either the ranking of interests must change or the categories of interests must be redefined, generally in a more abstract manner.[3] Recent shifts in attitudes toward religion have provoked changes of both these kinds. As religion (or, as it is more natural to say here, *one's* religion) has come to be seen more as a matter of private concern on a par with other private interests, it has become harder to justify assigning religious concerns the pre-eminent value they have traditionally received. In order to make contemporary sense of this traditional assignment of values, on the other hand, there has been a tendency to redefine "religion" more abstractly as "a person's ultimate values and deepest convictions about the nature of life," thereby preserving some plausibility for the claim that we can all agree on the importance of religion in one's life even though we may have different beliefs.

The categories of participant interests I have been discussing are naturally identified with familiar categories of expression: political speech, commercial speech, etc. But we should not be too quick to make this identification. The type of protection that a given kind of expression requires is not determined by participant values alone. It also depends on such factors as the costs and benefits to non-participants and the reliability of available forms of regulation. Not surprisingly, these other factors also play a role in how categories of expression are defined. As will later become apparent, the lack of clarity concerning these categories results in part from the difficulty of seeing how these different elements are combined in their definition.[4]

B. AUDIENCE INTERESTS

The interests of audiences are no less varied than those of participants: interests in being amused, informed on political topics, made aware of the pros and cons of alternatives available in the market, and so on. These audience interests conflict with those of participants in an important way. While participants sometimes aim only at communicating with people who are already interested in what they have to present, in a wide range of important cases their aims are broader: they want to gain the attention of people who would not otherwise consider their message. What audiences generally want, on the other hand, is to have expression available to them should they want to attend to it. Expression that grabs one's attention whether one likes it or not is generally thought of as a cost. But it should not be thought of only as a cost, even from the audience's point of view. As Mill rightly emphasized,[5] there is significant benefit in being exposed to ideas and attitudes different from one's own, though this exposure may be unwelcome. If we had complete control over the expression we are exposed to, the chances are high that we would use this power to our detriment. The important and difficult question however, is, when unwanted exposure to expression is a good thing from the audience's point of view.

This question is relatively easy to answer if we think of it as a problem of balancing temporary costs of annoyances, shock, or distraction against the more lasting benefits of a broadened outlook or deepened understanding. But it becomes more complicated if we take into account the possibility of more lasting costs such as being misled, having one's sensibilities dulled and cheapened, or acquiring foolish desires. This balancing task is simplified in the way we often think about expression by a further assumption about the audience's control. We are inclined to think that what would be ideal from the audience's point of view would be always to have the choice whether or not to be exposed to expression. Similarly, we have a tendency to assume that, having been exposed, an audience is always free to decide how to react: what belief to form or what attitude to adopt. This freedom to decide enables the audience to protect itself against unwanted long-range effects of expression. If we saw ourselves as helplessly absorbing as a belief every proposition we heard expressed, then our views of freedom of expression would be quite different from what they are. Certainly we are not like that. Nonetheless, the control we exercise over what to believe and what attitudes to adopt is in several respects an incomplete protection against unwarranted effects of expression.

To begin with, our decisions about what to believe are often mistaken, even in the best of circumstances. More generally, the likelihood of our not being mistaken, and hence the reliability of our critical rationality as a defense mechanism, varies widely from case to case depending on our emotional state, the degree of background information we possess, and the amount of time and energy we have to assess what we hear. As these things vary, so too does the value of being exposed to expression and the value of being able to avoid it. Commonly recognized cases of diminished rationality such as childhood, panic, and mental illness are just extreme instances of this common variation.

Quite apart from the danger of mistakenly believing what we hear, there is the further problem that a decision to disbelieve a messages does not erase all the effects it may have on us. Even if I dismiss what is said or shown to me as foolish and exaggerated, I am slightly different for having seen or heard it. This difference can be trivial but it can also be significant and have a significant effect on my later decisions. For example, being shown powerful photographs of the horrors of war, no matter what my initial reaction to them may be, can have the effect of heightening (or ultimately of dulling) my sense of the human suffering involved, and this may later affect my opinions about foreign policy in ways I am hardly aware of.

Expression influencing us in this way is a good thing, from the point of view of our interests as audiences, if it affects our future decisions and attitudes by making us aware of good reasons for them, so long as it does not interfere with our ability to weigh these reasons against others. Expression is a bad thing if it influences us in ways that are unrelated to relevant reasons, or in ways that bypass our ability to consider these reasons. "Subliminal advertising" is a good example of this. What is bad about it is not just that it is "subliminal," *i.e.* that we are influenced by it without being aware of that influence. This, I think, happens all the time and is, in many cases, unobjectionable. What is objectionable about subliminal advertising, if it works, is that it causes us to act—to buy popcorn, say, or to read Dostoevsky—by making us think we have a good reason for so acting, even though we probably have no such reason. Suddenly finding myself with the thought that popcorn would taste good or that *Crime and Punishment* would be just the thing is often good grounds for acting in the relevant way. But such a thought is no reason for action if it is produced in me by messages flickered on the screen rather than by facts about my present state that indeed make this a good moment to go out for popcorn or to lie down with a heavy book.

I have assumed here that subliminal advertising works by leading us to form a false belief: we acquire a positive feeling toward popcorn which we then take, mistakenly, to be a sign that we would particularly enjoy some popcorn. One can easily imagine, however, that the effect is deeper.[6] Suppose that what the advertising does is to change us so that we both have a genuine desire for popcorn and will in fact enjoy it. One can still raise the question whether being affected in this way is a good thing for us, but an answer to it cannot rely on the claim that we are made to think that we have a reason to buy popcorn when in fact we do not. For in this case we will have as good a reason to buy popcorn as we ever do: we want some and will enjoy it if we get it. Advertising of this kind will be a bad thing from the audience's point of view if one is worse off for having acquired such a desire, perhaps because it leads one to eat unhealthily, or because it distracts one from other pursuits, or for some other reason.

It is particularly galling to think of such effects being produced in us by another agent whose aim is to have us benefit him through actions we would not otherwise choose. But the existence of a conscious manipulator is not essential to the objections I have presented. It is a bad thing to acquire certain desires or to be influenced by false reasons, and these things are bad whether or not they are brought about by other agents. But while the existence of a conscious manipulator is not essential to this basic objection, it can be relevant in two further ways. What we should want in general is to have our beliefs and desires produced by processes that are reliable—processes whose effectiveness depends on the grounds for the beliefs and on the goodness of the desires it produces. We prefer to be aware of how we are being affected partly because this critical awareness increases the reliability of the process; although, as I have said, this safeguard is commonly overrated. Particularly where effects on us escape our notice, the existence of an agent controlling these effects can decrease the reliability of the process: the effects produced will be those serving this agent's purposes, and there may be no reason to think that what serves his purposes will be good from our point of view. (Indeed, the reverse is suggested by the fact that he chooses surreptitious means.) So the existence of a controlling agent can be relevant because of its implications for the reliability of the process. Beyond the question of reliability, however, we may simply prefer to have the choice of whether or not to acquire a given desire; we may prefer this even where there is no certainty as to which desire it is better to have. This provides a further reason for objecting to effects produced in us by others (although this reason seems to hold as well against effects produced by inanimate causes).

The central audience interest in expression, then, is the interest in having a good environment for the formation of one's beliefs and desires. From the point of view of this interest, freedom of expression is only one factor among many. It is important to be able to hear what others wish to tell us, but this is not obviously more important than having affirmative rights of access to important information or to basic education. Perhaps freedom of expression is thought to differ in being purely negative: it consists merely in not being denied something and is therefore more easily justified as a right than are freedom of information or the right to education, which require others to provide something for us. But this distinction does not withstand a careful scrutiny. To begin with, freedom of expression adequately understood requires affirmative protection for expression, not just the absence of interference. Moreover, even nonintervention involves costs, such as the annoyance and disruption that expression may cause. On the other side, restrictions on freedom of information include not only failures to provide information but also attempts to conceal what would otherwise become public. When a government makes such an attempt for the purpose of stopping the spread of undesirable political opinions, this contravenes the same audience interests as an attempt to restrict publication, and the two seem to be objectionable on the same grounds. The fact that there is in the one case no "participant" whose right to speak is violated, but only a fact that remains undiscovered, seems not to matter.

C. BYSTANDER INTERESTS

I have mentioned that both participants and audiences can sometimes benefit from restrictions on expression as well as from the lack thereof. But the most familar arguments for restricting expression appeal to the interests of bystanders. I will mention these only briefly. First are interests in avoiding the undesirable side effects of acts of expression themselves: traffic jams, the noise of crowds, the litter from leafletting. Second, and more important, are interests in the effect expression has on its audience. A bystander's interests may be affected simply by the fact that the audience has acquired new beliefs if, for example, they are beliefs about the moral character of the bystander. More commonly, bystanders are affected when expression promotes changes in the audience's subsequent behavior.

Regulation of expression to protect any of these bystander interests can conflict with the interests of audiences and participants. But regulation aimed at protecting bystanders against harms of the first type frequently strikes us as less threatening than that aimed at protecting bystanders against harmful changes in audience belief and behavior. This is true in part because the types of regulation supported by the two objectives are different. Protecting bystanders against harmful side effects of acts of expression calls for regulation only of the time, place, and manner of expression, and in many cases such regulation merely inconveniences audiences and participants. It *need* not threaten central interests in expression. Regulation to protect interests of the second kind, however, must, if it is successful, prevent effective communication of an idea. It is thus in direct conflict with the interests of participants and, at least potentially, of audiences as well. But this contrast is significant only to the degree that there are some forms of effective expression through which participant and audience interests can be satisfied without occasioning bystander harms of the first type: where there is no surplus of effective means of expression, regulation of time, place, and manner can be just as dangerous as restrictions on content.

III. THEORIES

Although "freedom of expression" seems to refer to a right of participants not to be prevented from expressing themselves, theoretical defenses of freedom of expression have been concerned chiefly with the interests of audiences and, to a lesser extent, those of bystanders. This is true, for example, of Mill's famous defense in *On Liberty*,[7] which argues that a policy of non-interference with expression is preferable to a policy of censorship on two grounds: first, it is more likely to promote the spread of true beliefs and, second, it contributes to the well-being of society by fostering the development of better (more independent and inquiring) individuals. A similar emphasis on audience values is evident in Alexander Meiklejohn's theory.[8] He argues that First Amendment freedom of speech derives from the right of citizens of a democracy to be informed in order that they can discharge their political responsibilities as citizens.

This emphasis can be explained, I think, by the fact that theories of freedom of expression are constructed to respond to what are seen as the most threatening arguments for restricting expression. These arguments have generally proceeded by calling attention to the harms that unrestricted expression may bring to audiences and bystanders: the harm, for example, of being misled, or that of being made less secure because one's neighbors have been misled or provoked into disaffection and unrest. The conclusion drawn is that government, which has the right and even the duty to protect its citizens against such harms, may and should do so by preventing the expression in question. Responding to this argument, theories of feedom of expression have tended to argue either that the interests in question are not best protected by restricting expression (Mill) or that "protecting" citizens in this way is illegitimate on other grounds (Meiklejohn).

The dialectical objective of Mill's argument helps to explain why, although he professes to be arguing as a utilitarian, he concentrates on just two goods, true belief and individual growth, and never explicitly considers how these are to be balanced off against other goods that would have to be taken into account in a full utilitarian argument.

The surprising narrowness of Meiklejohn's theory can be similarly explained. Meiklejohn was reacting against the idea that a "clear and present danger" could justify a government in acting to protect its citizens by curbing the expression of threatening political ideas. This seemed to him to violate the rights of those it claimed to protect. Accordingly, he sought to explain the "absolute" character of the First Amendment by basing it in a right to be informed and to make up one's own mind. But is there such a right? Meiklejohn saw the basis for one in the deliberative role of citizens in a democratic political order. But a right so founded does not apply to all forms of expression. Debates over artistic merit, the best style of personal life, or the promotion of goods in the marketplace may have their importance, but Meiklejohn saw these forms of expression as pursuits on a par with many others, unable to claim any distinct right to immunity from regulation. He was thus led to concede that these activities, in the main, fall outside the area of fundamental First Amendment protection or, rather, that they qualify for it only insofar as their general importance makes them relevant to political decisions.

This narrowness is an unsatisfactory feature of what is in many ways an interesting and appealing theory. Moreover, given this emphasis on political rights as the basis of First Amendment protection of speech, it is particularly surprising that Meiklejohn's theory should take audience values —the right of citizens to be informed—as the only fundamental ones. For prominent among the political rights of democratic citizens is the right to participate in the political process—in particular, the right to argue for one's own interests and point of view and to attempt to persuade one's fellow citizens. Such rights of participation do not entirely derive from the need of one's fellow citizens to be informed; the right to press one's case and to try to persuade others of its validity would not evaporate if it could be assumed that others were already perfectly informed on the questions at issue. Perhaps Meiklejohn would respond by saying that what is at stake is not a matter of being informed in the narrow sense of possessing all the relevant information. Democratic citizens also need to have the arguments for alternative policies forcefully presented in a way that makes their strengths and weaknesses more apparent, stimulates critical deliberation, and is conducive to the best decision. Surely, it might be asked, when political participation reaches the point where it becomes irrelevant to or even detracts from the possibility of good political decisions, what is the argument in its favor? I will return to this question of the relation between participant and non-participant interests in section five.[9]

Several years ago I put forward a theory of freedom of expression[10] that was very much influenced by Meiklejohn's views. Like him, I wanted to state a principle of freedom of expression which had a kind of absoluteness or at least a partial immunity from balancing against other concerns. But I wanted my theory to be broader than Meiklejohn's. I wanted it to cover more than just political speech, and I thought it should give independent significance to participant and audience interests. The basis of my theory was a single, audience-related principle applying to all categories of expression.

The Millian Principle:

There are certain harms which, although they would not occur but for certain acts of expression, nonetheless cannot be taken as part of a justification for legal restrictions on these acts. These harms are: (a) harms to certain individuals which consist in their coming to have false beliefs as a result of those acts of expression; (b) harmful consequences of acts performed as a result of those acts of expression, where the connection between the acts of expression and the subsequent harmful acts consists merely in the fact that the act of expression led the agents to believe (or increased their tendency to believe) these acts to be worth performing.[11]

I undertook to defend this principle by showing it to be a consequence of a particular idea about the limits of legitimate political authority: namely, that the legitimate powers of government are limited to those that can be defended on grounds compatible with the autonomy of its citizens—compatible, that is, with the idea that each citizen is sovereign in deciding what to believe and in weighing reasons for action.[12] This can be seen as a generalized version of Meiklejohn's idea of the political responsibility of democratic citizens.

The Millian Principle was intended to rule out the arguments for censorship to which Mill and Meiklejohn were responding. It did this by ruling that the harmful consequences to which these arguments appeal cannot count as potential justifications for legal restriction of expression. But there are other ways to arrive at policies that would strike us as incompatible with freedom of expression. One such way would be to restrict expression excessively, simply on the ground that it is a nuisance or has other undesirable consequences of a kind that the Millian Principle does allow to be weighed. So the second component in a theory of the type I described counters "excessive" restriction of this type by specifying that participant and audience interests in expression are to receive high values when they are balanced against competing goods. (As I have indicated, these values vary from one type of expression to another.) But freedom of expression does not only require that there should be "enough" expression. The two further components of the theory require that the goods of expression (for both participants and audiences) should be distributed in ways that are in accord both with the general requirements of distributive justice and with whatever particular rights there may be, such as rights to political participation, that support claims for access to means of expression.

This theory identifies the Millian Principle as the only principle concerned specifically with *expression* (as opposed to a general principle of justice) that applies with the same force to all categories of expression. If correct, then, it would answer one of the questions with which I began.[13] But is it correct? I now think that it is not.[14]

To begin with, the Millian Principle has what seems to be implausible consequences in some cases. For example, it is hard to see how laws against deceptive advertising or restrictions such as the ban on cigarette advertising on television could be squared with this principle. There are, of course, ways in which these objections might be answered. Perhaps the policies in question are simply violations of freedom of expression. If, on the other hand, they are acceptable this is because they are examples of justified paternalism, and my original theory did allow for the Millian Principle to be set aside in such cases.[15] But the theory provided for this exception only in cases of severely diminished rationality, because it took the view that any policy justified on grounds violating the Millian Principle would constitute paternalism of a particularly strong form.[16] The advertising cases seem to be clear counterexamples to this latter claim. More generally, clause (a) of the Millian Principle, taken as a limitation that can be set aside only in cases where our rational capacities are severely diminished, constitutes a rejection of paternalism that is too strong and too sweeping to be plausible. An acceptable doctrine of justified paternalism must take into account such factors as the value attached to being able to make one's own decisions, as well as the costs of so doing and the risks of empowering the government to make them on one's behalf. As the advertising examples show, these factors vary from case to case even where no general loss of rational capacities has occurred.

But the problems of the Millian Principle are not limited to cases of justified paternalism. The principle is appealing because it protects important audience interests—interests in deciding for one's self what to believe and what reasons to act on. As I have remarked earlier, these interests depend not only on freedom of expression, but also on other forms of access to information, education, and so on. Consideration of these other measures shows that there are in general limits to the sacrifices we are willing to make to enhance our decision-making capacity. Additional information is sometimes not worth the cost of getting it. The Millian Principle allows some of the costs of free expression to be weighed against its benefits, but holds that two important classes of costs must be ignored. Why should we be willing to bear unlimited costs to allow expression to flourish provided that the costs are of these particular kinds? Here it should be borne in mind that the Millian Principle is a restriction on the authority of legitimate governments. Now it may well be that, as I would argue, there is *some* restriction of this kind on the costs that governments may take as grounds for restricting expression, and that this is so because such a restriction is a safeguard that is more than worth the costs involved. But an argument for this conclusion, if it is to avoid the charge of arbitrariness and provide a convincing account of the exact form that the restriction takes, must itself be based on a full consideration of all the relevant costs.

What these objections mainly point to, then, is a basic flaw in the argument I offered to justify the Millian Principle. There are many ways in which the appealing, but notoriously vague and slippery notion of individual autonomy can be invoked in political argument. One way is to take autonomy, understood as the actual ability to exercise independent rational judgment, as a good to be promoted. Referring to "autonomy" in this sense is a vague, somewhat grandiloquent and perhaps misleading way of referring to some of the most important audience interests described in section two. The intuitive arguments I have offered in the present section appeal to the value of autonomy in this sense. These audience interests were also taken into account in the second component of my earlier theory. My argument for the Millian Principle, on the other hand, employed the idea of autonomy in a different way, namely as a constraint on justifications of authority. Such justifications, it was held, must be compatible with the thesis that citizens are equal, autonomous rational agents.[17]

The idea of such a constraint now seems to me mistaken. Its appeal derives entirely from the value of autonomy in the first sense, that is, from the importance of protecting central audience interests. To build these interests in at the outset as constraints on the process of justification gives theoretical form to the intuition that freedom of expression is based on considerations that cannot simply be outweighed by competing interests in the manner that "clear and present danger" or "pure balancing" theories of the First Amendment would allow. But to build these audience interests into the theory in this way has the effect of assigning them greater and more constant weight than we in fact give them. Moreover, it prevents us from even asking whether these interests might in some cases be better advanced if we could shield ourselves from some influences. In order to meet the objections raised to the Millian Principle, it is necessary to answer such questions, and, in general, to take account of the variations in audience interests under varying circumstances. But this is not possible within the framework of the argument I advanced.

Most of the consequences of the Millian Principle are ones that I would still endorse. In particular, I still think that it is legitimate for the government to promote our personal safety by restricting information about how to make your own nerve gas,[18] but not legitimate for it to promote our safety by stopping political agitation which could, if unchecked, lead to widespread social conflict. I do not think that my judgment in the latter case rests simply on the difficulty of predicting such consequences or on the idea that the bad consequences of allowing political controversy will in each such case be outweighed by the good. But I do not think that the difference between the two cases can be found in the distinction between restricting means and restricting reasons, as my original article suggested. The difference is rather that where political issues are involved governments are notoriously partisan and unreliable. Therefore, giving government the authority to make policy by balancing interests in such cases presents a serious threat to particularly important participant and audience interests. To the degree that the considerations of safety involved in the first case are clear and serious, and the participant and audience interests that might suffer from restriction are not significant, regulation could be acceptable.

In this way of looking at things, political speech stands out as a distinctively important category of expression. Meiklejohn's mistake, I think, was to suppose that the differences in degree between this category and others mark the boundaries of First Amendment theory. My mistake, on the other hand, was that in an effort to generalize Meiklejohn's theory beyond the category of political speech, I took what were in effect features particular to this category and presented them, under the heading of autonomy, as a priori constraints on justifications of legitimate authority.

In order to avoid such mistakes it is useful to distinguish several different levels of argument. At one extreme is what might be called the "level of policy," at which we might consider the overall desirability or undesirability of a particular action or policy, *e.g.*, an ordinance affecting expression. At the other extreme is what might be called the "foundational level." Argument at this level is concerned with identifying the ultimate sources of justification relevant to the subject at hand. In the case of expression, these are the relevant participant, audience, and bystander interests and the requirements of distributive justice applicable to their satisfaction. Intermediate between these levels is the "level of rights."[19] The question at this level is what limitations and requirements, if any, must be imposed on policy decisions if we are to avoid results that would be unacceptable with respect to the considerations that are defined at the fundamental level? To claim that something is a right, then, is to claim that some limit or requirement on policy decisions is *necessary* if unacceptable results are to be avoided, and that this particular limit or requirement is a *feasible* one, that is, that its acceptance provides adequate protection against such results and does so at tolerable cost to other interests. Thus, for example, to claim that a particular restriction on searches and seizures is part of a right of privacy would be to claim that it is a feasible form of necessary protection for our important and legitimate interests in being free from unwanted observation and intrusion. What rights there are in a given social setting at a given time depends on which judgments of necessity and feasibility are true at that place and time.[20] This will depend on the nature of the main threats to the interests in question, on the presence or absence of factors tending to promote unequal distribution of the means to their satisfaction, and particularly on the characteristics of the agents (private individuals or governments) who make the relevant policy decisions: what power do they have, and how are they likely to use this power in the absence of constraints?

Most of us believe that freedom of expression is a right. That is, we believe that limits on the power of governments to regulate expression are necessary to protect our central interests as audiences and participants, and we believe that such limits are not incompatible with a healthy society and a stable political order. Hundreds of years of political history support these beliefs. There is less agreement as to exactly how this right is to be understood—what limits and requirements on decision making authority are necessary and feasible as ways of protecting central participant and audience interests and insuring the required equity in the access to means of expression. This is less than surprising, particularly given the fact that the answer to this question changes, sometimes rapidly, as conditions change. Some threats are constant—for example the tendency of governments to block the expression of critical views—and these correspond to points of general agreement in the definition of the right. But as new threats arise— from, for example, changes in the form or ownership of dominant means of communication—it may be unclear, and a matter subject to reasonable disagreement, how best to refine the right in order to provide the relevant kinds of protection at a tolerable cost. This disagreement is partly empirical —a disagreement about what is likely to happen if certain powers are or are not granted to governments. It is also in part a disagreement at the foundational level over the nature and importance of audience and participant interests and, especially, over what constitutes a sufficiently equal distribution of the means to their satisfaction. The main role of a philosophic theory of freedom of expression, in addition to clarifying what it is we are arguing about, is to attempt to resolve these foundational issues.

What reasons are there for taking this view of rights in general and of freedom of expression in particular? One reason is that it can account for much of what we in fact believe about rights and can explain what we do in the process of defending and interpreting them. A second reason is that its account of the bases of rights appears to exhaust the relevant concerns: if a form of regulation of expression presents no threat to the interests I have enumerated, nor to the equitable distribution of the means to their satisfaction, what further ground might there be to reject it as violating freedom of expression? Beyond these two reasons, all I can do in defense of my view is to ask, what else? If rights are not instrumental in the way I have described, what are they and what are the reasons for taking them seriously?

IV. CATEGORIES

Let me distinguish two ways in which arguments about freedom of expression may involve distinctions between categories of expression. First, not every participant or audience interest is capable of exerting the same upward pressure on the costs freedom of expression requires us to bear. Freedom of expression often requires that a particular form of expression—leafletting or demonstrations near public buildings—be allowed despite high bystander costs because important participant or audience interests would otherwise be inadequately or unequally served. Such arguments are clearly category-dependent: their force depends on the importance of the particular participant or audience interests in question. But, once it is concluded on the basis of such an argument that a given mode of expression must be permitted, there is the further question whether its use must be permitted for any form of expression or whether it may be restricted to those types of expression whose value was the basis for claiming that this mode of expression must be allowed. If the latter, then not only will categories of interests be assigned different weights in arguments about the content of the right of freedom of expression, but the application of this right to particular cases will also involve determining the category to which the acts in question belong. I will refer to these two forms of categorization as, respectively, categories of interests and categories of acts.

This distinction can be illustrated by considering the ways in which "political speech" can serve as a category. For the purposes of this discussion, I will assume that "political" is to be interpreted narrowly as meaning, roughly, "having to do with the electoral process and the activities of government." We can distinguish a category of interests in expression that are political in this sense, including both participant interests in taking part in the political process and audience (and bystander) interests in the spread of information and discussion about political topics. As a category of acts, on the other hand, "political speech" might be distinguished[21] either by participant intent—expression with a political purpose—or by content and effect—expression that concerns political issues or contributes to the understanding of political issues. These two definitions correspond, roughly, to the two sets of interests just mentioned. I will assume for the moment that the category of political speech is to be understood to include acts falling under either of these definitions.

While the political interests in expression are not uniquely important, the fact that they are inadequately or very unequally served constitutes a strong reason for enlarging or improving available modes of expression. Their particular importance as a source of upward pressure is something that rational argument about freedom of expression must recognize. Must "political speech" be recognized as a category of acts as well? That is, can the fact that an act of expression has the relevant political intent or content exempt it from regulation that would otherwise be compatible with freedom of expression?

Special standards for defamation applicable to expression concerning "public officials," "public figures," or "public issues"[22] indicate that something like "political speech" does function as a category of acts in the current legal understanding of freedom of expression. Reflection on the *Skokie* case may also suggest that "political speech" has a special place in our intuitive understanding of this right. It seems unlikely that expression so deeply offensive to bystanders would be deemed to be protected by freedom of expression if it did not have a political character—if, for example, its purpose had been merely to provide entertainment or to promote commerce. But I do not see how this interpretation of freedom of expression can be defended, at least unless "political" is understood in a very broad sense in which any important and controversial question counts as a "political issue." Expression that is political in the narrow sense is both important and in need of protection, but it is not unique in either respect. Furthermore, even if "political" is understood broadly, the idea that access to a mode of expression can be made to depend on official determination of the "political" nature of one's purposes or one's message does not sit comfortably with the basic ideas of freedom of expression.

This suggests a second, more plausible analysis of the *Skokie* case, one which relies more heavily on categories of interests and less on categories of acts. The judgment that the Nazi march is protected may reflect the view that no[23] ordinance giving local authorities the power to ban such a march could give adequate protection to central interests in political expression. This argument avoids any judgment as to whether the content and purposes of this particular march were "genuinely political." It relies instead on the judgment that such a march could not be effectively and reliably distinguished from political expression that it is essential to protect.

The distinction between categories of interests and categories of acts can be used to explain some of the ambivalence about categories noted at the beginning of this article. Reference to categories of interests is both important and unavoidable in arguments about freedom of expression. Categories of acts may also be unavoidable—"expression" is itself such a category, and assault, for example, is distinguished from it on the basis of participant intent—but there are good reasons for being wary of categories of acts and for keeping their use to a minimum. Even where there is agreement on the relative importance of various interests in expression, the purposes and content of a given expressive act can be a matter of controversy and likely misinterpretation, particularly in those situations of intense conflict and mistrust in which freedom of expression is most important. (Well-known difficulties in the application of laws against incitement are a good illustration of this point.) Thus the belief that the fundamental principles of freedom of expression must transcend categories derives in part from the recognition that categories of acts rest on distinctions—of intent and content—that a partisan of freedom of expression will instinctively view with suspicion. Nonetheless, in interpreting freedom of expression, we are constantly drawn toward categories of acts as we search for ways of protecting central interests in expression while avoiding unacceptable costs. The current struggle to define the scope of special standards of defamation[24] is a good example of this process. Identifying the categories of acts that can actually be relied upon to give the protection we want is a matter of practical and strategic judgment, not of philosophical theory.

I have mentioned the possibility of official misapplication as one reason for avoiding categories of acts, but this is not the only problem. A second difficulty is the fact that it is extremely difficult to regulate one category of speech without restricting others as well. Here the recent campaign financing law is an instructive example.[25] The basic aim of restricting money spent during a campaign in order to increase the fairness of this particular competition is entirely compatible with freedom of expression. The problem is that in order to regulate spending effectively, it was deemed necessary to make campaign funds flow through a single committee for each candidate. In order to do this a low limit was placed on the amount any private person or group could spend on expression to influence the campaign. But since spending on expression to influence a campaign cannot be clearly separated from expression on political topics generally, the limit on private spending constituted an unacceptable restriction on expression. Limits on spending for "campaign speech" are in principle as compatible with freedom of expression as limits on the length of speeches in a town meeting: both are acceptable when they enhance the fairness of the proceedings. Unlike a town meeting, however, "campaign speech" is not easily separated from other expression on political topics, hence not easily regulated in a way that leaves this other expression unaffected.

In addition to the difficulty of regulating one category without affecting others, there is the further problem that the categories within which special regulation is held to be permissible may themselves suffer from dangerous overbreadth. I believe that this is true, for example, of the category of commercial speech. Presumably "commercial speech" is to be defined with reference to participant intent: expression by a participant in the market for the purpose of attracting buyers or sellers. It is not identical with advertising, which can serve a wide variety of expressive purposes, and it cannot be defined by its subject matter: *Consumer Reports* has the same subject matter as much commercial speech, but it is entitled to "full" First Amendment protection. Why, then, would anyone take commercial speech to be subject to restrictions that would not be acceptable if applied to other forms of expression? This view is widely held, or has been until recently,[26] and it appears to be supported by the acceptability of laws against false or deceptive advertising, the regulation of cigarette advertising and restriction on the form of classified advertisements of employment opportunities. One reason for this attitude may be that the participant and audience interests at stake in commerical speech—promoting one's business, learning what is available in the market—are not generally perceived as standing in much danger from overrestriction. There is, we are inclined to think, plenty of opportunity for advertising, and we are in no danger of being deprived of needed information if advertising is restricted. In fact, the relevant audience interests are in much more danger from excessive exposure to advertising, and from false and deceptive advertising. In addition, laws against such advertising seem acceptable in a way that analogous laws against false or deceptive political or religious claims would not be, first because there are reasonably clear and objective critieria of truth in this area, and second, we regard the government as much less partisan in the competition between commercial firms than in the struggle between religious or political views.

Much of this is no doubt true, but it does not support the generalization that commerical speech as a category is subject to less stringent requirements of freedom of expression. The restrictions I have mentioned, where they seem justified, can be supported by arguments that are applicable in principle to other forms of expression (for example, by appeals to qualified paternalism, or to the advantages for audiences of protection against an excessive volume of expression). It is a mistake to think that these arguments are applicable only to commercial speech or that all commercial speech is especially vulnerable to them. In particular, if, as I believe, the assumption that governments are relatively neutral and trustworthy in this area is one reason for our complacent attitude toward regulation of commercial speech, this assumption should be made explicit and treated with care. There are many cases that clearly count as commerical speech in which our traditional suspicions of governmental regulation of expression are as fully justified as they are elsewhere. One such example might be an advertising battle between established energy companies and anti-establishment commercial enterprises promoting alternative energy sources.[27]

V. PORNOGRAPHY

In this final section I will consider the category of pornography. This example will illustrate both the problems of categories, just discussed, and some of the problems concerning participant and audience interests that were discussed in section two above.

The question to ask about pornography is, why restrict it? I will consider two answers. The first appeals to the interest people have in not being unwillingly exposed to offensive material. By offense, I do not mean a reaction grounded in disapproval but an immediate discomfort analogous to pain, fear, or acute embarrassment. I am willing to assume for purposes of argument that many people do have such a reaction to some sexual material, and that we should take seriously their interest in being protected against it. I also agree that what offends most people will differ from place to place depending on experience and custom. Therefore the appropriate standards of protection may also vary. But if this were the only reason for restricting pornography the problem would have an easy solution: restrict what can be displayed on the public streets or otherwise forced on an unwilling audience but place no restrictions whatever on what can be shown in theaters, printed in books, or sent through the mails in plain brown wrappers. The only further requirement is that the inconvenience occasioned by the need to separate the two groups should be fairly shared between them.

The idea that this solution should be acceptable to all concerned rests on specific assumptions about the interests involved. It is assumed that consumers of pornography desire private enjoyment, that sellers want to profit from selling to those who have this desire, and that other people want to avoid being forced to see or hear what they regard as offensive. Rarely will one find three sets of interests that are so easily made compatible. There are of course certain other interests which are left out of this account. Perhaps some people want to enjoy pornography in public; their pleasure depends on the knowledge that they are disturbing other people. Also, sellers may want to reach a larger audience in order to increase profits, so they would like to use more stimulating advertisements. Finally, those who wish to restrict pornography may be offended not only by the sight of it but even by the knowledge that some people are enjoying it out of their sight; they will be undisturbed only if it is stopped. But none of these interests has significant weight. There is, to be sure, a general problem of explaining what makes some interests important and others, like these, less significant; but this is not a problem peculiar to freedom of expression.

Unfortunately, offense is not the only reason to restrict pornography. The main reason, I think, is the belief that the availability, enjoyment, and even the legality of pornography will contribute to undesirable changes in our attitudes toward sex and in our sexual mores. We all care deeply about the character of the society in which we will live and raise our children. This interest cannot be simply dismissed as trivial or illegitimate. Nor can we dismiss as empirically implausible the belief that the evolution of sexual attitudes and mores is strongly influenced by the books and movies that are generally available and widely discussed, in the way that we can dismiss the belief that pornography leads to rape. Of course, expression is not the only thing that can influence society in these ways. This argument against pornography has essentially the same form as well-known arguments in favor of restricting non-standard sexual conduct.[28] If the interest to which these arguments appeal is, as I have conceded, a legitimate one, how can the arguments be answered?

I think that transactions "between consenting adults" can sometimes legitimately be restricted on the ground that, were such transactions to take place freely, social expectations would change, people's motives would be altered, and valued social practices would as a result become unstable and decline. I think, for example, that some commercial transactions might legitimately be restricted on such grounds. Thus Richard Titmuss,[29] opposing legalization of blood sales in Britain, claims that the availability of blood on a commerical basis weakens peoples' sense of interdependence and leads to a general decline in altruistic motivation. Assuming for the purposes of argument that this empirical claim is correct, I am inclined to think that there is no objection to admitting this as a reason for making the sale of blood illegal. To ban blood sales for this reason seems at first to be objectionable because it represents an attempt by the state to maintain a certain state of mind in the population. What is objectionable about many such attempts, which violate freedom of expression, is that they seek to prevent changes of mind by preventing people from considering and weighing possible reasons for changing their minds. Such interventions run contrary to important audience interests. As far as I can see, however, the presence of a market in blood does not put us in a better position to decide how altruistic we wish to be.

There are of course other objections to outlawing the sale of blood, objections based simply on the value of the opportunity that is foreclosed. Being deprived of the opportunity to sell one's blood does not seem to me much of a loss. In the case of proposed restrictions on deviant sexual conduct, however, the analogous costs to the individuals who would be restricted are severe—too severe to be justified by the considerations advanced on the other side. In fact, the argument for restriction seems virtually self-contradictory on this score. What is the legitimate interest that people have in the way their social mores evolve? It is in large part the legitimate interest they have in not being under pressure to conform to practices they find repugnant under pain of being thought odd and perhaps treated as an outcast. But just this interest is violated in an even more direct way by laws against homosexual conduct.

The case for restricting pornography might be answered in part by a similar argument, but there is also a further issue, more intrinsic to the question of freedom of expression. Once it is conceded that we all have legitimate and conflicting interests in the evolution of social attitudes and mores, the question arises how this conflict can fairly be resolved. In particular, is majority vote a fair solution? Can the majority be empowered to preserve attitudes they like by restricting expression that would promote change? The answer to this question is clearly no. One reason is that, as Meiklejohn would emphasize, the legitimacy of majoritarian political processes themselves depends upon the assumption that the voters have free access to information and are free to attempt to persuade and convince each other. Another reason is that, unlike a decision where to build a road, this is an issue that need not be resolved by a clear decision at any one time. There is hence no justification for allowing a majority to squeeze out and silence a minority. A fair alternative procedure is available: a continuing process of "informal politics" in which the opposing groups attempt to alter or to preserve the social consensus through persuasion and example.

This response to the argument for restricting pornography has several consequences. First, since it rests upon viewing public interaction under conditions of freedom of expression as an informal political process that is preferable to majority voting as a way of deciding certain important questions, the response is convincing only if we can argue that the process is in fact fair. It will not be if, for example, access to the main means of expression, and hence the ability to have an influence on the course of public debate, are very unequally distributed in the society. Thus, equity in the satisfaction of participant interests, discussed above as one goal of freedom of expression, arises here in a new way as part of a defense of freedom of expression against majority control.

A second consequence of the argument is that time, place, and manner restrictions on obscene material, which at first seemed a satisfactory solution to the problem of offense, are no longer so obviously satisfactory. Their appeal as a solution rested on the supposition that, since the interests of consumers and sellers of pornography were either purely private or simply commercial, unwilling audiences were entitled to virtually complete protection, the only residual problem being the relatively trivial one of how to apportion fairly the inconvenience resulting from the need to shield the two groups from each other. But if what the partisans of pornography are entitled to (and what the restrictors are trying to deny them) is a fair opportunity to influence the sexual mores of the society, then it seems that they, like participants in political speech in the narrow sense,[30] are entitled to at least a certain degree of access even to unwilling audiences. I do not find this conclusion a particularly welcome one, but it seems to me difficult to avoid once the most important arguments against pornography are taken seriously. Let me conclude by considering several possible responses.

The argument I have presented starts from the high value to be assigned to the participant interest in being able to influence the evolution of attitudes and mores in one's society. But while some publishers of "obscene" materials have this kind of crusading intent, undoubtedly many others do not. Perhaps the proper conclusion of my argument is not that any attempt to publish and disseminate offensive sexual material is entitled to full First Amendment protection but, at most, that such protection can be claimed where the participant's intent is of the relevant "political" character. This would construe "pornography" as a category of acts in the sense defined above: sexually offensive expression in the public forum need not be allowed where the intent is merely that of the pornographer—who aims only to appeal to a prurient interest in sex—but must be allowed where the participant has a "serious" interest in changing society. To take "the obscene" as a category of acts subject to extraordinary regulation would involve, on this view, the same kind of overbreadth that is involved when "commerical speech" is seen as such a category. In each case features typical of at most some instances are taken to justify special treatment of the category as a whole.

As I indicated in section four above, distinctions based on participant intent cannot be avoided altogether in the application of the right of freedom of expression, but they are nearly always suspect. This is particularly so in the present case; expression dealing with sex is particularly likely to be characterized, by those who disapprove of it, as frivolous, unserious, and of interest only to dirty minds. To allow expression in this area to be regulated on the basis of participant intent would be to set aside a normal caution without, as far as I can see, any ground for doing so.

The conclusion that unwilling audiences cannot be fully protected against offensive expression might be avoided in a second way. Even if the "political interest" in expression on sexual topics is an important interest, and even if it supports a right of access to unwilling audiences, there is a further question whether this interest requires the presentation of "offensive" material. Perhaps it would be enough to be entitled to present material that "deals with" the question of sexual mores in a sober and non-offensive manner. Perhaps Larry Flynt and Ralph Ginzburg should, on the one hand, be free to sell as much pornography as they wish for private consumption, and they should on the other hand be free to write newspaper editorials and books, make speeches, or go on television as much as they can to crusade for a sexually liberated society. But the latter activity, insofar as it presses itself on people's attention without warning, is subject to the requirement that it not involve offense.

On the other side, it can be claimed that this argument rests on an overly cognitive and rationalistic idea of how people's attitudes change. Earnest treatises on the virtues of a sexually liberated society can be reliably predicted to have no effect on prevailing attitudes toward sex. What is more likely to have such an effect is for people to discover that they find exciting and attractive portrayals of sex which they formerly thought offensive or, vice versa, that they find boring and offensive what they had expected to find exciting and liberating. How can partisans of sexual change be given a fair chance to make this happen except through a relaxation of restrictions on what can be publicly displayed? I do not assume that the factual claims behind this argument are correct. My question rather is, if they were correct what would follow? From the fact that frequent exposure to material previously thought offensive is a likely way to promote a change in people's attitudes, it does not follow that partisans of change are entitled to use this means. Proponents of a change in attitude are not entitled to use just *any* expressive means to effect their aim even if the given means is the only one that would actually have the effect they desire: audience interests must also be considered. It must be asked whether exposure to these means leads to changes in one's tastes and preferences through a process that is, like subliminal advertising, both outside of one's rational control and quite independent of the relevant grounds for preference, or whether, on the contrary, the exposure to such influences is in fact part of the best way to discover what one really has reason to prefer. I think that a crucial question regarding the regulation of pornography and other forms of allegedly corrupting activity lies here.

It is often extremely difficult to distinguish influences whose force is related to relevant grounds for the attitudes they produce from influences that are the work of irrelevant factors. Making this distinction requires, in many cases, a clearer understanding than we have both of the psychological processes through which our attitudes are altered and of the relevant grounds for holding the attitudes in question. The nature of these grounds, in particular, is often a matter of too much controversy to be relied upon in defining a right of freedom of expression. The power to restrict the presentation of "irrelevant influences" seems threatening because it is too easily extended to restrict any expression likely to mislead.

Subliminal advertising is in this respect an unusual case, from which it is hard to generalize. A law against subliminal advertising could be acceptable on First Amendment grounds because it could be framed as a prohibition simply of certain techniques—the use of hidden words or images—thus avoiding controversial distinctions between relevant and irrelevant influences. Where we are concerned with the apparent—as opposed to the hidden—content of expression, however, things become more controversial (even though it is true that what is clearly seen or heard may influence us, and be designed to do so, in ways that we are quite unaware of).

The case for protecting unwilling audiences against influence varies considerably from one kind of offensive expression to another, even within the class of what is generally called pornography. The separation between the way one's attitudes are affected by unwanted exposure to expression and the relevant grounds for forming such attitudes is clearest in the case of pornography involving violence or torture. The reasons for being opposed to, and revolted by, these forms of behavior are quite independent of the question whether one might, after repeated exposure, come to find them exciting and attractive. This makes it plausible to consider such changes in attitude produced by unchosen exposure to scenes of violence as a kind of harm that an unwilling audience is entitled to protection against.[31] The question is whether this protection can be given without unacceptably restricting other persuasive activity involving scenes of violence, such as protests against war.

The argument for protection of unwilling audiences is much weaker where what is portrayed are mildly unconventional sexual attitudes or practices, not involving violence or domination. Here it is more plausible to say that discovering how one feels about such matters when accustomed to them is the best way of discovering what attitude towards them one has reason to hold. The lack of independent grounds for appraising these attitudes makes it harder to conceive of changes produced by expression as a kind of harm or corruption. Even here there are some independent grounds for appraisal, however.[32] Attitudes towards sex involve attitudes towards other people, and the reasons for or against holding *these* attitudes may be quite independent of one's reactions to portrayals of sex, which are, typically, highly impersonal. I believe that there are such grounds for regarding as undesirable changes in our attitudes towards sex produced by pornography, or for that matter by advertising, and for wanting to be able to avoid them. But, in addition to the problem of separability, just mentioned with regard to portrayals of violence, these grounds may be too close to the substantive issues in dispute to be an acceptable basis for the regulation of expression.

It seems, then, that an argument based on the need to protect unwilling audiences against being influenced could justify restriction of at most some forms of offensive expression. This leaves us with the residual question how much offense must be tolerated in order for persuasion and debate regarding sexual mores to go forward. Here the clearest arguments are by comparison with other categories of expression. The costs that audiences and bystanders are required to bear in order to provide for free political debate are generally quite high. These include very significant psychological costs, as the *Skokie* case indicates. Why should psychological costs of that particular kind occasioned by obscenity be treated differently (or given a particularly high value)? A low cost threshold would be understandable if the issues at stake were trivial ones, but by the would-be restrictors' own account this is not so. I do not find the prospect of increased exposure to offensive expression attractive, but it is difficult to construct a principled argument for restriction that is consistent with our policy towards other forms of expression and takes the most important arguments against pornography seriously.

NOTES

*Versions of this paper were presented at the University of Minnesota and the University of California at Berkeley as well as at the Pittsburgh symposium. I am grateful to members of all these audiences for helpful comments. I have also benefited greatly from discussions of this topic with Marshall Cohen, Clark Glymour, and Derek Parfit.

1. Village of Skokie v. National Socialist Party of America, 69 Ill. 2d 605, 373 N.E. 2d 21 (1978).

2. How the existence of an approximate consensus, even though it is only approximate, can contribute to the legitimacy of the agreed-upon values as a basis for justification is a difficult problem which I cannot here discuss.

3. I have assumed here that categories of interests are disrupted by a decrease in consensus and an increase in diversity of views since this is the course of change we are most familiar with. I suppose that the reverse process—in which increasing consensus makes an abstract category seem pointlessly abstract and leads to its being redefined to include what was before only a special case—is at least possible. On the former, more familiar kind of transition, see E. DURKHEIM, *Individualism and the Intellectuals*, in EMILE DURKHEIM ON MORALITY AND SOCIETY 43 (R. Bellah ed. 1973). *See also* E. DURKHEIM, DIVISION OF LABOR IN SOCIETY (G. Simpson trans. 1933). Perhaps Marx's view of the transition to a socialist society includes an instance of the latter kind.

4. Here libel provides a good example. One reason for assigning it low status as a category of expressive acts is the low value attached to the participant interest in insulting people and damaging their reputations. This is something we sometimes want to do, but it gets low weight in our social calculus. Another reason is the high value we attach to not having our reputations damaged. These are not unrelated, but they do not motivate concern with the same class of actions. Other relevant considerations include the interest we may have in performing or having others perform acts which incidentally damage reputations. A defensible definition of libel as a category of expressive acts will be some resultant of all these factors, not simply of the first or the second alone.

5. J. MILL, ON LIBERTY ch. 2 (C. Shields ed. 1956).

6. Here I am indebted to the discussion following the presentation of this paper at Berkeley and to comments by members of my graduate seminar for the Spring Term, 1979.

7. J. MILL, *supra* note 5.

8. A. MEIKLEJOHN, POLITICAL FREEDOM (1960).

9. *See* pp. 32–34 *infra.*

10. Scanlon, *A Theory of Freedom of Expression*, 1 PHILOSOPHY & PUB. AFF. 204 (1972).

11. *Id.* at 213.

12. *Id.* at 215.

13. *See* p. 140 *supra.*

14. In what follows I am indebted to a number of criticisms, particularly to objections raised by Robert Amdur and by Gerald Dworkin.

15. Scanlon, *supra* note 10, at 220.

16. *Id.* at 221.

17. *Id.* at 215.

18. *Id.* at 211–13.

19. For a presentation of this view at greater length, see Scanlon, *Rights, Goals and Fairness*, in PUBLIC AND PRIVATE MORALITY (S. Hampshire ed. 1978).

20. Of course there may be multiple solutions to the problem; that is, different ways in which a right might be defined to give adequate protection to the interests in question. In such a case what there is a right to initially is *some* protection of the relevant kind. At this point the right is incompletely defined. Once one adequate form of protection becomes established as a constraint on policy making, the other alternatives are no longer *necessary* in the relevant sense. In this respect our rights are partly determined by convention.

21. Distinguished, that is, from other forms of protected expression. I am concerned here only with what marks speech as political. A full definition of "political speech" (*i.e.* permissible political expression) would, in order to exclude such things as bombings, take into account features other than those mentioned here. *See* note 4 *supra.*

22. *See* the line of cases following New York Times Co. v. Sullivan, 376 U.S. 254 (1964). *See, e.g.,* Curtis Publishing Co. v. Butts, 388 U.S. 130 (1967); Gertz v. Robert Welch, Inc., 418 U.S. 323 (1974); Herbert v. Lando, 99 S.Ct. 1635 (1979); Hutchinson v. Proxmire, 99 S.Ct.

2675 (1979).

23. Of course an actual decision need only find a particular ordinance unconstitutional. I take it, however, that an intuitive judgment that an action is protected by freedom of expression is broader than this and implies that *no* acceptable ordinance could restrict that action.

24. *See* cases cited note 22 *supra*.

25. Buckley v. Valeo, 424 U.S. 1 (1976). Federal Election Campaign Act of 1971, Pub. L. No. 92–225, 86 Stat. 3 (1972), *as amended by* Federal Election Campaign Act Amendments of 1974, Pub. L. No. 93–443, 88 Stat. 1263 (1974), *as amended by* Federal Election Campaign Act Amendments of 1976, Pub. L. No. 94–283, 90 Stat. 475 (1976).

26. *See* Bates v. State Bar of Arizona, 433 U.S. 350 (1977) *reh. denied* 434 U.S. 881 (1977); Virginia Pharmacy Bd. v. Virginia Consumer Council, 425 U.S. 748 (1976).

27. It might be claimed that insofar as this example has the character I mention it is an instance of political, not merely commercial, speech. Certainly it does have a political element. Nonetheless, the intentions of the participants (and the interests of audiences) may be thoroughly commerical. The political element of the controversy triggers First Amendment reactions because it raises the threat of partisan regulation, not because the interests at stake, on the part of either participants or audience, are political.

28. *See* DEVLIN, THE ENFORCEMENT OF MORALS (1965).

29. R. TITMUSS, THE GIFT RELATIONSHIP chs. 13–15 (1971). *See also* Singer, *Altruism and Commerce*, 2 PHILOSOPHY & PUB. AFF. 312 (1973).

30. Perhaps Meiklejohn would defend "offensive" discussion of sexual topics in a similar fashion, construing it as a form of political speech. Several differences should be noted, however. First, my argument appeals to participant interests rather than to the audience interests Meiklejohn emphasizes. Second, the politics I am concerned with here is an informal process distinct from the formal democratic institutions he seems to have in mind. Participation in this informal process is not important merely as a preliminary to making decisions in one's offical capacity as a citizen. But even if Meiklejohn would not construe the political role of citizens this narrowly, a further difference remains. Having an influence on the evolving mores of one's society is, in my view, only one important participant interest among many, and I would not make the validity of all First Amendment claims depend on their importance for our role in politics of either the formal or the informal sort. It is true, however, that those ideas controversial enough to be in greatest need of First Amendment protection are likely also to be the subject of politics in one or both of these senses. *See* note 27 *supra*.

31. Prohibiting the display of such scenes for willing audiences is a separate question. So is their presentation to children. Here and throughout this article I am concerned only with adults.

32. Here the moral status of attitudes and practices may become relevant. Moral considerations have been surprisingly absent from the main arguments for restricting pornography considered in this section: the notion of offense quite explicitly abstracts from moral appraisal, and the importance of being able to influence the future mores of one's society does not depend on the assumption that one's concern with these mores is based in morality. A person can have a serious and legitimate interest in preserving (or eliminating) certain customs even if these are matters of no *moral* significance. But morality is relevant to the argument for audience protection since, if sexual attitudes are a matter of morality, this indicates that they can be appraised on grounds that are independent of subjective reaction, thus providing a possible basis for claiming that a person who has come to have a certain attitude (and to be content with having it) has been made worse off.

Susan Wendell

Pornography and Freedom of Expression

Although it is part of our present concept of pornography that it has some relationship to sexual feelings or activities, the most important and difficult social issues raised by pornography are not concerned with its sexual content. They are concerned with its sometimes recommending, condoning, or portraying acts of unjustified physical coercion, such as rape, involuntary bondage, torture and mutilation, and sex between adults and children.[1] Acts of physical coercion are morally wrong unless they are justified by such circumstances as self-defense, defense of others, or prevention of greater harms.[2] In addition, we have a right to society's efforts to protect us from unjustified physical coercion and an obligation to contribute to the protection of others from it. In contrast, nothing is immoral just in virtue of its being sexual, and we have no rights or duties with regard to protection from sexual activities that are voluntary. I think that these differences between the two kinds of actions have implications for the treatment of material which recommends, condones, or portrays them.

In this essay, I will not attempt to show that physical coercion requires justification or that we have rights and duties with regard to protection from unjustified physical coercion; I will take it for granted that the reader agrees with these assertions. Nor will I criticize the existing laws concerning pornography, except by implication, nor propose specific legislation or

This article has not been previously published.

enforcement procedures with regard to pornography. What I will do is define the sort of material which I believe ought to be restricted, distinguish among and consider various kinds of restriction, and offer justifications, based upon commitment to freedom of expression and commitment to the protection of citizens from involuntarily suffering serious harm, for restricting some forms of pornography.

I shall state my conclusions first and then discuss their meaning in more detail and the reasoning by which I arrived at them.

CONCLUSIONS

1. There are certain sorts of visual, audio, and written material to which children should not be exposed and to which adults should only be exposed voluntarily. These are expressions of opinion recommending or condoning actions of kinds *a* or *b* below and, with some exceptions, depictions, descriptions, and dramatizations of these actions:

   a. unjustified physical coercion of human beings, with or without additional harm being inflicted, such as murder, rape, torture, and involuntary bondage.

   b. sexual acts between adults and children (which are, in a sense, coercive, because children cannot properly be said to give their consent to adults).

   The exceptions are depictions and dramatizations that present these actions from the point of view of the victim or sincerely attempt to dissuade people from committing the actions, and depictions and descriptions that simply report that such actions have occurred.

2. The sale and distribution, as well as the display, of certain sorts of depictions and dramatizations should be prohibited. These are depictions and dramatizations that were created by coercive acts of kind *a* or *b* above, where these acts were committed or arranged by the creators at least in part for the purpose of creating the depictions or dramatizations of them.

   The onus should be on those people selling or distributing depictions or dramatizations of these acts to guarantee either that they were merely simulations of the acts or that the acts depicted were not committed or arranged by the depictors even in part to create the depictions, i.e., that the depictions are simply reports of the actions (such as newspaper photographs of acts of terrorism).

3. If the best evidence indicated that the sale or distribution of some material described in *#1* above causes a significant increase in the incidence of coercive actions of type *a* or *b* above, *and* if it were practically impossible to prevent those actions by other acceptable means, the sale and distribution

of that material should be prohibited. For example, if the sale and distribution of simulations that condoned sex between adults and children were shown to cause significant increases in sexual assaults on children, and if no other adequate and acceptable means of preventing most such assaults were available to a society, then that society should prohibit the sale and distribution of material that stimulates and condones sex between adults and children.

4. The display, sale, and distribution of all other forms of pornography should not be restricted.

DISCUSSION

In reaching these conclusions I am working with the premise that freedom of expression is a *prima facie* right in any good society, that is, that there is a presumption in favor of free expression and that, therefore, any restriction on expression must be justified by good reasons. Specifically, what counts as a justification for restriction on expression is that some form or act of expression tends to harm people other than those expressing themselves, that there is no effective and acceptable way to prevent the harm it does without restricting the expression, and that the harm it does outweighs the harm of restricting the expression.[3]

That there ought to be a presumption in favor of free expression is justified by the good consequences of a society's having such a presumption and the bad consequences of its not having one. John Stuart Mill has defended it on this basis far better than I can do here.[4] What I will do is discuss some of the conditions that I think override the presumption. If we take the right to free expression seriously, the presumption in its favor must be a strong one that cannot be overridden by minor bad consequences of its exercise. For example, annoyance or discomfort or even moral outrage at what is being expressed is not sufficient harm to justify restrictions of expression. In addition, if there are severely harmful consequences of a form of expression, as when people are persuaded by a speech to try to lynch a murder suspect, but we can prevent those harms by acceptable means other than restricting the expression, such as restraining and reasoning with the crowd and protecting the potential victim, then we should not restrict the expression. Not all alternative means of preventing very harmful consequences are acceptable, however. If the availability of some forms of pornography clearly incited so many men to commit rape that adequate protection could not be provided for women so long as men moved about freely, it would be better to restrict the availability of pornography than to have a curfew for all men.

I will now argue that the reasons for preventing involuntary exposure to the material described in conclusion #1 justify restricting its display; they meet all the criteria of a justification for restriction of expression.

THE HARM

The most immediate serious harm that this material (which, for convenience, I shall call coercive pornography) can cause when seen or heard involuntarily is like the harm caused by direct threats of violence or coercion. In those who identify with the victims of the acts portrayed, it can, and frequently does, cause fear and anxiety. In addition, the widespread display of coercive pornography can cause other important harms to the involuntary perceiver that I will discuss later.

The fear and anxiety produced by direct threats depend in part upon the threatened victims' beliefs about how likely it is that the threats will be carried out. Likewise, it seems reasonable to suppose that the fear and anxiety felt by those who identify with the victims portrayed in coercive pornography depends partly upon the social context in which the pornography occurs, especially upon the actual danger of violence and coercion for those who are viewing it and their awareness of that danger. Thus, depictions which condone violence against women will cause more fear and anxiety in women who live in a society like ours, where women know that such violence occurs frequently, than in a society where it rarely occurs; and although it is possible for anyone to identify with the victims depicted, coercive pornography will generally cause the most fear in members of those groups on whom violence and coercion is most often perpetrated when it depicts members of those groups as the victims. Those who will suffer the most fear and anxiety from involuntary exposure to coercive pornography in our society are women, children, and those subgroups of men who suffer from the most unprovoked violence, such as homosexuals; and they will suffer most when members of their own group are depicted as victims.

We recognize the need to protect people from the harm that direct threats cause; we do not regard threats just as indicators of probable harm to come, but as causes of significant harm in themselves. Consider two examples:

Someone you do not know calls you every day at an unpredictable time to tell you he is going to kill you. He demonstrates that he knows your habits, and he says that he will kill you one day when you least expect it. This will be most frightening if you believe that he is likely to kill you. Now suppose that the police know who the caller is, and they and his psychiatrist know that he calls purely for the satisfaction of frightening you and has no intentions of killing you. Do we not agree that they should nevertheless take steps to stop the threats and to inform you that they are false threats? This can only be because we realize that the threats themselves cause you harm. Furthermore, if we agree that it should be a punishable offense to threaten someone in this way, it is because we think that such threats cause a kind of harm from which we are entitled to society's protection.

Now imagine the life of a child whose father repeatedly threatens: "I'll break every bone in your body" or "I'll make you sorry you were ever born." Although the father often appears to be very angry and may even reach for a baseball bat or a knife and brandish it, he never physically hurts the child. Do we not believe that the harm probably done to the child by these threats justifies and even demands that we make an effort to protect her/him from them?

Of course, it is not the purpose of most coercive pornography to threaten anyone in particular; nor is most coercive pornography the expression of a particular person's intention to harm anyone. But the examples of direct threat demonstrate that we do sometimes consider the production of fear and anxiety sufficiently harmful to justify restricting freedom of expression. And in a society where violence and coercion occur often enough to be a source of realistic concern to potential victims, their involuntary exposure to the material described in conclusion #1 has four probable harmful effects that must concern us here:[5]

i. It may make them feel threatened, causing fear and anxiety.

ii. It may give them the impression, and they know it might give potential attackers the impression, that many people condone, or at least tacitly accept, their victimization. This could reasonably be expected to increase their fear and anxiety. This effect is likely to occur even if they know that the acts recommended, condoned, or portrayed in the pornography are crimes and therefore *officially* disapproved of by society.

iii. It may make them afraid that the material will incite potential attackers to commit the acts it recommends, condones, or portrays.

iv. It may damage their self-esteem. It is especially a danger to young people, whose sense of their own worth is often shaky and very subject to external influences, that seeing the abuse of people like themselves condoned or apparently accepted as commonplace by their neighbors may lead them to regard themselves as less worthy of respect than those who seem to do the abusing.

To my knowledge, the effects of involuntary exposure to coercive pornography have not been studied systematically by social scientists. Experimental study is, of course, ruled out by the ethical obstacles to running an experiment in which exposure to the material is truly involuntary, but well-designed surveys might give us valuable information on this issue. We do know from the testimony of women that many potential victims of coercion experience the harmful effects listed above, and I take this testimony seriously.[6]

Could we prevent these harms by acceptable means without restricting the display of coercive pornography? Let us examine the possibilities.

The most obvious possible means of reducing harm *i* is to reduce the occurrence of the acts portrayed in coercive pornography. For most people, their perception of the actual danger is a factor in how threatened they feel. Thus, if the incidence of violence and coercion in a society were very low, people would feel less threatened by its being recommended, condoned, or portrayed than they would in a society where they knew there was a significant danger of becoming a victim of one of these acts.[7] However, the following considerations show that this possible solution has limited effectiveness.

Children's emotional responses to portrayals of violence and coercion are not reliably affected by the real degree of danger. This is partly because they are often ignorant of the facts, partly because they are still developing the ability to distinguish fantasy from reality, and partly because, like adults, they have an immediate emotional response, which is not easily mitigated by realistic beliefs about the danger, to some portrayals of violence and coercion. If the public taste ran to pictures of adults mutilating children, and magazines covered with these pictures were displayed on newsstands and at grocery stores, we would not consider it adequate prevention of their harm to children to make sure that children were rarely mutilated by adults and to teach them that there is little real danger of its happening to them.

Even in adults, the immediate emotional response of feeling threatened is not easily alleviated by knowing that the real danger is slight. Our knowing that threatening phone calls were coming from a maximum security prison would not render them harmless to us; most people would agree that, if possible, they should be stopped. Likewise, knowing that there is no Ku Klux Klan and little racist sentiment in his community would not render involuntary exposure to Klan propaganda harmless to a black man. Even if a man lived alone with his bodyguards on an isolated island, but was reminded every day that some people wanted him dead, he would probably feel threatened.

Perhaps we could make it clear that most people do not condone, or even tacitly accept, the acts portrayed in coercive pornography. This might reduce the fear and anxiety an involuntary viewer would feel by preventing harm *ii*. If, as a matter of fact, very little coercive pornography were displayed, and if most people did disapprove of all the acts it portrays, this solution to harm *ii* might be effective. But if a lot of coercive pornography were displayed, the claim that most people disapprove of the acts it portrayed would be hard to believe in the face of the large market for depictions of the acts. Imagine the effect of assuring a visitor that, although the magazine racks are full of depictions of sadistic sex, most people disapprove of actually doing that sort of thing; our visitor would have to be more naive than most children not to suspect deception, or at least self-deception, in such circumstances. Moreover, if most people clearly did not disapprove of the acts portrayed, public assurances to the contrary would not comfort most potential victims. This solution could not be counted upon as a practice by which to alleviate the harms caused by free display of coercive pornography, since its effectiveness depends on how much coercive pornography is displayed and on most people's attitudes at a given time.

If people are rarely or never incited by exposure to coercive pornography to commit the acts it portrays, and if we could convince potential victims that that is the case, we could prevent harm *iii* by doing so.

The damage that involuntary exposure to coercive pornography may do to people's self-esteem can be mitigated by giving them messages that they are as worthy of respect as anyone; but such messages might only be confusing, and not reassuring, if coercive pornography were plentiful and widespread. Members of oppressed groups have written eloquently about the effects of conflicting social attitudes on their self-esteem.[8] There seems to be no way to counteract fully the damage done to children by numerous portrayals of people with whom they identify as victims.

In summary, the harmful effects of involuntarily viewing coercive pornography can at best be mitigated by acceptable practices other than restricting its display. If we could greatly reduce the incidence of the acts it portrays, this would probably reduce the fear and anxiety it produces in adult involuntary viewers, but we could not expect it to eliminate those reactions altogether in adults, and we could not expect it even to reduce the fear and anxiety of children. Countermeasures to harms *ii* and *iv*, such as publicizing most people's disapproval of the acts portrayed in coercive pornography, could only be effective if the pornography were not plentiful and widespread and if most people did in fact disapprove of the acts it portrays. Only the fear that coercive pornography will incite others to commit the acts portrayed could reliably be calmed in rational people, provided that we can prove that it does not in fact incite the crimes. We must now compare the remaining harm to the harm that would be done by restricting the display of the material in question.

A number of harms would follow from restricting the display of coercive pornography in such a way that no one would be exposed to it involuntarily. Individuals and political groups, such as the neo-Nazis, who include genocide or other forms of unjustified physical coercion in their ideologies would be unable to express their full views anywhere that people might be exposed to them involuntarily. Revolutionaries who advocate the overthrow of the government by physical coercion present a more difficult case than groups like the neo-Nazis, because there is more controversy about whether the coercion they advocate would be justified. If we use the test I discuss below, of justifiability under the laws of our society (see page 177), then publicly advocating revolution by physical coercion would not be allowed anywhere that people might be exposed to it involuntarily. This consequence of restricting the display of coercive material raises the concern that such restrictions open the way to dangerous political censorship, especially since the parties and individuals who advocate revolution by physical coercion are among those whose opinions governments most want to suppress.[9] But it is only advocating or condoning illegal physical coercion to involuntary audiences that would be prevented; advocating revolution (which does not imply the strategy of physical coercion) to any audience or advocating revolution by physical coercion to voluntary audiences would be permitted. Under the restrictions I propose, any individual or group could advocate illegal physical coercion at meetings or in printed material made available in such a way that exposure to it was only by consent, so long as the public was adequately warned about the content of the meetings or printed material. However, on posters or in street-corner speeches, "Trudeau is a hypocritical lackey of the bloodsucking capitalist imperialists" would be allowed, but "Death to Trudeau" would not. Whether someone is advocating illegal physical coercion can, I think, be determined at least as easily as whether she/he is inciting a riot or threatening another individual; it would not lead to political suppression unless we became careless about protecting our civil liberties.

Those who could increase their sales of coercive pornography by advertising it graphically, and those who could perhaps increase their sales of other things by association with it through advertising, would lose money because of the restrictions I propose.

Finally, in calculating the harms of restriction, we must also consider the social costs of detection and enforcement, including the likelihood of error and unfairness in the application of restrictions. All law enforcement involves some risk of error and unfairness. In addition, if we restrict the display of coercive pornography, judgments will have to be made about whether material fits one of the categories of exceptions described in conclusion *#1*. These judgments, which I will discuss further below, will sometimes be difficult, but not more difficult than many judgments we currently accept about such matters as whether false advertising has occurred. It must also be remembered that here we are only considering restricting the display of coercive pornography so that people are not exposed to it involuntarily; we are not considering making it unavailable to those who want to have access to it. Therefore, errors or unfairness in the enforcement of restrictions would not prevent willing audiences from obtaining any material or seeing or hearing anything they wish to in this category.

The harms of restricting the display of coercive pornography are not insignificant. They include some curtailment of the freedom to express one's views in public, some financial loss to those who would profit by advertising with coercive pornography, and the usual social costs of enforcing any such restrictions. However, if we recall the harms that would result from free display of coercive pornography, I think we must agree that they outweigh the harms of restricting display. If coercive pornography were displayed as freely as magazines are today, or if it were shown without warning on television or advertised on billboards, many citizens, including all children, would be forced to live in a much more frightening and anxiety-inducing atmosphere than they live in now.[10] Parents and children might be confronted at any movie house or grocery store with material condoning the rape of children. Anyone who could rent a billboard could advocate beating up immigrants who take scarce jobs or sterilizing welfare mothers without their permission. In addition to the fear and anxiety that such displays would cause, they are likely to damage the self-esteem of many young people. Preventing such harms is clearly worth incurring the harms of restriction.

THE EXCEPTIONS

Depictions and dramatizations that present the actions in question from the point of view of the victim or sincerely attempt to dissuade people from committing the actions do not cause all the same kinds of harm, and not usually the same degree of harm, as material that recommends, condones, or portrays the acts in other ways. They do not cause harms *ii* and *iv*, unless they are misunderstood, because they do not give potential victims the impression that society condones their victimization; on the contrary, they can inform potential victims that society stands for their protection from coercion. And although they can cause much fear and anxiety (harm *i*) in involuntary viewers, they may be effective means of preventing coercive actions.

Depictions and dramatizations that present these actions from the point of view of the victim virtually force us to identify with the victim by portraying vividly the victim's experiences in the situation. This usually makes them frightening; Hitchcock's *Psycho* is a good example. Such depictions and dramatizations may be the most effective means we have of influencing some potential offenders not to act. Being made vividly aware of the sorts of experience harmful actions are likely to cause often influences us to change our attitudes towards harming others, especially when we have not thought seriously about the consequences for the victims of those actions. Recent experimental results suggest that both sexual arousal to rape depictions and subsequent aggression toward female targets are inhibited in male viewers by the victim's showing a clear negative reaction in the rape depiction. (See Donnerstein and Berkowitz, 1981, and Malamuth and Check, 1981, in this volume.)

Potential offenders are not likely to seek out either the victim's point of view or attempts to dissuade them from acting. If this sort of material is to have any chance of affecting potential offenders, it will have to be possible to present it to the general public, for example on television and radio or in the newspapers. Some of the recent television programs about wife and child battering are good examples of this sort of thing. We do not know how effective these efforts to affect potential offenders will be, but the possibility that they might prevent substantial numbers of coercive acts is an important factor in weighing the harm they might cause against the harm of restricting their display. Furthermore, although presentations from the point of view of the victim and sincere attempts to dissuade people from committing coercive actions sometimes cause fear and anxiety in involuntary viewers, they are very good means of assuring potential victims that at least someone wants to prevent their victimization. These considerations lead me to believe that the good this sort of material might do and the harm it might prevent make the harm of restricting its display greater than the harm caused by involuntary exposure to it. I conclude that, unless we find that this sort of material has no significant potential to prevent coercion, its display should not be restricted.

It will not always be easy to distinguish material that sincerely attempts to dissuade people from committing coercive acts from material that really exploits portrayals of the acts. My intention in saying "sincerely attempts to dissuade" is to rule out material that clearly portrays the acts as desirable while tagging on a formal disclaimer such as, "The publishers disapprove of the acts portrayed herein." The latter sort of material does not do any good or prevent any harm to outweigh the harm it causes the involuntary viewer. The responsibility for distinguishing exploitative material from that which sincerely attempts to dissuade would have to be entrusted to a panel of reasonable citizens (a censorship board or a jury). Juries are frequently trusted to make similar difficult determinations, for example, in cases where fraud or false advertising is alleged.

The case of depictions and descriptions that are simply reports that the acts have occurred is different from that of the other two exceptions. The good they do is primarily that they provide information, and the circulation of information is itself one of the justifications of the presumption in favor of freedom of expression, for its long-range benefits are great. The freedom to report the occurrence of events is a freedom we must be particularly careful to protect. The ultimate harm of restricting reports is liable to be greater than almost any harm they can do. Therefore, free display of simple reports of the acts in question should be allowed, but it must be clear to citizens that the reports do not also recommend or condone the acts reported. Purveyors of coercive pornography will probably try to take advantage of the freedom we want news sources to have, but here too I think we could expect a panel of reasonable citizens to determine whether material is recommending or condoning the acts it also reports. In addition, the restriction described in conclusion #2 would prevent people displaying pornography that was created by the commission of the acts in question, where the acts were committed or arranged by the creators at least partly for the purpose of creating the pornography.

WHY "UNJUSTIFIED PHYSICAL COERCION" AND SEXUAL ACTS BETWEEN ADULTS AND CHILDREN?

Although material that recommends, condones, or portrays justified physical coercion, such as acts of self-defence, the arrest of murderers, and karate matches, may cause fear or anxiety in some people, material that recommends, condones, or portrays coercion of the apparently innocent victim is the important source of the harms I described above. In addition, I do not think there should be restrictions on publicly recommending, condoning, or portraying any act that is not immoral, and justified physical coercion is, by definition, not immoral. We might say that if the acts recommended, condoned, or (with the specified exceptions) portrayed by some material would be considered justified by the laws of a good society, then display or distribution of that material should not be restricted. In practice, we would probably have to use the test of whether the coercion recommended, condoned, or (with the specified exceptions) portrayed would be considered justified under the laws of our society, even when our laws fall short of what we would expect of a good society, as they do with regard to rape.[11] If we do use this latter test of justifiability, then we should also commit ourselves to creating the best possible set of laws about physical coercion.

Sex between adults and children is a kind of coercion, because children usually have a great deal less power over their lives and less understanding of the range of their choices and the consequences of their actions than adults have. We do not recognize contracts between adults and children for these reasons, and we should not recognize adults' (or children's) assertions that children have consented to sexual relations with them for the same reasons, even though it is certainly possible for a child genuinely to want to have sexual relations with an adult. We do, of course, condone other sorts of coercion of children by adults, which we believe to be justified because their aim is the children's own good. The claim that sexual relations between adults and children may take place for the good of the children is at least highly dubious, and the risk of harm to the children is too great to allow for exceptions.

The categories of material the display of which I think should be restricted include some things that we would not call pornography, for example, pamphlets advocating sterilization of welfare recipients without their permission and movies that condone bashing a man over the head with a chair because you didn't like what he said about your girlfriend. Since I think that what is most harmful about pornography is not its concern with sex, this result is not surprising. Nor is it surprising that much of what we would call pornography is not included in the categories that I think should not be freely displayed, for example, depictions of sex between consenting adults and depictions of people masturbating.

WHY NOT RESTRICT MORE?

There are all sorts of material that might upset or frighten significant numbers of people. Some people are frightened and/or disgusted by seeing pictures of sex between consenting adults, and this is a genuine sort of harm. Might not this harm justify restricting the display of such material? Consider what would be involved in protecting people from any serious psychological pain that might be caused by public displays. Some people are harmed, i.e., suffer anxiety, feelings of guilt, deep sadness, or depression, by seeing displays of affection between parents and children, perhaps because their own childhoods were very troubled or because their children were killed in an accident. Many people become deeply depressed at Christmas time, partly because of all the displays about family happiness and people giving expensive gifts that many cannot afford, and the suicide rate goes up in consequence. We could only prevent all such harms at the expense of virtually all freedom of expression.

Yet I do not think that the answer to this problem is to disallow psychological harms as justifications of restriction. I suggest instead that we should not consider restricting displays unless they recommend, condone, or (with the specified exceptions) portray actions that harm people other than those acting and from which people have a right to be protected by society and some obligation to contribute to the protection of others. This limitation is sufficiently narrow to allow for a very wide range of free expression. It prevents us from becoming involved in futile attempts to protect citizens from all socially caused psychological pain at the expense of all public displays. On the other hand, it meets our intuition that part of the point of protecting people from becoming victims of harms caused by the immoral actions of others is to prevent their having to live in fear of those harms. By restricting the display of material that recommends, condones, or portrays those actions that we feel society has an obligation to prevent, we can reduce one of the harms they cause, i.e., the fear and insecurity that potential victims feel.

Now there are more actions that harm others and that we expect society to protect us from than are included in my categories of coercive actions (p. 168). Theft is one, and the fear of theft can be a serious harm. I know retired people who will not leave their homes at night because of it. They would be upset, and their fear would be increased, by seeing, let us say, magazines for thieves advertising "Ten Great New Ways to Steal from Your Neighbors" displayed at the corner store (where they are now subjected to coercive pornography). It might be appropriate to restrict material that recommends or condones theft. I doubt that all displays recommending or condoning actions in the same category (call them "crimes with victims") should be restricted, however. Defrauding old people out of their life's savings is an action in the category, and reminders of it may cause some anxiety, but the fact that people can virtually prevent becoming victims of it by taking precautions that do not severely restrict their own freedom makes it much less fearful to contemplate than certain kinds of violence or even theft. The harm caused by display of material that recommends, condones, or (with specified exceptions) portrays these sorts of actions would have to be weighed against the harm of restriction in each case. There are not so many types of crimes with victims that this would be a burdensome problem. Since I am concerned here with pornography, and since the sorts of crimes with victims displayed in pornography are almost exclusively crimes of physical coercion, I will leave the problem here.

WHY BAN SOME THINGS REGARDLESS OF THEIR EFFECTS?
REASONS FOR CONCUSION #2

We should prohibit the display, sale, and distribution of material that was created by physically coercive acts, where the acts were committed or arranged by the creators at least in part for the purpose of creating the depictions or dramatizations of them. It undermines the purpose of prohibiting these acts (which are crimes in any decent society) to allow people to profit by committing them.

It will be relatively easy to distinguish material of this kind from simulations and reports of the acts if we put the onus on those displaying, selling, or distributing the material to prove that it was simulated or reported. Pornographers and reporters will take care to have believable witnesses to the acts or simulations and their roles with regard to them.

Of course we must recognize that any kind of pornography, including simulations of coercive acts, may be created by coercion that is not depicted. Threats and physical coercion (including drugging) are sometimes used to force models and actors to participate in making pornography.[12] In addition, economic conditions may be so desperate as to leave people little choice but to sell their services to pornographers. In these respects, however, making pornography is not different from anything else one may be forced to do. Laws should and do prohibit threats and physical coercion, and we must enforce them to the best of our ability; pornographers who have been proved to use these methods should be prohibited from selling the products. However, since posing for pornography is not clearly worse than many other legal things people do for money, the existence of economic coercion in making pornography is not an adequate reason for banning the pornography, although, like other kinds of economic coercion, it is a very good reason for eliminating poverty.

WHY NOT BAN MORE?

Why prohibit only the *display* of simulations and reports that recommend, condone, or (with the specified exceptions) portray coercive acts? Why not prohibit their sale and distribution too? The harm which this material causes people who are exposed to it involuntarily (see p. 171) justifies restricting its display. However, when people expose themselves to it voluntarily, i.e., when they know what they are going to see, hear, or read, and choose it, there is an obviously effective and acceptable way of preventing any harm they might suffer by their exposure, without banning the material. The potential consumers can stay away from it and avoid any harm. In the presence of such an excellent way of preventing the harms, the presumption in favor of freedom of expression means that we should not prohibit the sale and distribution of the material to prevent harm to the consumer. We should, however, make sure that every reasonable effort is made to inform potential customers of the nature of the material, so that their exposure to it is as voluntary as we can make it. In addition, all reasonable precautions should be taken to guarantee that children are not exposed to it at all, since most children's ability to consent or refuse is not as well developed or reliable as that of most adults. For the same reasons that we do not allow children to buy liquor, we should not allow them to consume coercive pornography.

What about harm—such as discomfort, anxiety, or disgust—that people may suffer by knowing that coercive pornography is available and that others are consuming it, even though they themselves need never be exposed to it? It seems to me that such harms are no worse than they might suffer from knowing that some people imagine the prohibited actions and even want to commit them. The harms are not sufficient to outweigh the harms of restriction, and it is reasonable to expect people to deal with them as they do with other kinds of unpleasant facts.

There are some conditions, besides those described in conclusion #2, under which sale and distribution of coercive pornography should be prohibited. Even if it were produced legitimately, if it clearly caused an increase in actions of the kind it recommends, condones, or portrays, and if it were practically impossible to prevent most of those actions by other acceptable means, we would be justified in prohibiting its sale and distribution. The harm it would cause under those conditions would outweigh the harm of restricting it, even though such a restriction would be a serious violation of freedom of expression. However, if we took such a measure, we would have an obligation to continue to seek acceptable alternative methods of preventing the actions in question and to lift the restrictions as soon as such methods were found. Moreover, we would not be justified in prohibiting the sale and distribution of any more than that subset of coercive pornography that clearly caused an increase in coercive crimes.

The evidence with regard to coercive pornography's possible indirect harms, i.e., its causal relationship to crimes of coercion, is inconclusive at this time.[13] There are three basic hypotheses about the indirect effects of coercive pornography. Some say that it incites people to commit coercive crimes. Some say that it creates an atmosphere of acceptability around coercive acts that leads to more coercive crimes than would otherwise be committed, because people who have some desire to commit them do not refrain as they would if they felt that it would be unacceptable to act. Others say that coercive pornography has a cathartic effect on some people who have desires to commit coercive acts. All three hypotheses are plausible.

On the one hand, widespread exposure to people treating certain other groups in cruel or humiliating ways does often influence us to do the same, especially if we have not been exposed to the point of view of the victim. Consider how ordinarily gentle men have learned to behave toward civilians of an enemy country during wartime. And anyone who has lived through a community's changing from open racism to a more tolerant attitude toward minority races knows that messages about what sorts of behavior are acceptable to the community are an important factor in motivating change. On the other hand, we all know that fantasies and fiction sometimes serve as excellent substitutes for the real thing, and that they often alert us to desires that we have hidden from ourselves, thereby creating the possibility of controlling them or expressing them in harmless ways. I am inclined to think that if display of coercive pornography were restricted, if we took much stronger action than we do now to prevent coercive crimes, and if we made it clear to everyone that coercive crimes of all sorts were considered abominable and stopped winking at some of them, we would make the best use of all three hypotheses until the evidence is in. The availability of coercive pornography would allow the cathartic function, if there is one, and the other measures would prevent any "tacit permission" effect and reduce the possibility of incitement.

SOME REMARKS ON OTHER SORTS OF PORNOGRAPHY

As I mentioned before, there is material we would call pornography that is not included in any of the categories I have been discussing. Much of it depicts women as passive objects for men's sexual desire, and the message it conveys to me is that both women and sex exist for men's pleasure. It seems probable that the prevalence of this sort of pornography has bad effects on women's self-images, on women's and men's repertoires of sexual enjoyment, and on our abilities to interact with responsibility and mutual care. Some of its effects are being studied now;[13] but even if social scientists prove that non-coercive pornography is harmful to us in these ways (and possibly others), we should not restrict it. To do so would open the door to unlimited efforts to eliminate by law the influences in society that tend toward results we do not want. If we restricted pornography because of its bad effects on our sexuality and relationships, think what we would have to do to television, to non-pornographic magazines and books, and to some sorts of religious teaching, if we were to be consistent.

If we value freedom of expression at all, we must not allow expression to be restricted unless the harm it does outweighs the harm of restriction and cannot be prevented by other acceptable means (see p. 169). In the case of non-coercive pornography, the harm that restriction would cause includes infringing on the freedom of people who want to have access to pornography, infringing on the freedom of those who want to sell or distribute pornography, creating a repressive enforcement apparatus that would inevitably infringe upon other freedoms and catch harmless expressions of sexuality in its net, and setting a precedent for restriction of all forms of expression which could be shown to cause similar harms. In addition, we have other acceptable means of preventing, or at least mitigating, the harm caused by non-coercive pornography. We can present people with more images, stories, and descriptions of people enjoying sex together as equals, more material that depicts the full range of non-coercive sexual pleasures for women as well as men and presents the possibility of combining intense pleasure with mutual respect and caring.[14] In other words, if non-coercive pornography is harming us, then we need better erotic material to compete with it.

NOTES

I thank David Copp, Don Brown, Lorenne Clark, and Bob Hadley for their very helpful comments on an earlier version of this paper.

1. Other feminists have been responsible for changing the focus of the debate over pornography to concern with its portrayal of violence and coercion. See, for example, Susan

Brownmiller, *Against Our Will* (New York: Simon and Schuster, 1975); Lorenne Clark, "Liberalism and Pornography," in this volume; and Helen Longino, "Pornography, Oppression, and Freedom: A Closer Look," in Laura Lederer, ed., *Take Back the Night, Women on Pornography* (New York: William Morrow and Co., 1980).

2. An excellent account of what is morally wrong with rape, which also applies to other forms of physical coercion, can be found in Carolyn M. Shafer and Marilyn Frye, "Rape and Respect," in Vetterling-Braggin, Elliston, and English, eds., *Feminism and Philosophy* (Totowa, N.J.: Littlefield, Adams, & Co., 1977), pp. 333–346.

3. See Robert Amdur's argument that rational autonomous citizens would almost certainly choose for the state to interfere with acts of expression that result in serious harms, in Amdur, "Scanlon on Freedom of Expression," *Philosophy and Public Affairs* 9, no. 3 (Spring 1980), pp. 287–300.

4. John Stuart Mill, *On Liberty* (New York: Bobbs-Merrill Co., 1956) (originally published in 1859).

5. I am not including such negative effects as annoyance, discomfort, or moral outrage, since I do not believe that these are ever severe enough to outweigh the presumption in favor of free expression.

6. See Lederer, *Take Back the Night.*

7. Concealing the actual incidence of physical coercion is not a realistic possibility, and in any case it would be wrong, since knowing about the danger enables people to take precautions against it.

8. See, for example, Maya Angelou, *I Know Why the Caged Bird Sings* and *Singin' and Swingin' and Gettin' Merry Like Christmas* (New York: Bantam, 1970 and 1974, respectively); Angela Davis, *With My Mind on Freedom* (New York: Bantam, 1974); Sheila Rowbotham, *Woman's Consciousness, Man's World* (Penguin, 1973); and, of course, Simone de Beauvoir, *The Second Sex* (New York: Bantam, 1961) (originally published in 1949).

9. I do not think that a distinction between personal coercion and political coercion will help us here, since I do not think that such a distinction can be made both clear and workable. Consider these examples: Does material that recommends wife beating as a way of keeping women in line recommend personal or political coercion? What about posters that say that all Arabs should be run out of the country because they are secretly buying it?

10. It might be argued that we would get used to coercive pornography, and its capacity to produce fear and anxiety would gradually diminish. There are three considerations I would like to raise about this: First, even if we can get used to it, children will not be born into the world emotionally immune to coercive pornography. Each child would be confronted by its full impact until she/he got used to it. Second, we know from experience with the development of pornography and even with advertising and television programming that when the public is no longer shocked by material designed to get and keep our attention, new shocks are presented to us; getting used to it all is likely to take a long time. Third, we must ask ourselves if we really want to be emotionally immune to all sorts of coercive pornography; would not such immunity be a harm at least as great as the fear and anxiety it would spare us?

11. See Lorenne Clark and Debra Lewis, *Rape: The Price of Coercive Sexuality* (Toronto: Canadian Women's Educational Press, 1977).

12. For example, see "Then and Now: An Interview with a Former Pornography Model," in Lederer, *Take Back the Night.*

13. See the Social Scientific Studies section of this volume.

14. For a discussion of the morality of pornography and the possibility of nonsexist pornography, see Ann Garry, "Pornography and Respect for Women," in this volume.

Committee on Obscenity and Film Censorship

Offensiveness, Pornography, and Art

INTRODUCTION

The following chapters are extracted from the report, published in 1979, of a British Government Committee on Obscenity and Film Censorship, of which I was chairman. The committee was appointed in 1977 "to review the laws concerning obscenity, indecency and violence in publication, displays and entertainments in England and Wales, except in the field of broadcasting, and to review the arrangements for film censorship. . . ." The omission of broadcasting (which attracted some criticism) was due basically to the fact that the Annan Committee on Broadcasting had reported not long before, and had dealt with these subjects in that area.

The committee was felt to be necessary because of the uncertainty and confusion of the English law on obscenity and related matters. There are several different laws that can be invoked, and they are not always consistent. In addition, the central statute, the Obscene Publications Act 1959 as later amended, defines the basic offense in terms of material which has an effect "such as to tend to deprave and corrupt persons who are likely . . . to read, see or hear. . . . it," and the interpretation of the deprave and corrupt formula (which in itself goes back to the nineteenth century) has given continuous trouble to the courts. In particular, this is because it imports the notion of a causal influence on character, but in fact it has often been understood, and with the sanction of higher courts, as referring rather to standards of public decency.

A further feature of the Obscene Publications Act, which was welcomed in liberal circles when it was passed, is that it provides a defense against conviction if the publication of an item is deemed to be "for the public good" on account of its literary, artistic, or scientific merit. The first and greatest achievement of this clause was the acquittal of D. H. Lawrence's *Lady Chatterley's Lover* soon after the act was passed. After this, the "public good defence" has had a rather chequered history. In one of the chapters that follow, our report argues that the provision, while in terms of the present law it has some liberal effect, is nevertheless misconceived in principle, and—very importantly—any law on these subjects will have to take account of that fact.

The main recommendations of our report can be summarized—very roughly and without legal precision—under three heads. First, the only material to be totally banned would be child pornography and material involving actual violence. The rationale of these prohibitions is to protect persons involved in the manufacture of such material. Apart from that, a class of offensive visual material should be restricted: this involves a number of provisions, in particular that it should not be sold to people under eighteen, and only on premises which permit no external display. The definition proposed for such material is that it should be ". . . such that its unrestricted availability is offensive to reasonable people by reason of the manner in which it portrays, deals with or relates to violence, cruelty or horror, or sexual, or faecal or urinary functions, or genital organs." An account of the main idea behind this recommendation is given in one of the chapters below.

Our third main recommendation was that material consisting entirely of the written word should be neither prohibited nor restricted. The rationale for this was that such material cannot involve the harms which invite prohibition, and very much less displays the kind of offensiveness that invites restriction; while, at the same time, this is the area (leaving aside the cinema for which separate proposals were made) which most involves questions of artistic merit and freedom of expression. It was not suggested—though some of our critics thought that it was—that the written word had less effect than photographs: our point was merely that it had less the effect of being immediately offensive, which was the feature that we suggested the law should address.

The proposals of our report have not been accepted nor acted upon, nor, on the other hand, have they been explicitly rejected. This is not altogether surprising. It is more often than not the fate met by reports of government committees and royal commissions in Britain—even in areas less sensitive than this.

A measure has been passed, the Indecent Displays (Control) Act, which aims to deal with the blatant offensive displays to which we referred. But this uses the existing concepts of the English law, and the rest of the apparatus that we criticized remains, at the time of writing, in place.

While our main aim in preparing our report was, of course, to report to the British government on what seemed to us the right way to change the English law, we were at the same time conscious that the chances of its actually being changed might be in any case not very great, and would certainly not depend simply on any merits that our recommendations might possess. So we consciously tried not only to produce a practical political document, but to make some contribution to the literature of the subject. The chapters that follow come from the section of our text entitled "Principles," and while they do relate in some obvious ways to English law, they are among parts of the report that raise issues which are wider and, I hope, of more general interest.

Bernard Williams

CHAPTER SEVEN

OFFENSIVENESS

7.1 The *deprave and corrupt* test of obscenity, the history of which we have already referred to, defines a concept of obscenity which is of course exactly suited to fit in with the harm condition: it is a causal notion of obscenity, based on the idea that the rationale of suppressing obscenity is the harm that it causes. But, as we noted, the actual use of the test in the past seems often to have had little to do with proving that there had been any harms at all. It has almost been as if people, accepting the harm condition, agreed that pornography should be suppressed only if it did harm; were quite clear that it should be suppressed; and concluded that somehow it must do harm.

7.2 One idea that may confuse the issue here is the assumption, which we touched on in discussing law and morality, that if something does no identifiable harm, then any objection to it must be (merely) a matter of taste. As we have said, some of those who have written to us do regard reactions to pornography as a matter of taste. Others go a little further, in saying that it

---

Chapters seven and eight of the *Report of the Committee on Obscenity and Film Censorship*, published by H. M. Stationery Office, London, 1979; reprinted (without appendices) by Cambridge University Press, 1981, as *Obscenity and Film Censorship: An Abridgement of the Williams Report*. This material is produced with the permission of The Controller of Her Britannic Majesty's Stationery Office.

is a matter of taste not just in the sense that some people have a taste for it and others do not, but that a taste for it is bad taste. This would make it, at any rate, a matter of aesthetic judgment.

7.3 Certainly most pornography is also trash; ugly, shallow, and obvious. (We will consider in Chapter 8 why this is so, and whether it is necessarily so —whether, that is to say, there could be a pornographic, or again obscene, work of art, a question which has constantly recurred to plague the Obscene Publications Act.) But this fact is not enough to explain its offensiveness; we are surrounded by shallow trash of all kinds but few people, however sensitive their taste, find it as upsetting and disagreeable as many people certainly find pornography. For many people, pornography is not only offensive, but deeply offensive.

7.4 Pornography essentially involves making public in words, pictures or theatrical performance, the fulfilment of fantasy images of sex or violence. In some cases the images are of forbidden acts: so it is with images of violence. In other cases, the line that is transgressed is only that between private and public; the acts represented in the images would be all right in private, but the same acts would be objectionable in public. There will of course be disagreement about how many acts are of this second sort rather than the first. Even the most puritanical will agree that there are some, if only straightforward sexual relations between husband and wife. Others may take more liberal views about what is legitimate sexual activity, but retain the view that the proper place for it is in private. People have strong sentiments attached to these notions of public and private, of what it is "unsuitable"—in its original sense, *indecent*—to show.

7.5 Obviously, as with the display of parts of the body, these perceptions vary over time. Some predict, indeed hope, that the time may come when such restrictions will have finally disappeared. One witness whom we saw made it clear that she looked forward to a society in which nothing one saw going on in the park would be more surprising than anything else, except perhaps in the sense of being more improbable. Most of us doubt whether this day will come, or that nothing would have been lost if it did. Still less do we look forward to a world in which sexual activity is not only freely conducted in public and can be viewed, but is offered to be viewed, copulating parties soliciting the interest of the passer-by. But this is, in effect, what publicly displayed pornography does.

7.6 Pornography crosses the line between private and public since it makes available in the form, for instance, of a photograph, some sexual act of a private kind and makes it available for a voyeuristic interest: since it is itself a public thing, a picture book or a film show, it represents already the projection into public of the private world—private, that is to say, to its participants—of sexual activity. The represented activity is in the first instance something offered to be seen, and can have the shock effect of something suddenly revealed. The consumer of the pornography does not of course necessarily, or perhaps typically, remain conscious of himself as an external viewer of what is represented. The material rather is incorporated into his fantasy; it is characteristic, for instance, that photographs, which must inevitably be records of sexual activity with the usual human limitations, will be incorporated in fantasies of the mythical, inexhaustible, limitless sexual activity which is the typical product of the pornographic imagination. The exact relation of pornographic material to the consumer and to his fantasies is a subtle matter. Even when it is taken up into fantasy, pornography often retains an assaulting quality—there is a sense in which it can be found offensive even while it is being enjoyed. In other cases, the sense of offensiveness evaporates for the consumer who involves himself in the images offered by photographs or films, or develops his own fantasy from the written word.

7.7 The basic point that pornography involves by its nature some violation of lines between public and private is compounded when the pornography not only exists for private consumption, but is publicly displayed. The original violation is then forced on the attention of those who have not even volunteered to be voyeurs. They are thus forced or importuned to see things which they do not think should be seen, and images are thrust into their mind which they reject. Whatever may be true of the willing consumer, pornography is straightforwardly offensive to those who do not want to take it in. There are some differences here between the visual and the written. Visual material displays its content to anyone within line of sight; when, moreover, it is photographic, real people and actual events are on display. Written material is further removed from any particular reality, and an activity is in any case needed in order to take in the content. These points help to explain the fact, to which everyone agrees, that written material, casually encountered, is less offensive than visual, and in particular photographic, material. It is probably a result of this that, as we have already explained, almost any printed book now seems likely to secure acquittal; it is worth recalling, too, that magazines with rather less explicit pictures, such as the DPP classifies as "Grade 2" and which are widely accepted at present, are sometimes prepared to carry written material which is straightforwardly hard-core pornography.

7.8 For those who are not disposed, as willing consumers are, to make the scenes of pornography into objects of their own fantasy, those scenes have a special and saddening ugliness. In people who are particularly resistant to such fantasy, either in general, or as involving objects such as these, anger,

disturbance, and oppression will be the reactions. It is tempting to speculate
—it cannot be more than speculation—that it is such reactions which are
understood by some who experience them as a perception that pornography
is intrinsically harmful and destructive. This perception, taken as a social
judgment, we believe may well be incorrect. But this does not mean that the
reactions themselves, or the less violent reactions of others who find the
display of such material in various degrees offensive, are incorrect. It seems
to us that they can be entirely appropriate, and that the world would not
necessarily be a better place if people ceased to have them.

7.9 When the material is violent, these reactions are typically intensified.
Here the scenes are such as no person who is not disturbed could want to
happen in reality. The scenes are offered in pornography as objects of sadomasochistic fantasy (we should repeat that there is no reason to believe that
this usually expresses itself in sadistic behavior in reality). For those
resistant to that sort of fantasy in general, or on this occasion, or who reject
fantasy on material as crude and explicit as this, these scenes will be totally
revolting. Similar reactions may be felt to fictional or pictorial violence
which, while it is not pornographic, in the sense of involving or invoking
sexual arousal, nevertheless is offered directly as an object of aggressive
fantasy. It is no doubt because aggressive impulses have to be contained and
denied expression in actual life to an even greater extent than is the case with
sexual impulses, that the reactions to sadistic and other violent material are
typically stronger and more alarming than to sexual material—except in so
far as an aggressive presentation of the sexual material, very characteristic
of pictorial pornography, is itself expressive of sadism. "I don't mind the
sex, it's the violence,"[1] as many people said to us.

7.10 In this discussion, we have inevitably been drawn a short distance into
the psychology of the experience of pornography, a subject in which we
would not feel confident in claiming that there existed any very definite
knowledge, let alone that we possessed it. But even if this account is not
quite right, something like it must be true. Such an account will explain how
it is that the reactions that many people experience to publicly displayed
pornography are not just a matter of arbitrary taste, but are deep reactions;
and how is it that the offensiveness it displays to them is, in both a
psychological and an ethical sense, a deep offensiveness.

7.11 The fact that one is being forced or importuned to see some unwanted
scene can be signalled without the scene itself being shown to one. If the
content is one in which such scenes are threatened (or, to the willing, prom-
ised) then associated material can take on an appropriate appearance, and
produce a milder version of the same reactions. This helps to explain the
fact which has always caused difficulty for legislation on these subjects,

that it is not an intrinsic degree of undress, for instance, nor even particular postures of the body (with some obvious unambiguous exceptions) which are found objectionable. It is notable for instance that a picture of a girl in underwear is perceived differently if it is on the cover of a woman's fashion magazine from the way it is seen if it is on the cover of a "man's magazine." This has an important consequence for any recommendation about the control of such material: it is not solely what is to be seen on the outside of a publication that governs the reaction appropriate to it. One and the same photograph in different contexts can mean something quite different, and become, in experience, effectively two different things. This means that a control simply on *indecent displays*, which has been proposed on various occasions, does not meet the case. Such proposals are based on a superficial view of what the offensive element is in publicly offered pornography.

7.12 Public sexual activity, except of the milder kinds, is prohibited, and this provides a clear and well-known example of legislation which is directed against the performance in public of acts which (with regard to many of them, at least) are legitimate in private. (Indeed, if the publicity is intentional, the acts are not, strictly speaking, the same as sexual acts done in private —they have a different motive.) Laws against public sex would generally be thought to be consistent with the harm condition, in the sense that if members of the public are upset, distressed, disgusted, outraged, or put out by witnessing some class of acts, then that constitutes a respect in which the public performance of those acts harms their interests and gives them a reason to object.

7.13 If there is an element of soliciting, that is all the more a nuisance to which citizens can reasonably object. It was in this spirit that the Wolfenden Committee recommended curbs on the public activities of prostitutes, recommendations which became law in the Street Offences Act 1959. In their report they wrote ". . . we feel that the right of the normal, decent citizen to go about the streets without affront to his or her sense of decency should be the prime consideration and should take precedence over the interests of the prostitute and her customers . . . ,"[2] and they made the point that these restrictions should properly apply both to loitering and to soliciting. The offensiveness of publicly displayed pornography seems to us to fall clearly within the sorts of considerations advanced by the Wolfenden Committee, and to be in line with traditionally accepted rules protecting the interest in public decency. Restrictions on the open sale of these publications, and analogous arrangements for films, thus seem to us to be justified.

7.14 Naturally, any system of restriction must involve some phenomena which themselves could, indirectly, offend someone. Thus pornography might be legitimately sold (as we shall propose) in shops which announced their nature but did not allow their contents to be seen from the outside. The presence of such shops is something which itself could be found offensive by someone; we have indeed received complaints about shops of some such kind (though we cannot be sure how reticent the particular examples may have been). If there were no such shops, but only mail-order distributors, then the advertisements for these, even if they displayed no material, would certainly be found offensive. If one goes all the way down this line, however, one arrives at the situation in which people objected to even knowing that pornography was being read in private; and if one accepted as a basis for coercing one person's actions, the fact that others would be upset even by the thought of his performing those actions, one would be denying any substantive individual liberty at all.[3] Any offence caused by such shops would clearly be much less vivid, direct, and serious than that caused by the display of the publications, and we do not accept that it could outweigh the rights of those who do wish to see this material, or more generally the arguments in favor of restricting, without suppressing, pornography.

7.15 We have suggested that proposals for restricting pornography would be clearly in line with existing provisions to deal with other kinds of offensiveness. We have also tried to explain why the offensiveness of pornography is found a serious matter, and reactions to it represent more than a mere divergence of taste. However, it seemed to us also that we should carry the argument further than this, and examine with rather greater precision what principle might justify legislation of this kind. For, as several witnesses said to us, to restrict publications "because they upset people" could be a dangerous precedent. There can be various public manifestations, publications, or other forms of utterance which may upset people, even deeply upset people, without those people thereby having a right to have those public manifestations suppressed. We think therefore that we should try to set out some considerations which would distinguish the kind of matter for which we propose restrictions from other cases in which restriction would be unjustifiable.

7.16 We suggest that there are two important characteristics of the case of restrictions on pornographic materials and of restrictions on them which help to distinguish that case from others where restriction would not be justifiable. An extended treatment of the subject of free expression would no doubt give an account of how far these considerations go, how they relate to one another, how they apply to difficult cases, and so on, but we do not think it either necessary or appropriate to pursue those further questions here.

(1) *The restriction is not directed against the advocacy of any opinion.*

7.17 Clearly some publications could have the effect of outraging or deeply upsetting many people because of the opinions or view of the world they advocated, which those who were outraged found deeply offensive to their own beliefs and outlook. However, many people would think that it would be contrary to basic principles of free expression even to resist, let alone suppress, publications *on this ground alone* (as opposed, for instance, to controlling them on the ground that they incited to riot). So it is important to the rationale for restricting pornographic publications that it is not for advocating any opinion that the restriction is proposed, and that the upset that they cause to the public is not a reaction to opinions which are found unacceptable. For the most part, this will be because the publications do not advocate any opinions at all. But some may do so; thus some pornographic magazines contain letterpress which advocates a "swinging" life-style, while there could also be a piece of pornography which as a whole was designed to advocate some opinion. But, in the first case, it would not be on the grounds of that part of the content that the magazine would be a candidate for restriction, and in the second example, it would not be because it had that character, but rather because the form of its advocacy was offensive, apart from what was being advocated.

7.18 Because we attach some weight to this principle, we do not entirely accept the emphasis given in their evidence by the Catholic Social Welfare Commission, among other witnesses, who particularly associated the harms of pornography with its encouraging a view of sex as trivial amusement or gratification. Whether or not that view is as distorted and damaging as the witnesses believe, the view that sex should not be taken seriously is at least an opinion, and if the bad character of pornography lay principally in its advocating such an opinion, then there would be, in our view, a difficulty of principle about one's right to restrict it.

(2) *Restricting the publication to a volunteer audience does not defeat its aims.*

7.19 If someone burns an IRA symbol or a photograph of the Ayatollah Khomeini, or sings an offensive political song, it *could* be that his purpose will be carried out if he is demonstrating or singing only to the converted. But it is much more likely that some part of his intention will be to make his point to people who would not originally have volunteered to see or hear him make it. This consideration obviously overlaps with the point about advocating opinions, but it goes further, since it applies also to activities which are not themselves the advocacy of opinions.

7.20 With pornographic publications, the restriction to a volunteer audience constitutes in general no hardship or defeat of the publications' intentions. The pornographer is offering a product, to be consumed by those who want to consume it. We say that there is no defeat of his *publicaton's* intentions. The pornographer himself may have some aims which would be impeded by restriction—thus it may be that he will make less money if his pornography is restricted and if his purpose in publishing it is to make money, that purpose will be impeded by restriction. But that is not the kind of purpose or intention that is in question.

7.21 There are exceptions among pornographic publications to this general point. There are some of a proselytising tendency, no doubt, and there are also pornographic works of a serious artistic intention, the writers of which might not necessarily be equally content with an audience who would volunteer under conditions of restriction. Moreover, the present point, that if the audience is restricted to volunteers this does not defeat the aim of the publication, is anyway not so directly related to a general principle about the restriction of publications as is the point that restriction is not directed against any opinions which are being advanced. It is plausible to claim that no publication should ever be restricted solely on the grounds of the opinions it advocates, but it is quite implausible that publications should be restricted only if those who produce them would be content with a volunteer audience. But it is nevertheless a relevant consideration that the nature of most pornography is such that there can be no complaint if its audience is confined to volunteers.

7.22 We have already remarked that works which consist only of written text are in fact found less offensive than pictorial matter, and that there are basic psychological reasons for this fact. If, as we have suggested, it makes a difference whether a proposed restriction is directed against opinions or not, this introduces a further point about the written word as contrasted with pictorial matter. Besides actual speech, it is the written word that is the principal medium for the advocacy of opinions, and which is accordingly likely to give rise to the most serious borderline cases in this connection. The written word, moreover, is the medium which, together with the film (for which we shall propose separate methods of control), has chiefly given rise to the traditional problem of serious artistic intent in supposedly obscene material. While written works can no doubt be found to some extent offensive, we believe that these various considerations provide a very strong case for withholding the possibility of restriction (let alone of suppression) from the written word, and we shall propose that, with respect to the area of the law we have been appointed to review, no publication shall be liable to either suppression or restriction in virtue of matter that it contains which consists solely of the written word.

7.23 We shall explain the details of our proposals for restriction in Chapter 9. The operative term that we have chosen for the characteristic which merits restriction is "offensive." "Indecent" seems to us too narrow in some respects (there is grossly offensive material, suitable for restriction, which would not naturally be called "indecent"), too wide in others (some material conventionally called "indecent" is not really offensive), and it suffers above all from having too long and disputed a legal history. The Defence of Literature and the Arts Society, whose carefully argued and constructive evidence we found helpful, offered us the term "outrage" in this connection, but we rejected this on the grounds that it seemed stronger than was appropriate. We also suspect that it may carry a misleading implication. "Outrage" is something chiefly felt towards actions, of an unjust or appalling character, but when it is applied to publications it seems usually to be on grounds of the opinions they express, which, as we have just explained, is something that we seek to exclude. "Offensiveness" is the term that seems to represent most clearly what is in question. To make clear, however, what kinds of offensiveness are at issue, we have thought it right to specify the kinds of respect in which material has to be offensive if it is to be restricted. Since, further, some people will be offended by almost anything, and others by nothing at all, it is also necessary to specify whose reactions in finding something offensive are to count, and we have decided in favor of the requirement that matter to be restricted should be "offensive to reasonable people." This seems to us to catch as well as any phrase can the central idea that at any given time there can be material which sensible people of mature tastes will quite properly demand, for the kinds of reasons we have discussed, not to have forced on their attention. We shall return in more detail to the terms of our formula in paragraph 9.29 and following.

CHAPTER EIGHT

PORNOGRAPHY, OBSCENITY, AND ART

8.1 In the course of Chapter 7, we have referred almost all our discussion to *pornography*, rather than to *obscenity*. This emphasis was deliberate. "Obscene," we shall suggest in this chapter, is a term which itself expresses the kinds of reactions we were discussing in Chapter 7, rather than telling one what kind of thing actually arouses those reactions. "Pornography," on the other hand, we take to be a rather more objective expression referring to a certain kind of writing, picture, etc. We have suggested that pornography does tend by its nature to be found offensive; and most of the publications and pictures which people find offensive are indeed pornographic. But we shall need to consider a little more precisely what pornography and obscenity are, in order to discuss an important question, the relations of pornography and obscenity to art. There is more than one reason why we thought that we should discuss this question. It has repeatedly surfaced in the history of this subject; it has constantly recurred, not surprisingly, in our own discussions; and it has been raised in various forms by many witnesses, some of whom were as certain that there could not possibly be an obscene work of art as others were that there could. The issues here are, moreover, deeply involved in both the theory and the practical use of the "public good defence" under section 4 of the Obscene Publications Act 1959. The discussion in this chapter directly bears on our recommendations and has, we believe important consequences for legislation on these subjects. We have not been convinced that it is impossible for any pornographic or obscene work to have artistic merit, and we shall try to explain why we have not. At the same time, we are convinced, for reasons that we shall give, that a public good defence with respect to artistic merit is inevitably unworkable. Any proposals for legislation must, we believe, accommodate both these conclusions.

Pornography

8.2 The term "pornography" always refers to a book, verse, painting, photograph, film, or some such thing—what in general may be called a *representation*. Even if it is associated with sex or cruelty, an object which is not a representation—exotic underwear, for example—cannot sensibly be said to be pornographic (though it could possibly be said to be obscene). We take it that, as almost everyone understands the term, a pornographic representation is one that combines two features: it has a certain function or intention, to arouse its audience sexually, and also a certain content, explicit representations of sexual material (organs, postures, activity, etc.). A work has to have both this function and this content to be a piece of pornography.

8.3 It is useful to distinguish works that extend over time (novels, films) from those that do not (paintings, photographs: series of pictures are obviously an intermediate case). The former offer the possibility that they may have some sections that are pornographic and others that are not, leaving room for borderline questions about whether the work as a whole is pornographic. Some such questions are unanswerable. However, it has proved to be the case up to now that there has been a demand for works which maximize pornographic content, so there is, in both the novel and the film, a definite *genre* of the pornographic work, which consists almost exclusively of pornographic representations of sexual activity, often complex. There is virtually no plot, no characters, no motivation except relating to sexual activity, and only a shadowy background, which may involve a standard apparatus of a remote and luxurious *chateau,* numerous silent servants, and so forth. This is the "ideal type" of a pornographic work evoked by Steven Marcus.[4]

"Obscene" and "Erotic"

8.4 We suspect that the word "obscene" may now be worn out, and past any useful employment at all. It is certainly too exhausted to do any more work in the courts. However, leaving aside the peculiar legal *deprave and corrupt* definition we have considered in earlier chapters, it seems to us that, insofar as it is not just used as a term of abuse, it principally expresses an intense or extreme version of what we have called "offensiveness." It may be that it particularly emphasizes the most strongly aversive element in that notion, the idea of an object's being repulsive or disgusting; that certainly seems to be the point when a person or animal is said to be, for instance, "obscenely" ugly or fat.

8.5 The term "erotic" sometimes seems to be used just as an alternative to "pornographic," being milder with regard to both the content and the intention: the content is by this interpretation more allusive and less explicit, and what is intended is not strong sexual arousal but some lighter degree of sexual interest. There is another interpretation[5] of the term, however, perhaps more accurate and certainly more interesting, under which the erotic is what expresses sexual excitement, rather than causes it—in the same way as a painting or a piece of music may express sadness without necessarily making its audience sad. Theorists have not found the notion of expression at all easy to explain, but a work which expresses a given feeling can at least be said to "fit" the feeling or to "match" it, and, in virtue of doing that, to put one in mind of the feeling. In this sense an erotic work will suggest or bring to mind feelings of sexual attraction or excitement. It may cause some such feelings as well, and put the audience actually into that state, but if so that is a further effect. This difference comes out rather clearly in the case of romantic love. Many erotic works— and of course many works that are not erotic—express the feelings of romantic love, and invoke images of them in their audience, but the state they bring about in their audience is very rarely that of being in love. On this kind of account of the erotic, it will follow that what is represented in an erotic work of art need not be a mild version of the pornographic at all. There are countless erotic works of art, many of which have no explicit sexual content of any kind.

8.6 As we understand these various notions, pornography, obscenity, and eroticism will be related in the following ways. Pornography will have some tendency to be obscene, but will not necessarily be so. We claimed in Chapter 7 that a tendency to be offensive is built into it, but it is not universally even offensive—it may have some other merit which cancels that effect. Still less must it inevitably be very strongly offensive or obscene. On the other hand, there will be obscene things which are not pornographic (e.g. it would be obscene to exhibit deformed people at a funfair, but that would not be a pornographic exhibition), some pornography is erotic, but it is not altogether easy for it to be so: the explicit content and the intention of arousal tend to work against the expressive effect of eroticism rather than with it. Many things, certainly, will be erotic without being pornographic. The most unlikely combination, on the present account, is that of the erotic and the obscene. Since the erotic is intended to attract and hold the attention by being, in the sexual dimension, pleasant or delightful, it is hard to see how this could be combined with the object being found at the same time disgusting and repulsive. The idea is so difficult, that this combination might be said to be impossible, except that human reactions in these areas are so complex that we hesitate to say that anything is impossible.

8.7 Some people may find it paradoxical to say that it is hard, if not impossible, for something to be both erotic and obscene. Several of our witnesses have certainly found it natural to say of many publications or films that they were both. We do not deny that these words, and the word "pornography," are often used with meanings which are more general and overlapping than those that we have just proposed. We claim only that there are significant and useful distinctions to be made here, and these words can helpfully be used, in the ways we suggest, to mark those distinctions. One body which submitted evidence to us, the Board for Social Responsibility of the Church of England, made some careful suggestions for distinguishing between these terms, and we found these helpful, even though the account we have given of the matter is not exactly the same as theirs.

Art.

8.8 We have already assumed that there can be an *erotic* work of art, and we take it that few would disagree with this. The questions now are: Can there be a work of art which is pornographic? Can there be one which is obscene? As we have already explained, these are for us two different questions. We take first the question about pornography.

8.9 As we said in an earlier chapter, it is incontestable that almost all the pornography sold across (or under) the counter, or seen in the cinema, is from any artistic point of view totally worthless. However, there is more than one possible explanation of that fact. The interesting question, which we shall be concerned with, is whether it just follows from the nature of pornography that it is bound to be worthless. If it does not just follow, then other and more circumstantial explanations may be considered (though we shall not consider them here): as that it is simply not worth anyone's while, at least in the modern world, to make pornography more artistically interesting than it is.

8.10 Several arguments have been put to us, or have been implicit in evidence we have received, to the effect that pornography cannot possibly have any artistic value. The most general argument to this effect is probably that which has been expressed by Steven Marcus in saying "literature possesses a multitude of intentions, but pornography possesses only one."[6] A related consideration is that the "one intention" of pornography—sexual arousal—is achieved through a blankly explicit, unmediated, content. Marcus' point is made with respect to literature, but if it is valid it can be applied just as well to the visual arts. It will be claimed that pornography is by its nature purely instrumental, a crude device for achieving a particular effect, and has nothing to do with the complex concerns and intentions which properly belong to a work of art.

8.11 However, it is not clear why it should be impossible to combine other aims with the "one intention" of pornography. In the case of the visual arts, there do exist some works which are indisputably pornographic in content and intention, but which are thought to succeed in realising other, artistic, concerns. There are many pornographic Japanese prints of the 18th century, works of the admired master Utamaro and others, which are regarded by critics as brilliant achievements. It can be reasonably claimed, moreover, that they are not merely of artistic interest despite being pornographic, but that their sexual intention is integrally bound up with their merits as expressive designs. Many great Western artists have of course produced pornographic works "on the side," to make money or for diversion, and some of these works no doubt have merit; the peculiarity of the Japanese case is that there was a tradition of very considerable artists applying their talents to this *genre*. Of course—to repeat ourselves—there is no suggestion that the existence of these erotic works somehow sheds artistic respectability on the vast range of current pornographic material. What they do prove, however, if their merits are agreed, is that it is not the simple fact that it is pornographic that makes all the material artistically worthless.

8.12 In the case of works which are extended in time, such as the novel and the film, more specific arguments are advanced to suggest that if they are pornographic, they must be no good. Their participants are not characters, but mere locations of sexual possibilities; there is no plot, no development, no beginning, middle, or end (a point made by the critic Adorno). Moreover, since there are no characters or genuine human presence, the whole effect is dehumanizing—destructive of any sense of personal individuality or life. These descriptions are obviously correct. It is perhaps worth adding that we do not entirely agree with those who in evidence to us or elsewhere have expressed this sort of idea by saying that the effect of pornography is to reduce everything to the *physical*. Among the various kinds of human presence which are lacking from literary pornography is, usually, any real sense of the human body. Because pornography ministers to fantasies of boundless sexual satisfaction, everything is weightless, untiring, effortlessly restored. The attempt to accommodate the same fantasies with photographs of actual people with actual bodies is partly what make so many pornographic photographs and films grotesque.

8.13 These descriptions apply more strongly, of course, the closer the fiction in question gets to the schema of the unrelievedly pornographic work. But obviously they would not apply unqualifiedly to a work which had only some pornographic sections along with other matter, even if those sections were integral to the work. Moreover, even works which are totally pornographic can occasionally break away from the "ideal type," and one or two writers have experimented with introducing psychological elements into the *genre*. Claims have been made by serious critics for the artistic merits of certain pornographic literary works (we have heard of none, as yet, with respect to thoroughly pornographic films). The arguments from the character of pornography do seem to suggest that concentratedly pornographic novels are going to be interesting pieces of literature only in rare cases, and then on a minor scale; but it does not seem to be impossible, even in the extreme case, and it would certainly be rash to claim on general grounds that any use of pornographic elements even in the context of other material must make a work worthless.

8.14 The arguments of the last four paragraphs have been concerned with questions of the intention and the structure of pornographic works. What has not yet been mentioned in this connection is their tendency to be offensive or obscene—in our present sense, that is to say, intensely or repellently offensive. This tendency raises a question about artistic value: can a work have any artistic interest and in that way command the attention of a reader or spectator, if it is at the same time found offensive? The question gets more pressing, the more insistent the offensiveness of the work. There may indeed be some pornographic works of artistic merit which do not even raise the question; these will be works in which the sexual content should not reasonably be regarded as offensive at all, and the merits of the work themselves contribute to cancelling the aspects of intrusion or violation that make other pornographic works offensive. The Japanese works already mentioned, and some Indian erotic sculptures, might be examples. Artistic merit can itself, in a case of this kind, contribute to the judgment whether a work is even offensive. There is another kind of work which may be experienced as offensive, and also be experienced as having aesthetic interest, but in the case of which these two experiences do not occur at the same time. These will be works which are found offensive at first, or by a spectator who remains distanced from them, but which lose that character for someone who is involved in them. The question of how one can combine at the same time aesthetic interest in the work and a sense that it is offensive will not then arise, though these works will still be "offensive works," in the sense of works which could prove offensive to a casual viewer or to someone who came across them and was unwilling or unable to involve himself in them.

8.15 Thus there can be pornographic works of merit which are not reasonably regarded as offensive; and there can be initially offensive works which can, once the offensiveness is past, display their merits. But it would be unwise to deny that, beyond all this, there could be works which were, and remained, offensive, indeed intensely offensive or obscene, and yet possessed real merits. Experience of those merits, in such a case, would surely have to involve the fact of their obscenity, and not just co-exist with it; the repulsiveness would have to be an integral part of what was being displayed by the artist. Where the work is itself pornographic, the repulsiveness will not just be forgotten in sexual arousal, but will be part of it. Some critics have claimed that certain pieces of French literary pornography, notably by Georges Bataille, are significant works of this extreme kind.

8.16 An extraordinary work which illustrates, in a unique way, some of the complexities involved here is Pasolini's last film *Salò*. This film came repeatedly into our discussions, both because of its nature, and also because it was, during our enquiries, the subject of legal action. Having been refused a certificate by the British Board of Film Censors, it was shown in a London club but was quickly seized by the police, and those who had shown it indicted. While they were awaiting trial, the Criminal Law Act 1977 came into force, which changed the law applying to the cinema from the test of indecency to the *deprave and corrupt* test. Because of this, the Director of Public Prosecutions withdrew the proceedings, but took the unusual step of announcing that anyone who subsequently showed the film would be prosecuted. It has however recently been shown, though in a cut version. It has appeared in most other European countries.

8.17 The film displays scenes of extraordinary cruelty and repulsiveness, supposedly happening under the short-lived Fascist republic set up at Salò in 1944. It has the ritual form of a pornographic work—indeed, it is specifically modelled on Sade's *120 Days of Sodom*. All of us agreed that it is obscene, in the sense that it is ruthlessly and almost unwatchably repellent. On its other qualities, and its merits, we found ourselves in great disagreement. Most of us felt that it was manifestly not designed to produce sexual excitement, and that it took great care not to do so, even incidentally; on this view of it, the work, though obscene, is not pornographic, despite its form. Some of us, however, were more suspicious of its intentions. Those who were most impressed by it thought that it presented an extraordinary metaphor of political power and was a remarkable work, perhaps a masterpiece. For anyone with that opinion of it, it is a work that combines artistic control and seriousness with a deep and sustained obscenity.

8.18 Our conclusion is that there is no intrinsic reason why pornography or even obscene works should not be capable of having artistic merit, though there are undoubtedly reasons in the nature of such works, and even more in the general conditions of their production, to make that an unlikely and marginal occurrence, and the works, even when successful, generally of minor stature.

The Public Good Defence

8.19 The conclusion that a work can be pornographic or even obscene and still be of artistic merit is one that of course agrees verbally with the assumptions of the Obscene Publications Acts which, as we have explained in Chapter 2, allow for the possibility that a work might be obscene and yet it be for the public good that it be published on account of its literary or artistic merit. But the agreement is only verbal, since the Obscene Publications Acts of course adopt the definition of obscenity in terms of the tendency to deprave and corrupt, rather than a notion of extreme offensiveness. Moreover, the merits of the work which would allow it to be acquitted of an offence, even though obscene, are themselves implicitly expressed in causal terms, to match the causal nature of the *deprave and corrupt* test. The work's tendency, as obscene, to produce bad effects has to be weighed against its tendency, as having artistic merit, to produce good effects, and the jury is expected to weigh one of these causal properties against the other. But if there is a difficulty, on the side of "obscenity," in ascribing harmful effects to a specific book (we shall take for the present discussion just the case of books), there is at least as much difficulty in ascribing good effects with respect to literary merit, and the task of showing why it was "for the public good" that some particular book, with its particular literary merits, should be published, is one that might understandably have baffled the expert witnesses who were called under this section.

8.20 We emphatically reject a view which a few witnesses put to us, that books have no good or bad effects at all. Quite certainly books have all sorts of effects, and in particular it is a reasonable assumption of much education that good books—for instance, masterpieces of imaginative literature—tend to have a certain kind of good effect, such as deepening a reader's understanding of human life: though one should not suppose that they are the only effects those books can have, nor that their merit is just to be calculated in terms of such effects. It has been said to us as an argument for the suppression of pornography: "If good books have good effects, then bad books must have bad effects." First, it must be said, this does not even follow: if good books have good effects it may be that all that bad books do is fail to have good effects. This is not a purely formal or verbal point. In the sense in which great works can draw the reader to new possibilities and extend his grasp, bad works may merely do nothing—they are inert, acquiescent, leave the reader as he was. Apart from this point, however, and indeed granting that bad books can have bad effects, the relevant contrast with good books does not of course lie in "bad books" in the sense of pornographic or obscene books—it lies rather in books which are "bad" because they fail to be works of creative literature, for instance because they are unoriginal and shallow and possibly, one may add, complacent or evasive as well, projecting some delusive image of life. There is room for much disagreement about the kinds of harms that might be ascribed to different kinds of bad literature, but if harm is done by bad fiction, there is certainly no reason to think that it is peculiarly done by obscene fiction, rather than by books that are bad because they are deceitfully sentimental, or even (some purist critics would suggest) just because they are badly written.

8.21 Critics, writers, and other expert witnesses called by the defence under section 4 have been required to speak of the merits of the work in question in terms of these causal concepts, supposedly relating some good effect specifically to the work, of such a kind as to outweigh any tendency to deprave or corrupt which the work might also possess.[7] The supposed causal character of these considerations, and the supposed weighing of them, constitute the first intractable feature of the public good defence. Moreover—and this point would apply to any such provision, even in less directly causal terms—the exercise has to be conducted in a court of law, the witnesses faced by cross-examination—circumstances which cannot make for the most sensible discussions of literary merit. It is not surprising that many absurd things have been said in the course of such proceedings, as by several expert witnesses for *Lady Chatterley's Lover*, or by the distinguished authority who was trapped into trying to think of otherwise unknown facts about 18th century London which one might learn from *Fanny Hill*. We have considerable sympathy for those who have gallantly gone to bat for works of art under these rules, but we can only regard the rules as absurd, as many of them must also have done.

8.22 Besides the causal nature of the concepts of section 4, and besides the drastic limitations of any court procedure, there is quite another reason of principle against any such exercise. The procedure involves weighing merit, but the merit will be possessed only by works which are, to some appropriate degree, *successful* works of art. The defence therefore has to take the form of claiming that the work in question is a good work; but this cannot be an appropriate requirement. If the law on obscenity is to protect artistic activity, it has to protect experimentation and the rights of new writers in particular, to try something out. It follows that it must protect the right to try and fail, and the experiment which issues in a bad book. The public good defence in terms of actual merit cannot do this, and it is entirely to be expected that its most famous victory was in defence of a work by a writer, D. H. Lawrence, who was absolutely outstanding, long dead, and already highly respectable. By contrast, the defence, using section 4, of *Last Exit to Brooklyn*, an indifferent book by an unknown writer, failed before a jury, though an appeal later was successful; in that case, the expert witnesses tended to exaggerate the book's merits, and they could scarcely have done anything else, granted the underlying idea of section 4.

8.23 Not only the requirement of merit, but the mere idea of the evidence being given by experts, tends in this same direction. It is as though informed persons, literary and artistic experts, are supposed to appear from the world of culture and inform the jury of how things stand there with the work under trial. Granted this, and the other features of the Act, it is not surprising that it has been criticized as elitist in conception, and as saying in effect that corrupting books are to be permitted so long as they are admired by professors. This criticism is largely unjust, but it hits at a basic fault in the Act, its absurd model of the role of expert opinion with regard to artistic or literary merit. The model is not so much elitist, as scholastic: it implies an informed consensus about merit which, for each work, already exists. In the real world, new works have to find their own way, and see whether they elicit any appreciation or not. No one may know, for some time, what to think about them. It is not just a matter of the *avante-garde:* works in some despised medium or style may subsequently turn out to have had more meaning than most experts would have originally supposed. (The recent history of critical taste with respect to Hollywood movies of the thirties and forties, compared to "art" films of that period, is an object lesson in this.) The critical reputation of a work can continue to vary. Expert consensus, if it comes at all, and if it stays the same, must come after the event, and to assume that expert opinion is available at the event, that is to say at the time of publication, is merely to make the deathly assumption that all forms of artistic significance have already been recognized.

8.24 For all these reasons, we conclude that the idea of a public good defence, relating to artistic or literary merit, is basically misconceived, not merely in the form presented by section 4 of the Obscene Publications Act, but quite generally. We have argued earlier in this chapter that it is not to be excluded in advance that pornographic or even obscene works can, to some degree, possess serious artistic interest. If our argument is correct, the law will have to accommodate that possibility, but without resting on the illusory hope of calling in experts to tell it when the possibility has come about.

NOTES

1. A phrase which has also been used by Mrs. Enid Wistrich as the title of her book about her experiences as Chairman of the Film Viewing Board of the GLC [Greater London Council].

2. Cmnd. 247, paragraph 249.

3. This point is very clearly shown by Hart: *Law, Liberty and Morality*, pp. 45 following.

4. "Pornotopia": *Encounter* 1966. The concept of an "ideal type" is applied to Marcus's account by Morse Peckham: *Art and Pornography* (New York 1969).

5. Suggested in a paper by Antonia Phillips, commissioned by us, to which the present chapter is indebted.

6. "Pornotopia": *Encounter* 1966. A similar point is made by Norman St. John-Stevas, *Obscenity and the Law* (London 1957), page 137.

7. For details of the history of the interpretation of section 4 of the Obscene Publications Act 1959, see paragraph 2.19 and following.

Bonnelle Strickling,
with David Copp and Susan Wendell

Selected Bibliography of Academic and Popular Philosophy

Allen. "What Those Women Want in Pornography." *The Humanist* (November/December 1978).

Amdur, R. "Scanlon on Freedom of Expression." *Philosophy and Public Affairs* 9 (Spring 1980).

Baier, Kurt. "Response: The Liberal Approach to Pornography." *University of Pittsburgh Law Review* 40 (1979).

Baker, Robert and Elliston, Frederick, eds. *Philosophy and Sex.* Buffalo, N.Y.: Prometheus Books, 1975.

Barnett, W. "Eroticism: The Disease of Our Age." *Film and Filming* (January 1961).

Barron, Jerome. *Freedom of the Press for Whom?* Bloomington, Ind.: University of Indiana Press, 1973.

Beauvoir, Simone de. "Must We Burn Sade?" In *The Marquis de Sade.* London: New English Library, 1972.

Berger, Fred. *Freedom of Expression.* Belmont, Ca.: Wadsworth Publishing Co., 1980.

Berlin, Isaiah. "Two Concepts of Liberty." In *Four Essays on Liberty.* London: Oxford University Press, 1969.

Berns, Walter. "Pornography vs. Democracy: The Case for Censorship." *The Public Interest* 22 (Winter 1971).

Buchanan, A. "Autonomy and Categories of Expression: A Reply to Professor Scanlon." *University of Pittsburgh Law Review* 40 (1979).

Care, Norman S., and Trelogan, Thomas K., eds. *Issues in Law and Morality.* Cleveland: Case Western Reserve University, 1973.

Carter, Angela. *The Sadian Woman and the Ideology of Pornography*. New York: Pantheon Books, 1979.

Clark, Lorenne M. G. "Privacy, Property, Freedom and the Family." In *Philosophical Law: Authority, Equality, Adjudication, Privacy*, edited by R. Bronaugh. Westport, Conn.: Greenwood Press, 1978.

————. *Towards a Feminist Political Theory*. Toronto: University of Toronto Press, forthcoming.

————, and Lewis, Debra J. *Rape: The Price of Coercive Sexuality*. Toronto: Canadian Women's Educational Press, 1977.

Cline, V. B., ed. *Where Do You Draw the Line? An Exploration into Media Violence, Pornography and Censorship*. Provo, Utah: Brigham Young Press, 1974.

Clor. "Obscenity and Freedom of Expression." In *Where Do You Draw the Line? An Exploration into Media Violence, Pornography and Censorship*, edited by V. B. Cline. Provo, Utah: Brigham Young Press, 1974.

Cragg, Wesley, ed. *Contemporary Moral Issues*. Toronto: McGraw-Hill Ryerson, 1983.

Davies and Dhavan, eds. *Censorship and Obscenity*. London: Macmillan, 1979.

Devlin, Patrick. *The Enforcement of Morals*. Oxford: Oxford University Press, 1965.

Dworkin, Gerald. "Paternalism." In *Morality and the Law*, edited by Richard Wasserstrom. Belmont, Ca.: Wadsworth Publishing Co., 1971.

Dworkin, Ronald. "Lord Devlin and the Enforcement of Morals." *Yale Law Journal* 75 (1966).

————. Review of *On Liberty and Liberalism: The Case of John Stuart Mill*, by Gertrude Himmelfarb. *New York Review of Books* 21, 31 October 1974.

Dybikowski, J. C. "Law, Liberty and Obscenity." *University of British Columbia Law Review* 7 (1972).

Epstein. "The Problem of Pornography." *Dissent* (Spring 1978).

Ernst, Morris L., and Schwartz, Alan U. *Censorship: The Search for the Obscene*. New York: The Macmillan Co., 1964.

Feinberg, Joel. " 'Harmless Immoralities' and Offensive Nuisances." In *Issues in Law and Morality*, edited by Norman S. Care and Thomas K. Trelogan. Cleveland: Case Western Reserve University, 1973.

————. "Limits to the Free Expression of Opinion." In *Philosophy of Law*, edited by Joel Feinberg and Hyman Gross. Encino and Belmont, Ca.: Dickinson Publishing Co., 1975.

————. "Obscenity, Pornography and the Arts: Sorting Things Out." In *Contemporary Value Conflicts*, edited by Burton M. Leiser. New York: Macmillan Publishing Co., 1981.

————. *Social Philosophy*. Englewood Cliffs, N.J.: Prentice-Hall, 1973.

————. "The Idea of the Obscene." The Lindley Lecture, University of Kansas, 5 April 1979. Lawrence, Kans.: Department of Philosophy, University of Kansas.

Fitch. "The Impact of Violence and Pornography on the Arts and Morality." In *Where Do You Draw the Line? An Exploration into Media Violence, Pornography and Censorship*, edited by V. B. Cline. Provo, Utah: Brigham Young Press, 1974.

Frye, Marilyn. "Rape and Respect." In *Feminism and Philosophy*, edited by

Vetterling-Braggin, Elliston, and English. Totowa, N.J.: Littlefield, Adams and Co., 1977.

Gastil, Raymond D. "The Moral Right of the Majority to Restrict Obscenity and Pornography through Law." *Ethics* 3 (1976).

Gerety, T. "Pornography and Violence." *University of Pittsburgh Law Review* 40 (1979).

Goodman, Paul. "Pornography, Art and Censorship." In *Perspectives on Pornography*, edited by D. A. Hughes. New York: St. Martin's Press, 1970.

Hart, Harold H., ed. *Censorship, For and Against.* New York: Hart Publishing Co., 1971.

Hart, H. L. A. *Law, Liberty and Morality.* Oxford: Oxford University Press, 1963.

Hausknecht. "The Problem of Pornography. *Dissent* (Spring 1978).

Himmelfarb, Gertrude. *On Liberty and Liberalism: The Case of John Stuart Mill.* New York: Alfred A. Knopf, 1974.

Holbrook, David. *The Case Against Pornography.* La Salle, Ill.: Library Press, 1974.

Hook, Sidney. *Paradoxes of Freedom.* Berkeley: University of California Press, 1962.

Hughes, Douglas A., ed. *Perspectives on Pornography.* New York: St. Martin's Press, 1970.

Hyman, Stanley Edgar. "In Defense of Pornography." In *Perspectives on Pornography*, edited by Douglas A. Hughes. New York: St. Martin's Press, 1970.

Keating, Charles H., Jr. *United States Commission on Obscenity and Pornography. Dissenting Report.* Washington, D.C.: U.S. Government Printing Office, 1970.

Kirkendall, Lester. "My Stance on Pornography." *The Humanist* (November/December 1978).

Kristol, Irving. "Pornography, Obscenity and the Case for Censorship." *New York Times Magazine*, 28 March 1971.

———. "The Case for Liberal Censorship." In *Where Do You Draw the Line? An Exploration into Media Violence, Pornography and Censorship*, edited by V. B. Cline. Provo, Utah: Brigham Young Press, 1974.

Kuh, Richard. *Foolish Figleaves?* New York: Macmillan, 1967.

Lawrence, D. H. "Pornography and Obscenity." In Lawrence's *Phoenix.* New York: Viking, 1973.

Lederer, Laura, ed. *Take Back the Night: Women on Pornography.* New York: William Morrow, 1980.

Longino, H. "Pornography, Oppression, and Freedom." In *Take Back the Night: Women on Pornography*, edited by Laura Lederer. New York: William Morrow, 1980.

Meiklejohn, A. *Political Freedom: The Constitutional Powers of the People.* New York: Oxford University Press, 1965.

Melden, A. I. *Human Rights.* Belmont, Ca.: Wadsworth Publishing Co., 1970.

Mill, John Stuart. *On Liberty.* Indianapolis: Bobbs-Merrill, 1956.

Miller, J. "Censorship and the Limits of Permission." *Proceedings of the British Academy* (1972).

Millett, Kate. *Sexual Politics.* New York: Avon Books, 1969.

Mishan, E. J. "Making the World Safe for Pornography." In *Making the World Safe for Pornography and Other Intellectual Fashions.* London: Alcove Press, 1973.

Murphy, C. F. "Response: Freedom of Expression—a Critique." *University of Pittsburgh Law Review* 40 (1979).

Peckham, Morse. *Art and Pornography.* New York: Basic Books, 1969.

Rembar. "Obscenity—Forget It." *Atlantic Monthly* (May 1977).

Richards, D. A. J. *The Moral Criticism of Law.* Encino and Belmont, Ca.: Dickinson Publishing Co., 1977.

Rist, Ray C. *The Pornography Controversy.* New Brunswick, N.J.: Transaction Press, 1975.

Rowbotham, Sheila. *Woman's Consciousness, Man's World.* Harmondsworth, Middlesex, England: Penguin, 1973.

Scanlon, T. "A Theory of Freedom of Expression." *Philosophy and Public Affairs* 1 (1972).

———. "Rights, Goals and Fairness." In *Public and Private Morality*, edited by Stuart Hampshire. Cambridge: Cambridge University Press, 1978.

Schauer, Frederick. "Pornography and the First Amendment." *University of Pittsburgh Law Review* 40 (1979).

Shear, Marie. "Free Meat Talks Back." *Journal of Communication* 26 (Winter 1976).

Smith, Marjorie M. " 'Violent Pornography' and the Women's Movement." *The Civil Liberties Review* (January/February 1978).

Sontag, Susan. "The Pornographic Imagination." In *Perspectives on Pornography*, edited by Douglas A. Hughes. New York: St. Martin's Press, 1970; also in Sontag's *Styles of Radical Will.* New York: Farrar, Straus & Giroux, 1966.

Spitz. "The Problem of Pornography." *Dissent* (Spring 1978).

Steiner, George. "Night Words: High Pornography and Human Privacy." In *Perspectives on Pornography*, edited by Douglas A. Hughes. New York: St. Martin's Press, 1970.

Tussman, Joseph. *Government and the Mind.* New York: Oxford University Press, 1977.

van den Haag, Ernest. "Democracy and Pornography." In *Where Do You Draw the Line? An Exploration into Media Violence, Pornography and Censorship*, edited by V. B. Cline. Provo, Utah: Brigham Young Press, 1974.

———. "Is Pornography a Cause of Crime?" *Encounter* 29 (1967).

———. Untitled essay. In *Censorship, For and Against*, edited by Harold H. Hart. New York: Hart Publishing Co., 1971.

Vanderveer. "Coercive Restraint of Offensive Actions." *Philosophy and Public Affairs* 8 (1979).

Wachtel, Eleanor. "Our Newest Battleground: Pornography." *Branching Out* 6 (1979).

Wasserstrom, Richard, ed. *Morality and the Law.* Belmont, Ca.: Wadsworth Publishing Co., 1971.

———, ed. *Philosophy and Women.* Belmont, Ca.: Wadsworth Publishing Co., 1979.

———, ed. *Today's Moral Problems.* New York: Macmillan, 1979.

Wollheim, Richard. "A Charismatic View of Pornography." *London Review of Books*, 7 February 1980.

Part Two:
Social Scientific Studies

Diana E. H. Russell

Research on How Women Experience the Impact of Pornography

Research on how women experience the impact of pornography has so far been of little interest to male researchers. I would therefore like to present some preliminary results from my own research.*

Nine hundred thirty-three women 18 years and older, who were living in San Francisco during the summer of 1978, were interviewed to ascertain the prevalence of sexual assault in that city. These women were drawn from a random-household sample obtained by a San Francisco public-opinion polling firm—Field Research Associates. The women in the study were asked the following question: "Have you ever been upset by anyone trying to get you to do what they'd seen in pornographic pictures, movies, or books?" Of the 929 women who answered this question, 89 (10 percent) said they had been upset by such an experience at least once, while 840 (90 percent) said they had no such experience. Since the sample is a representative one, one can predict from this finding that 10 percent of the adult female population in San Francisco would say that they have been upset by men having seen something in pornography and then trying to get the women to do what they'd seen. Of course, it is possible that the women may be wrong in thinking that the men were inspired by what they had seen in the pornographic pictures, movies, or books. On the other hand, there are

Excerpted from Diana E. H. Russell, "Pornography and Violence: What Does the New Research Say?" In Laura Lederer, editor, *Take Back the Night*, William Morrow (1980). Reprinted by permission of the author.

apt to be many instances of upsetting sexual contact in which the woman was unaware that the man's idea came from having viewed pornography; these instances would not get picked up by this question.

Those who answered "Yes" to the question were then asked to describe the experience that upset them the most. As will be noted in some of the replies quoted below, although most of the women were able to avoid doing what was asked or demanded of them, others were not so fortunate. And even in cases where the behavior was avoided, the woman often ended up feeling harassed and/or humiliated.

SELECTED ANSWERS TO PORNOGRAPHY QUESTIONS:

Have you ever been upset by anyone trying to get you to do what they'd seen in pornographic pictures, movies, or books? IF YES: Could you tell me briefly about the experience that upset you the most?

Ms. A: Urinating in someone's mouth.

Ms. B: It was a three-girls-and-him situation. We had sex. I was really young— like fourteen.

Ms. C: He was a lover. He'd go to porno movies, then he'd come home and say, "I saw this in a movie. Let's try it." I felt really exploited, like I was being put in a mold.

Ms. D: I was staying at this guy's house. He tried to make me have oral sex with him. He said he'd seen far-out stuff in movies, and that it would be fun to mentally and physically torture a woman.

Ms. E: It was physical slapping and hitting. It wasn't a turn-on; it was more a feeling of being used as an object. What was most upsetting was that he thought it would be a turn-on.

Ms. F: He'd read something in a pornographic book, and then he wanted to live it out. It was too violent for me to do something like that. It was basically getting dressed up and spanking. Him spanking me. I refused to do it.

Ms. G: He forced me to have oral sex with him when I had no desire to do it.

Ms. H: This couple who had just read a porno book wanted to try the groupie number with four people. They tried to persuade my boyfriend to persuade me. They were running around naked, and I felt really uncomfortable.

Ms. I: I was S & M stuff. I was asked if I would participate in being beaten up.

It was a proposition, it never happened. I didn't like the idea of it.

Interviewer: Did anything else upset you?
Ms. I: Anal intercourse. I have been asked to do that, but I don't enjoy it at all. I have *had* to do it, *very* occasionally.

Ms. J: My husband enjoys pornographic movies. He tries to get me to do things he finds exciting in movies. They include twosomes and threesomes. I always refuse.

Also, I was always upset with his ideas about putting objects in my vagina, until I learned this is not as deviant as I used to think. He used to force me or put whatever he enjoyed into me.

Ms. K: He forced me to go down on him. He said he'd been going to porno movies. He'd seen this and wanted me to do it. He also wanted to pour champagne on my vagina. I got beat up because I didn't want to do it. He pulled my hair and slapped me around. After that I went ahead and did it, but there was no feeling in it.

Ms. L: I was newly divorced when this date talked about S & M and I said, "You've got to be nuts. Learning to experience pleasure through pain! But it's your pleasure and my pain!" I was very upset. The whole idea that someone thought I would want to sacrifice myself and have pain and bruises. It's a sick mentality. This was when I first realized there were many men out there who believe this.

Ms. M: Anal sex. First he attempted gentle persuasion, I guess. He was somebody I'd been dating a while and we'd gone to bed a few times. Once he tried to persuade me to go along with anal sex, first verbally, then by touching me. When I said "No," he did it anyway—much to my pain. It hurt like hell.

Ms. N: This guy had seen a movie where a woman was being made love to by dogs. He suggested that some of his friends had a dog and we should have a party and set the dog loose on the women. He wanted me to put a muzzle on the dog and put some sort of stuff on my vagina so that the dog would lick there.

Ms. O: My old man and I went to a show that had lots of tying up and anal intercourse. We came home and proceeded to make love. He went out and got two belts. He tied my feet together with one, and with the other he kinda beat me. I was in the spirit, I went along with it. But when he tried to penetrate me anally, I couldn't take it, it was too painful. I managed to convey to him verbally to quit it. He did stop, but not soon enough to suit me.

Then one time, he branded me. I still have a scar on my butt. He put a little wax initial thing on a hot plate and then stuck it on my ass when I was unaware.

Ms. P: My boyfriend and I saw a movie in which there was masochism. After that he wanted to gag me and tie me up. He was stoned. I was not. I was really shocked at his behavior. I was nervous and uptight. He literally tried to force me, after gagging me first. He snuck up behind me with a scarf. He was hurting me with it and I started getting upset. Then I realized it wasn't a joke. He grabbed me and shook me by my shoulders and brought out some ropes, and told me to relax, and that I would enjoy it. Then he started putting me down about my feelings about sex and my inhibitedness. I started crying and struggling with him, got loose, and kicked him in the testicles, which forced him down on the couch. I ran out of the house. Next day he called and apologized, but that was the end of him.

As may be clear from some of the quotations cited, there was often insufficient probing by the interviewers to determine the exact nature of the unwanted sexual experience. This means that the number of clear-cut cases of forced intercourse (i.e., rapes) reported in answer to this question is likely to be a considerable underestimate (see Table 1).

Table 1.
SEXUAL ASSAULTS REPORTED IN ANSWER TO QUESTION:
Have you ever been upset by anyone trying to get you to do what they'd seen in pornographic pictures, movies or books?

Sexual Assault	Number
Completed vaginal intercourse with force	4
Completed oral, anal, or vaginal intercourse with foreign object, with force	10
Attempted oral, anal, vaginal intercourse with foreign object, with force	1
Total	15

While it cannot be concluded from these data that pornography is *causing* the behavior described, I think one can conclude that at minimum it *does* have some effect. The most notable is that 10 percent of the women interviewed felt they had been personally victimized by pornography. Regarding the men's behavior, at the very least it appears that some attempt to use pornography to get women to do what they want.[1] It also seems likely that some pornography may have reinforced and legitimized these acts, including the assaultive behavior, in those men's minds. In some cases the actual *idea* of doing certain acts appears to have come from viewing pornography—as in the suggestion that a dog be used on a woman, and in some of the S & M proposals.

Millions of dollars were spent on the research conducted by the Commission on Obscenity and Pornography, which came up with the false conclusions that pornography is harmless. Just the few questions cited here, included in a survey on another topic, are sufficient to refute their irresponsible conclusion.

NOTES

*This research was supported by Grant RO1 MH2890 from the National Institute of Mental Health, Rockville, Md.

1. Note Donald Mosher's finding that 16 percent of a sample of 256 male college students had "shown a girl pornography, or taken a girl to a sexy movie to induce her to have intercourse." Donald Mosher, "Sex Callousness toward Women," *Technical Reports of the Commission on Obscenity and Pornography*, Vol. 8, 1971, p. 314.

Edward Donnerstein

Pornography and Violence Against Women: Experimental Studies

Recently, the National Institute of Mental Health designated that an understanding of the conditions that lead to sexual attacks against women is a major problem area and requires an increased focus. While there are many potential avenues of investigation, one that seems to be of current concern is the role of media effects in the possible elicitation of such aggressive acts, particularly in the area of pornography. Although the 1970 Presidential Commission on Obscenity and Pornography concluded that there was no evidence of a relationship between exposure to erotic forms of presentations and subsequent aggression (particularly sexual crimes), recent criticisms of these findings (Berkowitz, 1971; Cline, 1974; Dienstbier, 1977)* have led a number of investigators to reexamine this issue. Specifically, research by a number of individuals in the social-psychological area has indicated that under appropriate conditions exposure to erotic forms of media presentations can facilitate subsequent aggressive behavior (Zillmann, 1971; Jaffe, Malamuth, Feingold, and Feshbach, 1974; Donnerstein, E., M. Donnerstein, and R. Evans, 1975; Baron and Bell, 1977; Donnerstein and Barrett, 1978). While this research has been directed at the effects of erotic media presentations on behavior, the issue of whether such presentations can in some manner be related to increased aggressive attacks against women has

---

*Essays cited in this and other articles in Part Two are listed in the Selected Bibliography of Social Scientific Essays.

Reprinted from *Annals of the New York Academy of Sciences*, Vol. 347 (1980), pp. 277–288, by permission of the New York Academy of Sciences and the author.

been only recently of concern (Donnerstein and Barrett, 1978; Donnerstein and Hallam, 1978). It is generally believed by a large proportion of the population that many sexual materials can precipitate violent sexual crimes, such as rape (U.S. Commission, 1971). Basic research directed at examining this concern, in regard to erotic forms of media and other presentations that depict women as victims of aggression, is an important goal of social research. The present series of studies was designed to examine this issue.

BRIEF HISTORICAL BACKGROUND

What are the effects of erotic or pornographic materials on antisocial behavior? An examination of recent research and reports in the area would suggest that the effects are, if anything, nonharmful. For example:

> It is concluded that pornography is an innocuous stimulus which leads quickly to satiation and that the public concern over it is misplaced. (Howard, Liptzin, and Reifler, 1973)

> If a case is to be made against "pornography" in 1970, it will have to be made on the grounds other than demonstrated effects of a damaging personal or social nature. Empirical research designed to clarify the question has found no reliable evidence to date that exposure to explicit sexual materials plays a significant role in the causation of delinquent or criminal sexual behavior among youth or adults. (U.S. Commission, 1971)

However, recent criticisms of these findings by a number of investigators (Cline, 1974; Dienstbier, 1977) have led to a reexamination of the issue of erotic exposure and subsequent aggressive behavior. While some individuals, like Cline (1974), have argued that there are major methodological and interpretation problems with the pornography commission report, others (Liebert and Schwartzberg, 1977) believe that the observations might be premature. The major reason for this concern comes, in part, from a recent series of experimental studies that suggests that the relationship between exposure to erotic materials and subsequent aggressive behavior is more complex than first believed. The brief review of this research that follows summarizes the current state of this issue.

AGGRESSION-ENHANCING EFFECTS OF EROTIC EXPOSURE

A number of studies in which subject have been angered, and later exposed to some form of erotic stimulation, have revealed increased aggressive behavior (Zillmann, 1971; Meyer, 1972). In fact, there is evidence to suggest that the facilitative effects are greater than those attributed to aggressive films (Zillmann, 1971; Zillmann, Hoyt, and Day, 1974). Such findings have been interpreted in terms of a general arousal model, stating that under conditions where aggression is a dominant response any source of emotional arousal will tend to increase aggressive behavior (Bandura, 1973). In accordance with this model, aggressive behavior, in subjects who have previously been angered, has been shown to be increased by exposure to arousing sources such as aggressive or erotic films (Zillmann, 1971), physical exercise (Zillmann, Katcher, and Milavsky, 1972), and noise (Donnerstein and Wilson, 1976). It would seem that because of their arousing properties erotic stimuli can have aggression-facilitating effects under certain conditions. Although there has been research indicating that erotic stimuli might increase aggression without prior anger arousal (Malamuth, Feshbach, and Jaffe, 1977), the majority of evidence to date would suggest that prior anger arousal is an important condition for a facilitative effect of erotic exposure.

AGGRESSION-INHIBITING EFFECTS OF EROTIC EXPOSURE

A second group of studies (Baron, 1974a; Frodi, 1977) have shown that exposure to erotic stimuli can actually reduce subsequent aggression. A number of explanations have been suggested for this effect: erotic stimuli are somehow incompatible, in their emotional state, with aggression (Baron, 1974a; Zillmann and Sapolsky, 1977); the level of anger arousal is inappropriate for an aggressive response (Frodi, 1977); or erotic exposure shifts attention away from previous anger arousal (Donnerstein, E., M. Donnerstein, and R. Evans, 1975). Whatever the explanation, there is sound evidence to suggest that under certain conditions erotic stimuli can reduce subsequent aggressive behavior.

A RECONCILIATION OF THE RESEARCH

While at first glance such results seem somewhat contradictory, recent studies by Donnerstein et al. (Donnerstein, E., M. Donnerstein, and R. Evans, 1975) and Baron and Bell (Baron and Bell, 1977) seem to have resolved this controversy. It is now believed that as erotic stimuli become more arousing, they give rise to increases in aggressive behavior. At a low level of arousal, however, such stimuli act to distract a subject's attention away from previous anger (Donnerstein, E., M. Donnerstein, and R. Evans, 1975) or act as an incompatible response with aggression (Baron and Bell, 1977), thus reducing subsequent aggressive behavior. The evidence for this curvilinear relationship between sexual arousal and aggression seems fairly well established. In fact, Baron and Baron, 1979, has shown that this type of relationship also occurs when females are exposed to mild and highly erotic stimuli.

The Issue of Erotic Stimuli and Aggression against Women

While the current theorizing on the relationship of erotic stimuli and aggression seems fairly conclusive, it is interesting to note that all of the aforementioned studies were concerned with same-sex, primarily male-to-male, aggression. Yet, the social implications of this research would be more applicable by an examination of male aggression toward females. For, as noted by the U.S. Commission on Obscenity and Pornography:

> It is often asserted that a distinguishing characteristic of sexually explicit materials is the degrading and demeaning portrayal of the role and the status of the human female. It has been argued that erotic materials describe the female as a mere sexual object to be exploited and manipulated sexually. (U.S. Commission, 1971)

In recent years there has been an increasing concern about the relationship of pornography and violence against women. Writers in both the popular media and the scientific community have addressed this issue. Generally, they have taken for granted that pornography and aggression against women are tightly linked:

> We are somewhat educated now as to the effects of rape on women, but we know less about the effects of pornography . . . we can admit that pornography is sexist propaganda, no more and no less. Pornography is the theory, and rape is the practice. (Morgan, 1978)

> Pornography is the undiluted essence of anti-female propaganda . . . does one need scientific methodology in order to conclude that the anti-female propaganda that permeates our nation's cultural output promotes a climate in which acts of sexual hostility directed against women are not only tolerated but ideologically encouraged. (Brownmiller, 1975)

> Even when they do not overtly depict scenes of violence and degradation of

women at the hands of men, such as rape, beatings, and subordination, the tone is consistently anti-feminist. . . . The intention would seem to be simply to degrade women, and it is noteworthy that in many cases of rape the men involved either act in the same manner . . . (Eysenck and Nias, 1978)

However, what is the evidence regarding the relationship of pornography and aggression against women?

Some studies have attempted to determine whether or not erotica has a differential effect on aggression against men and against women. The general conclusion has been that no differential effects occur. Thus, in one series of studies, Mosher (Mosher, 1971c; Mosher, 1971b) found no increase in "sex-calloused" attitudes, aggressive verbal remarks, or exploitive sexual behavior toward females. More recent research by Jaffe *et al.* (Jaffe, Malamuth, Feingold, and Feshbach, 1974) and Baron and Bell (Baron and Bell, 1973) have also indicated that erotic exposure does not differentially affect men's aggression toward males or females.

There are a number of problems with the research that has examined the link between pornography and male aggression toward females. First, there is strong evidence that prior or subsequent anger instigation is critically important in facilitating aggression following erotic exposure. Given the fact that males are usually hesitant about aggressing against females (Dengerink, 1976), and that in the above research subjects were not even instigated by their potential victim, it would seem unlikely that a differential facilitation in aggression would occur. In fact, except for the Jaffe *et al.* study (Jaffe, Malamuth, Feingold, and Feshbach, 1974), researchers found that exposing nonangered individuals to erotic films tended to *reduce* aggression or maintain it at a level comparable to that of subjects exposed to a neutral film (Baron, 1974a).

Second, previous researchers have found that only under conditions of high sexual arousal does a facilitative effect in aggression occur. Exposure to mild sexually arousing stimuli seems to reduce aggression, even in previously angered individuals (Baron, 1974a; Baron and Bell, 1977; Donnerstein, E., M. Donnerstein, and R. Evans, 1975). Again, except for Jaffe *et al.* (Jaffe, Malamuth, Feingold, and Feshbach, 1974), the research that has examined the relationship of erotic stimuli and aggression toward females has employed milder forms of sexually arousing stimuli.

It would seem, therefore, that an appropriate test of the effects of erotic stimuli on aggression toward females would need to employ both some form of anger instigation and high levels of sexual arousal. This particular combination of important factors, which seems to account for the facilitative effects of erotic stimuli on aggression, has not, until recently, been investigated in those studies in which females are the victims of aggression from males.

EXPERIMENT I

A recent study by Donnerstein and Barrett (Donnerstein and Barrett, 1978) was designed to examine these issues using the theory and data of past research in the erotic stimuli-aggression area as a framework. Male subjects were exposed to either a neutral or highly arousing erotic film. The type of erotic stimuli employed was similar to those used in previous studies that have indicated facilitative effects for aggression (Zillmann, 1971; Meyer, 1972). In addition, prior to stimulus exposure subjects were either angered or treated in a neutral manner by a male or female target of aggression. Both aggressive behavior, in the form of electric shock, and physiological reactions of the subject were observed.

Since the procedures in the studies in this series were all similar, a few words regarding the methodology employed are presented. All subjects were male undergraduates who volunteered for the study as part of receiving extra credit in their course work. They believed that they were interacting with another male or female subject in a study on the effects of stress and performance. Our male subjects were first given an opportunity to write an essay with the understanding that the essay would be evaluated by the "other subject" via the delivery of electric shock. If the subject was in a condition where they were to be angered, they received a large number of shocks plus a negative written evaluation of their essay from the other male or female subject. Nonangered subjects received only one shock and a very positive evaluation. This type of procedure is very common in the literature and produces both physiological responses and self-reports that indicate that subjects have, in fact, been angered. Following this procedure, subjects were then given an opportunity to deliver shock to the "subject" who had evaluated their essay. No shock was actually delivered, but subjects assumed that they were in fact administering various levels of shock to this person. At various times in the studies, physiological responses of the subjects in the form of blood pressure were measured. It should be noted that in addition to various consent forms that were signed by the subject, a complete debriefing as to the nature of the study was given to the subjects at the end of the session.

With this experimental procedure in mind, the first study in this series made a number of predictions based upon previous research in the area: (1) exposure to erotic films should increase aggressive behavior in angered individuals, while (2) no facilitation in aggressive behavior should occur for nonangered subjects. Of more immediate interest, however, were the following questions: (1) Would exposure to erotic stimuli differentially affect aggression toward males and females in subjects who have previously been instigated to aggress? (2) Might there be an increase in aggression toward females even without prior instigation due to implied sexually aggressive cues in the erotic films? and (3) What are the physiological patterns that emerge during film exposure? This third question was of special interest, in that from a theoretical perspective, the interaction of anger arousal and erotic-film-exposure arousal have been employed in an explanatory manner in this area (Zillmann, 1971). To date, however, such results were based upon interactions with only male targets of aggression. There is a suggestion from prior research (Taylor and Epstein, 1967) that although males display less aggression toward females following provocation, physiological arousal is maintained at a high level. It seemed important, in terms of past research in this area, to examine further not only the arousal component of anger instigation from males to females, but also its interaction with highly arousing sexual stimuli. Donnerstein and Barrett (Donnerstein and Barrett, 1978) also examined the effects of anger, erotic stimuli, and sex on a more prosocial or rewarding response. Since it was expected that less social restraints would be present with this reward response than with the shock response toward females, subjects were given an opportunity in this study to administer rewards (money) to their target. The major results for this first study are presented in TABLES 1 and 2. With regard to aggression, as measured by the intensity and durations of shocks administrated to the male or female, two interactions were found. The first, anger × sex of target, indicated that angered subjects were more aggressive than nonangered subjects and that subjects angered by a male were more aggressive than those angered by a female. The second, anger × films, indicated that under nonanger conditions there were no effects for the films shown, but, when subjects were angry the erotic film increased aggression. Thus, when subjects were exposed to highly arousing erotic stimuli there was a possibility for aggression to be facilitated. More important to the discussion is the fact that no differential aggression was observed toward females as a function of film exposure. In fact, as has been the case in past studies (Taylor and Epstein, 1967), less aggression was administered to the

Table 1
MEAN INTENSITY* × DURATION AS A FUNCTION OF
EXPERIMENTAL CONDITIONS

Condition	Means	
	Anger	No Anger
Anger × Sex of Target		
Male	1.86$_a$	0.95$_c$
Female	1.55$_b$	1.13$_c$
Anger × Films		
Erotic	1.90$_a$	0.93$_c$
Neutral	1.45$_b$	1.15$_c$

*Means with a different subscript differ from each other at the 0.05 level by Duncan's procedure.

Table 2
MEAN CHANGE* IN BLOOD PRESSURE AS A FUNCTION OF EXPERIMENTAL
CONDITIONS AFTER FILM EXPOSURE

	Film	
Condition	Erotic	Neutral
	Mean Blood Pressure	
Anger		
Males	1.8_b	-0.2_b
Females	9.4_a	-3.1_c
No Anger		
Males	8.2_a	-3.9_c
Females	7.2_a	-3.9_c
	Systolic Blood Pressure	
Anger		
Males	2.8_b	-1.4_b
Females	11.3_a	-4.8_c
No Anger		
Males	11.2_a	-5.6_c
Females	8.6_a	-6.2_c

*Means with different subscripts differ from each other at the 0.05 level by Duncan's procedure.

female targets. Does this imply, therefore, that erotic films do not influence aggression towards females as suggested by the pornography commission (U.S. Commission, 1971)? The physiological data obtained in this study would suggest that perhaps another process was operating with angered subjects. The blood pressure data indicated that higher levels of arousal were obtained with a female rather than a male target after erotic exposure, and that this arousal was still present after aggressing. It might have been expected, therefore, that aggression would have been higher toward females than males. Results, however, tended to indicate just the opposite. Under anger conditions females were aggressed against less than males. It is interesting to note that Taylor and Epstein (Taylor and Epstein, 1967) also found increased physiological arousal in male subjects who were less aggressive toward a female target under attack conditions. One possible explanation for this type of finding, suggested by Dengerink (Dengerink, 1976), is that aggression towards females is generally disapproved of, and that this fear of disapproval could act to inhibit aggression. Further evidence that males were inhibited from acting aggressively toward female targets in this study was suggested by the reward data. Under anger conditions a reduction in reward was found for females. It would seem reasonable to suggest that in the context of this study, changes in rewarding behavior would carry less social restraints than delivery of a noxious stimulus toward a female. If these results were a function of inhibitions toward aggressing against females, then conditions allowing for a reduction in inhibitions might reveal differential aggression toward males and females as a function of erotic exposure.

EXPERIMENT II

The purpose of this experiment was to create a condition in which male subjects would be less inhibited or restrained against aggressing toward a female, in order to examine the effects that erotic exposure would have upon such aggression. While there are many potential strategies to reduce aggressive inhibitions (e.g., aggressive models), the present study adopted a situation similar to that employed by Geen, Stonner, and Shope (Geen, Stonner, and Shope, 1975). These investigators found that when subjects were given two opportunities to aggress against an anger instigator, aggression was higher than in a condition in which subjects were not given this initial aggression opportunity. Furthermore, subjects in the double aggression condition reported less restraints against aggressing than individuals in all other conditions. Additional support for this increase in aggression, following an initial opportunity to aggress, has been provided by a number of investigators (e.g., Geen, Stonner, and Shope, 1975). In the context of the pres-

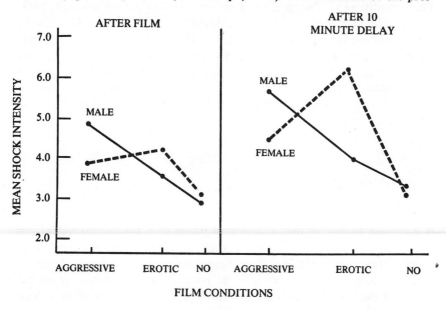

FIGURE 1. Mean shock intensity as a function of film conditions, sex of target, and time of aggression.

ent experiment, it was hypothesized that allowing male subjects an initial opportunity to aggress against a female would act to reduce any aggression inhibitions present. If erotic films are capable of facilitating aggression against females, then the present experiment, by incorporating both anger instigation and highly erotic films in addition to a reduction in inhibitions, should allow for a more judicious test of this possibility.

In this study, male subjects were angered by a male or female target prior to being placed into one of three film conditions. Before being given an opportunity to aggress, subjects viewed either a highly erotic film, aggressive film, or no film. After having one opportunity to aggress against the male or female target, subjects waited 10 minutes and were given a second opportunity to aggress.

The results of the present study, as seen in FIGURE 1, would suggest that highly erotic films can act to increase aggressive responses against females under certain conditions. When male subjects were given an opportunity to aggress immediately following film exposure, it was found that highly erotic films did increase aggression beyond that of the no-film controls. This finding corroborates those of other investigators (Donnerstein, E., M. Donnerstein, and R. Evans, 1971; Zillmann, 1971) who have found that highly arousing erotica can act as a facilitator of aggression in previously angered individuals. In addition, it was found that during this initial aggression opportunity there was no differential aggression toward males or females. These results are also supportive of previous studies (Baron and Bell, 1973; Donnerstein and Barrett, 1978; Jaffe, Malamuth, Feingold, and Feshbach, 1974) that have indicated no sex-of-target effects following erotic exposure. However, when male subjects were given a second opportunity to aggress against the target, 10 minutes later, aggressive responses were increased against female targets. This finding of an increase in aggression against women in the delayed condition is the first demonstration that this effect can, in fact, occur.

EXPERIMENT III

It has been suggested that a major problem with the conclusion of the pornography commission report (U.S. Commission, 1971) was the lack of research on "porno-violence," or aggressive content in erotic forms of materials (Cline, 1974). This lack of research was surprising given the results of the National Commission on the Causes and Prevention of Violence (U.S. National Commission, 1969), dealing with media aggression and its effect on subsequent aggressive behavior.

Given the nature of most erotic films, in which women are depicted in a

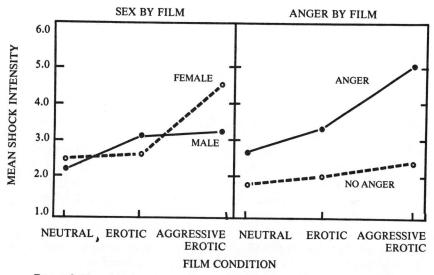

FIGURE 2. Mean shock intensity as a function of sex of target by films, and anger by films.

submissive, passive role, any subtle aggressive content could act to increase **aggression against females because of their association with observed aggression. As noted in the work of Berkowitz (Berkowitz, 1974), one important** determinant of whether an aggressive response is made is the presence of aggressive cues. Not only objects, but individuals can take on aggressive-cue **value if they have been associated with observed violence. Thus, in the con**text of the present research, the viewing of more sexually aggressive films might facilitate aggression towards females because of the aggression-eliciting stimulus properties of the female target from her repeated association with observed violence. This increase in aggression should be especially true for previously angered individuals who are already predisposed to aggress. In the research discussed up to this point the films employed did not contain acts of aggression. If they did, perhaps the results would have differed with respect to female victims.

In order to examine this issue, male subjects in the present study (Donnerstein, 1980b) were angered or treated in a neutral manner by a male or female. They were then shown one of three films. Two of the films were highly erotic but differed in aggressive content. While one film was entirely nonaggressive, the other depicted the rape of a women by a man who breaks into her house and forces her at gunpoint into sexual activity. The third film was a neutral (nonerotic and nonaggressive) presentation.

The major results are presented in FIGURE 2. Two interactions occurred which deserve attention. The first, anger × film, indicated that both the erotic and aggressive-erotic film increased aggression, primarily in angered individuals. The largest increase occurred, however, for subjects exposed to the aggressive-erotic film. The second interaction, sex of target × film, indicated that while both types of erotic films increased aggression against a male, only the aggressive-erotic film facilitated aggression against a female, and this level of aggression was higher than that directed against a male. Why would aggression be increased against the female after exposure to the aggressive-erotic film? One potential explanation is that the females' association with the victim in the film made her an aggressive stimulus that could elicit aggressive responses (e.g., Berkowitz, 1974). The combination of anger and arousal from the film heightened this response and led to the highest level of aggression against the female. But, even under nonanger conditions aggression was increased. This was not the case for subjects paired with a male. Under nonanger, the aggressive-erotic film did not influence aggression against the male target. It would seem, then, that the female's association with observed violence was an important contributor to the aggressive responses toward her. If this is the case then it would be expected that films that depict violence against women, even without sexual content, could act as a stimulus for aggressive acts toward women. It seems important, therefore, for future research to begin a systematic investigation into the context of women's association with violence in the media.

CONCLUSION AND IMPLICATIONS

It was the intention of the present research to examine the effects that certain media presentations have on aggression against women. Results from these investigations suggest that films of both an erotic *and* aggressive nature can be a mediator of aggression toward women. In addition to the theoretical implications of these results, there is a more applied question that has been the concern of the present paper. When it is found that (1) 50% of university females report some form of sexual aggression (Kanin and Parcell, 1977), (2) 39% of the six offenders questioned indicate that pornography had something to do with the crime they committed (Walker, 1971), and (3) the incidence of rape and other sexual assaults have increased then the question of what conditions precipitate such actions should be examined. The present research suggests that specific types of media account for part of these actions. Given the increase in sexual and other forms of violence against women depicted in the media, a concern over such presentations seems warranted. There is ample evidence that the observation of violent forms of media can facilitate aggressive response (e.g., Geen,

1978), yet to assume that the depiction of sexual-aggression could not have a similar effect, particularly against females, would be misleading. Given the findings of the present studies, it seems important for future investigations to a systematic examination of the role of the media in aggression against women.

ACKNOWLEDGEMENTS

The advice and encouragement of Prof. Len Berkowitz in this research is greatly appreciated.

NOTES

*This paper was written while the author was a visiting professor at the University of Wisconsin. Study III and the writing of this paper was supported by a grant from the National Institute of Mental Health, 1 F32 MH 07788-01.

Edward Donnerstein and Leonard Berkowitz

Victim Reactions in Aggressive Erotic Films as a Factor in Violence Against Women

There has been an increased concern in recent years about rape and other forms of aggression against women. While many explanations have been offered for this apparent increase in violence against women, a number of writers have indicted the mass media, and especially pornography, as one important contributor to these assaults (e.g., Brownmiller, 1975; Burt, 1980; Donnerstein, 1980a). Others disagree. The 1971 report of the Presidential Commission on Obscenity and Pornography had concluded that there was no direct relationship between exposure to pornography and subsequent sexual crimes. However, recent criticisms of the Commission's findings (e.g., Berkowitz, 1971; Cline, 1974; Dienstbier, 1977; Wills, 1977) have led several investigators to re-examine the issue. This later research has indicated that exposure to certain types of erotic materials can increase aggressive behavior (e.g., Baron and Bell, 1977; Donnerstein, in press; Donnerstein, Donnerstein, and Evans, 1975; Malamuth, Feshbach, and Jaffe, 1977; Meyer, 1972; Zillmann, 1971, 1979).

By and large, these investigations have been aimed primarily at the question of whether sexual scenes can influence aggressive behavior generally. The more specific issue of the effect of these media portrayals on aggression against women in particular has only recently been studied (e.g.,

Reprinted from the *Journal of Personality and Social Psychology*, Vol. 41, No. 4 (1981), pp. 710–724. Copyright 1981 by the American Psychological Association. Reprinted by permission of the publisher and Edward Donnerstein.

Donnerstein and Barrett, 1978; Donnerstein and Hallam, 1978; Donner-stein and Malamuth, in press). The experiments reported here are a continu-ation of these latter investigations within the framework of research on the stimulus qualities of the filmed event and the possible targets for aggression (e.g., Berkowitz, 1971, 1974). We basically ask whether the behavioral characteristics of the people in the erotic film and the nature of the targets available for aggression afterwards can affect the intensity of the aggression that is subsequently displayed.

One behavioral quality that could be quite important has to do with the amount of violence in the erotic scene. Several writers tell us the incidence of aggressively toned pornography has increased in the last few years (e.g., Eysenck and Nias, 1978; Malamuth and Spinner, 1980; Malamuth and Check, in press). Can it be that the addition of aggression heightens the chances that the erotic material will have an adverse impact on the viewers? Indeed, the violence in an aggressive erotic film could conceivably have a greater aggression-enhancing effect than the purely sexual nature of the film alone. According to Berkowitz's analysis of movie violence (1971, 1974), the stimuli on the screen tend to elicit reactions that are semantically associated with them. Observed aggression should therefore evoke aggres-sion-facilitating responses, whereas purely sexual stimuli should elicit primarily sexual reactions (although the general excitement that also accom-panies these latter reactions might energize whatever aggressive responses the observers are set to perform in the given situation). This increased ag-gressivity produced by the violent content obviously should be greatest for those viewers who are angry at the moment; since they are disposed to at-tack someone, the aggression-associated movie stimuli could readily evoke aggressive reactions from them. Donnerstein (1980b) has obtained support-ing evidence. Male subjects were angered or treated in a neutral manner by a male or female confederate and then were shown one of three films. Two of these movies were highly sexually arousing but one of them also had explicit aggressive content while the other did not. The third film was neither sex-ually or aggressively evocative. Donnerstein found that the men exposed to the aggressive erotic movie were subsequently more aggressive to the confederate than were those who had seen the purely sexual film, but par-ticularly if they had been angered by the confederate beforehand.

A nearby person's stimulus characteristics can also determine the extent to which aggression is directed against this individual. Berkowitz's research indicates that people with certain stimulus qualities tend to evoke the strongest aggression-facilitating reactions from those who are ready to be aggressive (Berkowitz, 1974; Berkowitz and Frodi, 1979). What is most relevant to us here is the available target's association with the victim of the movie violence. Perhaps because this association connects the possible target with the successful (or positively reinforced) aggression shown on the screen, a person bearing the same label as the victim of the observed violence tends to receive stronger attacks than those who have a different label (Berkowitz, 1974). Another of Donnerstein's (1980b) results can be interpreted in just this way. When his subjects had been angered by a man and then were given an opportunity to punish this male confederate, the aggressive erotic film did not lead to any more aggression than the sexual movie. However, if the subjects were paired with a female confederate, the aggressive erotica led to substantially stronger attacks than did the purely sexual film, and this happened, furthermore, even when the woman confederate had not provoked the subjects earlier. The female confederate's sex-linked connection with the victim of the witnessed violence could have strengthened her capacity to elicit aggressive responses from the men.

Yet another factor that might affect the audience's aggressive reactions has to do with the outcome of the observed sexual attack. Opponents of pornography have noted that women are typically portrayed in this material as enjoying the assault upon them (Brownmiller, 1975). From the viewers' perspective, the woman victim's pleasure could mean that she heightens the aggressor's enjoyment even further. They might then come to think, at least for a short while, that their own sexual aggression also would be profitable so that their restraints are reduced (Bandura, 1973). Malamuth and Check (in press, a) have recently reported evidence consistent with our analysis. In their study the male subjects' self-reported likelihood of raping a woman was highly correlated with both (a) their belief that the women in the aggressive erotic material presented to them had enjoyed being attacked and (b) their notion that women generally derive pleasure from being raped. These views lessen the moral reprehensibility of any witnessed assaults on women and, more than this, also suggest that the sexual attacks may have a highly desirable outcome—for the victim and for the aggressor. Men having such beliefs might therefore be more likely to attack a woman themselves after they see a supposedly "pleasurable" rape. Furthermore, since there is a substantial aggressive component in the sexual assault, we suggest that the favorable outcome lowers the observers' restraints against aggression toward women as well as against sexual behavior with them.

All this does not mean the victim's suffering will necessarily be taken as an unpleasant outcome. Angry people want to inflict injury (Baron, 1977; Berkowitz, Cochran, and Embree, 1981). Information that someone, and especially the person who had provoked them, has been hurt would be particularly rewarding for them. As a stimulus associated with reinforcements for aggression, this information could theoretically lead to heightened attacks by the provoked observers (Baron, 1977; Berkowitz, 1974). Now suppose that the male viewers of aggressive erotica happen to be very angry with women as they watch the movie. Seeing the woman victim being hurt by the assault on her might be very stimulating for them; her "pain cues" could elicit stronger aggression-facilitating reactions within them to the extent that they want to injure the women in their own lives.

EXPERIMENT I

The present paper reports two studies designed to investigate these and related notions. In the first experiment male subjects were first angered by a male or female confederate and then were shown one of four films. Three of the movies were highly erotic in nature but differed in their aggressive content. The first was a nonaggressive erotic film. The other two erotic films had an aggressive component but differed in terms of the scene's outcome: one had a positive conclusion while the other ended on a decidedly negative note. The fourth film was neutral with respect to both sex and aggression. Since any increase in aggression after the movies might be due to the physiological arousal engendered by the observed scene (e.g., Zillmann, 1971), all of the erotic films were chosen to be equal in the level of arousal they produced. Finally, immediately after the men saw their movie, each of them had an opportunity to punish the confederate in a socially sanctioned manner.

The research just reviewed led us to formulate several specific predictions. *First*, we expected the *purely sexual* erotic movie to lead to stronger attacks on the male than on the female confederate. On the basis of other studies (e.g., Donnerstein, in press), we assumed that the sexual arousal produced by the erotic film would intensify the aggressive reactions the angry men were disposed to make. However, we also thought the men would be fairly reluctant to punish a woman severely even though she had provoked them earlier (Donnerstein, 1980b). Unless these restraints were overcome—by conditions that lowered the men's inhibitions and/or strengthened the woman's capacity to evoke aggression-facilitating responses from them—the men should be more aggressive to another male than to a woman.

Second, we predicted that exposure to an aggressive erotic movie with a positive outcome (the woman victim apparently enjoyed the assault) would lead to a relatively high level of aggression against the female target. This aggression should be higher than that displayed in the pure erotica condition or in the same movie condition having a male target for aggression. In this case we reasoned that (a) the aggressive content of the sex film would evoke strong aggressive reactions from the angry viewers, (b) the positive outcome would lower their inhibitions against attacking women, and (c) the female target's sex-linked association with the victim of the assault on the screen would facilitate attacks on her.

Third, we also thought the negative outcome to the aggressive erotic film (in which the woman victim was shown suffering) would also *cause* the confederate to be punished relatively strongly when this target was a female but perhaps not as strongly as in the positive outcome condition. Here, too, the female confederate should draw stronger attacks than the male confederate in the same film condition. As we had suggested earlier, the reasoning was that the assaulted woman's suffering would serve as pain cues for these angry men and thus stimulate fairly strong aggressive reactions within them. However, some restraints against aggression should also be present in the viewers since the witnessed attack was not portrayed as "worthwhile" or "justified." As a result, the aggressive responses evoked by both the aggressive content and the depicted suffering should be somewhat inhibited. And finally, the female confederate's connection with the movie victim should lead to stronger punishment of her than of the male confederate.

METHOD

SUBJECTS

The subjects were 80 male undergraduates enrolled in a course in introductory psychology. Subjects participated to receive extra credit toward their final grade in the course.

APPARATUS AND SELECTION OF FILMS

Aggression, as measured by shock intensity ostensibly delivered to the aggressive target, was administered via a modified Buss (1961) "aggression machine" identical to that employed in previous investigations (e.g., Donnerstein, Donnerstein, and Barrett, 1976). A Narco Biosystem Electrosphygmomanometer was used to measure systolic and diastolic blood pressure. A Harvard Inductorium system was employed for the delivery of electric shock to the subject during the anger manipulation phase in the experiment. All films were shown over a SONY Video Recorder system.

Four films were prepared for the present study. All were 5 minutes in length and were in black and white. The neutral film was of a talk show interview and contained no aggressive or erotic content. It is similar to that used in previous investigations by the senior author (e.g., Donnerstein, 1980b). The purely erotic movie depicted a young couple engaged in various stages of sexual intercourse and was also used in the previous studies. It did not contain any aggressive content. The final two films were of an aggressive erotic nature. Both were the same except for the introductory narrative and the final 30 seconds. Each film depicted a young woman who comes to study with two men. Both men have been drinking and when she sits between them she is shoved around and also forced to drink. She is then tied up, stripped, slapped, and sexually attacked. In the *positive outcome-*

aggressive erotic movie the ending shows the woman smiling and in no way "resisting" the two men. The introduction to the film also told the subjects that by film's end the woman becomes a willing participant in the sexual activity. In the *negative outcome-aggressive erotic* film the woman's actions in the last 30 seconds of the scene indicate she is suffering. The introduction to this version of the film reports that she finds the experience humiliating and disgusting. Pretesting indicated that the woman in the latter film was seen as suffering more and as having enjoyed her experience less than the woman in the positive ending movie.

DESIGN AND PROCEDURE

The basic design was a 2×4 factorial, with sex of target (male, female) and films (neutral, erotic, positive/aggression, negative/aggression) treated as factors. Four undergraduate males were randomly assigned to the role of experimenter and confederate, and two females also served as confederates.

On arriving for the experiment, the subject was met by an experimental confederate (male or female) posing as another subject. The experimenter then arrived and conducted the confederate and subject into the first experimental room.

Prerecorded taped instructions to the subject explained that the experiment was concerned with the effects of stress on learning and physiological responses. The subject and the confederate were informed that the experiment would involve both receiving and delivering mild electric shocks to the fingertips. The two people were told they could refuse to participate and still receive full experimental credit. After this, an informed consent form was provided which the subject was to read and sign, acknowledging his agreement to participate in an experiment involving electric shock. The form also indicated that all information regarding the study would be given at the conclusion of the session. All subjects then completed a Medial Health Survey Questionnaire to assure that they were physically able to take part in the study and that they were under no medication which could influence blood pressure readings.

The taped instructions were then started again and described the remainder of the procedure more fully. In these instructions the subjects were told that each of them would be asked to perform a task under a stressful situation. Besides being interested in their performance on the task, the experimenter supposedly was interested in their physiological responses to the task and the experimental situation. Consequently, readings of blood pressure would be taken from each subject at various specified times during the experiment.

At this point, the experimenter selected one subject (always the confederate) to come into a second room ostensibly to begin studying for his/her task. After waiting about a minute, the experimenter returned to the subject, and conducted him to a second room. The subject was informed that his task was to assist the experimenter in administering the learning test which "the other subject" (the confederate) was studying. Subjects were told that the experimenter needed to remain free to measure physiological reactions during the entire experiment.

While the confederate studied, it was explained to the subject, he would perform his task. But first, a base level measure of blood pressure would be needed for both people. The experimenter then attached the arm cuff of the sphygmomanometer to the subject, returned to the adjoining room, and recorded the blood pressure reading (BP1-baseline).

Anger manipulation. After the first blood pressure measure was taken the experimenter returned to the subject's room and presented the next segment of pre-recorded instructions. The subjects were told that their task involved writing a short essay on the issue of the legalization of marijuana. The subjects were instructed to state their opinion on this issue and to write a short essay (approximately five minutes) supporting their stand. Stress was induced by telling the men that their essay would be evaluated by their partner in the other room by the use of electric shock and a short written evaluation. Following a procedure used in previous studies (e.g., Donnerstein and Wilson, 1976), it was noted that the shock evaluation could range from no shocks for a good rating to ten shocks for a very poor rating. The experimenter then left the room for five minutes while the subjects wrote their essays.

After this time had elapsed, the experimenter re-entered the room and said that he would now give the essay to the other person (the confederate) for evaluation. Upon returning to the subject (and while the confederate supposedly was "reading" the essay) the experimenter attached two electrodes to the fingers of the subjects in preparation for the evaluation. The experimenter then left, ostensibly to collect the partner's written evaluation of the subject's essay, and then returned to the subject's room. He then contacted the confederate by intercom and instructed him/her to deliver the shock "evaluation." All subjects received 9 shocks of mild intensity, each having .5-sec. duration. Following the shock evaluation, the subject was presented with the written evaluation of his task performance. This consisted of ratings on 4 5-point rating scales and showed that the subject's partner had a poor opinion of his essay. A second measure of the subject's blood pressure was then recorded (BP2).

When this was completed, the experimenter removed the electrodes and told the subjects that their partner (the confederate) would soon perform his or her task. It was explained that the subject would help in the administration of that task, but, as enough time had not elapsed for the confederate to finish studying, there would be a few minutes delay in beginning the new phase of the experiment.

Film conditions. At this point the rationale for the different film conditions was introduced. A subject assigned to the *neutral* movie condition was informed that while the "learner" was studying, the experimenter was interested in having the subject view a movie which he (the experimenter) was hoping to use in future research. Since it was not part of the initial experiment, the experimenter added, would the subject be willing to view the film, rate it on a number of dimensions, and have his blood pressure taken immediately following the film?

For the purely *erotic* and *aggressive-erotic* film conditions, in addition to being given the above rationale, the subject was informed that the movie to be shown was highly erotic and depicted a scene of explicit sexual behavior. It was made clear that the subject was free to choose not to see the film and that credit for participation in the experiment would not in any way be affected by his decision. If he chose to continue and view the film (all subjects did), he was given an appropriate informed-consent form to read and sign.

All of the men complied with the experimenter's request and subsequently saw the film while the experimenter returned to the control room. Upon completion of the movie (5 minutes later), the subject's blood pressure was taken (BP3) and a short questionnaire regarding the film content was completed. The subject was then informed that he could now proceed with the "learning under stress" experiment.

Aggression opportunity. For the second task of the experiment, the subject was asked to present a prepared list of nonsense syllables to the confederate, ostensibly freeing the experimenter to monitor the other person's task performance and physiological reactions. The subject was supplied with the correct answer for each trial of the task and was informed that if his partner responded correctly on a trial, he was to give this person a number of points (betwen 1 and 8), with each point equal to one cent. At the completion of the task, the partner was to receive the amount of money he/she had earned for correct responses. If the partner was incorrect, however, the subject was to deliver some level of shock (again on a scale between 1 and 8). The subject was also told that he could administer any number of points or level of shock he felt appropriate for any trial since the particular number or level would have no effect on the partner's performance.[1]

The task consisted of 24 trials, with the confederate making errors on 16 trials and correct responses on 8 trials. After the last trial a final measure of blood pressure (BP4) was taken.

Questionnaire and debriefing. Following the last BP measure, the subject completed a short questionnaire that asked him to rate, on a five-point scale, how he felt his essay was evaluated, how angry/not angry he felt after the rating, and how good/bad he felt. After completion of the rating scales the subject was completely debriefed as to the nature of the experiment and any questions he had were answered. Those men exposed to the aggressive erotic films were given an additional debriefing regarding the nature of the films. The subject was then thanked for his participation and dismissed.

Calculation of physiological arousal. Three measures of blood pressure were calculated: systolic, diastolic, and mean blood pressure. Mean blood pressure (Zillmann, 1971) was computed as mean blood pressure = diastolic + ⅔ (systolic – diastolic). All change scores are in comparison to base level (BP1).

RESULTS

EFFECTIVENESS OF MANIPULATIONS

Film ratings. All subjects were asked to respond to four questions regarding the film content. In addition, the men who saw the erotic and aggressive erotic films also completed three questions dealing with the movie victim. These results are presented in Table 1.

Table 1
MEAN SELF-REPORT AND PHYSIOLOGICAL CHANGES TO
VARIOUS FILM CONDITIONS

(Experiment 1)

| | FILM CONDITION | | | |
RATINGS OF FILM	NEUTRAL	EROTIC	POSITIVE	NEGATIVE
INTERESTING	1.6_a	3.4_b	3.3_b	3.2_b
SEXUALLY AROUSING	1.1_a	3.7_b	3.7_b	3.9_b
AGGRESSIVE	1.4_a	1.4_a	3.5_b	4.8_c
SEXUAL CONTENT	1.4_a	6.0_b	5.9_b	5.6_b
RATINGS OF VICTIM				
SUFFERING		1.7_a	2.7_b	4.8_c
ENJOYMENT		6.3_a	5.1_b	2.6_c
RESPONSIBLE		5.6_a	4.1_b	2.9_c
MEAN BLOOD PRESSURE	-0.9_a	$+6.1_b$	$+8.5_b$	$+5.5_b$

Note. Means with different subscripts differ from each other at the .05 level by Duncan's procedure. Film ratings are on a 7-point scale.

A main effect for films was obtained on the question of how interesting was the film, $F(3, 72) = 7.20$, p < .01; how aggressive was the content, $F(3, 72) = 23.35$, p .01; and how sexual was the content, $F(3, 72) = 47.37$, p < .01. As can be seen in Table 1, all three erotic films were considered more interesting, more sexually arousing, and as containing more sexual content than the neutral film, while not differing from each other. Thus, according to these measures at least, any behavioral differences among the erotic movie groups cannot be attributed to differences in the films' level of interest or excitement. On the rating of the aggressiveness of the movie, the negative outcome-aggressive erotic film was seen as more aggressive than the positive version, with both films differing reliably from the neutral and erotic presentations.

Main effects for films were also obtained on the question of how much the victim in the film suffered, $F(2, 54) = 51.81$, p < .01; how much she enjoyed the experience, $F(2, 54) = 50.11$, p < .01; and how responsible she was for what happened, $F(2, 54) = 15.02$, p < .01. Looking at the means in Table 1, the woman in the negative-aggressive erotic film was thought to have suffered more, enjoyed her experience less, and assigned less responsibility for the incident than her counterpart in the positive outcome film. Along with the pretesting data, these results support the effectiveness of the movie variations.

Essay evaluation and anger. Analyses of the items dealing with the subjects' reactions to the ratings they received for their essay and their feelings after the shock-evaluation did not reveal any sex of target or film effects. The mean rating of how good/bad the essay was, evaluated on a 5-point scale, was 4.38, suggesting that the manipulation was effective. Subjects also reported feeling a mean of 3.53 on the good/bad scale and 2.68 on the not angry/angry scale in response to how they felt after receiving the evaluation.

PHYSIOLOGICAL AROUSAL

Mean blood pressure. A 2×4 analysis of variance (ANOVA) with sex of target and films as factors was conducted on the BP2 measure (after the anger manipulation). This analysis did not reveal any significant effects. However, an additional test comparing the overall increase in mean blood pressure ($M = 10.67$) over the base level indicated that the anger manipulation did significantly increase the subjects' physiological arousal (p < .01), indicating that the confederate's treatment of them had provoked the men.

A 2×4 ANOVA was also conducted on the BP3 scores (after film exposure). This analysis yielded a main effect for films, $F(3, 72) = 5.29$, p < .01, with the purely erotic and aggressive erotic films not differing in physiological arousal but significantly different (see Table 1) from the neutral film. These latter findings are consistent with the film ratings mentioned earlier, and again indicate that behavioral differences among the erotic movie groups cannot be attributed to differences in movie-produced arousal.

A 2×4 ANOVA on BP4 scores (after aggression) did not reveal any significant sources of variation.

Systolic blood pressure. The analysis of the systolic blood pressure data revealed results identical to that of mean blood pressure and will not, consequently, be elaborated on further.

Diastolic blood pressure. The analysis of the diastolic blood pressure data revealed a significant increase in arousal ($p < .01$) after the anger manipulation, as well as a marginally significant effect ($p < .15$) for films on BP3 (after film exposure). The results were similar to those obtained for the other blood pressure measures.

AGGRESSIVE BEHAVIOR

A 2×4 ANOVA on the mean intensity of the shocks administered to the confederate revealed significant effects for films, $F(3, 72) = 3.82$, $p < .02$; and for the interaction of Sex of Target $\times$ Films, $F(3, 72) = 8.34$, $p < .01$. This interaction is presented in Figure 1.

This interaction indicated that for male targets there were no increases in aggression as a function of film exposure. For those subjects paired with a female target, however, the movie condition did affect the subsequent aggressive behavior significantly. While the purely erotic film did not heighten aggression, exposure to either aggressive erotic film increased the level of aggression to the female target (p's $< .05$, Duncan's procedure), significantly above that displayed in the neutral film and purely erotic groups. The positive and negative film versions did not differ from each other. This level of aggression toward the females in the two aggressive erotic conditions was significantly ($p < .05$) higher than all other male target conditions except for the men in the purely erotic film condition.

REWARDING BEHAVIOR

Rewarding behavior was calculated as the average number of points administered to the target on each correct trial of the learning task. An ANOVA on these data did not reveal any significant effects.

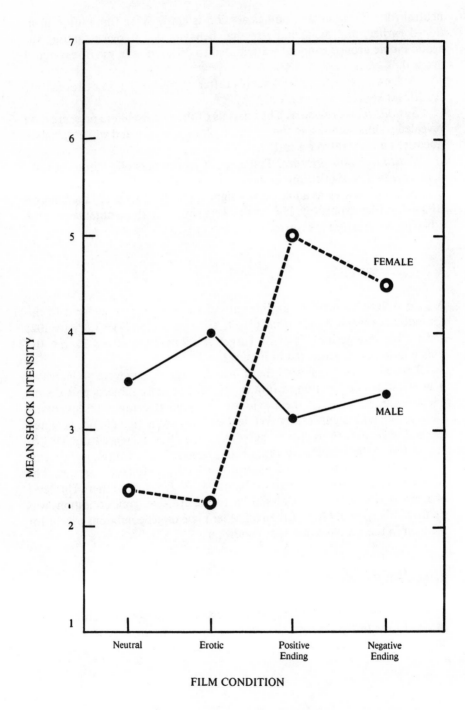

FIGURE 1. Mean shock intensity as a function of sex of target and film condition.

DISCUSSION

Our first prediction was that aggression would be increased against a male target, but not a female, after exposure to the erotic film. Contrary to this expectation, however, although somewhat more aggression was directed against a male than a female in the erotic film group, the movie conditions did not differ reliably in the level of aggression against the male target, although the results were in the predicted direction. While this absence of differences is not consistent with other findings in the literature (e.g., Donnerstein, 1980b; in press), this lack of effect could be due in part to the unusually high level of aggression in the neutral condition. An examination of the shock data from the previous studies which have made use of these same two films (e.g., Donnersteing, 1080b; in press) showed that shock levels in the present neutral movie group are unusually high. The scores for the purely erotic film were, however, quite similar to the present data.[2]

The effects of exposure to the purely erotic film on aggression toward females essentially replicates other studies using similar stimuli (e.g., Donnerstein, 1980b; in press). These results tend to suggest, once again, that unless aggressive restraints are reduced and/or the stimulus value of the target is enhanced, exposure to highly arousing but nonaggressive erotica will not significantly increase violence toward women relative to men (e.g., Donnerstein and Hallam, 1978).

Our second prediction was that exposure to the positive outcome-aggressive erotic film would heighten the angry viewers' attacks on a female target. Not only did this increase result, but the level of aggression was greater than that administered to a male target in the same condition. This latter difference points to the importance of the female target's association with the victim in the aggressive movie. Our final prediction was that the negative outcome-aggressive erotic film would also increase aggression against a female by angered male subjects, presumably because the filmed victim's suffering stimulated the angry observers. The present results were highly supportive of this prediction.

The results of the present study once again suggest that aggressive erotica can increase aggression against women under certain conditions. While the observed assault's outcome did not seem to produce substantial differences in aggression, it could be, nevertheless, that the intensified attacks occurred for different reasons in the two aggressive erotic movies. As we had conjectured earlier, in addition to the aggressive stimulation produced by the aggressive content, the positive ending might have lowered the men's inhibitions against attacking an available target. In a sense, the movie outcome suggested that aggression could have a worthwhile result. A recent study by Malamuth (1978) gives some support to this suggestion. When the male subjects in his study were angered by a female and then exposed to pictures combining sex and violence, aggression was increased when the men were led to believe it was permissible to behave aggresively. A similar process might have operated in the present study, in the positive outcome-aggressive erotic movie condition.

On the other hand, the subjects exposed to the negative outcome-aggressive film could have been stimulated to intensified aggression by the sight of the victim's suffering. Since they were angry at the time so that they were instigated to hurt someone (Berkowitz, Cochran, and Embree, 1981), the pain cues from the victim were associated with this goal and thus might have evoked a heightened aggressive inclination in them (Berkowitz, 1974; Swart and Berkowitz, 1976).

EXPERIMENT 2

The second experiment was designed to be a further test of this last-mentioned possibility. All of the subjects in the initial study had been angered by the available target, and this anger arousal had presumably caused the movie victim's suffering to be an aggression eliciting cue for them. If our reasoning is correct, nonangry viewers should not be stimulated to increased attacks on a female target on seeing the film victim's pain and distress. We tested this expectation in the second investigation by having half of the male subjects believe that their female partner had deliberately insulted them, whereas the remaining participants were treated in a neutral fashion by her so that they were not angry at the time. Thus, in keeping with our initial findings, we predicted that the negative outcome-aggressive erotic film would lead to increased aggression toward the female confederate when the men were angry with her, but would have no such effect when the men had not been provoked. Indeed, other research (cf. Baron, 1977) suggests that the movie pain cues might actually produce a lowered level of overt aggression.

On the other hand, as our second prediction, we thought that the positive outcome-aggressive erotic movie would produce heightened attacks on the woman target (above that displayed in the neutral and purely erotic film groups) whether the subjects had been angered or not. In this case the film's aggressive content theoretically would stimulate intensified aggressive inclinations in both the angered and nonangered men (although more strongly so in the former group), and the depicted positive outcome would lower their restraints against attacking the target.

METHOD

SUBJECTS

The subjects were 80 male undergraduates enrolled in a course in introductory psychology. Subjects participated to receive extra credit toward their final grade in the course. None of the subjects had participated in Experiment 1.

DESIGN AND PROCEDURE

The basic design was a 2×4 factorial with anger (anger, no anger) and films (neutral, erotic, positive outcome-aggressive erotic, negative outcome-aggressive erotic) treated as factors. Two undergraduate males served as experimenters and four undergraduate females served as confederates so that the possible target was always a woman. All subjects were randomly assigned to conditions.

The experimental procedure was identical to that of Experiment 1 except for the inclusion of the nonangered condition. Subjects in the non-angered groups received 1 mild intensity shock of .5-sec. duration rather than the 9 received by angered subjects. In addition, the written evaluation judged the subject's essay positively on the four 5-point rating scales.

DEBRIEFING FOLLOWUP

Two weeks to four months after the subjects participated in the present study, they were again contacted in their introductory psychology classes and asked to complete a questionnaire in order to determine what effects their participation in the study had on them. The questionnaire contained 7 items from the Burt (1980) Rape Myth Acceptance and Acceptance of Interpersonal Violence scales. The return rate was 77%.

EFFECTIVENESS OF MANIPULATIONS

Film ratings. All of the subjects responded to four questions regarding the film content after they saw the movie. In addition, subjects viewing the three erotic films answered additional questions concerning the victim in the film shown them. These results are presented in Table 2. A main effect for films was obtained on the questions of (1) interest, $F(3, 72) = 11.70$, p < .01, (2) sexual arousal, $F(3, 72) = 22.13$, p < .01, (3) aggressive content, $F(3, 72)$

Table 2

MEAN SELF-REPORT AND PHYSIOLOGICAL CHANGES TO
VARIOUS FILM CONDITIONS

(Experiment 2)

	FILM CONDITION			
RATINGS OF FILM	NEUTRAL	EROTIC	POSITIVE	NEGATIVE
INTERESTING	1.6_a	3.8_b	3.8_b	3.2_b
SEXUALLY AROUSING	1.6_a	4.7_b	3.7_c	3.7_c
AGGRESSIVE	1.2_a	1.8_a	4.3_b	6.2_c
SEXUAL CONTENT	1.3_a	6.4_b	5.9_{bc}	5.5_c
RATINGS OF VICTIM				
SUFFERING		1.7_a	3.0_b	5.7_c
ENJOYMENT NO ANGER		5.6_{ac}	5.9_{ac}	1.6_b
ANGER		6.5_a	4.9_c	3.2_d
RESPONSIBLE		5.6_a	4.3_b	2.3_c
MEAN BLOOD PRESSURE	-0.5_a	$+8.3_b$	$+10.7_b$	$+8.9_b$

Note. Means with a different subscript differ from each other at the .05 level by Duncan's procedure. Film ratings are on a 7 point scale.

$=95.38$, p ‹ .01, and (4) sexual content, $F(3, 72) = 77.15$, p ‹ .01. As can be seen in Table 2, all three erotic films were regarded as reliably more interesting, sexually arousing, and containing more sexual content than the neutral movie. Interestingly, the purely erotic film was rated as sexually more arousing than both aggressive erotic movies. On the perceived aggression measure the two aggressive erotic films were seen as more aggressive than the neutral or erotic stimuli, with the negative version viewed as more aggressive than the positive version.

Main effects for films were also obtained on the question of how much the woman in the film suffered, $F(2, 54) = 62.70$, p ‹ .01, and how responsible she was for what happened, $F(2, 54) = 19.53$, p ‹ .01. As Table 2 indicates, the woman in the negative outcome-aggressive erotic film was seen to suffer more, and be less responsible for what transpired than her counterpart in the positive outcome-condition. On the question of enjoyment there was a main effect for films, $F(2, 54) = 47.22$, p ‹ .01, as well as an Anger × Films interaction, $F(2, 54) = 5.64$, p ‹ .01. This interaction indicated that under both anger and nonanger conditions the woman in the negative condition was seen to enjoy the situation less than her positive counterpart for some reason. However, she was thought to have enjoyed the situation more when the subjects were angered. Along with the pretesting data and the results of Experiment 1, these data once again support the film manipulations effectiveness.

Essay evaluation and anger. An analysis of the ratings that subjects indicated they received from the confederate for their essay revealed a main effect for anger, $F(1, 72) = 327.63$, p $<$ .01, with the nonangered subjects reporting a reliably better rating (M = 4.42) than their angered counterparts (M = 1.45). Significant effects for anger were also obtained on the measures of how good/bad subjects felt, $F(1, 72) = 256.11$, p $<$ .01, and how angry they were, $F(1, 72) = 72.68$, p .01. Angered subjects reported feeling worse (M = 3.57 vs. M = 1.30, respectively) and more angry (M = 2.60 vs. M = 1.05, respectively) than their nonangered peers. Again, these data support the effectiveness of the anger manipulation.

PHYSIOLOGICAL AROUSAL

Mean blood pressure. A 2×4 ANOVA with anger and films as factors was conducted on the BP2 (after the anger manipulation) scores. This analysis yielded a main effect for anger, $F(1, 72) = 51.12$, p $<$ .01, with angered subjects showing a higher increase in arousal (M = 11.55) than nonangered subjects (M = 2.11).

An analysis of the BP3 (after film exposure) data revealed a main effect for films, $F(3, 72) = 11.36$, p $<$ .01, with the erotic and aggressive erotic films not differing in arousal, but significantly different (see Table 2) from the neutral film.

The analysis on BP4 (after aggression) did not reveal any significant sources of variation.

Systolic blood pressure. The analysis on systolic blood pressure revealed results identical to that of mean blood pressure and will, consequently, not be elaborated upon further.

Diastolic blood pressure. The analysis on diastolic blood pressure revealed results like those of mean and systolic blood pressure. Consequently, the results will not be discussed further.

AGGRESSIVE BEHAVIOR

A 2×4 ANOVA on the mean intensity of the shocks administered to the female confederate revealed significant effects for anger, $F(1, 72) = 28.26$, p $<$ .01; films, $F(3, 72) = 36.16$, p $<$ .01; and Anger × Films, $F(3, 72) = 4.76$, p $<$ .01. This interaction is presented in Figure 2.

The interaction indicates that for the angered subjects both the positive and negative outcome-aggressive erotic films increased aggression above that displayed in the neutral and purely erotic film conditions. The reliable

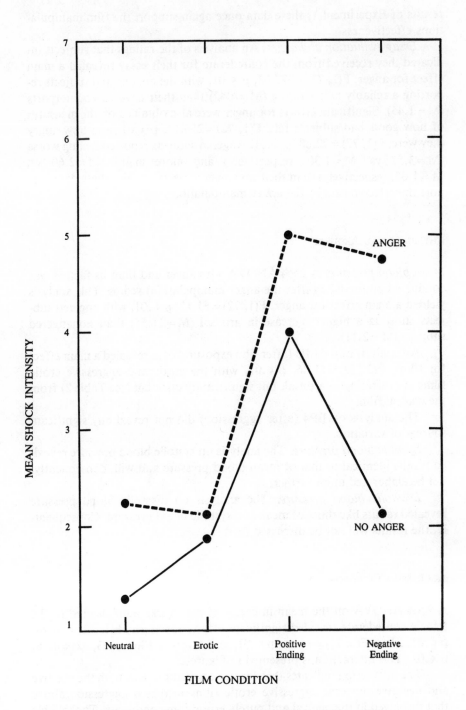

FIGURE 2. Mean shock intensity as a function of anger and film condition.

difference for these provoked men between the aggressive erotic subjects and the others (p < .05 by Duncan's test) confirms the results obtained when there was a female target in Experiment 1. Moreover, just as we had expected, under nonangered conditions only the positive outcome-aggressive erotic film resulted in significantly higher aggression than that shown in the neutral and purely erotic movie groups (p < .05 by Duncan's test). In sum, the viewers apparently had to be disposed to hurt someone before the movie victim's suffering could evoke heightened aggression from them.

REWARDING BEHAVIOR

The analysis on the number of points administered to the female confederate revealed a marginally significant effect for anger only, $F(1, 72) = 3.75$, p < .06, with angered subjects administering less (M = 5.51) points than their nonangered (M = 6.15) counterparts.

DEBRIEFING FOLLOWUP

For each of the 7 questions assessing the subjects' attitudes toward rape and

Table 3
MEAN RESPONSES TO THE RAPE MYTH ACCEPTANCE SCALE AND SIGNIFICANT
LEVELS FOR DEBRIEFED AND NONDEBRIEFED SUBJECTS.

1. One reason that women falsely report rape is that they frequently have a need to call attention to themselves
   A. Control 3.65   B. Debriefed 2.39   (p < .01)

2. In the majority of rapes, the victim is promiscuous or has a bad reputation
   A. Control 2.47   B. Debriefed 1.88   (p < .10)

3. If a woman engages in necking or petting and she lets things get out of hand, it is her own fault if her partner forces sex on her
   A. Control 4.00   B. Debriefed 2.70   (p < .01)

4. Women who get raped while hitching a ride get what they deserve
   A. Control 2.82   B. Debriefed 2.27   (NS)

5. Many women have an unconscious wish to be raped, and may then unconsciously set up a situation in which they are likely to be attacked
   A. Control 2.82   B. Debriefed 2.70   (NS)

6. What percentage of women who report a rape would you say are lying because they are angry and want to get back at the man they accuse
   A. Control 33%   B. Debriefed 13%   (p < .01)

7. Being roughed up is sexually stimulating to many women
   A. Control 3.88   B. Debriefed 2.55   (p < .01)

Note. Ratings were made on 7 point scales. Item 7 comes from the Acceptance of Interpersonal Violence scale. All p levels are by t tests. NS = not significant.

violence a *t* test was conducted comparing the scores of the debriefed and control subjects (the latter were shown only the neutral film). The means and questions are presented in Table 3.

Significant effects were obtained on questions 1, 3, 6, and 7, with a marginally significant (p < .10) effect for question 2. In all cases, the debriefed subjects indicated *less* acceptance of rape myths. For the remaining two questions (items 4 and 5) there was no difference between the two groups, although the means were again in the less accepting direction for the debriefed subjects. All in all, then, the debriefing had evidently sensitized the subjects so that they were now less inclined to go along with the standard myths regarding rape and rape victims.

GENERAL DISCUSSION

The results of the present two experiments have important theoretical as well as practical implications. For one thing, they can help us gain a greater understanding of the processes causing scenes of violence in the mass media to heighten the audience's aggressive inclinations. Consider the possible role of the excitement engendered by the movie. Some writers (e.g., Tannenbaum and Zillmann, 1975) have suggested that film violence leads to increased aggression primarily because of the movie's exciting nature; the viewers' film-produced arousal supposedly energizes their existing aggressive dispositions. Contrary to this contention, however, the condition differences in self-reported or measured arousal did not parallel the group differences in the intensity of the attacks on the available target. In Experiment 1, as an example, the purely erotic movie was just as arousing as the aggressive erotic films (according to both the subjects' ratings and their mean blood pressure), and yet the latter evoked stronger aggression toward the female confederate.

A variation on this "it is only the arousal" theme holds that the consequences of movie violence depend upon how the viewers label their own feelings after they see the film; they presumably would display aggression only if they thought they were angry (Konecni, 1975; Rule and Nesdale, 1976), and the violent film supposedly leads the observers to interpret their arousal in this manner (Zillmann, 1971). This analysis receives little support in our experiments. In both studies the film conditions did not differ in how angry the subjects believed they were even though there were group differences in attacks on the female target. From some discussions of "misattribution" or "excitation transfer" effects, we might have expected a film-produced mislabeling of feelings in the provoked men shown the purely erotic movie. They could have attributed the arousal engendered by the film to their previous insult so that they regarded themselves as highly angry and then behaved accordingly. But in actuality, this misattribution apparently did not occur. At any rate, there are no good indications that the condition differences in overt aggression follow similar differences in reported anger.

All this is not to say, of course, that the viewers' arousal level does not have any effect on the behavior they show after seeing the movie. Their general arousal probably interacts with the specific content of the film to influence their actions.

Yet another commonly held interpretation of movie violence emphasizes disinhibitory processes (although other kinds of processes are acknowledged as well) (e.g., Bandura, 1973). According to this view, the filmed scene reduces the observers' inhibitions against aggression so that they are more willing to attack the available target. In our estimation the relatively high level of aggression exhibited by the subjects in the positive outcome-aggressive erotica condition in both experiments is probably due to this kind of disinhibition, as we suggested earlier. The indication that the woman had enjoyed being raped implied that the assault on her had been worthwhile from the attackers' perspective, and this implication could have given the observers the idea that their own aggression would also pay off. However, while disinhibitory processes undoubtedly are important, they probably are not the only factors producing the media effects. In the realm of sexual behavior, Mann, Berkowitz, Sidman, Starr, and West (1974) demonstrated that married couples were more apt to make love after viewing erotic films than after seeing sexually neutral movies, apparently not because their restraints had been lowered but because they had been sexually stimulated. Berkowitz (1970) has suggested that a conceptually analogous process occurs in the case of aggressive scenes. Just as sexual stimuli can evoke sexual reactions, the sight of aggression can elicit transient, aggression-facilitating responses. These responses are usually only fairly weak and short-lived, but at times they can be translated into open behavior. Such an effect arose, we believe, in the subjects shown the aggressive erotic movies. The aggressive content in these films could have stimulated the viewers aggressively. Then energized by their high level of arousal, these reactions led to heightened attacks on the female target. Furthermore, as we had also discussed earlier, we also think that S-R associations had produced the greater level of aggression toward the female than the male target in Experiment 1. The woman confederate's sex-linked connection with the woman victim on the screen had apparently strengthened her aggressive cue value so that she drew stronger attacks from the angry men. And similarly, we also suggested that the woman victim's suffering in the negative outcome movie had stimulated the angry men to increased aggression because her pain was associated with prior reinforcements for aggression. All in all, our findings point to the multiplicity of processes that can determine the audience's reactions to events in the mass media. Arousal level, lowered inhibitions, the viewers' interpretations and understandings, and S-R associations as well, all play some part.

The findings reported here can also give us a greater insight into the effects of pornography on people in the audience. Most obviously, they indicate that the addition of aggression to the sex in pornographic materials is probably more dangerous (in terms of possibly aggressive consequences) than the display of pure erotica. As we noted earlier, this combination seems to be increasingly prevalent in pornographic material, and the aggressive content could stimulate aggressively disposed men with weak inhibitions to assault an available woman.

Another important factor has to do with the reactions of the woman in the sexual scene to the attack on her. A common theme in pornography is that women enjoy being victimized (e.g., Barry, 1979; Gager and Schurr, 1976). Results in both studies suggest that depictions consistent with this theme, that the woman has enjoyed the assault on her, can act to justify aggression and reduce the observers' general inhibitions against aggression (e.g., Malamuth, 1978).

Victim reactions also tended to affect responses other than the overt display of aggression. In both studies subjects exposed to the positive outcome-aggressive erotic film found the film less aggressive and the victim more responsible for her plight than those subjects who were exposed to the negative version. The finding regarding perceived aggression in the film seems to support the results obtained by other researchers (e.g., Malamuth and Check, in press, a) who have found that exposure to sexual violence reduces the audience's sensitivity to rape. The results for responsibility would also have important implications. At least in the present study, a positive reaction on the part of the rape victim, independent of the events which have occurred previously, makes the victim more responsible for her actions. This "shifting" of responsibility to the victim might be one factor which accounts for the increased calloused attitudes toward rape and the self-reported willingness to commit rape observed in subjects who have been exposed to aggressive erotica (e.g., Malamuth and Check, in press, a). This change in responsibility might also effect judicial decisions in rape cases. It would seem important, then, for future research to examine more closely the reasons and implications for this apparent change in attribution.

One question which could be raised at this point is whether the type of aggression measured in the present experiments is in any way related to rape or other forms of sexual aggression directed against women. Recent research by Malamuth (in Malamuth and Donnerstein, in press) has assessed the validity of the measure used in the present studies as they relate to "real" world sexually-linked aggression against women. Malamuth found that the present type of aggression was significantly related to a self-reported "desire to hurt" a particular woman and also to an attitude and emotion which taps the subjects' proclivity to rape. As suggested by Malamuth, these findings seem to attest to the construct validity of the measures employed in laboratory studies of aggression against women.

Another interesting aspect of the present research is the results obtained with the debriefing manipulation. Some critics have recently questioned the ethicality of research which exposes subjects to rape depictions (e.g., Sherif, 1980). These concerns seem legitimate and were, in fact, the basis for the debriefing followup in Experiment 2. The results of this followup, however, strongly suggest that a proper debriefing can have quite beneficial effects. As we have seen, subjects who viewed aggressive erotica and were debriefed revealed *less* acceptance of the standard rape myths. A very similar finding has recently been obtained by Malamuth and Check (1981). The results of the present study and that of Malamuth and Check (1981) point to the possibility of future research which is directed at reducing the acceptance of rape myths, an attitude which has been shown to be related to many asocial behaviors (e.g., Burt, 1980; Malamuth and Check, in press, b).

NOTES

*This research was supported by Grant MH 07788-02 from the National Institute of Mental Health to the first author.

1. These instructions, indicating that the shocks would not help the other subjects' learning, were used to reduce the possibility that subjects administered higher shocks out of a desire to help the victim (e.g., Baron, 1977).

2. One possible explanation for this high level of aggression in the neutral film group is that subjects in the present study tended to be angrier than subjects in the previous study. An examination of the self-reported anger scores for subjects paired with a male target in the present study and the earlier Donnerstein (1980b) study revealed anger ratings of 2.7 and 2.0, respectively, with 3.2 generally being the highest score given on this scale. While it is not possible without additional data to explain this apparent increase in anger, the greater apparent anger in the neutral film group could account for the higher level of aggression in this condition.

Neil M. Malamuth and James V. P. Check

Penile Tumescence and Perceptual Responses to Rape as a Function of Victim's Perceived Reactions

The present experiment is part of a series of studies focusing on college students' responses to rape stimuli.[1] The impetus for this research program comes from two important areas of theorizing and research. The first is the work of Gene Abel and his colleagues on developing objective assessment techniques for use in the treatment of rapists. The second area is the writings of feminists on the subject of sexual violence.

Abel, Barlow, Blanchard, and Guild (1977) report clear differences between the sexual responsiveness of rapists and non-rapists to portrayals of sexual assault. Whereas rapists in their sample evidenced high levels of penile tumescence to audio-taped portrayals of both rape and consenting sexual acts, the non-rapist comparison group showed substantial sexual arousal to the mutually-consenting depictions only. These investigators therefore suggest that sexual responsiveness to the depiction of sexual violence relative to sexual arousal to consenting themes serves as a measure of the "proclivity to rape" that can be used in the diagnosis and treatment of rapists. (See also Abel, Blanchard, and Becker, 1976; 1978). The question of what is or is not sexually arousing to "normals" is therefore not

Reprinted from the *Journal of Applied Social Psychology*, Vol. 10, No. 6 (1981), pp. 528–547. Reprinted by permission of V. H. Winston and Sons and Neil M. Malamuth.

257

only of theoretical interest but has important implications for the type of "rape proclivity" measure developed by Abel et al. (1977). This type of measure has recently been extended to the identification and treatment of pedophiles (Abel, Becker, Murphy, and Flanagan).

Both the rapist and non-rapist samples studied by Abel and his colleagues were male patients referred for evaluation of their deviant sexual arousal. A recent study by Barbaree, Marshall, and Lanthier (1979), however, successfully replicated Abel et al. (1977) findings using college students as the non-rapist sample. These studies thus suggest that the portrayal of rape is not sexually arousing to non-deviants.

Such a conclusion appears incongruous with content analyses revealing that a great deal of "hard core" pornography (McConahay and McConahay, 1973; Smith, 1976) and to an increasing degree "soft core" erotica (Malamuth and Spinner, 1980; *Time*, 1976; 1977) incorporate violent themes. It seems likely that publishers' decision to include violent pornography is to some degree a reflection of buyers' interests. It may well be, therefore, that certain dimensions distinguish the type of sexual violence found in commercially available erotica from that used in the research studies cited above. Consistent with this possibility are the data reported by Schmidt (1975) and by Farkas (1979). Schmidt found that both male and female students were highly aroused by a pornographic film depicting rape. Unfortunately, this investigator's description of the rape stimulus is not sufficiently detailed to pinpoint how it may have differed from the stimuli used by Abel et al. (1977). Farkas found that rape stimuli tended to elicit non-significantly greater sexual arousal (as measured by penile tumescence) than non-rape stimuli in subjects from the university community. Farkas' stimuli differ from those of Abel et al. along several dimensions. Any one or combination of these dimensions may account for the conflicting findings.

Malamuth, Heim, and Feshbach (1980) recently attempted to pinpoint the basis for such conflicting data by systematically varying the content of written portrayals of rape along several dimensions. They found that only manipulation of the victim's reactions significantly affected self-reported sexual arousal: Male and female college students reported relatively high levels of sexual arousal to a rape depiction when the victim was depicted as involuntarily experiencing sexual arousal (as is typically the portrayal in pornography) as compared to when the victim responded with nausea. The stimuli used by Abel et al. (1977) and Farkas (1979) do indeed differ along the dimension of victim arousal: Abel et al. employed stimuli that stressed the victim's abhorrence whereas Farkas' rape depictions were judged by raters to be extremely sexually arousing to the female victim. In the experiment by Malamuth et al. (1980, b), however, a non-rape portrayal was not included. The first purpose of the present experiment was to extend Malamuth et al. findings by using a penile tumescence measure of sexual arousal and by including both rape and non-rape depictions within the same experiment.

A second interrelated issue addressed concerns the effects of sexually violent stimuli that portray rape in a "positive" or negative light on subsequent reactions to rape. Feminist writers have forcefully contended that pornographic depictions that portray sexual violence in "positive" terms (e.g., resulting in victim arousal) constitute "hate literature" against women that have antisocial effects (Brownmiller, 1975; Gager and Schurr, 1976; Kostach, 1978).

These assertions seem inconsistent with the research of the President's Commission on Pornography (1970) which concluded that there was no evidence of adverse effects of pornography. However, specific hypotheses regarding the effects of sexual violence were not adequately tested by the Commission, for it did not clearly distinguish between materials that merely depicted explicit sexual content from those involving violent and/or coercive-exploitative portrayals of sexual relationships. In fact, materials of the latter type were generally not employed in the Commission's studies. There were a few studies that included extreme sadomasochistic materials (e.g., Mann, Sidman, and Starr, 1971) but not the type of violence that is common in today's pornography and elsewhere.

A recent study by Malamuth, Haber, and Feshbach (1980) yielded some suggestive data consistent with the feminist position. Subjects were exposed to either a "mild" sadomasochistic or a non-violent version of the same sexual passage and then all subjects were exposed to a portrayal of rape. Some nonsignificant trends were noted suggesting that the exposure to the sadomasochistic portrayal in which the violence inflicted on the woman was, to her own surprise, sexually arousing may have affected males' sexual responsiveness to rape. Moreover, it was found that self-reported sexual arousal to sexual violence (both as portrayed in the sadomasochistic version and the rape) but not arousal to sexual non-violence was correlated with a self-reported likelihood of engaging in rape. This self-reported proclivity to rape was in turn associated with a generally callous attitude toward rape and rape victims. The present study was also intended to extend these data by examining the impact of exposure to relatively "favorable" (i.e., resulting in victim's sexual arousal) vs. unfavorable (i.e., resulting in victim's abhorrence) rape depictions on subsequent sexual responsiveness to and perceptions of rape.

METHOD

SUBJECTS

One hundred nine male Introductory Psychology students at the University of Manitoba signed up for an experiment described as investigating the use of physiological measures of sexual arousal. Subjects were given experimental credit for arriving at the laboratory, irrespective of whether or not they chose to actually participate in the experiment. Thirty-four subjects decided not to participate after being given a complete description of the measures to be used. An analysis of the number of subjects who decided not to participate indicated no significant difference as a function of sex of experimenter. The remaining 75 subjects were randomly assigned to the various experimental conditions.

OVERVIEW OF THE EXPERIMENT

In Phase 1, subjects were exposed to one of three audio-taped versions of a passage and their arousal assessed. Group A listened to a rape story in which the rapist perceives that the victim becomes sexually aroused.[2] Group B heard a rape in which the victim continuously abhors the assault. Group C heard a mutually-desired intercourse story.

In Phase 2, all of these three groups listened to the same "rape-criterion" story in order to determine the effects of the prior exposures on subsequent responses to rape.

About half of the subjects in each group had a male experimenter for both phases and half had a female experimenter for both phases. The dependent measures consisted of sexual arousal (penile tumescence and self-reported) in each phase and perceptions of the rape in the rape-criterion story, assessed by means of a questionnaire.

MATERIALS

Stories. Four stories were constructed and presented via an audio tape recorder. Except for the rape-criterion story, the depictions were directly based on those used by Abel et al. (1977). They were recorded by a male speaker.

Rape Arousal Story. The rape-arousal story was a rape story, told from the perspective of the rapist. This story was of about equal length and very similar in content to the rape-abhorrence depiction described below, *except* that the rapist perceived that the victim became sexually aroused. The following portion illustrates the arousal aspect of the passage content:

> You're holding her down, forcing yourself on her and you can tell she likes it. She's telling you to stop, to please stop. You can tell she's getting excited now. She's really aroused. She's pleading with you and it's no use. You just hold her down screwing her and fucking her. You've got her just where you want her.

Rape-Abhorrence Story. The rape abhorrence story was virtually identical to that reported by Abel et al. (1977). It depicted a victim that continuously abhors the assault. The following is an illustration of the story's content:

> . . . and she's fighting you. You slap her a little. You tell her to quieten down, to remain still. She's starting to scream now and cry. You slap her and you tell her to be quiet, and you take her hand and you muffle her voice there. You're holding her down, you've got her pinned down there, just forcing yourself on her.

Mutually-Desired Intercourse. The mutually-desired intercourse depiction was a somewhat shorter version of the non-violent story employed by Abel et al. (1977) in which both partners are portrayed as obviously desiring and enjoying the experience. The two rape stories were just slightly over 2 minutes duration, whereas the mutually-desired depiction was 1 minute and 33 seconds.

Rape-Criterion. The rape-criterion story was that used by Malamuth et al. (1980, a). The story was of a male student raping a female student in an alley, and was in the third person. This story was 3 minutes and 38 seconds in duration.

VALIDATION STUDY

To validate the intended manipulation of the audio tapes, 81 male and female introductory psychology students fulfilling part of a course requirement were randomly distributed one of the four stories (Rape-Arousal, Rape-Abhorrence, Mutually-Desired, and Rape-Criterion) in written format. They were asked to indicate their judgments concerning their own perceptions of the woman's willingness and how much pleasure, if any, she derived from the act. Raters were also requested to indicate their judgments of the perceptions of the man depicted in the story.

Perceptions of the Woman's Pleasure. The two items measuring perceptions of the woman's pleasure were each subjected to a one-way ANOVA with the four stories as levels of the independent variable. These analyses yielded a significant effect for raters' own perceptions of the woman's pleasure, $F(3,77) = 67.56$, $p < .001$, and judgments of the man's perceptions of the woman's pleasure, $F(3,77) = 15.41$, $p < .001$. Mean ratings on these two items for the four stories appear in rows 1 and 2 of Table 1. These data indicate that as expected, the rape-arousal as well as the mutually-desired intercourse were associated with greater perceived woman's pleasure than the victim-abhorrence and rape-criterion stories.

Table 1

PERCEPTIONS OF THE WOMAN'S PLEASURE AND WILLINGNESS AS A
FUNCTION OF DEPICTION

	DEPICTION			
	Rape-Arousal	Rape-Abhorrence	Mutually-Desired	Rape-Criterion
	$(n=21)$	$(n=20)$	$(n=20)$	$(n=20)$
ITEMS RATED				
Woman's Pleasure				
Rater's Perceptions	3.14_b	1.80_a	7.60_c	1.85_a
Man's Judged Perception	7.81_b	4.70_a	8.45_b	5.45_a
Woman's Willingness				
Rater's Perceptions	3.00_a	2.35_a	9.35_b	2.75_a
Man's Judged Perception	7.71_b	4.55_a	9.55_c	6.40_b

Note: Higher numbers indicate greater pleasure/willingness. Degree of pleasure was rated on scales ranging from 1 (no pleasure) to 10 (complete pleasure). Willingness was rated on a scale from 1 (completely willing) to 9 (completely unwilling). (For consistency, the willingness scale has been reversed). Within each row, means with common subscripts do not differ from each other at the .05 level using the Newman-Keuls procedure.

This was true for judgments of both rater-perceived woman's pleasure and the man's perception of the woman's pleasure.

Perceptions of the Woman's Willingness. Analysis of the two woman's willingness items yielded a significant effect for rater's ratings of their own perceptions of the woman's willingness, $F(3.77) = 70.76$, $p < .001$, and raters' judgments of the man's perception of the woman's willingness, $F(3,77) = 16.09$, $p < .001$. Mean ratings of the woman's willingness from both the raters' perspective and the man's perspective for each of the four stories can be found in rows 3 and 4 of Table 1. As expected, the woman was generally rated as less willing in the three rape depictions than in the mutually-desired intercourse depiction.

In summary, the results of the validation study suggest that that the victim was effectively portrayed as unwilling in the three rape depictions and that the woman was effectively portrayed as experiencing pleasure in the rape-arousal and mutually-desired intercourse depictions.

ASSESSMENT INSTRUMENTS

Penile Tumescence. Penile tumescence was monitored by the use of a mercury-in-rubber strain gauge (Parks Electronics Laboratory, Beaverton, Oregon), a device recommended in recent analyses of differing measuring instruments (Laws, 1977; Rosen and Keffe, 1978). Changes in resistance of the gauge as a function of changes in penile diameter were amplified through a Wheatstone Bridge and recorded using a Fisher Recordall Series 5000 Chart Recorder (Fisher Instruments, Winnipeg, Manitoba, Canada). The strain gauge was sterilized by both a two-hour exposure to ultra-violet light and cleansing with an alcohol solution. Penile tumescence to a story was computed on the basis of the maximum positive deflection from baseline, measured just prior to the story's beginning. A comparison between this approach and that of computing the area under the curve has shown that the two procedures yield very similar results (Abel, Blanchard, Murphy, Becker, and Djenderdjian, in press).

Self-Reported Arousal. After each erotic phase, subjects were asked to indicate how sexually erotic they felt. They were asked to indicate their responses on an eleven-point scale ranging from 0 percent (not sexually erotic) to 100 percent (extremely erotic).

Rape Questionnaire. After the second phase exposure, subjects filled out a sixteen-item questionnaire asking their perceptions of the rape-criterion story. This questionnaire was similar to that employed by Malamuth et al. (1980, a). On the basis of factor analysis data described in detail in the Results section, the questionnaire items were classified in five factors reflecting perceptions of the *Victim's Experience*, the *Normality of Rape*, the *Criminal* aspect of rape, the *Victim* herself, and the *Rapist*.

PROCEDURE

Subjects were run individually. The experimenter signed the subject's experimental credit card as soon as the subject arrived at the laboratory. The subject was then escorted to a soundproof room, handed a set of written instructions, and left alone. The instructions indicated that the subject's responses were anonymous and that he was free to leave at any time during the experiment without loss of credit and without any notice to the experimenter. If the subject chose to remain, he then closed the door, signed or initialled a consent to participate form, placed the strain gauge on his penis, did his trousers back up, and turned on the tape recorder.

The instructions on the tape indicated that there would be stories interspersed with music, and that the subject was to imagine the events described in the stories but not to fantasize sexually during the musical interludes. After the initial instructions there was a two-minute musical interlude and then the first erotic passage (Phase 1). At the end of the first passage the voice on the tape asked the subject to indicate on the scale provided how sexually erotic he found the story. A 10-minute musical interlude followed (during which all subjects returned to baseline levels of arousal) and then the rape-criterion story was presented followed by instructions to rate how erotic the passage was (Phase 2). A third phase followed in which subjects were instructed to reach 100 percent arousal without touching the penis. This procedure was intended to enable the transformation of the physiological arousal scores to a percentage of maximum arousal. Following the 100 percent erection phase, the subject removed the strain gauge and notified the experimenter by intercom that he was finished. At this point, he was told to go to a corner of the room and fill out questionnaires in separate envelopes on the shelf.[3] After filling out the questionnaires, the subject buzzed the experimenter again, was brought a debriefing sheet and personally thanked for his participation. The debriefing sheet cautioned the subject that the rape passages were pure fiction and pointed out that rape was in fact a terrible crime abhorred by women and a serious criminal offense.

RESULTS

EFFECTS OF OUTCOME ON INITIAL AROUSAL

Penile Tumescence. A 3 (story) × 2 (sex of experimenter) ANOVA was calculated on the penile tumescence scores. This analysis yielded a significant main effect for story, F (2,65) = 4.97, $p < .01$, but no sex of experimenter effect nor interaction effect. Mean levels of arousal for each story are presented in Figure 1. Follow-up simple effects tests on these means using the Newman-Keuls procedure with a significance criterion of $p < .05$, revealed that as predicted, the rape-arousal story generated significantly more arousal than the rape-abhorrence story. There were no other significant paired comparisons.

Self-Reported Arousal. Self-reported arousal to the first erotic presentation correlated r(69)[4] = 0.54, $p < .001$ with penile tumescence. This correlation is similar to those found in previous research (e.g., Heiman, 1977). The ANOVA yielded no significant effects, although the mean differences were in the same direction as those of the penile tumescence measure (e.g., 28.6 percent for the rape-arousal vs. 20.4 percent for the rape-abhorrence).

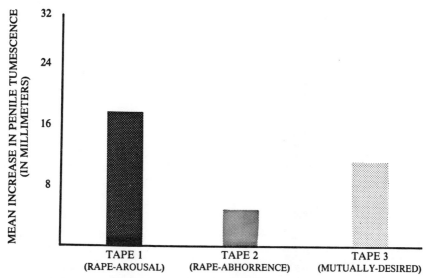

Note: The mutually-desired depiction was somewhat shorter than the rape portrayals. When length is controlled for by calculating arousal for all subjects at the same point (i.e., at a duration equivalent to the mutually-desired story) the means for the rape-arousal, rape-abhorrence, and mutually-desired portrayals are 12.79, 5.20, and 10.07, respectively.

FIGURE 1. Penile Tumescence (Measured as Deflection from Baseline) as a Function of Story.

EFFECTS OF PRIOR EXPOSURE ON SUBSEQUENT AROUSAL TO RAPE

To reiterate, the second erotic presentation was the rape-criterion story for all groups so as to assess the effects of prior exposure on subsequent sexual arousal to rape and perceptions of rape.

Penile Tumescence. A 3 (prior exposure) × 2 (sex of experimenter) ANOVA calculated on penile tumescence to the rape-criterion story (Phase 2) yielded a significant effect for prior exposure, $F(2,63) = 4.46$, $p < .02$, and an effect for sex of experimenter, $F(1,63) = 6.67$, $p < .02$, but no interaction effect. The means for each condition are presented in Figure 2. As predicted, subjects who were previously exposed to the rape-arousal outcome depiction were subsequently more aroused to the rape-criterion story than subjects who listened to the rape-abhorrence story prior to exposure to the rape-criterion. This difference was statistically significant using the Newman-Keuls procedure with a criterion of $p < .05$. However, subjects who had first heard the mutually-desired intercourse story were also subsequently highly aroused to the rape-criterion story, significantly higher than those who listened to the rape-abhorrence story prior to hearing the rape-criterion story. The sex experimenter effect occurred as a result of subjects being more aroused if the experimenter was male than if the experimenter was female (means 26.59 and 16.28, respectively).

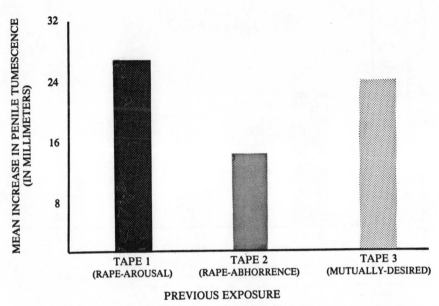

FIGURE 2. Penile Tumescence (Measured as Deflection from Baseline) in Response to Rape-Criterion as a Function of Previous Exposure.

Self-Reported Arousal. Self-reported arousal to the second erotic presentation correlated r (67) = 0.31, $p < .01$ with penile tumescence. The ANOVA yielded no significant effects, although the means were again in the same direction as the penile tumescence means (e.g., 48.6 percent for rape-arousal vs. 39.6 percent for rape-abhorrence).

100% AROUSAL PHASE

A large percentage of subjects indicated in their self-reports that they did not reach 100 percent erection during the third phase of the experiment, in which they were instructed to reach as high a level as possible without external physical stimulation. Consequently it was not feasible to translate the physiological arousal scores from Phases 1 and 2 into percentage of full erection scores. Self-reports of arousal during this phase indicated that subjects reached an average of 65 percent full erection. In order to determine whether there was any generalized effect as a function of earlier exposure, levels of arousal during this phase were analyzed. ANOVAS calculated for both penile tumescence scores and self-reported arousal yielded no effects, with the means being virtually identical in all of the conditions.

QUESTIONNAIRE DATA

The 16 questionnaire items were factor analyzed by means of a principal components factor analysis followed by varimax rotation. Table 2 presents the item loadings for the five factors which were extracted using a minimum eigen-value of 1.0 as the criterion for extraction. The first three factors had multiple questionnaire items, whereas the remaining two factors had only one item each. These five factors accounted for 64 percent of the total variance of the original 16 questionnaire items.

Table 2
VARIMAX ROTATED FACTOR LOADINGS FOR THE QUESTIONNAIRE ITEMS

	FACTORS				
Questionnaire Item	I "Normality" of Rape	II Victim's Experience	III Criminal Aspect	IV Victim	V Rapist
Would you rape if not caught?	.809[1]	.141	.009	−.024	.118
% of women who would derive pleasure	.791[1]	−.207	−.034	−.126	−.047
% of men who would rape	.790[1]	−.193	−.031	.047	−.278
Would you rape?	.660[1]	−.286	−.224	.009	.353
Identify with rapist	.530[1]	−.112	−.048	−.369	.249
Woman shares responsibility	.404[1]	−.153	−.106	−.390	−.367
Woman's Pain	.084	.877[2]	−.081	.010	−.134
Woman's Trauma	−.131	.724[2]	.315	−.227	.170
Woman's Resistance	−.053	.578[2]	.066	.334	.124
Woman's Pleasure	.477	−.554[2]	−.252	−.232	.213
Man's danger to society	−.204	.152	.758[3]	−.110	−.118
Recommended sentence	.098	−.076	.740[3]	−.033	−.125
Should have gone to police	−.106	.241	.533[3]	.439	−.081
Woman's Unwillingness	−.120	.197	.497[3]	.424	.283
Woman's attractiveness	−.043	−.044	−.087	.795[4]	.016
Rapist's Intelligence	.116	−.052	−.211	.022	.843[5]

[1]Factor I items
[2]Factor II items
[3]Factor III items
[4]Factor IV items
[5]Factor V item

The three sets of items corresponding to the three multiple-item factors were each analyzed by a multivariate analysis of variance (MANOVA). For each of the three multi-item factors, a 3 (prior exposure) × 2 (sex of experimenter) MANOVA was performed. A significant multivariate effect was obtained as a function of the exposure variable on the four items in the perceptions of the *Victim's Experience* factor (Factor 2, Table 2), Multivariate $F (8,132) = 2.45$, $p < .02$. Univariate effects tests in this item set indicated a significant F value only on the item assessing perceptions of the woman's trauma, $F (2,69) = 6.33$, $p < .004$. Follow-up analyses using the Newman-Keuls procedure revealed that subjects who first listened to the rape-arousal story rated the woman as experiencing less trauma in the rape-criterion story ($\bar{x} = 3.00$) than subjects who had heard the rape-abhorrence story ($\bar{x} = 3.96$) or those who had listened to the mutually-desired intercourse prior to hearing the rape-criterion story ($\bar{x} = 3.83$).

There were no other significant multivariate effects for the questionnaire data or univariate effects for the two single item factors. There was, however, a significant univariate effect as a function of the exposure variable on the item which asked subjects what percentage of men they thought might engage in rape, $F (2,69) = 3.34$, $p < .05$. Examination of the means indicated that subjects who had first listened to the rape-arousal passage followed by the rape-criterion story believed that a greater percentage of men ($\bar{x} = 10.79$) would rape than subjects who had first listened to the rape-abhorrence story ($\bar{x} = 8.25$) or the mutually-desired story ($\bar{x} = 6.83$) prior to hearing the rape-criterion depiction. (Note that the rating scale on this item ranged from one to twenty with ten representing 45–50 percent.) Follow-up analyses with the Newman-Keuls procedure indicated that the difference between subjects who had first heard the rape-arousal depiction and those who had first listened to the mutually-desired intercourse was the only effect that reached statistical significance.

SELF-REPORTED PROCLIVITY TO RAPE

Correlations with Questionnaire Items. Of the 75 subjects who responded to the rape proclivity questions (1 = not at all likely, 5 = very likely) 17 percent indicated a 2 or above in response to whether they personally would be likely to act as the rapist did in the same circumstances. Sixty-nine percent similarly responded when questioned about their behavior if they could be assured of not being punished. Furthermore, 37 percent chose the middle of the scale (3) or above in response to the latter question. Since these two items correlated highly, $\underline{r} (73) = .63$, $p < .001$, only the correlations for the "not caught" item with the other questionnaire items are presented in Table 3. Consistent with the results of Malamuth et al. (in press, a), the correlational pattern shows that this self-report was associated with a generally

Table 3
CORRELATIONS BETWEEN SELF-REPORTED PROCLIVITY TO RAPE
AND QUESTIONNAIRE ITEMS (n = 75)

QUESTIONNAIRE ITEM	CORRELATION WITH RAPE PROCLIVITY
Identification with Rapist	.39**
Woman Shares Responsibility	.31*
Woman Derived Pleasure from the Rape	.32*
Other Men Would Rape if Not Punished	.44**
Women Would Enjoy Victimization	.44**

* $p < .01$
** $p < .005$

callous attitude about rape that is similar to the reported attitudes of many convicted rapists (Clark and Lewis, 1977; Gager and Schurr, 1976).

Stepwise multiple correlations were computed to ascertain which combination of attitudes, taking into consideration correlations among items, would best predict self-reported proclivity to rape. In conducting this analysis, only variables entering the regression equation at a significant level ($p < .05$) are reported. The resulting multiple correlation was significant R $(2,100) = .49$, $p < .011$. The two items retained in the regression equation collectively accounted for 24 percent of the variance. These items were the belief that women in general would derive pleasure from being raped (accounting for 19 percent of the variance) and the extent to which the subject identified with the rapist (accounting for the other 5 percent of the variance).

It is interesting that not only did the manipulation of victim arousal in Phase 1 affect sexual arousal to rape, but also that self-reported proclivity to rape correlated with the two items assessing subjects' beliefs concerning whether women enjoy being raped. In order to further explore this interrelationship between rape and perceived victim pleasure, an analysis was performed to determine whether there was a correlation between sexual arousal to the rape-criterion story (a depiction which in no manner implied victim arousal) and the two "pleasure" items. This analysis yielded a significant correlation between the belief that, in general, women would derive pleasure from rape for both penile tumescence, $r (67) = 0.25$, $p < .02$, one-tailed, as well as self-reported arousal, $r (73) = 0.24$, $p < .02$, one-tailed. With respect to the perception of the woman's pleasure in the rape-criterion depiction, the correlations were in the same direction, but only significant for self-reported arousal, $r (73) = 0.34$, $p < .002$, one-tailed.

Proclivity and Sexual Arousal. Malamuth et al. (1980, a) found that self-reported proclivity to rape correlated with sexual arousal to sexual violence rather than sexual responsiveness *per se.* In the present investigation, subjects also listened to both violent and nonviolent passages. For purposes of comparison, self-reported proclivity was correlated with self-reported arousal separately for each type of story. The correlations are presented in Table 4.

Table 4
CORRELATIONS BETWEEN SELF-REPORTED AROUSAL AND
SELF-REPORTED PROCLIVITY TO RAPE

	GROUP		
	A (Rape-Arousal)	*B* (Rape-Abhorrence)	*C* (Mutually-Desired)
PHASE 1 STORIES			
ʳarousal, proclivity	− .16	.35*	.07
PHASE 2 STORIES		Rape Criterion	
ʳarousal, proclivity	.42*	.42*	− .16

* *p* ᐸ .05, one-tailed

As can be seen from the table, in Phase 1 self-reported proclivity correlated with arousal to the rape-abhorrence story, but not with arousal to the mutually-desired intercourse depiction nor to the rape-arousal depiction. In Phase 2, the correlations with the rape-criterion were generally significant, except for subjects who had earlier heard the mutually-desired depiction. The correlation between self-reported proclivity to rape and self-reported arousal to the. rape-criterion story collapsed across all three groups was $\underline{r}$ (73) = 0.26, p ᐸ .02, one-tailed. Correlations between penile tumescence and self-reported proclivity to rape were generally in the same direction as for self-reported sexual arousal but did not reach acceptable significance levels.

These data suggest that not only is self-reported proclivity to rape associated with a callous attitude towards rape, it also correlates with self-reported arousal to sexual violence rather than sexual responsiveness *per se.*

DISCUSSION

Sexual Responsiveness

With respect to the first issue addressed in this study, the sexual responsiveness of "normals" to rape depictions, the results very clearly extended the earlier findings of Malamuth et al. (1980, b). As indicated by the penile tumescence data, subjects were considerably more sexually aroused to a rape depiction in which the victim was perceived by the rapist to become involuntarily sexually aroused than when she continuously abhorred the assault. These data may thus explain the conflicting findings described earlier concerning non-deviants' arousal to sexual violence.

Additional data obtained in the present study point to the importance of the belief in victim pleasure. Correlational data indicated that those subjects who were inclined to perceive victim pleasure in the rape-criterion depiction, a portrayal which gave no indication of such pleasure, were more inclined to report sexual arousal to this rape depiction and to report that they would rape if they could be assured of not being caught. Similarly, men who were more inclined to believe that women in general would enjoy being victimized were more sexually aroused to the rape-criterion portrayal (as indicated by penile tumescence and self-reports) and reported a greater likelihood of raping. These data are of particular interest in light of reports by several investigators that many rapists believe that their victims derived pleasure from being assaulted regardless of how brutalized or traumatized the victim actually was (Gager and Schurr, 1976; Clark and Lewis, 1977).

While the present data do not enable a selection among the varied possible explanations outlined by Malamuth et al. (1980, b) for the effect of perceived victim pleasure, the data obtained in the validation study reported herein are inconsistent with one of these explanations. The possibility that subjects re-interpret the events so that in the context of victim pleasure the assault is not perceived as coercive in nature is contradicted by ratings of the woman's willingness: Raters did not indicate any significant difference in their own perceptions of how willing the victim was in the rape-arousal as compared with the rape-abhorrence depictions, although they did believe that the rapist in the story would be more inclined to believe that the woman was willing if she was perceived as sexually aroused.

Effects of Exposure

Sexual Arousal. The data bearing upon the second issue addressed, the effects of exposure to sexual violence on subsequent responses to rape, formed a somewhat complex pattern. While consistent differences on both the sexual arousal and questionnaire data were found between those earlier exposed to the rape-arousal and rape-abhorrence portrayals, comparison with the control condition revealed somewhat different effects on these dependent measures.

The sexual arousal data suggest that those first exposed to the rape-abhorrence depiction were inhibited in their sexual responsiveness to the rape-criterion portrayal as compared to subjects first exposed to the rape-arousal depiction or to the mutually-desired depiction. These data are in keeping with the finding that the sexual responsiveness of non-deviants may be particularly sensitive to inhibitory cues (Barbaree, et al., 1979). This inhibition effect may be labeled an "educational impact" in that exposure to a depiction stressing the true horror of a rape victim's experience lessened subjects' sexual arousal to a subsequent pornographic rape portrayal. The fact that during the 100 percent arousal phase no differences were found among the various exposure conditions suggests that a generalized inhibitory effect did not occur, but that the effects of exposure to the rape-abhorrence depiction were specific to rape portrayals.

Sexual responsiveness to the rape-criterion depiction was not found to significantly differ between those earlier exposed to the rape-arousal as compared to the mutually-desired portrayal. These data thus fail to show an enhancement effect on arousal as a function of exposure to "favorable" depictions of sexual violence as reported in a nonsignificant trend by Malamuth et al. (1980a). However, the fact that sexual arousal to the rape-criterion for those first exposed to the mutually-desired portrayal was very high for a brief audio-tape presentation seriously limited the opportunity of finding such an enhancement effect. Future research employing a similar design should utilize a rape portrayal (in Phase 2) that generates relatively low levels of sexual arousal to assess the possibility that exposures to sexual violence that portray rape in a "positive" manner may have undesirable effects on sexual responsivity.

Perceptions of Rape. On rape perceptions, significant differences were found between those earlier exposed to the rape-arousal as compared to both the rape-abhorrence and the mutually-desired portrayals. Since the degree of sexual arousal generated in the first phase was comparable in the rape-arousal and mutually-desired depictions (and since a delay was interposed between the two phases in which arousal was found to dissipate completely), arousal *per se* could not account for the perceptual effects obtained in phase two. Differences in perception occurred in multivariate analyses on the set of items assessing perceptions of the rape victim's experience. This finding is expected since it was the perceived victim reaction that was manipulated in the stories used in Phase 1. Within this set of items, univariate analyses revealed a significant effect for the item measuring perceptions of victim trauma: Those earlier exposed to the rape-arousal portrayal perceived little victim trauma in the rape-criterion depiction relative to those earlier exposed to the rape-abhorrence or the mutually-desired depictions. This finding supports assertions regarding the antisocial impact of exposure to materials that portray rape in a relatively "positive" manner, causing and/or perpetuating undesirable myths. It is consistent with other recent data indicating that exposure to violent pornography may stimulate rape fantasies (Malamuth, in press) and increase behavioral aggression (as measured by the administration of electric shock) in comparison with neutral, sexual, or aggressive stimuli (Donnerstein, 1980; Malamuth, 1978).

An additional cognitive-perceptual difference reflecting an antisocial effect was found on a univariate analysis of the item assessing beliefs regarding the percentage of men who would rape if they could be assured of not being caught. Those first exposed to the rape-arousal portrayal believed that a higher percentage of men would rape than subjects in the other two conditions, although the difference between the rape-arousal and rape-abhorrence conditions did not reach acceptable statistical significance. To the extent that subjects first exposed to the rape-arousal perceived less victim trauma in the rape-criterion depiction, it is understandable that they would expect other men to be relatively likely to commit such a violent act.

Taken as a whole, the data suggest that exposure to depictions that portray rape in a relatively "favorable" or unfavorable manner may affect subsequent responses to acts of sexual violence. The fact that the type of effect observed differed for the two dependent measures highlights the need to examine exposure effects on multiple measures, each of which may be relatively more sensitive to certain manipulations.

Possibility of Raping. Self-reported possibility of engaging in rape was found to relate to general attitudes to rape as well as to self-reported sexual arousal. With respect to attitudes, generally callous attitudes toward rape similar to those of many convicted rapists were found to be associated with self-reported proclivity to rape. In general, self-reported sexual responsivity to sexual violence but not to sexual non-violence was found to correlate with the reported likelihood of raping.

In the first phase of the experiment, the relationship between sexual arousal and likelihood of raping was found for the rape-abhorrence but not for the rape-arousal depiction. These data may be understood by considering the fact that most subjects were relatively aroused to the rape-arousal depiction. Thus, sexual responsiveness to this type of stimulus did not discriminate among those who reported being relatively likely or unlikely to engage in rape. Relatively few subjects, on the other hand, were not inhibited by the description of the victim's abhorrence. Arousal to such rape-abhorrence depictions has been shown to discriminate between the responses of rapists and non-rapists (Abel et al., 1977; Barbaree et al., 1979). Therefore, the significant correlation between arousal to this abhorrence portrayal and self-reported likelihood of raping provides additional support for the contention that such self-reported proclivity is a meaningful measure predictive of important arousal and cognitive-attitudinal responses (Malamuth et al., 1980, a). The similar correlation obtained overall between the rape-criterion passage (Phase 2) and self-reported rape proclivity is consistent with these data in that raters' judgments of this story were virtually identical to those of the rape-abhorrence passage.

In light of the fact that the relationship between sexual arousal to sexual violence and proclivity to rape was significant for self-reported arousal but not for penile tumescence, it may be hypothesized that a self-perception process (Bem, 1972) mediates this relationship. A subject who perceives that he is aroused to portrayals of sexual violence, irrespective of whether corresponding tumescence changes occur, may infer that he would be sexually aroused by an actual assault. The inferences drawn from such self-perceived arousal merit further examination in that they may not only help account for the relationship with self-reported proclivity to rape, but also for the development of the motivation to actually commit acts of sexual assault, an area that is presently totally devoid of any empirical research.

NOTES

1. Portions of this paper were presented at the Annual Convention of the Canadian Psychological Association, Quebec City, June 1979. This project was supported by a grant from the University of Manitoba Research Grants Committee. The authors would like to thank Kathleen DeLeon for serving as the female experimenter, Heather Mullen for conducting the validation study, and Phil Gerson and Les Bell for technical assistance in the development of the mechanical instruments. Requests for reprints should be addressed to N. Malamuth, Dept. of Psychology, University of Manitoba, Winnipeg, Man. R3T 2N2, Canada.

2. As indicated below, a strong statement concerning the absolute falsehood of such depictions and the true horror of rape was given to all subjects (in both the validation study and the experiment) following exposure. Recent data (Malamuth and Check, Note 4; Donnerstein, Note 5) indicates that such debriefings are effective in counteracting any possible adverse effects of exposure to sexually violent depictions. Moreover, these studies indicate that the experience of exposure to rape portrayals followed by a debriefing results in less acceptance of rape myths than control subjects on assessments conducted days or weeks following exposure.

3. The questionnaires consisted of the 16-item rape questionnaire described above as well as a postexperimental questionnaire. The latter questionnaire was designed to determine whether any subjects were aware of the hypothesis regarding the effects of exposure in Phase 1 on reactions to the rape criterion story presented in Phase 2. Subjects were asked if they had heard anything about the experiment and what they felt psychologists could learn from an experiment of this sort. No one indicated any awareness of the prior exposure hypothesis, and so all 75 subjects were included in the analyses.

4. There are slight variations in the degrees of freedom reported due to a few instances of missing data for the physiological measure at either phase 1 or phase 2. These were due to mechanical failure.

Dolf Zillmann, Jennings Bryant, Paul W. Comisky, and
Norman J. Medoff

Excitation and Hedonic Valence in the Effect of Erotica on Motivated Intermale Aggression

Research on the effects of visual erotica on motivated aggressive behavior
has produced findings which may appear to be contradictory. In one set of
experiments (e.g., Zillmann, 1971; Meyer, 1972; Zillmann, Hoyt, and Day,
1974; Baron, 1979; Cantor, Zillmann, and Einsiedel, 1978; Donnerstein and
Hallam, 1978), provoked persons exhibited more aggressiveness after exposure to erotica than after exposure to communications with nonerotic
contents. This apparent facilitation of aggression due to exposure to erotica
has also been demonstrated in comparison to conditions under which
subjects were not exposed to particular communications (Meyer, 1972;
Sapolsky, 1977). In another set of experiments (Baron and Bell, 1973, 1977;
Baron, 1974a, 1974b, 1979; Donnerstein, Donnerstein, and Evans, 1975;
White, 1979), however, provoked persons were found to aggress less against
their tormentor after exposure to erotica than after exposure to neutral fare;
and this apparent reduction of aggression was also observed relative to a no-
exposure control condition (White, 1979).

Clearly, if all visual erotica had similar properties and elicited uniform
responses, such discrepant findings would be difficult to reconcile. The
erotica employed in the various investigations differ vastly along many
conceptual dimensions, however. Some investigators used photographs of

Reprinted from the *European Journal of Social Psychology*, Vol. 11, No. 3 (1981), pp.
233–252, permission of John Wiley and Sons Ltd. and Dolf Zillmann.

attractive females in the nude (e.g., Baron and Bell, 1973); others used hard-core films featuring a great variety of sexual interactions, including fellatio, cunnilingus, and anal intercourse (e.g., Donnerstein and Hallam, 1978). Differences, then, were with regard to mode of representation, the degree of sexual explicitness, the potential to arouse, etc. In reconciling the conflicting findings, the apparent task became to determine the properties of erotica that are capable of enhancing motivated aggression and the properties of those other erotica capable of reducing such behavior.

The conflicting findings also made it clear that, in terms of a theoretical accounting of the various effects, the models employed to predict either a facilitation or a reduction of aggression, while potentially valid for a particular domain of erotica, could not explain the effects of all conceivable erotica. The aggression-facilitating effect of some erotica, for instance, has usually been explained as the result of the excitatory capacity of these erotica. Specifically, it has been argued (a) that exposure to erotica elevates the level of sympathetic excitation, (b) that sympathetic excitation does not dissipate abruptly and thus extends into postexposure behavior, (c) that residues of erotica-induced excitation combine with excitation from provocation, and (d) that, because at higher levels of excitation feelings of annoyance and anger are likely to be experienced as more intense, the provoked person who is still aroused from exposure to erotica will behave more aggressively than he or she otherwise would (cf. Zillmann, 1971, 1978). It is the residual "sexual" arousal, then (or more accurately, its sympathetic concomitant), that is viewed as transferring into anger and aggression, making these behaviors "artificially" intense. Such reasoning obviously does not account for the aggression-reducing effects of certain other erotica. This aggression-reducing effect, on the other hand, has been explained as the result of hedonic incompatibilities between sexual and aggressive response tendencies (cf. Baron, 1974b). The provoked person's exposure to pleasant erotica, according to this view, diminishes the experience of negative affect resulting from provocation, and the experience of pleasant sexual excitement makes it difficult for the person to return to anger even when such a reaction is indicated by situational cues. Fromm (1973) has similarly proposed an incompatibility between arousal and destructive behavior, hinting at the evolutionary necessity of a separation between reproductive and destructive response tendencies. It has also been suggested that erotica, among other types of absorbing stimuli, simply distract the annoyed person from the circumstances of the annoyance, thereby effecting relief and a reduction in aggression (Bandura, 1973; Zillmann and Johnson, 1973; Donnerstein, Donnerstein, and Evans, 1975; Bryant and Zillman, 1977). All these proposals fail, of course, to account for the aggression-facilitating effects of some erotica.

Inspection of the stimuli used in the research on the effects of visual erotica on motivated aggression reveals an eye-catching correspondence:

Aggression-facilitating effects were almost exclusively observed after exposure to rather explicit and highly arousing motion pictures; aggression-reducing effects, in contrast, were almost exclusively observed after exposure to minimally explicit and, at best, moderately arousing, presumably pleasant and absorbing photographs. It appears, then, that "mild" erotica (such as females in sexually provocative poses) and "strong" erotica (such as explicit films of sexual intercourse) may have different effects and that their unique effects might be the result of a differential involvement of established mechanisms. This circumstance led Donnerstein, Donnerstein, and Evans (1975) to propose a two-factor account for erotica generally, the rationale being that the arousal factor dominates the effect of strong erotica toward a faciliation of aggression and that absorption or distraction, the second factor, dominates the effect of mild erotica toward a reduction of aggression. Subsequent research on the distraction factor (Zillmann and Sapolsky, 1977; Sapolsky, 1977) has failed, however, to support the assumption that erotica, especially "mild" erotica, are particularly absorbing and that a reduction of aggression is mediated by the respondent's involvement with the stimuli. Instead, this research implicated the hedonic valence of erotic stimuli as a critical factor in the mediation of motivated aggression, and it suggested a two-component model of erotica effects in which (a) the excitatory potential and (b) the hedonic valence of a stimulus are jointly considered.

The excitation and valence model of erotica projects an additive combination of any aggression-facilitating response tendencies due to excitatory potential with any aggression-reducing response tendencies due to positive hedonic valence. It further incorporates the aggression-facilitating effect of erotica associated with negative hedonic valence (cf. White, 1979; Sapolsky, 1977), projecting again a simple summation of the effects of excitation and hedonic valence. Exposure to "mild" erotica with a negligible excitatory capacity, then, is expected to decrease motivated aggressiveness when the stimuli are appraised as pleasant, but to increase it when the stimuli are appraised as displeasing and disturbing. Exposure to moderately arousing, pleasant erotica, in contrast, should produce a negligible effect only because the aggression-modifying response tendencies due to excitation and valence cancel each other out. Exposure to similarly arousing but disturbing erotica, however, should lead to increased motivated aggression. Finally, exposure to "strong" erotica with a great excitatory capacity and with positive hedonic valence is expected to increase aggression somewhat, the countereffect of valence removing much of the arousal effect. The strongest facilitation of motivated aggression is, of course, expected after exposure to erotica that are both highly arousing and greatly disturbing.

The present investigation was designed as a test of the excitation and valence model of erotica effects on motivated aggression. Excitatory potential (low, high) and hedonic valence (negative, positive) were varied orthogonally to permit an evaluation of the proposed additive combination of their respective effects. A no-exposure control was included to assess the direction of exposure effects.

It has often been alleged that sexual arousal and aggression are uniquely linked. Fromm (1973), for instance, proposed that such arousal fosters assertiveness, at least in males, but reduces destructive inclinations. Consequently, to the extent that erotica arouse the respondent sexually, pain-inducing and injurious behaviors should be inhibited. Feshbach and his associates (Malamuth, Feshbach, and Jaffee, 1977; Feshbach and Malamuth, 1978), on the other hand, have recently suggested that exposure to erotica is likely to foster aggressive behavior, even in unprovoked persons, because the disinhibition of tabued sexual behavior will generalize to tabued aggression.

In order to determine whether or not the effect of erotica is unique, the present design involved a further variation: erotica vs. nonerotica, with both types of stimuli being matched on excitatory potential and on hedonic valence in all conditions. If, under these experimental conditions, erotica produce effects on motivated aggression that are critically different from those produced by nonerotica, other factors, among them the uniqueness of the sexual thematic, will have to be drawn upon to explain the effects in question. However, if erotica and nonerotica which are matched on both excitatory potential and hedonic valence have very similar, potentially identical effects, an explanation in terms of excitatory and hedonic stimulus properties may be considered adequate, and claims of unique effects of erotica on aggression may be called into question.

METHOD

Selection of Experimental Materials

Ninety-six photographs and 56 film segments were sampled from a large collection of erotic and nonerotic photographs and motion pictures. Twenty-four erotic photographs and 14 erotic films were considered likely to induce positive hedonic reactions in male undergraduates; erotic photographs and erotic films of an equal number were considered to be likely to induce negative hedonic reactions.[1] The nonerotic stimuli, both photographs and films, were subjected to the same initial classification.

The presumed hedonic reactions were empirically determined in a pretest.[2] Twenty male undergraduates at Indiana University served as subjects. They were enrolled in an introductory communications course and received course credit for their participation. Each session accommodated two subjects who were separated by a partition to avoid interactions. Ten subjects were exposed to all of the photographs and ten to all of the films. In both conditions, the stimuli were presented in orders randomized by session. Each photograph was projected from a slide for 10 seconds. The duration of each film segment was one minute. Films were presented via videocassette on a large-size (25") color monitor. Each stimulus was evaluated immediately after exposure. Ratings were made on several bipolar scales which ranged from − 100 to 100. Hedonic valence was assessed on a scale labeled "extremely displeasing" (− 100) and "extremely pleasing" (100). All other scales served to disguise the pertinence of the hedonic variable.

On the basis of the ratings, stimuli that initially had been misclassified were discarded. Several sets of stimuli with the required hedonic properties were subjected to analyses of variance to determine the degree to which the needed stimulus differentiations and compatibilities were achieved. Sets of 15 photographs each and of six films each were considered to best approximate the required structure of hedonic stimulus properties. The analysis of variance performed on the ratings of these sets of stimuli, which cross-varied mode of representation (photographs, films) as the only independent-measures factor with the two repeated measures-factors contents (erotica, nonerotica) and hedonic valence (positive, negative), yielded a strong overall differentiation for hedonic valence: In the positive-valence condition, the mean rating was 32; in the negative-valence condition, it was − 49, the difference being associated with $F(1,18) = 120.23$, $p < .001$. A significant main effect was also observed for mode of representation: $F(1,18) = 16.01$, $p < .001$. The associated differentiation (for photographs, $M = 2$; for films, $M = − 20$) derives from the fact that the negative-valence films produced stronger negative reactions than the negative-valence photographs. The main effect of contents was trivial ($F = .17$). All interactions were similarly unreliable. In all, then, the results of the pretest show the experimental stimuli to differ in hedonic valence as required; at the same time, and also as required, there were no appreciable differences whatever between erotica and nonerotica at any condition of hedonic valence or mode of representation.

It can be considered well documented that in male respondents motion pictures of sexual behaviors produce stronger excitatory reactions than photographs of the same activities (e.g., McConagy, 1974; Sandford, 1974; Zillmann and Sapolsky, 1977; Sapolsky, 1977). On the basis of this research and on the assumption that this difference in reactivity also applies to the representation of nonerotic events capable of inducing strong affective reactions, the variation in mode of representation was expected to manifest an arousal differentiation: Specifically, films were expected to produce stronger excitatory reactions than photographs, other things being equal. Validation of this expectation was possible only in the main experiment, however, through the peripheral assessment of excitatory reactions.

EXPERIMENTAL MATERIALS

Eight different sets of stimuli were created by transferring the pretest-selected photographs or film segments onto separate videocassettes. Each of the four low-excitatory-potential sets was composed of 15 photographs, each photograph being displayed for 24 seconds. Each of the four high-excitatory-potential sets was composed of six film segments, each segment being displayed for 60 seconds. All presentations thus were of six-minute duration. The low-excitation sets (i.e., photographs) were presented without sound. In the high-excitation sets, the original sound track of the motion picture was presented; some erotic segments (off 8 mm film) were without sound.

The *nonerotic, low excitatory potential, negative hedonic valence* presentation featured photographs of chronically diseased human faces, disfiguring tumors of the eyes and the neck, scarred and burned tissue of victims of child abuse, gaunt victims of starvation, crying children, and soldiers lying in pools of blood. The *nonerotic, low excitatory potential, positive hedonic valence* presentation featured photographs of appetizingly displayed gourmet food, children playing with pets, baby animals, and spectacular nature scenes. The *nonerotic, high excitatory potential, negative hedonic valence* presentation featured film segments of the bloody slaughter of baby seals, an eye operation in close-ups, and a scene of a distraught child overhearing his parents engaged in a hostile argument. The *nonerotic, high excitatory potential, positive hedonic valence* presentation featured film segments of rock concerts and scenes from commercials showing young people exuberantly dancing, singing, and otherwise joyously interacting. The *erotic, low excitatory potential, negative hedonic valence* presentation featured photographs of obviously pregnant women masturbating with mechanical devices or dildos; of women bound, gagged, and beaten in bondage rituals; of an extremely obese female fellating a gaunt male; and, in close-ups, of the deformation of female genitalia by pliers and metal clips. The *erotic, low excitatory potential, positive hedonic valence* presentation featured photographs of attractive nude or scantily clothed females characteristic of soft-core "girlie" magazines. The *erotic, high excitatory potential, negative hedonic valence* presentation featured segments from sado-masochistic and bestiality films: A male being beaten by a female during cunnilingus; a male being whipped while his genitalia were tied and abused; a woman and a large male dog engaged in intercourse; and a woman fellating and masturbating a dog. The *erotic, high excitatory, positive hedonic valence* presentation featured film segments from so-called "high quality," hard-core pornography movies; these segments explicitly depicted a variety of forms of heterosexual precoital and coital behaviors devoid of elements of aggression.

SUBJECTS

Seventy-four male undergraduates at the University of Massachusetts served as subjects. All were enrolled in an introductory communications course and received course credit for their participation. Two subjects were dismissed prior to data analysis; both had expressed the suspicion that the person presented as another subject was an experimental accomplice.

All subjects consented to participating in an experiment that involves deception and were informed of their right to withdraw from the experiment at any time.

PROCEDURE

Subjects were randomly assigned to one of the nine experimental conditions and tested individually. Upon arriving in the laboratory, the subject was met by a male experimenter. The experimenter told the subject that they would have to wait for another subject who was involved in the study. A short time later, the individual purported to be the other subject arrived. This individual was actually an experimental confederate.[3] The experimenter led the subject and the confederate to an experimental room and presented taperecorded instructions. The session was introduced as part of an investigation of the use of offensive and defensive game strategies as a function of knowledge of certain characteristics of the opponent and of feedback about the success of offensive maneuvers. A one-way version of the battleship game was then described (cf. Zillmann and Bryant, 1974; Zillmann, Johnson, and Day, 1974b).[4] In brief, by a bogus "random" decision the subject is assigned to defense and the confederate to offense. The confederate attacks according to fixed, prepared schedules, ostensibly trying to hit the target in a minimal number of trials. The subject has to find a "safe" location for the target and to move it between trials so as to minimize the chances for it to be hit. In addition, he provides the offensive player with *deceptive* feedback about the trials. The declared objective of this feedback is to mislead the offensive player about any progress made toward hitting the target. Feedback consists of punishment, operationalized in the ostensible delivery of noxious noise via headphone to one ear of the offensive player, and of negative reinforcement, operationalized in the removal of noxious noise from the offensive player's other ear. The intensity of both the negative feedback (i.e., punishment) and the positive feedback (i.e., reinforcement) is variable. Frequency and intensity of negative feedback used by the annoyed subject serve as measures of retaliatory behavior.

The players were informed about the mechanics of the game and familiarized with the apparatus. Several intensities of positive and negative feedback were demonstrated. They were then told that three different types of games would be played: fixed-position defense, in which the target remains stationary; partially-variable defense, in which the target can be relocated only in three-trial intervals; and totally-variable defense, in which the target can be moved after every trial.

The subject and the confederate were told that the offensive player would later receive special instructions that should enable him to play superior strategy. These instructions would be time-consuming, and since the defensive player would be idle during that time, his participation in a minor, unrelated study would be appreciated. This study was said to examine physiological responses to various visual and audiovisual stimuli capable of producing strong affective reactions. It was pointed out that explicit and potentially disturbing erotica might be involved, and it was explained that subjects who, for whatever reason, did not want to be exposed to such stimuli would be free to leave without losing credit for participation. No subject voiced objections to participating in the supplementary study. After permitting ample time for the examination of specific consent forms, the experimenter collected the signed forms from both the subject and the confederate.

After responding to any questions for clarification of the procedure, the experimenter pretended to have drawn a random number which assigned the subject to defense and the confederate to offense. He then escorted the confederate to the adjoining room where the apparatus for offense was said to be located. Returning to the experimental room, he spoke via intercom to the confederate and gave final instructions to the subject.

The subject was instructed to play fixed-position defense. He was led to believe that such defense typically requires eight trials before the target is hit. The subject then placed his target, the confederate missed it, and the subject administered feedback. In all, the confederate (always knowing the target's location) missed on 10 trials, the proximity of his misses according to a fixed schedule. The fact that the subject managed to have his target hit only on the eleventh trial should have made him confident that he played effective defense. The subject's feedback responses were fed into an event recorder. The 10 preprovocation responses served as a potential covariate for the later measures of retaliatory behavior.

After this initial game, both players were informed that the offensive player now would begin to study superior offensive strategies and that, at the same time, the defensive player would respond to questionnaires assessing his experience with games and his position on several important societal issues. The latter was said to constitute the information about the person playing defense that would be provided to the offensive player. Actually, the information served the provocation treatment.

The key issue on the questionnaire concerned the female liberation movement. The subject was asked: "Are you generally in favor of the women's liberation movement?" and "Do you support the push toward more and stronger female lead characters in prime-time suspense dramas and situation comedies?" He was to check "Yes" or "No" and to briefly justify his position in a space provided for that purpose. After the subject had answered all questions, the experimenter brought the issues questionnaire to the confederate for examination.

Upon the experimenter's return, the subject was informed that he would now watch the television segments of the unrelated study. After the physiological measurement devices were attached and time for relaxation was permitted, basal readings of systolic and diastolic blood pressures and of heart rate were obtained (t_1, base). Thereafter, the confederate informed the experimenter via the intercom that he had completed his examination of the opponent's responses. The experimenter again left for the adjoining room, returning with the confederate's written reactions to the subject's responses. In all instances, the confederate had put down similar insulting remarks to the two critical responses of the subject. If the subject had expressed support for women's liberation, the confederate had written: "Anyone who supports women's lib is really stupid! They want to take our rights!" If the subject had expressed opposition, the confederate's comment read: "Anyone who doesn't support women's lib is really stupid! Women have rights too!" Analogously, if the subject had been supportive of women on television, the confederate had written: "There are already enough female lead characters on TV. Men are losing all of their rights. This is really stupid!" If the subject had expressed opposition, the confederate remarked: "There are not enough female lead characters on TV. It's about time women got a break. This is really stupid!" To add force to the written provocation, the confederate also insulted the subject orally. After the subject had read the evaluative comments, the experimenter addressed the confederate over the intercom, asking if he had completed the reading of his strategy instructions. The confederate's response, which had been previously taperecorded and was played back under auditory conditions identical with the live verbal exchanges, was: "No, but I don't think I'll need them for him." The experimenter quickly replied: "We'll give you some more time." He then told the subject that they were about ready now for the unrelated study, but that he first would have to take basal physiological measures once more (t_2, post provocation).

After all the measures were taken, the subject was exposed to one set of the experimental stimuli or, in the control condition, made to wait for the period of time that in the other conditions was consumed by exposure. In the control, the experimenter told the subjects that they would be running late with this session, and that they would simply skip the unrelated study. Following exposure or waiting, a third set of physiological measures was obtained (t_3, post exposure). The experimenter, who during exposure or waiting had busied himself in a remote corner of the experimental room, returned to the subject and removed all physiological measuring devices.

The experimenter then addressed the confederate, informing him that they would have to start the game with partially variable strategy. The subject was told that the average number of trials for hitting the target under these conditions was twelve. In this second game, the subject's target was hit on the eleventh trial. Upon hitting the target, the confederate opened the intercom and spontaneously insulted the subject again. He arrogantly quipped: "I told you I could beat a guy like that easy." The experimenter responded in a nonpunitive but firm manner: "Please don't use the intercom except when requested. Are you ready to begin the final game?" The confederate's "Sure!" was once again spoken arrogantly. As before, these comments of the confederate came off a recorder. The third game with a totally variable strategy was then played, the subject's target being hit on the sixteenth trial.

At the end of the game, the subjects who had been exposed to erotic or nonerotic materials were requested to evaluate these materials on a questionnaire. The three initial rating scales were bipolar and involved the following adjectives: exciting/boring, displeasing/pleasing, and calming/disturbing. The questions read: "How _____ or how _____ were these scenes?" The associated scales ranged from − 10 through 0 to 10, had marks at regular intervals, and were labeled "extremely _____" at both ends. All subsequent rating scales were unipolar, using the following adjectives: amusing, erotic, arousing, satisfying, beautiful, sickening, captivating, annoying, disgusting, appealing, shocking, frustrating, and cruel. The questions read: "How _____ was this segment?" The associated scales ranged from 0 to 10, had marks at regular intervals, and were labeled "not at all _____" and "extremely _____" at the respective ends.

After completion of this questionnaire, subjects were requested to evaluate their opponents. They were led to believe that their opponents would evaluate them as well. Subjects were asked to assist the experimenter in determining the amount of credit their opponents were to receive for their performance of the experimental tasks. Credit recommendations were made on a scale ranging from zero to three credit points. The four choices were labeled: "poor," "mediocre," "good," and "superb."

Measures of excitation. Relative to the basal measures (t_1), t_2-measures assessed the effect of provocation and t_3-measures that of exposure to communication. All measures (systolic and diastolic blood pressure, heart rate, and skin temperature) were employed as peripheral indices of sympathetic activity.

Measures of hedonic valence. The variation in the hedonic valence of the stimuli that had been secured in the pretest could be further validated through the analysis of pertinent scales drawn from the questionnaire assessing judgmental responses to the stimuli.

Measures of aggression and hostility. Frequency and accumulated intensity of punishing noxious noises, as negative feedback ostensibly administered to the opponent in thwarting the successful completion of his task, served as the primary measures of aggressiveness. Frequency and accumulated intensity of positive feedback were employed as secondary, negative indices of aggressiveness. Since subjects could also retaliate against their annoyers in a nonphysical manner by recommending minimal or no credit for their participation in the experiment, the subjects' credit recommendations were considered to assess hostile behavior.

APPARATUS

Blood pressures were measured by the cuff method and heart rate photoelectrically from the tip of the index finger. The measures were taken from the nonwriting arm and hand of the subject and recorded on Whittaker apparati. Skin temperature was taken from the tip of the subject's middle finger of his nonwriting hand and recorded on a Nihon Kohden thermistor thermometer.

The experimental materials were presented on a 19" Sony Trinitron color monitor.

Frequency, intensity, and duration of aggressive responses were recorded on an Esterline-Angus event recorder.

RESULTS

EXCITATORY REACTIONS TO PROVOCATION

The increase in sympathetic activity expected to be produced by the provocation treatment was analyzed in the changes from the basal (t_1) to the post-provocation measures (t_2) of the various indices employed. All nine communication conditions, which up to this point did not differ in treatments received, were incorporated in this analysis. In accord with expectations, the provocation treatment was found to produce significant $(p < .001)$ activity increases on all indices. Across communication conditions, systolic blood pressure increased from $M = 117.9$ to $M = 125.7$ mm Hg, the difference being associated with $F(1,63) = 100.23$. Similarly, diastolic blood pressure increased from $M = 70.6$ to $M = 73.7$; $F(1,63) = 21.66$. Heart rate increased substantially from $M = 79.9$ to $M = 88.2$ bpm; $F(1,63) = 111.98$. Furthermore, skin temperature declined from $M = 31.42$ to $31.07\,°C$; $F(1,63) = 19.62$. This decline indicates, of course, increased vasoconstriction and, thus, increased sympathetic activity. The main effects of communication conditions and the interactions between communication conditions and repeated measures were all entirely negligible ($F < 1$) for all indices of excitation. The excitatory impact of the provocation treatment was consequently not only strong, but also very homogeneous in the various experimental conditions.

EXCITATORY REACTIONS TO THE EXPERIMENTAL MATERIALS

The eight conditions in which subjects were exposed to materials were arranged in a 2^3 design varying nonerotica/erotica, excitatory potential, and hedonic valence. The differential excitatory impact of exposure to communication was assessed in the postexposure scores relative to basal scores $(t_3 - t_1)$. The analysis of these scores yielded various significant effects on systolic blood pressure and heart rate. As can be seen from Tables 2 and 3, the required differentiation between stimuli of a low vs. a high excitatory potential was obtained for both indices. Also as required, systolic blood pressure was at extremely similar levels for both negative and positive hedonic valence. On heart rate, however, the stimuli of negative valence had a somewhat stronger impact than those of positive valence. As shown in Table 2, the only other reliable effect was observed on systolic blood pressure: Overall, erotica ($M = 6.1$) had a stronger excitatory effect than nonerotica ($M = 0.7$).

Although the pattern of effects for diastolic blood pressure paralleled that described for systolic blood pressure, none of the effects proved statistically reliable. On skin temperature, all effects were trivial ($F < 1$). The physiological data were also analyzed in toto (comparing t_1, t_2, and t_3). This analysis produced results redundant with those reported.

Taken together, the analysis of excitatory reactions to the experimental materials shows that the required overall differentiation of the excitatory potential of the stimuli was achieved, but that there was a tendency for negative stimuli to be stronger overall than positive ones (heart rate) and for erotic stimuli to be stronger overall than nonerotic ones (systolic blood pressure).

The ratings on the "arousing" scale were more directly supportive of the required differentiation in excitatory potential: for low: $M = 2.2$; for high: $M = 4.9$; $F(1,56) = 17.42$, $p < .001$. All other effects on that scale were negligible.

HEDONIC VALENCE OF THE EXPERIMENTAL MATERIALS

The subjects' ratings of the stimuli's hedonic properties corroborate the results of the pretest. As can be seen from Tables 2 and 3, the valence dif-

Table 1

RETALIATORY AGGRESSION AFTER EXPOSURE TO EROTIC AND NONEROTIC
STIMULI AND EXCITATORY AND HEDONIC PROPERTIES OF THESE STIMULI

MEASURE	NO-EXPOSURE CONTROL	TYPE OF STIMULUS	HEDONIC VALENCE			
			Negative		Positive	
			Excitatory potential		Excitatory potential	
			Low	High	Low	High
Noxious noise delivered						
Frequency	9.8	Nonerotica	14.1	16.0*	9.0	11.2
		Erotica	13.8	17.1*	9.4	12.2
Intensity	52.5	Nonerotica	85.5	125.2*	55.0	75.2
		Erotica	86.4	115.0*	49.4	73.5
Excitatory response						
▲ Systolic BP	2.2	Nonerotica	0.5	3.0	−2.4	1.5
		Erotica	1.6	9.5	3.8	9.5
▲ Heart rate	1.4	Nonerotica	5.0	7.5	−3.8	0.1
		Erotica	6.2	9.1	−3.0	9.1
Perception of stimulus						
Displeasing-pleasing	————	Nonerotica	−5.6	−6.5	3.6	4.9
		Erotica	−5.2	−6.2	3.2	4.8
Disturbing-calming	————	Nonerotica	−3.1	−4.1	3.4	2.4
		Erotica	−2.6	−3.9	3.2	1.5

Note: Frequency of noxious noise could vary from 0 to 25. Intensity was accumulated over trials. On each trial, it could vary from 1 to 10. Blood pressure is in mm Hg, heart rate in bpm. Difference scores (▲) were obtained by subtracting basal from postexposure measures. Ratings could vary from −10 (displeasing, disturbing) to 10 (pleasing, calming).

On both the frequency and the intensity measure of noxious noise, all treatment means were compared against the control-condition mean by Dunnett's test. Treatment means significantly ($p <$ .05) different from that of the control are identifed by asterisk. The application of Newman-Keuls' a posteriori procedure to all means produced the same statistical decisions.

ferentiation was pronounced on both the "displeasing/pleasing" and "disturbing/calming" scales. All other main effects and all interactions were of trivial magnitude.

Other pertinent ratings were entirely redundant. For example, highly significant ($p <$ .001) main effects for hedonic valence were observed for "satisfying" [negative: $M = 1.4$; positive: $M = 4.8$; $F(1,56) = 25.34$], for "annoying" (6.0, 1.2; $F = 58.02$), for "disgusting" (7.2, 0.5; $F = 173.10$),

Table 2
SUMMARY OF *F* RATIOS FROM ANALYSES OF VARIANCE
PERFORMED ON MEASURES OF RETALIATORY AGGRESSION, EXCITATORY
POTENTIAL, AND HEDONIC VALENCE

SOURCE OF VARIATION	NOXIOUS NOISE DELIVERED		EXCITATORY RESPONSE		PERCEPTION OF STIMULUS	
	Frequency	Intensity	▲ Systolic BP	▲ Heart Rate	Displeasing-pleasing	Disturbing-calming
Type of stimulus (A)	.30	.18	10.26**	1.62	.00	.00
Excitatory potential (B)	7.23**	8.35**	8.67**	4.65*	.07	1.89
Hedonic valence (C)	24.56***	16.61***	.11	6.55*	137.73***	44.52***
AB interaction	.30	.03	1.14	.76	.00	.08
AC interaction	.03	.00	.92	.48	.11	.23
BC interaction	.00	.38	.01	1.14	1.83	.02
ABC interaction	.05	.15	.27	.63	.01	.02
MS$_{error}$	14.90	1,521.80	46.13	98.35	11.69	13.21

*p <.05; **p <.01; ***p <.001.

Note: All *F* ratios are associated with 1,56 degrees of freedom.

Table 3
EXCITATORY AND HEDONIC PROPERTIES OF STIMULI AND THEIR EFFECTS
ON RETALIATORY AGGRESSION

MEASURE	EXCITATORY POTENTIAL		HEDONIC VALENCE	
	Low	High	Negative	Positive
Noxious noise delivered				
Frequency	11.6	14.2**	15.2	10.5***
Intensity	69.1	97.2**	103.0	63.3***
Excitatory response				
▲ Systolic BP	0.9	5.9**	3.7	3.1
▲ Heart rate	1.1	6.5*	.7.0	0.6*
Perception of stimulus				
Displeasing-pleasing	−1.0	−0.8	−5.9	4.1***
Disturbing-calming	0.2	−1.0	−3.4	2.6***

*p <.05; **p <.01; ***p <.001.

Note. Comparisons are within factors and measures only. Evaluations are by *F* test (main effects of factor B or factor C, respectively).

and for "frustrating" (5.0, 0.8; $F = 37.55$). All other main effects and all interactions were negligible for all these measures. The findings on other scales also proved redundant. It was observed, for example, that the negative stimuli were judged to be significantly ($p < .001$) less beautiful, more sickening, less appealing, and more shocking than the positive ones, with other effects again being negligible. On related scales, the negative stimuli were found to be significantly ($p < .05$) less captivating and more boring than the positive ones. Finally, a significant main effect of hedonic valence was obtained on the "cruel" scale: $M = 6.2$ for negative and $M = 0.4$ for positive; $F(1,56) = 130.08$, $p < .001$; no other effects were reliable.

In the light of these consistent findings, the differentiation in hedonic valence can be considered pronounced and homogeneous.

Ratings on the "arousing" scale confirmed the reported differentiation in excitatory potential: for low: $M = 2.2$; for high: $M = 4.9$; $F(1,56) = 17.42$, $p < .001$. All other effects on that scale were negligible.

RETALIATORY AGGRESSION

The feedback responses were initially analyzed in a $2 \times 2 \times 2 \times 5$ design, the last factor being a repeated-measure factor with five blocks of five responses each. All repeated-measures effects, including all interactions involving repeated measures, proved negligible for both the frequency and the intensity of negative and positive feedback. The blocks were consequently collapsed for all further analyses.

Preliminary analyses of variance were also performed on the preprovocation feedback responses. No appreciable effects were observed on any measure. The preprovocation responses were further employed as a covariate in analyses of covariance on the various measures of retaliatory aggression. All results were redundant with those from the analyses of variance reported below.

Frequency of punitive feedback. As can be seen from Tables 2 and 3, significant main effects were obtained for excitatory potential and hedonic valence, both in the expected direction. The main effect of type of stimulus (nonerotic, erotic) and all interactions were trivial, however.

The incorporation of the no-exposure control condition yielded $F(8,63) = 4.39$, $MS_e = 15.74$, $p < .001$ in a one-factor arrangement. Subsequent comparisons between means showed exposure to stimuli that combined high excitatory potential and negative hedonic valence, whether erotic or nonerotic, to foster levels of punitive-feedback use that were significantly above the level of the control (Dunnett's test, $p < .01$) and the levels associated with exposure to stimuli with a low excitatory potential and positive hedonic valence (Newman-Keuls' test, $p < .05$). Table 1 exhibits the high degree of parallelity in the effect of erotic and nonerotic stimuli with comparable excitatory and hedonic properties.

Accumulated intensity of punitive feedback. The effects on this measure were totally redundant with those reported for the frequency of usage. Tables 2 and 3 display the expected effects of excitatory potential and hedonic valence. Again, all other effects were trivial. The incorporation of the control yielded $F(8,63) = 4.02$, $MS_e = 1,426.20$, $p < .001$; and subsequent comparisons on the means, shown in Table 1, led to statistical decisions identical with those reported for the frequency of usage.

Use of reinforcing feedback. The frequency of positive feedback is, of course, simply the inverse of the frequency of punitive feedback, with identical statistical decisions. The accumulated intensity of positive feedback is free to vary, but nonetheless proved to be the mirror image of the use of punitive feedback. All statistical decisions were the same in both the factorial design and the one-factor arrangement. And again, subsequent tests showed the erotica and nonerotica conditions in which high excitatory potential combined with negative hedonic valence to be the only ones significantly different from the control. The greater usage of punitive feedback in these conditions thus corresponded very closely with a lesser use of reinforcing feedback.

RETALIATORY HOSTILITY

The consistency in the findings regarding retaliatory behavior is further evident from the analysis of the credit recommendations. Again, the main effects of excitatory potential [$F(1,56) = 5.62$, $p < .025$; $M = 1.59$ (low) and $M = 1.16$ (high)] and of hedonic valence [$F(1,56) = 16.52$, $p < .001$; $M = 1.00$ (negative) and 1.75 (positive)] were significant, and all other effects were of trivial magnitude ($F < 1$). Inclusion of the no-exposure control yielded $F(8,63) = 3.37$, $MS_e = .53$, $p < .005$, in the one-factor arrangement. Subsequent comparisons (Dunnett's test) once more showed the conditions in which high excitatory potential combined with negative hedonic valence ($M = .75$ for the nonerotica condition and $M = .88$ for the erotica condition) to be the only ones significantly ($p < .05$) different from the control ($M = 1.88$). In these conditions, then, the observed increase in hostile behavior closely corresponded with that of aggressive behavior reported earlier.

DISCUSSION

The findings lend strong support to the excitation and valence model of erotica effects on motivated aggression. Both the excitatory potential and the hedonic valence of stimuli affected aggressive behavior as predicted; and as the highly consistent absence of interactions indicates, the contributions of both factors combine additively in the effect on aggression.

On the other hand, the findings challenge the view that the effect of erotica is mediated by a specific sex-aggression incompatibility (Fromm, 1973) or by the generalization of disinhibition from sex to aggression (Feshbach and Malamuth, 1978). The pattern of the effects of excitationally and hedonically matched erotic and nonerotic stimuli on motivated aggression was identical. According to the findings, then, the effect of erotica is not due to their sexual thema per se (or to the *sexual* arousal they may induce), but rather to their impact on automatic arousal and their evocation of pleasure or disturbance. Erotica, in other words, affect aggression because they are arousing and pleasant or irritating—not simply because they display "sex."

Although the findings demonstrate that, overall, residues from communication-induced excitation facilitate motivated aggression, the findings do not fully accord with the pardigm of excitation transfer (cf. Zillmann, 1978). This paradigm leads to the expectation that similarly arousing stimuli should, under identical circumstances, produce similar effects on subsequent behavior. The independent effect of hedonic valence observed in the present investigation obviously does not conform to this expectation and, in fact, suggests a modification of the paradigm (i.e., the possibility of an impediment of excitation transfer by the hedonic incompatibility of antecedent states has to be acknowledged).

Assessed against the no-exposure control, exposure to arousing and disturbing erotica proved to have a strong aggression-facilitating effect. In practical terms, this finding can be taken to mean that a great majority of male college students is both aroused and disturbed by exposure to such sexual activities as flagellantism and bestiality and that, because of this, erotic themes of this kind have the capacity to promote antisocial behaviors, at least temporarily. These consequences are not necessarily restricted to erotica that feature rather extreme sexual practices, however. They accrue to all erotica that elicit, for whatever reason, a negative reaction. The evaluative response that mediates the hedonic valence of the reaction to erotica has been explored by Byrne and his associates (e.g., Byrne, Fisher, Lamberth, and Mitchell, 1974) and appears to be highly variable, especially in males. Dependent upon a person's upbringing, erotica can be hailed or condemned and elicit affective reactions accordingly. Persons with limited sexual socialization experiences, in particular, have been found to respond negatively to erotica (e.g., Fisher and Byrne, 1978). Such persons, the so-called *erotophobes*, appear to be especially vulnerable to behaving more aggressively after exposure to erotica, even to comparatively mild erotica—innocuous as these stimuli may seem to others. Apparently, one person's "turn-on" is another's "turn-off." With such individual variation in the hedonic response to erotica, the accurate prediction of erotica effects depends to a high degree on personality considerations. This acknowledgement amounts to saying that attempts to predict the effects of visual erotica on aggression solely on the basis of what is being depicted are bound to be imprecise and that experiential factors will have to be considered in the construction of adequate predictive models.

Relative to the control, exposure to comparatively nonarousing, pleasant erotica did not reduce motivated aggressive behavior. This finding fails to corroborate earlier observations (White, 1979) and seems inconsistent with the proposal that pleasant erotic fare has a beneficial effect on annoyed persons (Baron, 1977). It is conceivable, however, that in the present investigation this failure resulted from the exclusion of nonarousing erotica that were rated as being extremely pleasant. The exclusion was necessary to match erotica and nonerotica on hedonic valence. In operational terms, the most attractive nude females in the most provocative poses made a poor hedonic match for gourmet food and baby animals and had to be replaced by somewhat less appealing women. But it is also possible that the annoyance accomplished by the provocation treatment used in the present investigation was considerably more intense than that created by the procedures employed in the earlier investigations, and that the well documented annoyance-diminishing effect of exposure to pleasant, nonarousing erotic fare (cf. Zillmann and Sapolsky, 1977) was simply not strong enough, in the present case, to produce a reduction in retaliatory behavior.

ALTERNATIVE EXPLANATIONS

In the present investigation, erotic and nonerotic stimuli associated with negative valence contained acts of aggression. The erotica featured such scenes as the mutual whipping of a male and female prior to and during intercourse [The whipping constitutes aggression only to the extent that it is perceived to be without mutual consent (cf. Zillmann, 1979).], and the nonerotica depicted events such as the killing of seals. The number of aggressive acts in the erotica was above that in the nonerotica; the destructive impact of these acts, on the other hand, was greater for nonerotica than for erotica. In addition, it will be remembered that events depicted in the stimuli associated with negative valence were rated to be crueler than those depicted in the stimuli associated with positive valence. Negative valence, then, was confounded with aggressiveness; and this circumstance makes possible the argument that the observed effects of valence actually resulted from the pertinence of aggressive cues in the respective stimulus condition (cf. Berkowitz, 1965, 1970). In recent research on the effects of nonaggressive and aggressive erotica (Donnerstein, personal communication), it has, in fact, been found that after exposure to aggressive erotica male aggression against females is at a higher level than after exposure to similarly arousing but nonaggressive erotica. No such difference was observed for intermale aggression, however.

In order to determine whether or not aggressive cues were significantly involved in the hedonic-valence effect obtained in the present investigation, a follow-up experiment was conducted (Zillmann, Bryant, and Carveth, in press). An "aggressive" erotic film featuring sadomasochistic behavior was successfully matched on both excitatory potential and negative hedonic valence with a film featuring bestiality (with cooperative animals). Compared against a no-exposure control, both films increased motivated aggression substantially, but to virtually identical degrees. Consistent with Donnerstein's observations, then, aggressiveness in highly arousing erotic films seems of little consequence for *intermale* aggression. [This assessment excludes rapists. There is reason to expect that "aggressive" erotica might further aggressive action in this subpopulation (cf. Abel, Barlow, Blanchard, and Guild, 1977).] Independent of general implications, however, the results of the follow-up experiment give no support to the aggressive-cue hypothesis and thus rule it out as an alternative explanation to the present findings.

The follow-up experiment also included a stimulus condition low in excitatory potential and very high in positive hedonic valence. This communication was composed of the photographs that had to be dismissed as too pleasant (i.e., beautiful female nudes in sexually provocative poses). There was a tendency for exposure to these "hyperpleasant" stimuli to reduce intermale aggression (relative to the no-exposure control), but this tendency again failed to be reliable statistically. It appears, then, that the earlier reported failure to observe a reduction of retaliatory behavior after exposure to pleasant, nonarousing erotica was not due to the stimuli's insufficient pleasantness, but may indeed have resulted from the severity of the provocation treatment. Taken together, these failures to replicate can be interpreted as suggesting that the aggression-reducing effect of the erotic fare in question is limited to minor and moderate provocations. This suggestion, needless to say, constitutes a post-hoc account of the findings, and it remains to be determined, through experimentation, whether or not the effect of these erotica is, as projected, a function of the magnitude of provocation and annoyance.

NOTES

*This investigation was supported by Grant BNS77-07194 from the National Science Foundation to Dolf Zillmann. Paul Cominsky was at the University of Massachusetts and Norman Medoff at Indiana University when the study was completed.

1. The authors gratefully acknowledge the assistance of the Institute for Sex Research at Indiana Univeristy in securing appropriate erotic stimuli.

2. NJM conducted the pretest.

3. PWC served as the experimenter. The authors are indebted to Chester Mysliewicz, who served as the confederate.

4. Alternative procedures for the measurement of aggressive reactions have employed a teaching task and have come under criticism (e.g., Baron, 1977) because the delivery of noxious stimuli in response to errors made by a learner can be construed as help-giving behavior. The battleship procedure rules out such interpretations by setting up a competitive exchange that focuses on destruction.

Berl Kutchinsky

The Effect of Easy Availability of Pornography on the Incidence of Sex Crimes: The Danish Experience

One of the traditional fears about pornography is that exposure to such material may trigger bizarre sexual responses in certain abnormal individuals, leading to the commitment of serious sex crimes (Clor, 1969; Commission on Obscenity and Pornography, 1970; Berkowitz, 1971). If this conjecture were well-founded, one would have to expect an increase in the number of sex crimes in a country like Denmark, where pornography during recent years has been easily available (Ben-Veniste, 1971; Kutchinsky, 1971a, in press). As can be seen in Figure 1, there has been no such increase—in fact, the number of sex crimes has decreased rather dramatically since 1967. From a fairly steady annual average of 85 cases of sexual offenders per 100,000 inhabitants, the number was reduced within three years to an average of less than 50 cases. Clearly, the trigger hypothesis of pornography must be rejected. The question is whether the opposite theory, often called the "safety-valve" theory [Kronhausen and Kronhausen, 1964], has gained any support. Does the decrease in registered sex crimes in Denmark have anything to do with the easy availability of pornography?

This article presents a digest of a number of investigations aimed at answering this question.[1] For various practical reasons we shall concentrate on Copenhagen and on sex crimes committed by males against females.

Reprinted from the *Journal of Social Issues*, Vol. 29, No. 3 (1973), pp. 163–181, by permission of the Society for the Psychological Study of Social Issues and the author.

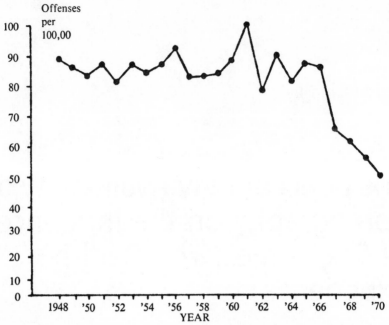

FIGURE 1. Incidence of all sex offenses (except incest) known to the police in Denmark during the period 1948-1970.

The analysis consists of two parts: a descriptive one (was there really a decrease?) and an explanatory one (why did the decrease occur there and then?).

The change in the total yearly number of sex crimes against females known to the police in Copenhagen during the period 1959-1970 is presented in Figure 2. It can be seen that there was a somewhat irregular downward trend until 1965, but thereafter the decrease became steady and substantial. In Table 1 these data are broken down into various types of crime, showing that there has been a considerable decrease in all types of sexual offenses except rape. The largest changes were found in *peeping, verbal indecency*, and *offenses against girls* (mainly cases of child molestation).

Descriptions of trends in crime statistics are in themselves not very informative. These figures only represent registrations made by the police, and it is well known that such registrations are the result of a complicated selection process. This process may be viewed as a chain of "decisions": A person decides whether or not to commit a criminal act; the object of this act "decides" whether or not to consider itself a victim of a crime and whether or not to report it to the police; the police, finally, decide whether or not to accept the complaint and to register an offense. The chain begins and ends with the legislative decision whether or not certain types of acts should be included in the criminal law—and accordingly in the crime statistics. At each of these junctures there may have been changes in the "deci-

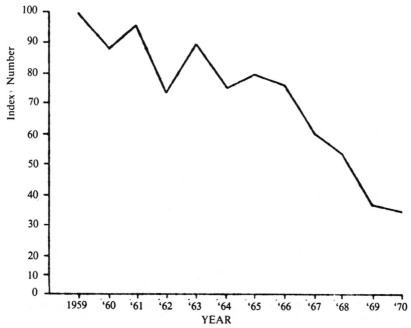

FIGURE 2. Sex offenses against females, known to the police in Copenhagen during the period 1959-1970. Index 100 = 895 cases.

sion process" leading to the exclusion of acts from the crime statistics which would earlier have been included. The factors responsible for the decrease may of course differ from one type of crime to another, and changes may have occurred at more than one juncture.

Two possible reasons for the decrease in the statistics examined here may immediately be excluded. During the period in question and concerning the crimes in question there were no legislative changes *nor* any changes in the official registration procedures which could have excluded any act, earlier included, from being registered. In other words, the decrease was not merely a technical artifact. Given that, the following possibilities remain:

1. The actual number of crimes committed may have decreased. (Only in this case need we consider the possibility of a safety-valve effect of pornography.)
2. The reporting frequency may have been reduced due to a change in the victims' definition of these acts as being criminal or not, and/or their tendency to report to the police when they felt victimized.
3. The police may have changed their reaction to people reporting sex crimes; they may have stopped filing complaints which they would earlier have accepted.

Three different types of data were gathered in order to assess these possibilities. A survey of victimization and attitudes in the general popula-

Table 1
SEX OFFENSES AGAINST FEMALES IN COPENHAGEN
BASED ON POLICE RECORDS

Offenses Registered	1959	1960	1961	1962	1963	1964	1965	1966	1967	1968	1969	1970	1959–69 Relative Decrease %	1959–70 Total No. of Cases	%
Rape	32	21	25	29	22	20	24	34	23	28	27	31	—	316	4.1
Exhibitionism	249	233	285	226	303	225	203	208	163	154	104	84	58.2	2437	31.3
Peeping	99	66	73	55	60	61	76	65	40	40	20	11	79.8	666	8.6
Coitus with minors	51	37	46	46	38	18	31	21	24	19	19	23	62.7	375	4.8
Verbal indecency	45	47	53	35	51	43	40	29	34	24	13	7	71.1	421	5.4
Incest	—	5	4	7	3	2	4	3	6	3	1	2	—	40	0.5
Other offenses against women	137	111	126	96	118	103	125	135	90	107	60	56	56.2	1264	16.2
Other offenses against girls	282	270	250	178	219	204	220	190	160	106	87	96	69.1	2262	29.1
	895	790	862	672	814	676	723	685	540	481	331	310	63.0	7779	100.0

tion was carried out with the purpose of ascertaining whether there had been a change in the social definition of and the readiness to report sex crimes. A series of interviews and a pilot study on legal attitudes gave some information about changes in the attitudes and unofficial registration procedures of the police. Finally, certain comparisons of all cases known to the police in various years could be used to test hypotheses concerning the decrease. This article presents a brief account of the major (and in some cases preliminary) findings, concentrating on four types of sex crimes: *exhibitionism, peeping, physical indency towards women*, and *physical indecency towards girls*—with a special emphasis on the two latter types. These four types constitute about 85% of all cases of heterosexual sex crimes known to the police in Copenhagen.

PUBLIC ATTITUDES TOWARDS SEX CRIMES

The possibility of changes in the victims' definitions of and attitudes towards reporting sexual offenses was investigated in an interview study of 198 men and 200 women, carried out in Copenhagen in December 1969. The respondents constituted a representative sample of the Copenhagen population, aged 18 to 60 (for a detailed account of this study, see Kutchinsky, in press).

A series of questions were designed to obtain some idea about what people in general considered "a sex crime." As suggested above, the idea was that due to a more relaxed atmosphere a number of sexual acts earlier considered criminal might no longer be seen in that light. They might still be considered annoying or even offensive, but they had lost their quality of being "criminal," a quality which is probably a necessary condition for reporting an act to the police. Eight different cases of sexual interference, phrased in one or two sentences, were described to the respondents. In each case the respondents were asked to tell whether, in their personal opinion, this act was to be considered criminal or not. Although no directly comparable data from earlier studies are available, the results nevertheless provide some important clues.

While the definition of an act as criminal may be considered a necessary condition for reporting it to the police, it would certainly not be a sufficient condition. For a number of reasons, a person who feels victimized by a sex crime may decide not to report it (see Kutchinsky, in press). Even if there had been no change in people's conceptions about sex crimes, serious changes in the readiness to report such acts might account for at least part of the decrease in the police figures. Therefore another part of the interview was designed to bear on attitudes towards reporting sex crimes, as well as changes in such attitudes. Four different crimes were described, each representing one typical example of the four types that we are concerned with. The respondents were asked how they would react if they themselves (occasionally the respondent's child or wife) were the victims. Furthermore, respondents over 25 years of age were asked what they would have done if the same thing had happened 10 years ago.

Finally, questions were asked about the respondents' own experience as victims of sex crimes. Comparisons with the police statistics indicated that, in spite of the low numbers, the victimization data were fairly valid; nevertheless they will only be used to indicate approximations of actual reporting frequencies of the various types of crime.

EXHIBITIONISM

The interview survey findings indicated that between 1959 and 1969 there was a change in people's attitudes towards exhibitionism, which may account for at least a major part of the 58% decrease in the number of cases known to the police. Indecent exposure probably has the lowest reporting frequency of all sex crimes. However, it was estimated that while 10 years ago the actual reporting frequency was not higher than 10%, it might easily have dropped since to about 4%—equal to a 60% decrease in the number of cases reported. The changing views on exhibitionism were also indicated by considerable differences[2] between younger and older age groups, both in the number of respondents who would consider such a case a criminal act, and in the number of respondents who would report it to the police (Kutchinsky, 1972b; in press).

PEEPING

The survey data indicated that only a small fraction of the 80% decrease in police statistics on peeping between 1959 and 1969 could be explained by changes in public attitudes. Reporting frequencies of this type of crime are fairly high. It was estimated that a minimum of 40% of all cases detected were reported to the police (although not necessarily registered by the police)—and extremely few respondents indicated that they had changed their minds about this. The conclusion was corroborated by the fact that all age groups shared more or less the same attitudes towards peepers and towards reporting such cases to the police. The fact about peeping seems to be that it is considered an intrusion upon privacy more than an act of sexual indecency. Accordingly, it is not so much influenced by the changing views on sex and on minor sex crimes.

PHYSICAL INDECENCY TOWARDS WOMEN

The survey data indicated that the 56% decrease in registered cases of physical indecency towards women might fully, or at least to a large extent, be explained by a reduced reporting frequency of this type of incidence. This conclusion was based on several facts. First, reporting frequency was generally rather low (there is little point in making numerical estimates, since the degree of seriousness varies considerably) and a fairly large proportion of respondents mentioned that they had changed their attitudes towards reporting such incidents. Second, women tended to look considerably more leniently upon minor cases of indecency than did men. Finally, among female respondents there were highly significant differences between younger and older age groups, both in the definition of indecency as "a criminal act" and in the tendency to report such cases to the police. For instance, when comparing female respondents under the age of 30 to those of 40 and above there were about twice as many among the older as among the younger who would consider a case of "touching woman's breast in streetcar" a criminal act (about 40% and 20%, respectively). These age differences among the female respondents are especially significant, since the majority of victims of physical indecency are very *young* women. Thus, the decrease in the number of cases reported to the police may not only be due to a generally more tolerant view of minor sexual interferences. First and foremost, perhaps, it may be due to the fact that a "new generation of victims" has come of age—a group less concerned about these things than the older generation.

PHYSICAL INDECENCY TOWARDS GIRLS

The category *physical indecency towards girls* constitutes mainly child molestation. Findings indicated that only a slight fraction of the 69% decrease from 1959 to 1969 in cases registered by the police could be explained as being due to a reduced reporting frequency. No less than 93% of the respondents would consider a specified and typical case of child molestation criminal, a viewpoint which was shared by men and women and all age groups alike. This fact rather excludes the liability of any change in the social definition of this type of crime. Furthermore, reporting frequency of offenses against children is rather high (it could be estimated to be at least 50%, depending of course upon the severity of the case), and very few respondents said they had changed their views in this respect. When comparing parents to nonparents of children aged 3 to 14 years, a highly significant difference in reporting readiness appeared. Parents (either sex) in the 25-29 age range, would tend to report a case of "indecency towards a 5-year-old girl" considerably more often than nonparents in the same age group (73% vs. 39%). In fact, the high percentage of potential reporters to the police was found in this category of respondents—the young parents—who could be expected to have both the most realistic and the most consequential views on this type of sex crimes. Thus, in contrast to the "new generation of *adult* female victims" there is no indication of a "new generation of parents of child victims" who are less concerned about having the offender punished. The possibility does remain that the child *victims* may have changed in their reaction to sexual interference as well as their tendency to tell parents about such incidents. If such a change has occurred, however, it would likely be in the direction of greater awareness of such incidents on the part of the children as well as an increased tendency to talk to the parents about it. In other words, changes in child victim attitudes combined with unchanged parental attitudes toward child molestation would likely have led to an increased rather than a reduced reporting frequency.

In conclusion, the survey of attitudes towards sex crimes in Copenhagen offered a tentative solution to the puzzle of the apparent decrease in two types of crime, exhibitionism and physical indecency towards adult females. It may well be that crimes in these two categories are less often reported. Other factors may also have served to reduce the number, but the information so far available suggests that such factors are not necessary. As far as peeping and child molestation are concerned, the survey excluded, convincingly although tentatively, the possibility that the decrease in registered cases could be due to changing attitudes among the general populace, leaving only two possibilities. Either the decrease is due to a change in police attitudes or there has been a real decrease in the number of criminal acts of these types committed.

CHANGES IN POLICE ATTITUDES

I shall now deal briefly with the possibility that the decrease in registered sex crimes may have been due to an unofficial change in police attitudes towards such crimes, resulting in a reduced tendency to register reports. Two minor investigations provided information about this question. One study provided quantitative data about the attitudes of 50 young policemen towards sex crimes compared to their attitudes towards other types of crimes, as well as the attitudes of various other groups. A Danish version of the Sellin-Wolfgang questionnaire for the measurement of attitudes towards crime was used in this pilot study (Sellin and Wolfgang, 1964). In another study, qualitative information about sex crimes was obtained through a series of semistructured interviews with police officers from various ranks.

The former investigation showed that policemen tend to consider sex crimes rather seriously, both in comparison to other groups of persons and when compared to other types of crimes such as crimes of property. For example, a case of sexual assault on a woman (with no physical harm done) obtained the same average score as a $1000 robbery, while a case of indecent exposure ranked the same as "breaking into a locked car, driving, and leaving it unharmed in another place." The list did not contain any cases of peeping.

The information obtained through interviews with police officers was also rather inconclusive as far as peeping is concerned. While high ranking officers would maintain that all cases reported were duly registered, some officers of lower rank said that policemen sometimes try to calm people down instead of taking action when minor cases of sexual interference are reported, and sometimes these cases would not be filed. On the other hand, all officers strongly and spontaneously asserted that all cases of indecency towards children (including attempts) were not only carefully registered, but also seriously investigated.

The conclusions that can be drawn from these findings vary with the category of offense. As far as exhibitionism and indecency towards women are concerned, it is possible that the decrease in the most trifling cases of these two types may be due to the combined effects of a more relaxed public attitude and a more relaxed police attitude. In general, I would tend to consider the former much more important than the latter.

For peeping, no firm conclusion can be reached. While it seems quite certain that the decrease cannot be due to a change in reporting frequency among the general population, the possibility cannot be excluded that at least part of the decrease may be attributed to an unofficial change in the handling of this type of crime by the police. On the other hand, there are reasons (see below) to think that the real cause of the decrease may be found in changes in offender behavior rather than police behavior.

In the category "indency toward girls," our findings so far have excluded both the possibility of a change in reporting frequency by the public and in registration frequency by the police. Accordingly, the only possibility left seems to be that there has been a very substantial decrease in the actual number of crimes of this type committed.

SUBSTANTIATING THE CONCLUSIONS

Is there a way of testing these tentative conclusions through more direct observation of crime data? An immediate answer to the question, How many cases of this or that type were *actually* committed, for instance, in

1959 and 1969?, cannot be obtained. Even the most refined victimization survey would fail in such a task. However, there is another way of comparing crime data from the two years. A comparison of some of the characteristics of the cases reported "then" and "now" yields evidence sufficient to either falsify or support some of our conclusions.

In a comparative study, all cases of sexual offenses registered by the police in Copenhagen in 1959, 1965, 1969, and 1970 were analyzed in detail on the basis of available records, and the seriousness of each case was assessed by means of objectively defined criteria. Some of the evidence on seriousness and on age of the victim in two types of sex crimes, namely physical indecency towards women and physical indecency towards girls, will be considered.

PHYSICAL INDECENCY TOWARDS WOMEN

A decrease during the 1960s in the registered number of cases of physical indecency towards women is thought to be due primarily to a change in women's conceptions of minor sexual interferences as criminal and a decrease in the readiness to report such cases to the police. If it were true that such a change had occurred, the decrease in reporting frequency would be expected to vary according to the seriousness of the crime—the more trifling the crime, the greater the reduction. In other words, when comparing cases of indecency towards women reported a decade ago and reported today, one would expect to find a significantly greater reduction in the nonserious than in the serious cases.

This expectation was fulfilled. When all registered cases were divided into three categories of seriousness (low, medium, and high), there was an 84% decrease in the low seriousness category between 1959 and 1970 while the cases with high seriousness only decreased by 32%. Significantly, in cases of rape, the *most* serious type of sex crime against women, there was no decrease at all.

Important evidence for the above conclusion concerning the decrease in reporting frequency was the finding of a difference between the attitudes of younger and older women towards sex crimes. In fact, it was proposed that a major reason for the decrease might be that a "new generation of victims" had appeared on the scene who were less concerned about minor sexual interferences. If this were true, one would expect to find a significantly greater reduction of cases reported by young victims than by older ones. This expectation was fulfilled: The number of registered victims aged 15–21 years decreased by 85% between 1959 and 1970, while during the same period the number of victims who were over 21 only decreased by 32%.

PHYSICAL INDECENCY TOWARDS GIRLS

Our investigations so far seemed to exclude the possibility that there has been a reduction in reporting frequency for child molestation. Based on the same logic as above, this conclusion would be strongly supported—in fact confirmed—if a comparison between cases reported "then" and "now" did not show a larger decrease in the nonserious cases than in the serious ones. This expectation was fulfilled: The reduction in registered cases was about the same at all levels of seriousness. In fact, the mean "seriousness score" for this type of crime was exactly the same in 1959 as in 1969.

In respect to indecency towards children, seriousness and age are related. If, then, the decrease were due to a reduced reporting frequency, a larger decrease would be expected in the number of older children victimized than in the number of very young victims. The comparison showed that there was not a larger reduction among older victims—rather, the greatest reduction was seen in cases where the victims were 4–7 years of age.

A comparison of the ages of the victims of child molestation in the four years, 1959, 1965, 1969, and 1970, showed a very interesting trend. *The decrease in the registered number of cases occurred earlier in the decade for the younger victims.* This finding not only clearly serves to reject a hypothesis of the decrease being due to a reduction in reporting frequency, it also strongly supports the conclusion that the decrease must primarily have been a real one. Whatever factor influenced offenders of children towards committing fewer offenses, it had an early and strong impact on cases involving girls 4–5 years of age (it had little effect on the few cases where the victims were below the age of 4). It had a somewhat later, but eventually just as strong, influence on cases involving victims aged 6–11 years. Finally, the decrease in cases involving victims aged 12–14 years occurred rather late and was less substantial.

The figures concerning offenses against girls 4–5 years of age are especially illustrative. In 1959, 52 cases were registered by the police in Copenhagen; by 1964 the number had gone down to 36; one year later, in 1965, the figure dropped to 16 cases. The subsequent years showed no further decrease; there were 19 cases of offenses against girls in this age group in 1969 and 1970. The year 1965, which alone counted for a 56% decrease in child molestation of this age group, was incidentally the year in which the first hard-core pornographic picture magazines appeared in Denmark, selling, according to one estimate, over two million copies (Ben-Veniste, 1971).

IN SEARCH OF A CAUSAL EXPLANATION

Having localized the decrease in some types of crimes primarily with the offender, in other types primarily with the victim, we now search for a causal explanation. To come out even, we would have to point out one (set of) causal factor(s) which influenced the peepers and the offenders against little girls, but not (or only to a slight extent) the exhibitionists and the offenders against adult women. And we would have to find another (set of) causal factor(s) which influenced the victims of indecent exposure and indecency towards adult women, but not the victims of peeping and child molestation. This is not the occasion for an exhaustive analysis of possibilities. I shall restrict myself to a brief discussion of two obviously relevant factors, both of which appear to have a temporal coincidence with the decrease.

The first one has to do with the *general change in sexual mores and attitudes* which has taken place in Denmark during recent years. The indications of such a change are numerous, the alleged results being greater sexual freedom for both men and women, fewer prejudices, less double morality, more openness, and so on. On the whole, however, there is hardly any doubt that to the vast majority of people, the "sexual revolution" is a revolution of the mind rather than the body: The change is a change of attitudes rather than of behavior.

It is conceivable that some sex offenders may have benefited from this general change in the sexual climate, obtaining adequate sexual relationships to the exclusion of the need to commit sex crimes. It is also to be expected that, in the long run, a more sensible sex education may serve to reduce the number of sex crimes committed. It is quite unthinkable, however, that this "sexual mores" factor through influencing potential offenders could be responsible for, for instance, the 60% reduction in cases of child molestation within the period 1965-69.

Rather, the "sexual mores" factor may have affected certain victims, making them less inclined to report minor sex offenses to the police. That such a change has indeed taken place was clearly demonstrated with respect to such types of sex crimes as indecent exposure and indecency towards adult women. Our investigations also showed that there has been no change or only a slight change in public attitudes towards serious sex crimes (rape, child molestation) or frightening sex crimes (peeping).

In other words, the general change in the sexual climate in Denmark could directly explain the decrease in indecency towards adult women and in exhibitionism, but not the very substantial decreases in peeping and child molestation. We are forced to look for another factor, and we need not search for long. The *high availability of pornography* in Denmark is too spectacular to be overlooked. During the 1960s Denmark experienced a "porno wave" with two rather distinctive phases. After 1961 a steeply accelerating number of pornographic books were sold in Denmark. This phase culminated in 1967, the year in which a penal law ban on pornographic literature was repealed—and very soon the porno books were out

(Kutchinsky, 1973). However, after 1965 the second phase of the porno wave took over: Millions of hard-core pornographic picture magazines in increasing numbers, variety, and audacity became available. This second wave culminated in 1969, the year in which the sale of pornographic pictures was legalized to persons 16 years of age and over.

There is some indication that the availability of pornography may have directly affected attitudes towards indecent exposure, while it had no effects on the victims of physical indecency. More interesting, however, is the question of whether the availability of pornography has affected potential or earlier sex offenders.

The likelihood that peepers may have welcomed the pornography as an adequate substitute for peeping needs no discussion. In a certain sense, Denmark during recent years has been a "peepers paradise" (Kutchinsky, 1972a).

Less evident would seem to be the idea that potential or former offenders of little children should have been able to use pornography instead. Two objections to this idea come to mind. The first objection is based on the findings in several studies that sex offenders are, as a rule, not more acquainted with pornography nor more sexually aroused by such material than are other males—in fact, such differences as are found tend to be in the opposite direction (Gebhard, Gagnon, Pomeroy, and Christenson, 1965; Thorne, Haupt, and Allen, 1966; Goldstein, Kant, Judd, Rice, and Green, 1971; Walker, 1971; Cook and Fosen, 1971; Johnson, Kupperstein, and Peters, 1971; Davis and Braucht, 1971). One reason for this could be that the use of pornography requires the ability to empathize and fantasize, an ability which is correlated with education. The poorly educated, a group to which the majority of sex offenders belong, "are apt to be much more pragmatic and require something more concrete in order to respond" (Gebhard et al., 1965, p. 671).

This objection seems relevant to the "pornographic factor" theory of the decrease as far as the effects of pornographic literature are concerned. The abundance of pornographic books could be expected to serve as "safety valves" only for the better educated (or more intelligent) potential sex offenders. Picture pornography, on the other hand, is not affected by this objection; on the contrary, one might expect that these full-color magazines and films with the reputation of "leaving nothing to fantasy" would be very well suited as a means of sexual stimulation for persons with a poor imagination, persons who need "something more concrete." Indeed, our survey of the general population in Copenhagen showed that in Denmark, unlike even the most recent studies in the United States (e.g., Abelson, Cohen, Heaton, and Sudor, 1971), there is no relation between the use of pornography and level of education. The findings in Denmark, in fact, indicate that the relation between acquaintance with pornography and level of education may simply be a function of the accessibility and the cost of the material. When pornography is scarce and expensive, it is naturally more often obtained by the privileged groups.

The second objection that might be raised against the idea of pornography as an adequate substitute to offenses against children concerns the content of pornographic magazines and films. Without exception, the visual pornography of the late 1960s depicted adult models; how could this type of pornography appeal to pedophile offenders? The answer may be found in the literature concerning this type of offender. According to Gebhard et al. (1965), only one-fourth to one-third of the sexual offenders of girls examined were classified as pedophiles, and in about half of those cases "some degree of socio-sexual deprivation existed at the time of the offense, which may have triggered the behavior [p. 74]." Gebhard et al. further mentioned that "the term 'pedophile' is somewhat unfortunate since these men did not consciously prefer children as sexual partners, but simply found them acceptable [p. 74]." In other words, to the majority of sexual offenders against children the criminal interference with children was not a coveted goal in itself; rather it served as a poor substitute for a pre-ferred, but unobtainable, normal heterosexual experience. A number of other facts about the heterosexual offender of children (discussed by Geb-hard et al., 1965) are relevant: he is usually "moralistic and conservative . . . . caught in a conflict between [his] morals and [his] behavior [p. 81]"; in contrast to most other sex offenders he responds rather positively to por-nography; he tends to masturbate rather frequently; and his masturbation fantasies are quite average, that is, he does not especially fantasize about children.

The changes in the pornographic scene in Copenhagen coincide exactly with the general decrease in sex offenses against female children. This holds both for the rapid decrease in offenses between 1965 and 1969 (the years of the "picture porno wave") and for the fact that there was in 1970 neither any further decrease nor any significant increase. The 1970 pornography did not differ in quality or in quantity from the 1969 pornography. In other words, those who were able to make use of this kind of substitute—appar-ently about two-thirds—had done so before 1970 (for developments after 1970, see Kutchinsky, in press). So far no one has been able to point to any factor other than the availability of pornography which could explain the specific course of the decrease in sex offenses against girls.

For the sake of completeness, the question of why the availability of pornography apparently did not affect exhibitionists as well as offenders against adult women, including rapists, must be examined.

The possibility that some exhibitionists have been able to use pornog-raphy should not be excluded. On the whole, however, one can hardly expect that a person who enjoys so much being looked at that he scorns the risk of arrest and punishment would readily substitute looking at others for self-exposure.

As far as offense against adult women are concerned, the explanation is quite simple—with Gebhard et al. at hand. According to these investigators, the offender against adult women is in almost every respect a striking contrast to the offender against children. As a rule, the former is *not* sociosexually deprived, rather he is "very strongly heterosexual and . . . interested (and singularly successful) in gratifying [his] sexual desires with adult females. The other outlets . . . were unimportant [1965, p. 131]." He is a "simple, unimaginative, impulsive opportunist [who] seeks gratification of [his] desires by the easiest and most immediate route with a minimum of reflection . . . He is the sort of man who is doomed to land in jail on some minor charge sooner or later, and the sexual element is almost fortuitous [p. 132]." In other words, the offender against women (and here we may include the rapist) would be the last one of whom to expect that he could use pornography instead of the offense. The criminal act was not a substitute, therefore it could not be substituted by pornography.

CONCLUSION

The unexpected outcome of this analysis is that the high availability of hard-core pornography in Denmark was most probably the very direct cause of a considerable decrease in at least one type of serious sex offense, namely, child molestation. Between 1965 (the first year of the availability of hard-core pornographic pictures) and 1969 (the year of the repeal of the Penal Law ban, and of peak production), the number of cases of this type dropped from 220 to 87. The implication of our conclusion is that a large number of such offenses have been avoided since the late 1960s, because potential offenders obtained sufficient sexual satisfaction through the use of pornography, most probably combined with masturbation.

The task ahead is to submit this implication to a number of direct tests. This would seem to be fairly easy. In Denmark we may compare, among other things, the use of pornography by sexual recidivists and nonrecidivists (data not yet published show that the number of recidivists has decreased just as much as the number of first offenders). In countries where pornography is not readily available, controlled experiments might be conducted in which pornography is used in the therapy of "child molesters" and "peepers" on probation. The pornography and the way it is placed at the disposal of potential sex offenders in such experiments should perhaps resemble the "Danish experiment" rather closely. It is quite likely that the type, the dosage, and not least the relaxed community attitudes towards pornography are important aspects of any "substitution" process.

NOTES

Correspondence regarding this article may be addressed to B. Kutchinsky, Institute of Criminal Science, 17 Rosenborggade, DK-1130 Copenhagen K, Denmark.

1. The studies were initiated by the Commission on Obscenity and Pornography and supported financially partly by the Commission, partly by the Danish Social Science Research Council. Preliminary results appeared in Kutchinsky, 1971b; a fuller and documented account of the studies can be found in Kutchinsky, in press.

2. All "differences" mentioned in this article refer to differences that were statistically significant at or beyond the .05 level of significance, usually estimated by a χ^2 analysis.

Bonnelle Strickling, with David Copp and
Susan Wendell

Selected Bibliography of Social Scientific Essays

Abel, G. G., and Blanchard, E. B. "The Measurement and Generation of Sexual Arousal in Male Sexual Deviation. In *Progress in Behavior Modification*, vol. 2, edited by Hersen, Eisler, and Miller. New York: Academic Press, 1976.

————, Blanchard, E. B., and Becker, J. V. "Psychological Treatment of Rapists." In *Sexual Assault: The Victim and the Rapist*, edited by M. Walker and S. Brodsky. Lexington, Mass.: Lexington Books, 1976.

————; Barlow, D. H.; Blanchard, E. B.; and Guild, D. "The Components of Rapists' Sexual Arousal." *Archives of General Psychiatry* 34 (1977): 895-903.

————, Blanchard, E. B., and Becker, J. V. "An Integreated Treatment Program for Rapists." In *Clinical Aspects of the Rapist*, edited by R. Rada. New York: Grune and Stratton, 1978.

————, Blanchard, E. B., Murphy, W. D., Becker, J. V., and Djenderdjian, A. "Two Methods of Measuring Penile Response." *Behavior Therapy* 12

Abelson, H. et al. "National Survey of Public Attitudes toward and Experience with Erotic Manuals." *Technical Reports of the Commission on Obscenity and Pornography*, vol. 6. Washington, D.C.: U.S. Government Printing Office, 1970: 1-137.

Bandura, A. *Aggression: A Social Learning Analysis*. Englewood Cliffs, N.J.: Prentice-Hall, 1973.

Barbaree, H. E., Marshall, W. L., and Lanter, R. D. "Deviant Sexual Arousal in Rapists." *Behavior Research and Therapy* 17 (1979): 215-222.

Barclay, A. M. "The Effect of Hostility on Physiological and Fantasy Responses." *Journal of Personality* 37 (1969): 651-667.

Barclay, A. M. "The Effect of Female Aggressiveness on Aggressive and Sexual Fantasies."

Journal of Projective Techniques and Personality Assessment 34 (1970): 19–26.
———. "Linking Sexual and Aggressive Motives: Contributions of 'Irrelevant' Arousals." *Journal of Personality* 39 (1971): 481–492.
Barlow, D. H. "Assessment of Sexual Behavior." In *Handbook of Behavioral Assessment*, edited by A. R. Ciminero. New York: Wiley-Interscience, 1977.
Baron, R. A. "Aggression as a Function of Audience Presence and Prior Anger Arousal." *Journal of Experimental Social Psychology* 7 (1971): 505–523 (a).
———. "Aggression as a Function of Magnitude of Victim's Pain Cues, Level of Prior Anger Arousal, and Aggressor-Victim Similarity." *Journal of Personality and Social Psychology* 18 (1971): 48–54 (b).
———. "Exposure to an Aggressive Model and Apparent Probability of Retaliation from the Victim as Determinants of Adult Aggressive Behavior." *Journal of Experimental Social Psychology* 7 (1971): 343–355 (c).
———. "Heightened Sexual Arousal and Physical Aggression: An Extension to Females." *Journal f Research in Personality* 13 (1979): 41–102.
———. "Reducing the Influence of an Aggressive Model: The Restraining Effects of Discrepant Modeling Cues." *Journal of Personality and Social Psychology* 20 (1971): 240–245 (d).
———, and Eggleston, R. J. "Performance on the 'Aggression Machine': Motivation to Help or Harm?" *Psychonomic Science* 26 (1972): 321–322.
———, and Bell, P. A. "Effects of Heightened Sexual Arousal on Physical Aggression." *Proceedings of the 81st Annual Convention of the American Psychological Association* 8 (1973): 171–172.
———. "The Aggression-Inhibiting Influence of Heightened Sexual Arousal." *Journal of Personality and Social Psychology* 30, 318 (1974) (a).
———. "Sexual Arousal and Physical Aggression: The Inhibiting Influence of 'Cheesecake' and Nudes." *Bulletin of the Psychonomic Society* 3, 337 (1974) (b).
———, and Bell, P. A. "Aggression and Heat: The Influence of Ambient Temperature, Negative Affect, and a Cooling Drink on Physical Aggression." *Journal of Personality and Social Psychology* 33 (1976): 245–255.
———. *Human Aggression.* New York: Plenum Press, 1977.
———, and Bell, P. A. "Sexual Arousal and Aggression by Males: Effects of Type of Erotic Stimuli and Prior Provocation." *Journal of Personality and Social Psychology* 35 (1977): 79–87.
———, and Byrne, D. *Social Psychology: Understanding Human Interaction.* Boston: Allyn and Bacon, 1977.
———. "Aggression-Inhibiting Influence of Sexual Humor." *Journal of Personality and Social Psychology* 36, 189 (1978).
———. "Heightened Sexual Arousal and Physical Aggression: An Extension to Females." (1979). Reprinted in this volume.
Barry, K. *Female Sexual Slavery* Englewood Cliffs, N.J.: Prentice-Hall, 1979.
Beach, F. A. *Human Sexuality in Four Perspectives.* Baltimore: Johns Hopkins University Press, 1976.
Bem, D. J. "Self-Perception Theory." In *Advances in Experimental Social Psychology*, vol. 6, edited by L. Berkowitz. New York: Academic Press, 1972: 1–62.
Ben-Veniste, R. "Pornography and Sex Crimes: The Danish Experience." *Technical Reports of the Commission on Obscenity and Pornography*, vol. 7. Washing-

ton, D.C.: U.S. Government Printing Office, 1971.

Berger, A. S., Simon, W., and Gagnon, J. H. "Youth and Pornography in Social Context." *Archives of Sexual Behavior* 4 (1973).

Berkowitz, L. "The Concept of Aggressive Drive: Some Additional Considerations." In *Advances in Experimental Social Psychology*, vol. 2, edited by L. Berkowitz. New York: Academic Press, 1965.

——, and Geen, R. G. "Film Violence and the Cue Properties of Available Targets." *Journal of Personality and Social Psychology* 4 (1966): 525–530.

——, Lepinski, J. P., and Angulo, E. J. "Awareness of Own Anger Level and Subsequent Aggression." *Journal of Personality and Social Psychology* 11 (1969): 293–300.

——. "The Contagion of Violence: An S-R Mediational Analysis of Some Effects of Observed Aggression." In *Nebraska Symposium on Motivation*, edited by W. J. Arnold and M. M. Page. Lincoln, Neb.: University of Nebraska Press, 1970.

——. "Sex and Violence: We Can't Have It Both Ways." *Psychology Today*, 1971.

——. "Some Determinants of Impulsive Aggression: The Role of Mediated Associations with Reinforcements for Aggression." *Psychological Review* 81 (1974): 165–176.

——, and Frodi, A. "Reactions to a Child's Mistakes as Affected by Her/His Look and Speech." *Social Psychology Quarterly* 42 (1979): 420–425.

——, Cochran, S. T., and Embree, M. C. "Physical Pain and the Goal of Aversively Stimulated Aggression." *Journal of Personality and Social Psychology (1981): in press.*

Bjorksten, O. J. W. *"Sexually Graphic Material in the Treatment of Sexual Disorders." In Clinical Management of Sexual Disorders*. Baltimore: Williams and Wilkins, 1976.

Brownmiller, Susan. *Against Our Will: Men, Women and Rape*. New York: Simon and Schuster, 1975.

Bryant, J., and Zillmann, D. "The Mediating Effect of the Intervention Potential of Communications on Displaced Aggressiveness and Retaliatory Behavior." In *Communication Yearbook 1*, edited by B. D. Ruben. New Brunswick, N.J.: Transactions, Intercommunication Association, 1977.

Burt, M. R. "Cultural Myths and Supports for Rape." *Journal of Personality and Social Psychology* 38 (1980): 217–230.

Buss, A. H. *The Psychology of Aggression*. New York: Wiley, 1961.

Byrne, D., Fisher, J. D., Lamborth, S., and Mitchell, H. E. "Evaluations of Erotica: Facts or Feelings?" *Journal of Personality and Social Psychology* 29 (1974).

——. "The Imagery of Sex." In *Handbook of Sexology*, edited by J. Money and H. Mustaph. Amsterdam: Excerpts Medica, 1977.

——, and Byrne, L., eds. *Exploring Human Sexuality*. New York: Crowell, 1977.

Cantor, J. R., Zillmann, D., and Einsiedel, E. F. "Female Responses to Provocation after Exposure to Aggressive and Erotic Films." *Communication Research* 5 (1978): 395–411.

Cline, V. B. "Another View: Pornography Effects, the State of the Art." In *Where Do You Draw the Line?* edited by V. B. Cline. Provo, Utah: Brigham

Young University Press, 1974.

Clor, H. M. *Obscenity and Public Morality.* Chicago: University of Chicago Press, 1969.

Colson, C. E. "The Evaluation of Pornography: Efforts of Attitude and Perceived Physiological Reaction." *Archives of Sexual Behavior* 3 (1973).

Cook, R. F., and Fosen, R. H. "Pornography and the Sex Offender: Patterns of Exposure and Immediate Arousal Effects of Pornographic Stimuli." In *Technical Reports of the Commission on Obscenity and Pornography*, vol. 7. Washington, D.C.: U.S. Government Printing Office, 1970.

Corey, S. H. "Sex-Guilt and Punishment of Sexua Behavior of Others." Master's thesis. University of Connecticut, 1970.

Court, J. H. "Pornography—Personal and Societal Effects." In *Geigy Psychiatric Symposium*, edited by N. McConaghy. (1974).

———. "Pornography and Sex Crimes: A Re-evaluation in the Light of Recent Trends around the World." *International Journal of Criminology and Penology* 5 (1976): 129.

———. *Law, Light and Liberty.* Adelaide: Lutheran Publishing House, 1975.

Davis, K. E., and Braucht, G. N. "Exposure to Pornography, Character, and Sexual Deviance: A Retrospective Survey." *Journal of Social Issues* 29 (1973): 183–196.

Dengerink, H. A. "Personality Variables as Mediators of Attack-Instigated Aggression." In *Perspectives on Aggression*, edited by R. Geen and E. O'Neal. New York: Academic Press, 1976.

Dienstbier, R. A. "Sex and Violence: Can Research Have It Both Ways?" *Journal of Communications* 27 (1977): 176–188.

Donnerstein, E., Donnerstein, M., and Evans, R. "Erotic Stimuli and Aggression: Facilitation of Inhibition." *Journal of Personality and Social Psychology* 32 (1975): 237–244.

———, and Wilson, D. W. "Effects of Noise and Perceived Control on Ongoing and Subsequent Aggressive Behavior." *Journal of Personality and Social Psychology* 34 (1976): 774–781.

———, Donnerstein, M., and Barrett, G. "Where Is the Facilitation of Media Violence: The Effects of Nonexposure and Placement of Anger Arousal." *Journal of Research in Personality* 10 (1977): 386–398.

———, and Hallam, J. "Facilitating Effects of Erotica on Aggression against Females." *Journal of Personality and Social Psychology* 36 (1978): 1270–1277.

———, and Barret, G. "The Effects of Erotic Stimuli on Male Aggression towards Females." *Journal of Personality and Social Psychology* 36 (1978): 180–188.

———. "Pornography and Violence against Women." (1980). Reprinted this volume, (a).

———. "Pornography Commission Revisited: Aggression-Erotica and Violence against Women." *Journal of Personality and Social Psychology* 39 (1980): 269–277 (b).

———. "Pornography and Violence: Current Research Findings." In *Aggression: Theoretical and Empirical Reviews.* New York: Academic Press, in press.

———, and Malamuth, N. "The Effects of Aggressive-Erotic Stimuli." In *Advances in Experimental Social Psychology*, vol. 15, edited by L. Berkowitz. New York; Academic Press, 1982.

Eysenck, H. J. *Sex and Personality.* London: Open Books, 1976.

————, and Nias, H. *Sex, Violence and the Media*. London: Spector, 1978.

Farkas, G. M. "Trait and State Determinants of Male Sexual Arousal to Descriptions of Coercive Sexuality." Ph.D. thesis. University of Hawaii, 1979.

Feshbach, S., and Malamuth, N. "Sex and Aggression: Proving the Link. *Psychology Today* (November 1978).

Fisher, J. L., and Harris, M. B. "Modeling Arousal and Aggression." *Journal of Social Psychology* 100 (1976): 219–226.

Fisher, W. A., and Byrne, D. "Individual Differences in Affective, Evaluative, and Behavioral Responses to an Erotic Film." *Journal of Applied Social Psychology* 8 (1978): 355–365.

Freud, S. *New Introductory Lectures on Psycho-Analysis*. New York: Norton, 1953.

Frodi, A. "Sexual Arousal, Situational Restrictiveness, and Aggressive Behavior." *Journal of Research in Personality* 11 (1977): 48–58.

Fromkin, H. L., and Brock, T. C. "Erotic Materials: A Commodity Theory Analysis of the Enhanced Desirability That May Accompany Their Unavoidability." *Journal of Applied Social Psychology* 3 (1973): 219–231.

Fromm, E. *The Anatomy of Human Destructiveness*. New York: Holt, Rinehart, and Winston, 1973.

Gager, N., and Schurr, C. *Sexual Assault: Confronting Rape in America*. New York: Grosset and Dunlap, 1976.

Galbraith, G. G., and Mosher, D. L. "Associative Sexual Responses in Relation to Sexual Arousal, Guilt, and External Approval Contingencies." *Journal of Personality and Social Psychology* 10 (1968): 142–147.

————, and Mosher, D. L. "Effects of Sex-Guilt and Sexual Stimulation on the Recall of Word Associations." Journal of Consulting and Clinical Psychology 34 (1970): 67–71.

Gebhard, P. H., Gagnon, J. H., Pomeroy, W. B., and Christenson, C. V. *Sex Offenders*. New York: Harper and Row, 1965.

Geen, R. G. "Effects of Frustration, Attack, and Prior Training in Aggressiveness upon Aggressive Behavior." *Journal of Personality and Social Psychology* 9 (1968): 316–321.

————, Stonner, D., and Shope, G. L. "The Facilitation of Aggression by Aggression: A Study of Response Inhibition and Disinhibition. *Journal of Personality and Social Psychology* 31 (1977): 721–726.

————. "Some Effects of Observing Violence upon the Behavior of the Observer." In *Progress in Experimental Personality Research*, edited by Davies and Dhavan. London: Macmillan, 1978.

Goldstein, M. J.; Kant, H. S.; Judd, L. L.; Rice, C. G.; and Green, R. "Exposure to Pornography and Sexual Behavior in Deviant and Normal Groups." *Technical Reports of the Commission on Obscenity and Pornography*, vol. 7. Washington, D. C.: U.S. Government Printing Office, 1971.

————. "A Behavioral Scientist Looks at Obscenity." In *Perspectives in Law and Psychology*, vol. 1, *The Criminal Justice System*, edited by B. D. Sales. New york: Plenum, 1977.

Harris, M. B., and Huang, L. C. "Arousal and Attribution." *Psychological Reports* 34 (1974): 747–753.

Herrell, J. M. "Sex Differences in Emotional Responses to 'Erotic Literature.' " *Journal of Consulting and Clinical Psychiatry* 43 (1975): 921.

Higgins, J. W., and Katzman, M. B. "Determinants in the Judgement of Obscenity." *American Journal of Psychiatry* 125 (1969): 1733–1738.

Howard, J. L., Liptzin, M. B., and Reifler, C. F. "Is Pornography a Problem?" *Journal of Social Issues* 29 (1973): 133–145.

Jaffe, Y., Malamuth, N., Feingold, J., and Feshbach, S. "Sexual Arousal and Behavioral Aggression." *Journal of Personality and Social Psychology* 30 (1974): 759–764.

James, P. B., and Mosher, D. L. "Thematic Aggression, Hostility-Guilty, and Aggressive Behavior." *Journal of Projective Techniquus and Personality Assessment* 31 (1967): 61–67.

Johnson, W. T., Kupperstein, L. R., and Peters, J. J. "Sex Offenders' Experience with Erotica." *Technical Reports of The Commission on Obscenity and Pornography*, vol. 7. Washington, D.C.: U.S. Government Printing Office, 1971.

Kanin, E. G., and Parcel, S. R. "Sexual Aggression: A Second Look at the Offended Female." *Archives of Sexual Behavior* 6 (1977): 67–76.

Kenyon, F. E. "Pornography, the Law and Mental Health." *British Journal of Psychiatry* 126 (1975): 225–233.

Kerater, G. A., and Walker, C. E. "Reactions of Convicted Rapists to Sexually Explicit Stimuli." *Journal of Abnormal Psychology* 81 (1973): 46–50.

Konecni, V. G. "Annoyance, Type and Duration of Post-Annoyance Activity, and Aggression: The 'Cathartic Effect.' " *Journal of Experimental Psychology: General* 104 (1975): 76–102.

Kostach, M. "Pornography: A Feminist View." *This Magazine* 12 (1978): 4–7.

Kraft-Ebbing, Richard von. *Psycopathia Sexualis.* 11th edition. Stuttgart: 1901.

Kronhausen, D., and Kronhausen, P. *Pornography and the Law.* Revised edition. New York: Ballantine, 1964.

Kutchinsky, B. "Pornography in Denmark: Pieces of a Jigsaw Puzzle Collected around New Year 1970." *Technical Reports of the Commission on Obscenity and Pornography*, vol. 4. Washington, D.C.: U.S. Government Printing Office, 1971 (a).

———. "Towards an Explanation of the Decrease in Registered Sex Crimes in Copenhagen." *Technical Reports of the Commission on Obscenity and Pornography*, vol. 7. Washington, D.C.: U.S. Government Printing Office, 1971 (b).

———. "Deviance and Criminality: The Case of Voyeur in a Peeper's Paradise." Paper presented at the conference on Ethnomethodology, Labelling Theory, and Deviance. University of Edinburgh, 1972 (a).

———. "Sociological Aspects of the Perception of Deviance and Criminality." In *Collected Studies in Criminological Research*, vol. 9, edited by the European Committee on Crime Problems. Strasbourg: Council of Europe, 1972 (b).

———. "Eroticism without Censorship: Sociological Investigations on the Production and Consumption of Pornographic Literature in Denmark." *International Journal of Criminology and Penology* 1 (1973): 217–225.

———. "The Effects of Not Prosecuting Pornography." *British Journal of Sexual Medicine* 3 (1976).

———. *Law, Pornography and Crime: The Danish Experience.* London, Martin Robertson, in preparation.

Lamb, C. "Personality Correlates of Humor Enjoyment Following Motivational

Arousal." *Journal of Personality and Social Psychology* 9 (1968): 237-241.

Laws, D. R. "A Comparison of the Measurement Characteristics of Two Circumferential Penile Tranducers." *Archives of Sexual Behavior* 6 (1977): 45-51.

Lehman, R. E. "The Disinhibiting Effects of Visual Material in Treating Orgasmically Dysfunctional Women." *Behavioral Engineering* 1 (2) (1974): 1-3.

Liebert, R. M., and Schwartzberg, N. S. "Effects of Mass Media." *Annual Review of Psychology* 28 (1977): 141-173.

Love, R. E., Sloan, L. R., and Schmidt, M. J. "Viewing Pornography and Sex Guilt: The Priggish, the Prudent and the Profligate." *Journal of Counseling and Clinical Psychology* 44 (1976): 624-629.

Malamuth, N. M., Feshbach, S., and Jaffe, Y. "Sexual Arousal and Aggression: Recent Experiments and Theoretical Issues." *Journal of Social Issues* 33 (1977): 110-133.

———. "Erotica, Aggression and Perceived Appropriateness." Paper presented at the Annual Meeting of the American Psychological Association, Toronto, 1978.

———, Heim, M., and Feshbach, S. "Sexual Responsiveness of College Students to Rape Depictions: Inhibitory and Disinhibitory Effects. *Journal of Personality and Social Psychology* 3 (1980): 399-408 (b).

———, Haber, S., and Feshbach, S. "Testing Hypotheses Regarding Rape: Exposure to Sexual Violence, Sex Differences, and the 'Normality' of Rape." *Journal of Research in Personality* 14 (1980): 121-137 (a).

———, and Spinner, B. "A Longitudinal Content Analysis of Sexual Violence in the Best-Selling Erotica Magazines." *The Journal of Sex Research* 16 (1980): 226-237.

———, and Check, J. "The Effectiveness of a Debriefing Following Exposure to 'Sexual' Violence." In preparation, 1981.

———. "Rape Fantasies as a Function of Exposure to Violent Sexual Stimuli." *Archives of Sexual Behavior*, in press.

———, and Check, J. "Penile Tumescence and Perceptual Responses to Rape as a Function of Victim's Perceived Reactions." Reprinted in the volume, (a).

———, and Check, J. "The Effects of Mass Media Exposure on Acceptance of Violence against Women: A Field Experiment." *Journal of Research in Personality*, in press. (b)

Mann, J., Sidman, J., and Starr, S. "Effects of Erotic Films on Sexual Behavior of Married Couples." *Technical Reports of the Commission on Obscenity and Pornography*, vol. 8. Washington, D.C.: U.S. Government Printing Office, 1971.

———; Berkowitz, L.; Sidman, J.; Starr, S.; and West, S. "Satiation of the Transient Stimulating Effect of Erotic Films." *Journal of Personality and Social Psychology* 30 (1974): 565-570.

Mendelsohn, M. J. "Sex-Guilt and Role-Played Moral Reactions." Master's thesis. The University of Connecticut, 1970.

Meyer, T. P. "The Effects of Sexually Arousing and Violent Films on Aggressive Behavior." *Journa of Sex Research* 8 (1972): 324-333.

Money, J., and Athanasiou, R. "Pornography: Review and Bibliographic Annotations." *American Journal of Obstetrics and Gynecology* 115 (1973): 130-146.

———. "Pornography in the Home: A Topic in Medical Education." In *Critical Issues in Contemporary Sex Research*, edited by J. Zubin and J. Money. Baltimore: Johns Hopkins Press, 1973.

Morgan, R. *Going Too Far.* New York: Vintage Press, 1978.

Mosher, D. L. "A Pilot Study to Develop a Laboratory Measure of Verbal Aggression." (Final report, RGLP No. 044.) Columbus, Ohio: Ohio State University, 1965.

———. "The Interaction of Fear and Guilt in Inhibiting Unacceptable Behavior." *Journal of Consulting Psychology* 29 (1965): 161–167 (b).

———. "The Development and Multitrait-Multimethod Matrix Analysis of Three Measures of Three Aspects of Guilt." *Journal of Consulting Psychology* 30 (1966): 25–29.

———. "Measurement of Guilt in Females by Self-Report Inventories." *Journal of Consulting and Clinical Psychology* 32 (1968): 690–695.

———, Mortimer, R. L., and Grebel, M. "Verbal Aggressive Behavior in Delinquent Boys." *Journal of Abnormal Psychology* 73 (1968): 454–460.

———, and Proenza, L. M. "Intensity of Attack, Displacement, and Verbal Aggression." *Psychonomic Science* 12 (1968): 359–360.

———, and Greenberg, I. "Females' Affective Reactions to Reading Erotic Literature." *Journal of Consulting and Clinical Psychology* 33 (1969): 472–477.

———, Farina, A., and Gliha, D. "Moral Stigma, Punishment, and Guilt." Unpublished manuscript. The University of Connecticut, 1970.

———, and Cross, H. J. "Sex-Guilt and Pre-Marital Sexual Experiences of College Students." *Journal of Consulting and Clinical Psychology* (1970), in press.

———. "Sex Callousness toward Women." *Technical Reports of the Commission on Obscenity and Pornography*, vol. 8. Washington, D.C.: U.S. Government Printing Office, 1971, pp. 255–312 (b).

———. "Pornographic Films, Male Verbal Aggresion against Women, and Guilt." In *United States Government Report of the Commission on Obscenity and Pornography.* Washington, D.C.: U.S. Government Printing Office, 1970.

New Zealand Psychological Society. "Submission to the Select Committee on the Cinematographic Films Bill and the Cinematographic Films Amendment Bill." *New Zealand Psychologist* 5 (1976): 98–105.

Okel, E., and Mosher, D. L. "Changes in Affective States as a Function of Guilt over Aggressive Behavior." *Journal of Consulting and Clinical Psychology* 32 (1968): 265–270.

Pascal, C. B. "A Question of Censorship: Science of Moral Persuasion." *Contemporary Psychology* 22 (1977): 579–580.

Romano, K. "Psychophysiological Responses to a Sexual and an Unpleasant Motion Picture." Bachelor's thesis. University of Manitoba, 1969.

Rosen, R. C., and Keefe, F. J. "The Measurement of Human Penile Tumescence." *Psychophysiology* 15 (1978): 366–376.

Rosene, J. M. "The Effects of Violent and Sexually Arousing Film Content: An Experimental Study." Ph.D. thesis. Ohio State University, 1971.

Rotter, J. B. *Social Learning and Clinical Psychology.* New York: Prentice-Hall, 1954.

Rule, B. G., and Hewitt, L. S. "Effects of Thwarting on Cardiac Response and Physical Aggression." *Journal of Personality and Social Psychology* 19 (1971): 181–187.

———, and Nesdale, A. R. "Emotional Arousal and Aggressive Behavior." *Psy-*

chological Bulletin 83 (1976): 851–863.

Russell, Diana E. H., and Van de Ven, Nicole, eds. *Crimes against Women: Proceedings of the International Tribunal.* Millbrae, Calif.: Les Femmes, 1976.

Sandford, D. A. "Patterns of Sexual Arousal in Heterosexual Males." *Journal of Sex Research* 10 (1974): 150–155.

Sapolsky, B. S. "The Effect of Erotica on Annoyance and Hostile Behavior in Provoked and Unprovoked Males." Ph.D. thesis. Indiana University, 1977.

Schacter, S. "The Interaction of Cognitive and Physiological Determinants of Emotional State." In *Advances in Experimental Social Psychology*, edited by L. Berkowitz. New York: Academic Press, 1964.

Schmidt, G., and Sigsch, V. "Psychosexual Stimulation by Films and Slides: A Further Report on Sex Differences." *Journal of Sex Research* 6 (1970).

———. "Male-Female Differences in Sexual Arousal and Behavior." *Archives of Sexual Behavior* 4 (1975): 353–364.

Sellin, T., and Wolfgang, M. E. *The Measurement of Delinquency.* New York: Wiley, 1964.

Sherif, C. "Comment on Ethical Issues in Malamuth, Heim and Feshbach's 'Sexual Responsiveness of College Students to Rape Depictions: Inhibitory and Disinhibitory Effects.' " *Journal of Personality and Social Psychology* 38 (1980): 409—412.

Slade. "Recent Trends in Pornographic Films." *Society* 77 (September/October 1975).

Smith, D. D. "The Social Content of Pornography." *Journal of Communication* 26 (1976): 16–33.

Spengler. "Manifest Sadomasochism of Males: Results of an Empirical Study." *Archives of Sexual Behavior* 6 (1977).

Stauffer, J., and Frost, R. "Male and Female Interest in Sexually Oriented Magazines." *Journal of Communication* 26 (1976): 25–30.

Stoller, Robert. *Perversion: The Erotic Form of Hatred.* New York: Pantheon, 1975.

———. "Sexual Excitement." *Archives of General Psychiatry* 33 (1976).

Swart, C., and Berkowitz, L. "Effects of a Stimulus Associated with a Victim's Pain in Later Aggression." *Journal of Personality and Social Psychology* 33 (1976): 623–631.

Tannenbaum, P. H., and Zillmann, D. "Emotional Arousal in the Facilitation of Aggression through Communication." In *Advances in Experimental Social Psychology*, vol. 8, edited by L. Berkowitz. New York: Academic Press, 1975.

Taylor, S. P., and Epstein, S. "Aggression as a Function of the Interaction of the Sex of the Aggressor and the Sex of the Victim." *Personality* 35 (1967): 474–486.

Thorne, F. C., Haupt, T. D., and Allen, R. M. "Objective Studies of Adult Male Sexuality Using the Sex Inventory." *Journal of Clinical Psychology* 21 (Monograph Supplement) (1966): 1–43.

Time Magazine. "Pornography." April 5, 1976, pp. 58–63.

———. "Really Socking It to Women." Februury 7, 1977, pp. 42–43.

United States. *Commission on Obscenity and Pornography.* The Report. Chairman: William B. Lockhart. Washington, D.C.: U.S. Government Printing Office, 1970; New York: Bantam Books, 1970.

———. *Commission on Obscenity and Pornography.* Technical Reports. Washington, D.C.: U.S. Government Printing Office, 1971.

————. *National Commission on the Causes and Prevention of Violence.* Washington, D.C.: U.S Government Printing Office, 1969.

Walker, E. C. "Erotic Stimuli and the Aggressive Sexual Offender." In *Technical Report of the Commission on Obscenity and Pornography*, vol. 8. Washington, D.C.: U.S. Government Printing Office, 1971.

Waring, E. M., and Jeffries, J. S. "The Conscience of a Pornographer." *Journal of Sex Research* 10 (1974): 40–46.

White, L. A. "Erotica and Aggression: The Influence of Sexual Arousal, Positive Affect, and Negative Affect on Aggressive Behavior." *Journal of Personality and Social Psychology* 37 (1979): 591–601.

Wills, G. "Measuring the Impact of Erotica." *Psychology Today* (1977).

Wilsons, W. C., and Goldstein, M. U., eds. "Pornography: Attitudes, Use and Effects." *Journal of Social Issuus* 29 (1973).

Wilson, J. Q. "Violence, Pornography and Social Science." In *Where Do You Draw the Line?* edited by V. B. Cline. Provo, Utah: Brigham Young University Press, 1974.

Yaffe, M. "Research Survey on Pornography." In *The Pornography Report*, edited by Longford. London: Coronet, 1972.

————, and Tennent, T. G. "Pornography: A Psychological Appraisal." *British Journal of Hospital Medicine* 9 (1973): 379–383.

————. "Pornography and Violence." *Bethlem and Maudsley Hospital Gazette* (Winter 1976): 11–14.

————. "Violence and Pornography." *British Journal of Sex Medicine* (1979).

————, ed. *The Influence of Pornography on Behavior.* London: Academic Press, 1979.

Zellinger, D. A.; Fromkin, H. L.; Speller, D. E.; and Kohn, C. A. "A Commodity Theory Analysis of the Efforts of Age Restrictions upon Pornographic Materials." Krannert Graduate School of Industrial Administration. Purdue University, Indiana. Paper No. 440. (1974).

Zillmann, D. "Excitation Transfer in Communication-Mediated Aggressive Behavior." *Journal of Experimental Social Psychology* 7 (1971): 419–434.

————, Katcher, A., and Milavsky, B. "Excitation Transfer from Physical Exercise to Subsequent Aggressive Behavior." *Journal of Experimental Social Psychology* 8 (1972): 247–259.

————, and Johnson, R. C. "Motivated Aggressiveness Perpetuuted by Exposure to Aggressive Films and Reduced by Exposure to Nonaggressive Films." *Journal of Research in Personality* 7 (1973): 261–276.

————, Hoyt, J. L., and Day, K. D. "Strength and Duration of the Effect of Aggressive, Violent, and Erotic Communications on Subsequent Aggressive Behavior." *Communication Research* 1 (1974): 286-306.

————, Johnson, R. C., and Day, K. D. "Attribution of Apparent Arousal and Proficiency of Recovery from Sympathetic Activation Affecting Activation Transfer to Aggressive Behavior." *Journal of Experimental Social Psychology* 10 (1974): 503–515 (a).

————, Johnson, R. C., and Day, K. D. "Provoked and Unprovoked Aggressiveness in Athletes." *Journal of Research in Personality* 8 (1974): 139–152 (b).

————, and Bryant, J. "Effect of Residual Excitation on the Emotional Response to Provocation and Delayed Aggressive Behavior." *Journal of Personality and Social Psychology* 30 (1974): 782-791.

Zillmann, D., and Cantor, J. B. "Effect of Timing of Information about Mitigating Circumstances on Emotional Responses to Provocation and Retaliatory Behavior." *Journal of Experimental Social Psychology* 12 (1976): 38-55.

———, and Sapolsky, B. S. "What Mediates the Effect of Mild Erotica on Annoyance and Hostile Behavior in Males?" *Journal of Personality and Social Psychology* 35 (1977): 587-596.

———. "Attribution and Misattribution of Excitatory Reactions." In *New Directions in Attribution Research*, vol. 2, edited by J. H. Harvey, W. J. Ickes, and R. F. Kidd. Hillsdale, N.J.: Erlbaum, 1978.

———. *Hostility and Aggression.* Hillsdale, N.J.: Erlbaum, 1979.

———, Bryant, J., and Carveth, R. A. "The Effect of Erotica Featuring Sadomasochism and Bestiality on Motivated Intermale Aggression." *Personality and Social Psychology Bulletin*, in press.

PART THREE: JUDICIAL ESSAYS

Regina v. Hicklin

The Queen on the Prosecution of Henry Scott, appellant
v. Benjamin Hicklin and another,
Justices of Wolverhampton, respondents

Court of Queen's Bench

(1868) LR 3 QB 360

[Editors' Note: Henry Scott was a member of the Protestant Electoral Union. Acting under the authority of the Obscene Publications Act 1857, police seized from his premises copies of a pamphlet entitled *The Confessional Unmasked; shewing the depravity of the Romanish priesthood, the iniquity of the Confessional and the questions put to females in confession.* The magistrates, one of whom was Hicklin, found the pamphlet obscene and ordered the copies destroyed. Scott appealed to Quarter Sessions, and the recorder found in his favor; but the Court of Queen's Bench reversed the judgement of the recorder, holding that the magistrates had been correct. This case is famous for the enunciation, by the Lord Chief Justice Cockburn, of the criterion of obscenity known as the "deprave and corrupt" test. The following is an excerpt from the report.]

COCKBURN, C.J.

This was a proceeding under 20 & 21 Vict. c. 83, s. 1, whereby it is provided that, in respect of obscene books, &c., kept to be sold or distributed,

Reprinted by permission of the Incorporated Council of Law Reporting for England and Wales.

magistrates may order the seizure and condemnation of such works, in case they are of opinion that the publication of them would have been the subject-matter of an indictment at law, and that such a prosecution ought to have been instituted. Now, it is found here as a fact that the work which is the subject-matter of the present proceeding was, to a considerable extent, an obscene publication, and, by reason of the obscene matter in it, calculated to produce a pernicious effect in depraving and debauching the minds of the persons into whose hands it might come. The magistrates must have been of opinion that the work was indictable, and that the publication of it was a fit and proper subject for indictment. We must take the latter finding of the magistrates to have been adopted by the learned recorder when he reversed their decision, because it is not upon that ground that he reversed it; he leaves that. ground untouched, but he reversed the magistrates' decision upon the ground that, although this work was an obscene publication, and although its tendency upon the public mind was that suggested upon the part of the information, yet that the immediate in-·tention of the appellant was not so to affect the public mind, but to expose the practices and errors of the confessional system in the Roman Catholic Church. Now, we must take it, upon the finding of the recorder, that such was the motive of the appellant in distributing this publication; that his intention was honestly and bona fide to expose the errors and practices of the Roman Catholic Church in the matter of confession; and upon that ground of motive the recorder thought an indictment could not have been sustained, inasmuch as to the maintenance of the indictment it would have been necessary that the intention should be alleged and proved, namely, that of corrupting the public mind by the obscene matter in question. In that respect I differ from the recorder. I think that if there be an infraction of the law the intention to break the law must be inferred, and the criminal character of the publication is not affected or qualified by there being some ulterior object in view (which is the immediate and primary object of the parties) of a different and of an honest character. It is quite clear that the publishing an obscene book is an offence against the law of the land. It is perfectly true, as has been pointed out by Mr. Kydd, that there are a great many publications of high repute in the literary productions of this country the tendency of which is immodest, and, if you please, immoral, and possibly there might have been subject-matter for indictment in many of the works which have been referred to. But it is not to be said, because there are in many standard and established works objectionable passages, that therefore the law is not as alleged on the part of this prosecution, namely, that obscene works are the subject-matter of indictment; and I think the test of obscenity is this, whether the tendency of the matter charged as obscenity is to deprave and corrupt those whose minds are open to such immoral influences, and into whose hands a publication of this sort may fall. Now, with regard to this work, it is quite certain that it would suggest to the minds of the young of either sex, or even to persons of more advanced years, thoughts of a most impure and libidinous character. The very reason why this work is put forward to expose the practices of the Roman Catholic confessional is the tendency of questions, involving practices and propensities of a certain description, to do mischief to the minds of those to whom such questions are addressed, by suggesting thoughts and desires which otherwise would not have occurred to their minds. If that be the case as between the priest and the person confessing, it manifestly must equally be so when the whole is put into the shape of a series of paragraphs, one following upon another, each involving some impure practices, some of them of the most filthy and disgusting and unnatural description it is possible to imagine. I take it therefore, that, apart from the ulterior object which the publisher of this work had in view, the work itself is, in every sense of the term, an obscene publication, and that, consequently, as the law of England does not allow of any obscene publication, such publication is indictable. We have it, therefore, that the publication itself is a breach of the law. But, then, it is said for the appellant, "Yes, but his purpose was not to deprave the public mind; his purpose was to expose the errors of the Roman Catholic religion especially in the matter of the confessional." Be it so. The question then presents itself in this simple form: May you commit an offence against the law in order that thereby you may effect some ulterior object which you have in view, which may be an honest and even a laudable one? My answer is, emphatically, no. The law says, you shall not publish an obscene work. An obscene work is here published, and a work the obscenity of which is so clear and decided, that it is impossible to suppose that the man who published it must not have known and seen that the effect upon the minds of many of those into whose hands it would come would be of a mischievous and demoralizing character. Is he justified in doing that which clearly would be wrong, legally as well as morally, because he thinks that some greater good may be accomplished? In order to prevent the spread and progress of Catholicism in this country, or possibly to extirpate it in another, and to prevent the state from affording any assistance to the Roman Catholic Church in Ireland, is he justified in doing that which has necessarily the immediate tendency of demoralizing the public mind wherever this publication is circulated? It seems to me that to adopt the affirmative of that proposition would be to uphold something which, in my sense of what is right and wrong, would be very reprehensible. It appears to me the only good that is to be accomplished is of the most uncertain character. This work, I am told, is sold at the corners of streets, and in all directions, and of course it falls into the hands of persons of all classes, young and old, and the minds of those hitherto pure are exposed to the danger of contamination and pollution from the impurity it contains. And for what? To prevent them, it is said, from becoming Roman Catholics, when the probability is, that nine hundred and ninety-nine out of every thousand into whose hands this work would fall would never be exposed to the chance of being converted to the Roman Catholic religion. It seems to me that the effect of this work is mischievous and against the law, and is not to be justified because the immediate object of the publication is not to deprave the public mind, but, it may be, to destroy and extirpate Roman Catholicism. I think the old sound and honest maxim, that you shall not do evil that good may come, is applicable in law as well as in morals; and here we have a certain and positive evil produced for the purpose of effecting an uncertain, remote, and very doubtful good. I think, therefore, the case for the order is made out, and although I quite concur in thinking that the motive of the parties who published this work, however mistaken, was an honest one, yet I cannot suppose but what they had that intention which constitutes the criminality of the act, at any rate that they knew perfectly well that this work must have the tendency which, in point of law, makes it an obscene publication, namely, the tendency to corrupt the minds and morals of those into whose hands it might come. The mischief of it, I think, cannot be exaggerated. But it is not upon that I take my stand in the judgment I pronounce. I am of opinion, as the learned recorder has found, that this is an obscene publication. I hold that, where a man publishes a work manifestly obscene, he must be taken to have had the intention which is implied from that act; and that, as soon as you have an illegal act thus established, quoad the intention and quoad the act, it does not lie in the mouth of the man who does it to say, "Well, I was breaking the law, but I was breaking it for some wholesome and salutary purpose." The law does not allow that; you must abide by the law, and if you would accomplish your object, you must do it in a legal manner, or let it alone; you must not do it in a manner which is illegal. I think, therefore, that the recorder's judgment must be reversed, and the order must stand.

Shaw v.
Director of Public Prosecutions

House of Lords

(1961) 2 All E.R. 446

[Editors' Note: Shaw published a directory of prostitutes called *Ladies Directory*. He was convicted of conspiring to corrupt public morals by means of the magazine and of living on the earnings of prostitution. Shaw's convictions on both counts were affirmed on appeal. This case is important for its discussion of the common law offense of conspiracy to corrupt public morals. We have included excerpts from the judgments of Viscount Simonds and Lord Morris of Borth-y-Gest. Footnotes have been renumbered as appropriate.]

VISCOUNT SIMONDS:

My Lords, as I have already said, the first count in the indictment is "Conspiracy to corrupt public morals", and the particulars of offence will have sufficiently appeared. I am concerned only to assert what was vigorously denied by counsel for the appellant, that such an offence is known to the common law and that it was open to the jury to find on the facts of this case that the appellant was guilty of such an offence. I must say categorically

Reprinted from the *All England Law Reports* by permission of Butterworth and Co. Ltd., London.

that, if it were not so, Her Majesty's courts would strangely have failed in their duty as servants and guardians of the common law. Need I say, my Lords, that I am no advocate of the right of the judges to create new criminal offences? I will repeat well-known words:

> "Amongst many other points of happiness and freedom which your Majesty's subjects have enjoyed there is none which they have accounted more dear and precious than this, to be guided and governed by certain rules of law which giveth both to the head and members that which of right belongeth to them and not by any arbitrary or uncertain form of government."

These words are as true today as they were in the seventeenth century and command the allegiance of us all. But I am at a loss to understand how it can be said either that the law does not recognise a conspiracy to corrupt public morals or that, though there may not be an exact precedent for such a conspiracy as this case reveals, it does not fall fairly within the general words by which it is described. I do not propose to examine all the relevant authorities. That will be done by my noble and learned friend. The fallacy in the argument that was addressed to us lay in the attempt to exclude from the scope of general words acts well calculated to corrupt public morals just because they had not been committed or had not been brought to the notice of the court before. It is not thus that the common law has developed. We are, perhaps, more accustomed to hear this matter discussed on the question whether such and such a transaction is contrary to public policy. At once the controversy arises. On the one hand it is said that it is not possible in the twentieth century for the court to create a new head of public policy, on the other it is said that this is but a new example of a well-established head. In the sphere of criminal law, I entertain no doubt that there remains in the courts of law a residual power to enforce the supreme and fundamental purpose of the law, to conserve not only the safety and order but also the moral welfare of the state, and that it is their duty to guard it against attacks which may be the more insidious because they are novel and unprepared for. That is the broad head (call it public policy if you wish) within which the present indictment falls. It matters little what label is given to the offending act. To one of your Lordships it may appear an affront to public decency, to another, considering that it may succeed in its obvious intention of provoking libidinous desires, it will seem a corruption of public morals. Yet others may deem it aptly described as the creation of a public mischief or the undermining of moral conduct. The same act will not in all ages be regarded in the same way. The law must be related to the changing standards of life, not yielding to every shifting impulse of the popular will but having regard to fundamental assessments of human values and the purposes of society. Today a denial of the fundamental Christian doctrine, which in past centuries would have been regarded by the ecclesiastical courts as heresy and by the common law as blasphemy, will no longer be an offence if the decencies of controversy are observed. When LORD MANSFIELD, speaking long after the Star Chamber had been abolished, said[1] that the Court of King's Bench was the custos morum of the people and had the superintendency of offences contra bonos mores, he was asserting, as I now assert, that there is in that court a residual power, where no statute has yet intervened to supersede the common law, to superintend those offences which are prejudicial to the public welfare. Such occasions will be rare, for Parliament has not been slow to legislate when attention has been sufficiently aroused. But gaps remain and will always remain since no one can foresee every way in which the wickedness of man may disrupt the order of society. Let me take a single instance to which my noble and learned friend, LORD TUCKER, refers. Let it be supposed that, at some future, perhaps, early, date homosexual practices between adult consenting males are no longer a crime. Would it not be an offence if, even without obscenity, such practices were publicly advocated and encouraged by pamphlet and advertisement? Or must we wait until Parliament finds time to deal with such conduct? I say, my Lords, that, if the common law is powerless in such an event, then we should no longer do her reverence. But I say that her hand is still powerful and that it is for Her Majesty's judges to play the part which LORD MANSFIELD pointed out to them. . . .

I will say a final word on an aspect of the case which was urged by counsel. No one doubts—and I have put it in the forefront of this opinion—that certainty is a most desirable attribute of the criminal and civil law alike. Nevertheless, there are matters which must ultimately depend on the opinion of a jury. In the civil law I will take an example which comes, perhaps, nearest to the criminal law—the tort of negligence. It is for a jury to decide not only whether the defendant has committed the act complained of but whether, in doing it, he has fallen short of the standard of care which the circumstances require. Till their verdict is given, it is uncertain what the law requires. The same branch of the civil law supplies another interesting analogy. For, though in the Factory Acts and the regulations made under them the measure of care required of an employer is defined in the greatest detail, no one supposes that he may not be guilty of negligence in a manner unforeseen and unprovided for. That will be a matter for the jury to decide. There are still, as has recently been said, "unravished remnants of the common law". So, in the case of a charge of conspiracy to corrupt public morals, the uncertainty that necessarily arises from the vagueness of general words can only be resolved by the opinion of twelve chosen men and women. I am content to leave it to them.

The appeal on both counts should, in my opinion, be dismissed. . . .

LORD MORRIS OF BORTH-Y-GEST:

I join, however, with those of your Lordships who affirm that the law is not impotent to convict those who conspire to corrupt public morals. The declaration of LORD MANSFIELD (see *Jones* v. *Randall*[2]) that

> "Whatever is contrary, bonos mores est decorum, the principles of our law prohibit, and the King's court, as the general censor and guardian of the public manners, is bound to restrain and punish"

is echoed and finds modern expression in KENNY'S OUTLINES OF CRIMINAL LAW (17th Edn.) in the statement that agreements by two or more persons may be criminal if they are agreements to do acts which are outrageously immoral or else are in some way extremely injurious to the public. There are certain manifestations of conduct which are an affront to and an attack on recognised public standards of morals and decency, and which all well-disposed persons would stigmatise and condemn as deserving of punishment. The cases afford examples of the conduct of individuals which has been punished because it outraged public decency or because its tendency was to corrupt the public morals.

It is said that there is a measure of vagueness in a charge of conspiracy to corrupt public morals, and also that there might be peril of the launching of prosecutions in order to suppress unpopular or unorthodox views. My Lords, I entertain no anxiety on those lines. Even if accepted public standards may to some extent vary from generation to generation, current standards are in the keeping of juries who can be trusted to maintain the corporate good sense of the community and to discern attacks on values that must be preserved. If there were prosecutions which were not genuinely and fairly warranted, juries would be quick to perceive this. There could be no conviction unless twelve jurors were unanimous in thinking that the accused person or persons had combined to do acts which were calculated to corrupt public morals. My Lords, as time proceeds, our criminal law is more and more being codified. Though it may be that the occasions for presenting a charge such as that in count 1 will be infrequent, I concur in the view that such a charge is contained within the armour of the law and that the jury were in the present case fully entitled to decide the case as they did.

I would dismiss the appeal.

NOTES

1. In *R.* v. *Delaval,* (1763), 3 Burr. at p. 1438.
2. (1774), Lofft at p. 385. The quotation above exactly accords with the report; but it seems that for "est" the conjunction "et" should be read. The corresponding passage in the report in 1 Cowp. at p. 39 reads "for the law of England prohibits everything which is contra bonos mores; or it must be against principles of sound policy;".

United States of America v. Samuel Roth

United States Court of Appeals

Second Circuit

237 F. 2d 796 (2ᵈ cir., 1956)

[Editors' Note: Samuel Roth was convicted on four counts of mailing books, periodicals, and photographs in violation of a federal statute which punished the mailing of "obscene, lewd, lascivious or filthy . . . " materials. Roth appealed, attacking the constitutionality of the statute. The Court of Appeals sustained his conviction, as did the U.S. Supreme Court in an important decision. The Supreme Court's ruling is discussed below in the excerpt from *Miller* v. *California*. Here is an excerpt from the decision of the Court of Appeals. Judge Jerome Frank concurred with his colleagues on the Court of Appeals, despite having reservations about the constitutionality of the federal statute. He agreed with his colleagues that since the Supreme Court had said that the statute was valid, the Court of Appeals could not hold to the contrary. Nevertheless, in the Appendix to his decision, Judge Frank eloquently set out his reservations. We have deleted a few lengthy citations of cases, much of the judge's discussion of empirical research, and a few footnotes, and we have renumbered the footnotes as necessary.]

FRANK, CIRCUIT JUDGE (CONCURRING)

I have much difficulty in reconciling the validity of that statute with opinions of the Supreme Court, uttered within the past twenty-five years,[1] relative to the First Amendment as applied to other kinds of legislation. The doctrine expressed in those opinions, as I understand it, may be summarized briefly as follows: Any statute authorizing governmental interference (whether by "prior restraint" or punishment) with free speech or free press runs counter to the First Amendment, except when the government can show that the statute strikes at words which are likely to incite to a breach of the peace,[2] or with sufficient probability tend either to the overthrow of the government by illegal means or to some other overt anti-social conduct.[3]

The troublesome aspect of the federal obscenity statute—as I shall try to explain in the Appendix to this opinion—is that (a) no one can now show that, with any reasonable probability obscene publications tend to have any effects on the behavior of normal, average adults, and (b) that under the statute, as judicially interpreted, punishment is apparently inflicted for provoking, in such adults, undesirable sexual thoughts, feelings, or desires—not overt dangerous or anti-social conduct, either actual or probable.

Often the discussion of First Amendment exceptions has been couched in terms of a " 'clear and present danger' ". However, the meaning of that phrase has been somewhat watered down by Dennis v. United States, 341 U.S. 494, 71 S.Ct. 857, 865, 95 L.Ed. 1137. The test now involves probability: " 'In each case (courts) must ask' ", said Chief Justice Vinson in Dennis, " 'whether the gravity of the "evil," discounted by its improbability, justifies such invasion of free speech as is necessary to avoid the danger.' " It has been suggested that the test now is this: "The more serious and threatened the evil, the lower the required degree of probability."[4] It would seem to follow that the less clear the danger, the more imminent must it be. At any rate, it would seem that (1) the danger or evil must be clear (i. e., identifiable) and substantial, and (2) that, since that statute renders words punishable, it is invalid unless those words tend, with a fairly high degree of probability, to incite to overt conduct which is obviously harmful. For, under the First Amendment, lawless or anti-social "acts are the main thing. Speech is not punishable for its own sake, but only because of its connection with those * * * acts * * * But more than a remote connection is necessary * * *"[5]. . .

APPENDIX

As a judge of an inferior court, I am constrained by opinions of the Supreme Court concerning the obscenity statute to hold that legislation valid. Since, however, I think (as indicated in the foregoing) that none of those opinions has carefully canvassed the problem in the light of the Supreme Court's interpretation of the First Amendment, especially as expressed by the Court in recent years, I deem it not improper to set forth, in the following, factors which I think deserve consideration in passing on the constitutionality of that statute.

1. Benjamin Franklin, in 1776 unanimously designated Postmaster General by the First Continental Congress, is appropriately known as the "father of the Post Office." Among his published writings are two[6]—*Letter of Advice to Young Men on the Proper Choosing of a Mistress* and *The Speech of Polly Baker*—which a jury could reasonably find "obscene," according to the judge's instructions in the case at bar. On that basis, if tomorrow a man were to send those works of Franklin through the mails, he would be subject to prosecution and (if the jury found him guilty) to punishment under the federal obscenity statute.[7]

That fact would surely have astonished Jefferson, who extolled Franklin as an American genius,[8] called him "venerable and beloved" of his countrymen,[9] and wrote approvingly of Franklin's *Polly Baker*.[10] No less would it have astonished Madison, also an admirer of Franklin (whom he described as a man whose "genius" was "an ornament of human nature")† and himself given to telling "Rabelaisian anecdotes."[11] Nor was the taste of these men unique in the American Colonies: "Many a library of a colonial planter in Virginia or a colonial intellectual in New England boasted copies of Tom Jones, Tristram Shandy, Ovid's Art of Love, and Rabelais. * * *"[12]

As, with Jefferson's encouragement, Madison, in the first session of Congress, introduced what became the First Amendment, it seems doubtful that the constitutional guaranty of free speech and free press could have been intended to allow Congress validity to enact the "obscenity" Act. That doubt receives reinforcement from the following:

In 1799, eight years after the adoption of the First Amendment, Madison, in an Address to the General Assembly of Virginia,[13] said that the "truth of opinion" ought not to be subject to "imprisonment, to be inflicted by those of a different opinion"; he there also asserted that it would subvert the First Amendment[14] to make a "distinction between the freedom and the licentiousness of the press." Previously, in 1792, he wrote that "a man has property in his opinions and free communication of them," and that a government which "violates the property which individuals have in their opinion * * * is not a pattern for the United States."[15] Jefferson's proposed Constitution for Virginia (1776), provided: "Printing presses shall be

†Footnote omitted.

free, except so far as by commission of private injury cause may be given of private action.''[16] In his Second Inaugural Address (1805), he said: "No inference is here intended that the laws provided by the State against false and defamatory publications should not be enforced * * * The press, confined to truth, needs no other restraint * * *; and no other definite line can be drawn between the inestimable liberty of the press and demoralizing licentiousness. If there still be improprieties which this rule would not restrain, its supplement must be sought in the censorship of public opinion.''

The broad phrase in the First Amendment, prohibiting legislation abridging "freedom of speech, or of the press", includes the right to speak and write freely for the public concerning any subject. As the Amendment specifically refers to "the free exercise [of religion]" and to the right "of the people * * * to assemble" and to "petition the Government for a redress of grievances", it specifically includes the right freely to speak to and write for the public concerning government and religion; but it does not limit this right to those topics. Accordingly, the views of Jefferson and Madison about the freedom to speak and write concerning religion are relevant to a consideration of the constitutional freedom in respect of all other subjects. Consider, then, what those men said about freedom of religious discussion: Madison, in 1799, denouncing the distinction "between the freedom and the licentiousness of the press" said, "By its help, the judge as to what is licentious may escape through any constitutional restriction," and added, "Under it, Congress might denominate a religion to be heretical and licentious, and proceed to its suppression * * * Remember * * * that it is to the press mankind are indebted for having dispelled the clouds which long encompassed religion * * *"[17] Jefferson, in 1798, quoting the First Amendment, said it guarded "in the same sentence, and under the same words, the freedom of religion, of speech, and of the press; insomuch, that whatever violates either, throws down the sanctuary which covers the others.''[18] In 1814, he wrote in a letter, "I am really mortified to be told that in the United States of America, a fact like this (the sale of a book) can become a subject of inquiry, and of criminal inquiry too, as an offense against religion; that (such) a question can be carried before the civil magistrate. Is this then our freedom of religion? And are we to have a censor whose imprimatur shall say what books may be sold and what we may buy? * * * Whose foot is to be the measure to which ours are all to be cut or stretched?''[19]

Those utterances high-light this fact: Freedom to speak publicly and to publish has, as its inevitable and important correlative, the private rights to hear, to read, and to think and to feel about what one hears and reads. The First Amendment protects those private rights of hearers and readers.

We should not forget that, prompted by Jefferson,[20] Madison (who at one time had doubted the wisdom of a Bill of Rights)[21] when he urged in Congress the enactment of what became the first ten Amendments, declared, "If they are incorporated into the Constitution, independent tribunals of justice will consider themselves in a peculiar manner the guardian of those rights; they will be an impenetrable barrier against every assumption of power in the Legislative or Executive; they will be naturally led to resist every encroachment upon rights expressly stipulated for in the Constitution by the declaration of rights."[22] In short, the Bill of Rights, including the First Amendment, was not designed merely as a set of admonitions to the legislature and the executive; its provisions were to be enforced by the courts.

Judicial enforcement necessarily entails judicial interpretation. The question therefore arises whether the courts, in enforcing the First Amendment, should interpret it in accord with the view prevalent among those who sponsored and adopted it or in accord with subsequently developed views which would sanction legislation more restrictive of free speech and free press.

So the following becomes pertinent: Some of those who in the 20th Century endorse legislation suppressing "obscene" literature have an attitude towards freedom of expression which does not match that of the framers of the First Amendment (adopted at the end of the 18th Century) but does stem from an attitude, towards writings dealing with sex, which arose decades later, in the mid-19th Century, and is therefore labelled—doubtless too sweepingly—"Victorian." It was a dogma of "Victorian morality" that sexual misbehavior would be encouraged if one were to "acknowledge its existence or at any rate to present it vividly enough to form a life-like image of it in the reader's mind"; this morality rested on a "faith that you could best conquer evil by shutting your eyes to its existence,"[23] and on a kind of word magic.[24] The demands at that time for "decency" in published words did not comport with the actual sexual conduct of many of those who made those demands: "The Victorians, as a general rule, managed to conceal the 'coarser' side of their lives so thoroughly under a mask of respectability that we often fail to realize how 'coarse' it really was * * * Could we have recourse to the vast unwritten literature of bawdry, we should be able to form a more veracious notion of life as it (then) really was." The respectables of those days often, "with unblushing license," held "high revels" in "night houses."[25] Thanks to them, Mrs. Warren's profession flourished, but it was considered sinful to talk about it in books.[26] Such a prudish and purely verbal moral code, at odds (more or less hypocritically) with the actual conduct of its adherents[27] was (as we have seen) not the moral code of those who framed the First Amendment.[28] One would suppose, then, that the courts should interpret and enforce that Amendment according to the views of those framers, not according to the later "Victorian" code.[29]

The "founding fathers" did not accept the common law concerning freedom of expression

It has been argued that the federal obscenity statute is valid because obscenity was a common law crime at the time of the adoption of the First Amendment. Quite aside from the fact that, previous to the Amendment, there had been scant recognition of this crime, the short answer seems to be that the framers of the Amendment knowingly and deliberately intended to depart from the English common law as to freedom of speech and freedom of the press. . . .†

Of course, the legislature has wide power to protect what it considers public morals. But the First Amendment severely circumscribes that power (and all other legislative powers) in the area of speech and free press.

Subsequent punishment as, practically, prior restraint

For a long time, much was made of the distinction between a statute calling for "prior restraint" and one providing subsequent criminal punishment;[30] the former alone, it was once said, raised any question of constitutionality *vis-a-vis* the First Amendment.[31] Although it may still be true that more is required to justify legislation providing "preventive" than "punitive" censorship,[32] this distinction has been substantially eroded. . . .

The statute, as judicially interpreted, authorizes punishment for inducing mere thoughts, and feelings, or desires

For a time, American courts adopted the test of obscenity contrived in 1868 by Cockburn, L.J., in Queen v. Hicklin, L.R. 3 Q.B. 360: "I think the test of obscenity is this, whether the tendency of the matter charged as obscenity is to deprave and corrupt those whose minds are open to such immoral influences, and into whose hands a publication of this sort might fall." He added that the book there in question "would suggest * * thoughts of a most impure and libidinous character."

The test in most federal courts has changed: They do not now speak of the thoughts of "those whose minds are open to * * * immoral influences" but, instead, of the thoughts of average adult normal men and women, determining what these thoughts are, not by proof at the trial, but by the standard of "the average conscience of the time," the current "social sense of what is right." . . . Yet the courts still define obscenity in terms of the assumed average normal adult reader's sexual thoughts or desires or impulses, without reference to any relation between those "subjective" reactions and his subsequent conduct. The judicial opinions use such key

†Footnote omitted.

phrases as this: "suggesting lewd thoughts and exciting sensual desires;"[33] "arouse the salacity of the reader,"[34] " 'allowing or implanting * * * obscene, lewd, or lascivious thoughts or desires' ",[35] "arouse sexual desires".[36] The judge's charge in the instant case reads accordingly: "It must tend to stir sexual impulses and lead to sexually impure thoughts." Thus the statute, as the courts construe it, appears to provide criminal punishment for inducing no more than thoughts, feelings, desires.

No adequate knowledge is available concerning the effects on the conduct of normal adults of reading or seeing the "obscene"

Suppose we assume, *arguendo,* that sexual thoughts or feelings, stirred by the "obscene," probably will often issue into overt conduct. Still it does not at all follow that that conduct will be antisocial. For no sane person can believe it socially harmful if sexual desires lead to normal, and not anti-social, sexual behavior since, without such behavior, the human race would soon disappear.[37]

Doubtless, Congress could validly provide punishment for mailing any publications if there were some moderately substantial reliable data show-ing that reading or seeing those publications probably conduces to seriously harmful sexual conduct on the part of normal adult human beings. But we have no such data.

Suppose it argued that whatever excites sexual longings might *possibly* produce sexual misconduct. That cannot suffice: Notoriously, perfumes sometimes act as aphrodisiacs, yet no one will suggest that therefore Con-gress may constitutionally legislate punishment for mailing perfumes. It may be that among the stimuli to irregular sexual conduct, by normal men and women, may be almost anything—the odor of carnations or cheese, the sight of a cane or a candle or a shoe, the touch of silk or a gunnysack. For all anyone now knows, stimuli of that sort may be far more provocative of such misconduct than reading obscene books or seeing obscene pictures. Said John Milton, "Evil manners are as perfectly learnt, without books, a thousand other ways that cannot be stopped." . . .

Effect on conduct of young people

Most federal courts (as above noted) now hold that the test of obscenity is the effect on the "mind" of the average normal adult, that effect being determined by the "average conscience of the time," the current "sense of what is right"; and that the statute does not intend "to reduce our treat-ment of sex to the standard of a child's library in the supposed interest of a salacious few"; United States v. Kennerley, D.C., 209 F. 120, 121.

However, there is much pressure for legislation, designed to prevent juvenile delinquency, which will single out children, i. e., will prohibit the sale to young persons of "obscenity" or other designated matter. . . .

Maybe some day we will have enough reliable data to show that obscene books and pictures do tend to influence children's sexual conduct adversely. Then a federal statute could be enacted which would avoid constitutional defects by authorizing punishment for using the mails or interstate shipments in the sale of such books and pictures to children.[38] It is, however, not at all clear that children would be ignorant, in any considerable measure, of obscenity, if no obscene publications ever came into their hands. Youngsters get a vast deal of eductaion in sexual smut from companions of their own age.[39] A verbatim report of conversations among young teen-age boys (from average respectable homes) will disclose their amazing proficiency in obscene language, learned from other boys.[40] Replying to the argument of the need for censorship to protect the young Milton said: "Who shall regulate all the * * * conversation of our youth * * * appoint what shall be discussed * * *?" Most judges who reject that view are long past their youth and have probably forgotten the conversational ways of that period of life: "I remember when I was a little boy," said Mr. Dooley, "but I don't remember how I was a little boy."

The obscenity statute and the reputable press

Let it be assumed, for the sake of the argument, that contemplation of published matter dealing with sex has a significant impact on children's conduct. On that assumption, we cannot overlook the fact that our most reputable newspapers and periodicals carry advertisements and photographs displaying women in what decidedly are sexually alluring postures,[41] and at times emphasizing the importance of "sex appeal." That women are there shown scantily clad, increases "the mystery and allure of the bodies that are hidden," writes an eminent psychiatrist. "A leg covered by a silk stocking is much more attractive than a naked one; a bosom pushed into shape by a brassiere is more alluring than the pendant realities."[42] Either, then, the statute must be sternly applied to prevent the mailing of many reputable newspapers and periodicals containing such ads and photographs, or else we must acknowledge that they have created a cultural atmosphere for children in which, at a maximum, only the most trifling additional effect can be imputed to children's perusal of the kind of matter mailed by the defendant.

The obscenity statute and the newspapers

Because of the contrary views of many competent persons, one may well be sceptical about Dr. Wertham's thesis. However, let us see what, logically, his crusade would do to the daily press: After referring repeatedly to the descriptions, in "comic books" and other "mass media," of violence combined with sadistic sexual behavior, descriptions which he says contribute to juvenile delinquency, he writes, "Juvenile delinquency reflects the social values current in a society. Both adults and children absorb these social values in their daily lives, * * * and also in *all the communications through the mass media* * * * Juvenile delinquency holds up a mirror to society * * * It is self-understood that such a pattern in a mass medium does not come from nothing * * * Comic books are not the disease, they are only a symptom * * * The same social forces that made comic books make other social evils, and the same social forces that keep comic crime books keep the other social evils the way they are." (Emphasis added.)

Now the daily newspapers, especially those with immense circulations, constitute an important part of the "mass media"; and each copy of a newspaper sells for much less than a "comic book." Virtually all the sorts of descriptions, of sex mingled with violence, which Dr. Wertham finds in the "comic books," can be found, often accompanied by gruesome photographs, in those daily journals. Even a newspaper which is considered unusually respectable, published prominently on its first page, on August 26, 1956, a true story of a "badly decomposed body" of a 24 year old woman school teacher, found in a clump of trees. The story reported that police had quoted a 29 year old salesman as saying that "he drove to the area" with the school teacher, that "the two had relations on the ground, and later got into an argument," after which he "struck her three times on the back of the head with a rock, and, leaving her there, drove away." Although today no one can so prove, one may suspect that such stories of sex and violence in the daily press have more impact on young readers than do those in the "comic books," since the daily press reports reality while the "comic books" largely confine themselves to avowed fiction or fantasy.† Yet Dr. Wertham, and most others who propose legislation to curb the sale of "comic books" to children, propose that it should not extend to newspapers.† Why not?

The question is relevant in reference to the application of the obscenity statute: Are our prosecutors ready to prosecute reputable newspaper publishers under that Act? I think not. I do not at all urge such prosecutions. I do suggest that the validity of that statute has not been vigorously challenged because it has not been applied to important persons like those publishers but, instead, has been enforced principally against relatively inconspicuous men like the defendant here.

†Footnotes omitted.

Da Capo: Available data seem wholly insufficient to show that the obscenity statutes come within any exception to the First Amendment

I repeat that, because that statute is not restricted to obscene publications mailed for sale to minors, its validity should be tested in terms of the evil effects of adult reading of obscenity on adult conduct.[43] With the present lack of evidence that publications probably have such effects, how can the government discharge its burden of demonstrating sufficiently that the statute is within the narrow exceptions to the scope of the First Amendment? One would think that the mere possibility of a causal relation to misconduct ought surely not be enough.

Even if Congress had made an express legislative finding of the probable evil influence, on adult conduct, of adult reading or seeing obscene publications, the courts would not be bound by that finding, if it were not justified in fact. See, e. g., Chastleton Corp. v. Sinclair, 264 U.S 543, 44 S.Ct. 405, 406, 68 L.Ed.841, where the Court (per Holmes, J.) said of a statute (declaring the existence of an emergency) that "a Court is not at liberty to shut its eyes to an obvious mistake, when the validity of the law depends upon the truth of what is declared." And the Court there and elsewhere has held that the judiciary may use judicial notice in ascertaining the truth of such a legislative declaration.[44]

If the obscenity statute is valid, why may Congress not validly provide punishment for mailing books which will provoke thoughts it considers undesirable about religion or politics?

If the statute is valid, then, considering the foregoing, it would seem that its validity must rest on this ground: Congress, by statute, may constitutionally provide punishment for the mailing of books evoking mere thoughts or feelings about sex, if Congress considers them socially dangerous, even in the absence of any satisfactory evidence that those thoughts or feelings will tend to bring about socially harmful deeds. If that be correct, it is hard to understand why, similarly, Congress may not constitutionally provide punishment for such distribution of books evoking mere thoughts or feelings, about religion or politics, which Congress considers socially dangerous, even in the absence of any satisfactory evidence that those thoughts or feelings will tend to bring about socially dangerous deeds.

2. The Judicial Exception of the "Classics"

As I have said, I have no doubt the jury could reasonably find, beyond a reasonable doubt, that many of the publications mailed by defendant were obscene within the current judicial definition of the term as explained by the trial judge in his charge to the jury. But so, too, are a multitude of recognized works of art found in public libraries. Compare, for instance, the books which are exhibits in this case with Montaigne's Essay on Some Lines of Virgil or with Chaucer. Or consider the many nude pictures which the defendant transmitted through the mails, and then turn to the reproductions in the articles on painting and sculpture in the Encyclopedia Britannica (14th edition):† Some of the latter are no less "obscene" than those which led to the defendants' conviction. Yet these Encyclopedia volumes are readily accessible to everyone, young or old, and, without let or hindrance, are frequently mailed to all parts of the country. Catalogues, of famous art museums, almost equally accessible and also often mailed, contain reproductions of paintings and sculpture, by great masters, no less "obscene."†

To the argument that such books (and such reproductions of famous paintings and works of sculpture) fall within the statutory ban, the courts have answered that they are "classics,"—books of "literary distinction" or works which have "an accepted place in the arts," including, so this court has held, Ovid's Art of Love and Boccacio's Decameron.[45] There is a "curious dilemma" involved in this answer that the statute condemns "only books which are dull and without merit," that in no event will the statute be applied to the "classics," i. e., books "of literary distinction."[46] The courts have not explained how they escape that dilemma, but instead seem to have gone to sleep (although rather uncomfortably) on its horns.

This dilemma would seem to show up the basic constitutional flaw in the statute: No one can reconcile the currently accepted test of obscenity with the immunity of such "classics" as e. g., Aristophanes' Lysistratra, Chaucer's Canterbury Tales, Rabelais' Gargantua and Pantagruel, Shakespeare's Venus and Adonis, Fielding's Tom Jones, or Balzac's Droll Stories. For such "obscene" writings, just because of their greater artistry and charm, will presumably have far greater influence on readers than dull inartistic writings.

It will not do to differentiate a "classic," published in the past, on the ground that it comported with the average moral attitudes at the time and place of its original publication. Often this was not true. It was not true, for instance, of Balzac's Droll Stories,[47] a "classic" now freely circulated by many public libraries, and which therefore must have been transported by mail (or in interstate commerce). More to the point, if the issue is whether a

†Footnotes omitted.

book meets the American common conscience of the present time, the question is how "average" Americans now regard this book, not how it was regarded when first published, here or abroad. Why should the age of an "obscene" book be relevant? After how many years—25 or 50 or 100—does such a writing qualify as a "classic"?

The truth is that the courts have excepted the "classics" from the federal obscenity statute, since otherwise most Americans would be deprived of access to many masterpieces of literature and the pictorial arts, and a statute yielding such deprivation would not only be laughably absurd but would squarely oppose the intention of the cultivated men who framed and adopted the First Amendment.

This exception—nowhere to be found in the statute[48]—is a judge-made device invented to avoid that absurdity. The fact that the judges have felt the necessity of seeking that avoidance, serves to suggest forcibly that that statute, in its attempt to control what our citizens may read and see, violates the First Amendment. For no one can rationally justify the judge-made exception. The contention would scarcely pass as rational that the "classics" will be read or seen solely by an intellectual or artistic elite; for, even ignoring the snobbish, undemocratic, nature of this contention, there is no evidence that that elite has a moral fortitude (an immunity from moral corruption) superior to that of the "masses." And if the exception, to make it rational, were taken as meaning that a contemporary book is exempt if it equates in "literary distinction" with the "classics," the result would be amazing: Judges would have to serve as literary critics; jurisprudence would merge with aesthetics; authors and publishers would consult the legal digests for legal-artistic precedents; we would some day have a Legal Restatement of the Canons of Literary Taste.

The exception of the "classics" is therefore irrational. Consequently, it would seem that we should interpret the statute rationally—i. e., without that exception. If, however, the exception, as an exception, is irrational, then it would appear that, to render the statute valid, the standard applied to the "classics" should be applied to all books and pictures. The result would be that, in order to be constitutional, the statute must be wholly inefficacious.

3. How censorship under the statute actually operates:

(A) Prosecutors, as censors, actually exercise prior restraint

Fear of punishment serves as a powerful restraint on publication, and fear of punishment often means, practically, fear of prosecution. For most men dread indictment and prosecution; the publicity alone terrifies, and to defend a criminal action is expensive. If the definition of obscenity had a limited and fairly well known scope, that fear might deter restricted sorts of publications only. But on account of the extremely vague judicial definition of the obscene,[49] a person threatened with prosecution if he mails (or otherwise sends in interstate commerce)[50] almost any book which deals in an unconventional, unorthodox, manner with sex,† may well apprehend that, should the threat be carried out, he will be punished. As a result, each prosecutor becomes a literary censor (i. e., dictator) with immense unbridled power, a virtually uncontrolled discretion.[51] A statute would be invalid which gave the Postmaster General the power, without reference to any standard, to close the mails to any publication he happend to dislike.[52] Yet, a federal prosecutor, under the federal obscenity statute, approximates that position: Within wide limits, he can (on the advice of the Postmaster General or on no one's advice) exercise such a censorship by threat, without a trial, without any judicial supervision, capriciously and arbitrarily. Having no special qualifications for that task, nevertheless, he can, in large measure, determine at his will what those within his district may not read on sexual subjects.[53] In that way, the statute brings about an actual prior restraint of free speech and free press which strikingly flouts the First Amendment.[54]

(B) Judges as censors

When a prosecution is instituted and a trial begins, much censorship power passes to the trial judge: If he sits without a jury, he must decide whether a book is obscene. If the trial is by jury, then, if he thinks the book plainly not obscene, he directs a verdict for the accused or, after a verdict of guilt, enters a judgment of acquittal. How does the judge determine whether a book is obscene? Not by way of evidence introduced at the trial, but by way of some sort of judicial notice. Whence come the judicial notice data to inform him?

Those whose views most judges know best are other lawyers. Judges can and should take judicial notice that, at many gatherings of lawyers at Bar Association or of alumni of our leading law schools,† tales are told fully as "obscene" as many of those distributed by men, like defendant, convicted for violation of the obscenity statute. Should not judges, then set aside such convictions? If they do not, are they not somewhat arrogantly concluding that lawyers are an exempt elite, unharmed by what will harm the multitude of other Americans? If lawyers are not such an elite then, since, in spite of the "obscene" tales lawyers frequently tell one another, data are lacking that lawyers as a group become singularly addicted to depraved sexual

†Footnotes omitted.

conduct, should not judges conclude that "obscenity" does not importantly contribute to such misconduct, and that therefore the statute is unconstitutional?

(C) Jurors as censors

If in a jury case, the trial judge does not direct a verdict or enter a judgment of acquittal, the jury exercises the censorship power. Courts have said that a jury has a peculiar aptitude as a censor of obscenity, since, representing a cross-section of the community, it knows peculiarly well the "common conscience" of the time. Yet no statistician would conceivably accept the views of a jury—twelve persons chosen at random—as a fair sample of community attitudes on such a subject as obscenity. A particular jury may voice the "moral sentiments" of a generation ago, not of the present time.

Each jury verdict in an obscenity case has been sagely called "really a small bit of legislation ad hoc".[55] So each jury constitutes a tiny autonomous legislature. . . . Any one such tiny legislature, as experience teaches, may well differ from any other, in thus legislating as to obscenity. And, one may ask, was it the purpose of the First Amendment, to authorize hundreds of divers jury-legislatures, with discrepant beliefs, to decide whether or not to enact hundreds of divers statutes interfering with freedom of expression? (I shall note, infra, the vast difference between the applications by juries of the "reasonable man" standard and the "obscenity" standard.)

4. The dangerously infectious nature of governmental censorship of books

Governmental control of ideas or personal preferences is alien to a democracy. And the yearning to use governmental censorship of any kind is infectious. It may spread insidiously. Commencing with suppression of books as obscene, it is not unlikely to develop into official lust for the power of thought-control in the areas of religion, politics, and elsewhere. Milton observed that "licensing of books * * * necessarily pulls along with it so many other kinds of licensing." J. S. Mill noted that the "bounds of what may be called moral police" may easily extend "until it encroaches on the most unquestionable legitimate liberty of the individual." We should beware of a recrudescence of the undemocratic doctrine uttered in the 17th century by Berkeley, Governor of Virginia: "Thank God there are no free schools or preaching, for learning has brought disobedience into the world, and printing has divulged them. God keep us from both."

The people as self-guardians: censorship by public opinion, not by government

Plato, who detested democracy, proposed to banish all poets; and his rulers were to serve as "guardians" of the people, telling lies for the people's good, vigorously suppressing writings these guardians thought dangerous.[56] Governmental guardianship is repugnant to the basic tenet of our democracy: According to our ideals, our adult citizens are self-guardians, to act as their own fathers, and thus become self-dependent.[57] When our governmental officials act towards our citizens on the thesis that "Papa knows best what's good for you," they enervate the spirit of the citizens: To treat grown men like infants is to make them infantile, dependent, immature.

So have sagacious men often insisted. Milton, in his Areopagitica, denounced such paternalism: "We censure them for a giddy, vicious and unguided people, in such sick and weak (a) state of faith and discretion as to be able to take down nothing but through the pipe of a licensor." "We both consider the people as our children," wrote Jefferson to Dupont de Nemours, "but you love them as infants whom you are afraid to trust without nurses, and I as adults whom I freely leave to self-government." Tocqueville sagely remarked: "No form or combination of social policy has yet been devised to make an energetic people of a community of pusillanimous and enfeebled citizens." "Man," warned Goethe, "is easily accustomed to slavery and learns quickly to be obedient when his freedom is taken from him." Said Carl Becker, "Self-government, and the spirit of freedom that sustains it, can be maintained only if the people have sufficient intelligence and honesty to maintain them with a minimum of legal compulsion. This heavy responsibility is the price of freedom."[58] The "great art," according to Milton, "lies to discern in what the law is to bid restraint and punishment, and in what things persuasion only is to work." So we come back, once more, to Jefferson's advice: The only completely democratic way to control publications which arouse mere thoughts or feelings is through non-governmental censorship by public opinion.

5. The seeming paradox of the First Amendment

Here we encounter an apparent paradox: The First Amendment, judicially enforced, curbs public opinion when translated into a statute which restricts

348   *Pornography and Censorship*

freedom of expression (except that which will probably induce undesirable conduct). The paradox is unreal: *The Amendment ensures that public opinion—the "common conscience of the time"—shall not commit suicide through legislation, which chokes off today the free expression of minority views which may become the majority public opinion of tomorrow.*

Private persons or groups, may validly try to influence public opinion

The First Amendment obviously has nothing to do with the way persons or groups, not a part of government, influence public opinion as to what constitutes "decency" or "obscenity." The Catholic Church, for example, has a constitutional right to persuade or instruct its adherents not to read designated books or kinds of books.

6. The fine arts are within the First Amendment's Protection

"The framers of the First Amendment," writes Chafee, "must have had literature and art in mind, because our first national statement on the subject of 'freedom of the press,' the 1774 address of the Continental Congress to the inhabitants of Quebec, declared, 'The importance of this (freedom of the press) consists, beside the advancement of truth, science, morality and *arts* in general, in its diffusion of liberal sentiments on the administration of government.'"[59] 165 years later, President Franklin Roosevelt said, "The arts cannot thrive except where men are free to be themselves and to be in charge of the discipline of their own energies and ardors. The conditions for democracy and for art are one and the same. What we call liberty in politics results in freedom of the arts."[60] The converse is also true.

In our industrial era when, perforce, economic pursuits must be, increasingly, governmentally regulated, it is especially important that the realm of art—the noneconomic realm—should remain free, unregimented, the domain of free enterprise, of unhampered competition at its maximum.[61] An individual's taste is his own, private, concern. *De gustibus non disputandum* represents a valued democratic maxim.

Milton wrote: "For though a licenser should happen to be judicious more than the ordinary, yet his very office * * * enjoins him to let pass nothing but what is vulgarly received already." He asked, "What a fine conformity would it starch us all into? * * * We may fall * * * into a gross conformity stupidly * *" In 1859, J. S. Mill, in his essay on Liberty, maintained that conformity in taste is not a virtue but a vice. "The danger," he wrote, "is not the excess but the deficiency of personal impulses and preferences. By dint of not following their own nature (men) have no nature to follow * * * Individual spontaneity is entitled to free exercise * * * That so few men dare to be eccentric marks the chief danger of the time." Pressed by the demand for conformity, a people degenerate into "the deep slumber of a decided opinion," yield a "dull and torpid consent" to the accustomed. "Mental depotism" ensues. For "whatever crushes individuality is despotism by whatever name it be called * * * It is not by wearing down into uniformity all that is individual in themselves, but by cultivating it, and calling it forth, within the limits imposed by the rights and interests of others, that human beings become a noble and beautiful object of contemplation; and as the works partake the character of those who do them, by the same process human life also becomes rich, diversified, and animating * * * In proportion to the development of his individuality, each person becomes more valuable to himself, and is therefore capable of being more valuable to others. There is a greater fullness of life about his own existence, and when there is more life in the units there is more in the mass which is composed of them."

To vest a few fallible men—prosecutors, judges, jurors—with vast powers of literary or artistic censorship, to convert them into what J. S. Mill called a "moral police," is to make them despotic arbiters of literary products. If one day they ban mediocre books as obscene, another day they may do likewise to a work of genius. Originality, not too plentiful, should be cherished, not stifled. An author's imagination may be cramped if he must write with one eye on prosecutors or juries; authors must cope with publishers who, fearful about the judgments of governmental censors, may refuse to accept the manuscripts of contemporary Shelleys or Mark Twains or Whitmans.[62]

Some few men stubbornly fight for the right to write or publish or distribute books which the great majority at the time consider loathsome. If we jail those few, the community may appear to have suffered nothing. The appearance is deceptive. For the conviction and punishment of these few will terrify writers who are more sensitive, less eager for a fight. What, as a result, they do not write might have been major literary contributions.[63] "Suppression," Spinoza said, "is paring down the state till it is too small to harbor men of talent."

7. The motive or intention of the author, publisher or distributor cannot be the test

Some courts once held that the motive or intention of the author, painter, publisher or distributor constituted the test of obscenity. That test, the courts have abandoned: That a man who mails a book or picture believes it entirely "pure" is no defense if the court finds it obscene. United States v. One Book Entitled Ulysses, 2 Cir., 72 F.2d 705, 708.[64] Nor, conversely, will he be criminally liable for mailing a "pure" publication—Stevenson's Child's Garden of Verses or a simple photograph of the Washington Monument—he mistakenly believes obscene. Most courts now look to the "objective" intention, which can only mean the effect on those who read the book or see the picture;[65] the motive of the mailer is irrelevant because it cannot affect that effect.

8. Judge Bok's decision as to the causal relation to anti-social conduct

In Commonwealth v. Gordon, 1949, 66 Pa.Dist. & Co.R. 101, Judge Bok said: "A book, however sexually impure and pornographic * * * cannot be a present danger unless its reader closes it, lays it aside, and transmutes its erotic allurement into overt action. That such action must inevitably follow as a direct consequence of reading the book does not bear analysis, nor is it borne out by general human experience; too much can intervene and too many diversions take place * * * The only clear and present danger * * * that will satisfy * * * the Constitution * * * is the commission or the imminence of the commission of criminal behavior resulting from the reading of a book. Publication alone can have no such automatic effect." The constitutional operation of "the statute," Judge Bok continued, thus "rests on narrow ground * * * I hold that (the statute) may constitutionally be applied * * * only where there is a reasonable and demonstrable cause to believe that a crime or misdemeanor has been committed or is about to be committed as the perceptible result of the publication and distribution of the writing in question: the opinion of anyone that a tendency thereto exists or that such a result is self-evident is insufficient and irrelevant. The causal connection between the book and the criminal behavior must appear beyond a reasonable doubt."

In confess that I incline to agree with Judge Bok's opinion. But I think it should be modified in a few respects: (a) Because of the Supreme Court's opinion in the Dennis case, 1951, 341 U.S. 494, 71 S.Ct. 857, 95 L.Ed. 1137, decided since Judge Bok wrote, I would stress the element of probability in speaking of a "clear danger." (b) I think the danger need not be that of probably inducing behavior which has already been made criminal at common law or by statute, but rather of probably inducing any seriously anti-social conduct (i. e., conduct which, by statute, could validly be made a state or federal crime). (c) I think that the causal relation need not be between such anti-social conduct and a particular book involved in the case on trial, but rather between such conduct and a book of the kind or type involved in the case.[66]

9. The void-for-vagueness argument.

There is another reason for doubting the constitutionality of the obscenity statute. The exquisite vagueness of the word "obscenity" is apparent from the way the judicial definition of that word has kept shifting: Once (as we saw) the courts held a work obscene if it would probably stimulate improper thoughts or desires in abnormal persons; now most courts consider only the assumed impact on the thoughts or desires of the adult "normal" or average human being. A standard so difficult for our ablest judges to interpret is hardly one which has a "well-settled" meaning, a meaning sufficient adequately to advise a man whether he is or is not committing a crime if he mails a book or picture . . . .

If we accept as correct the generally current judicial standard of obscenity—the "average conscience of the time"—that standard still remains markedly uncertain as a guide to judges or jurors—and therefore to a citizen who contemplates mailing a book or picture. To be sure, we trust juries to use their common sense in applying the "reasonable man" standard in prosecutions for criminal negligence (or the like); a man has to take his chances on a jury verdict in such a case, with no certainty that a jury will not convict him although another jury may acquit another man on the same evidence.[67] But that standard has nothing remotely resembling the looseness of the "obscenity" standard.

There is a stronger argument against the analogy of the "reasonable man" test: Even if the obscenity standard would have sufficient definiteness were freedom of expression not involved, it would seem far too vague to justify as a basis for an exception to the First Amendment.

NOTES

1. "For nearly 130 years after its adoption, the First Amendment received scant attention from the Supreme Court"; Emerson, The Doctrine of Prior Restraint, 20 L. & Cont.Problems (1955) 648, 652.

2. See, e. g., Chaplinsky v. State of New Hampshire, 315 U.S. 568, 572, 62 S.Ct. 766, 86 L.Ed. 1031.

3. The judicial enforcement of some private rights—as in suits, e. g., for defamation, injury to business, fraud, or invasion of privacy—comes within the exception.

4. Lockhart and McClure, Obscenity and the Constitution, 38 Minn.L.Rev. (1954) 295, 357; cf. Kalven, The Law of Defamation and the First Amendment, in (University of Chicago) Conference on the Arts, Publishing and the Law (1952) 3, 12.

5. Chafee, The Blessings of Liberty (1956) 69.

6. See Van Doren, Benjamin Franklin (1938) 150-151, 153-154. Franklin's *Letter to The Academy of Brussels* (see Van Doren, 151-152) might be considered "filthy."

7. 18 U.S.C. § 1461.

8. Jefferson, Notes on the State of Virginia (1781-1785), Query VI; See Padover, The Complete Jefferson (1943) 567 at 612.

9. Jefferson, Autobiography (1821); See Padover, loc. cit., 1119 at 1193.

10. Jefferson, Anecdotes of Franklin (1818); see Padover, loc. cit., 892 at 893.

11. Padover, the Complete Madison (1953) 8-9. . . .

12. Ernst and Seagle, To The Pure (1928) 108. . . .

13. See Padover, The Complete Madison (1953) 295-296.

14. Madison referred to the "Third Amendment," but the context shows he meant the First.

15. See Padover, The Complete Madison (1953) 267, 268-269.

16. Padover, The Complete Jefferson (1943) 109.

17. Madison, Address to the General Assembly of Virginia, 1799; see Padover, The Complete Madison (1953) 295.

18. See Padover, The Complete Jefferson (1943) 130.

19. See Padover, The Complete Jefferson (1943) 889.

20. Jefferson's Letter to Madison (1789); Padover, The Complete Jefferson (1943) 123-125. See also Brant, James Madison, Father of the Constitution (1950) 267.

21. The Federalist No. 84; Cahn, The Firstness of the First Amendment, 65 Yale L.J. (1956) 464.

22. Madison, Writings (Hunt ed.) V, 385; Corwin, Liberty Against Government (1948) 58-59; Cahn, The Firstness of the First Amendment, 64 Yale L.J. (1956) 464, 468.

23. Wingfield-Stratford, Those Earnest Victorians (1930) 151.

24. See Kaplan, Obscenity as an Esthetic Category, 20 Law & Contemp. Problems (1955) 544, 550: "In many cultures, obscenity has an important part in magical rituals. In our own, its magical character is betrayed in the puritan's supposition that words alone can work evil, and that evil will be averted if only the words are not uttered."

25. Wingfield-Stratford, loc. cit., 296-297.

26. Paradoxically, this attitude apparently tends to "create" obscenity. For the foundation of obscenity seems to be secrecy and shame: "The secret becomes shameful because of its secrecy." Kaplan, Obscenity As An Esthetic Category, 20 Law & Contemp. Problems (1955) 544, 556.

27. To be sure, every society has "pretend-rules" (moral and legal) which it publicly voices but does not enforce. Indeed, a gap necessarily exists between a society's ideals, if at all exalted, and its practices. But the extent of the gap is significant. See, e. g., Frank, Lawlessness, Encyc. of Soc. Sciences (1932); cf. Frank, Preface to Kahn, A Court for Children (1953).

28. It is of interest that not until the Tariff Act of 1824 did Congress enact any legislation relative to obscenity.

29. For discussion of the suggestion that many constitutional provisions provide merely minimum safeguards which may properly be enlarged—not diminished—to meet newly emerging needs and policies, see Supreme Court and Supreme Law (Cahn ed. 1954) 59-64.

30. Blackstone, most influentially, made this distinction; 4 Blackstone, Commentary, 151-162. . . .

31. See Holmes, J. in Patterson v. State of Colorado, 1907, 205 U.S. 454, 27 S.Ct. 556, 51 L.Ed. 879 citing Blackstone. But compare his subsequent dissenting opinion in Abrams v. United States, 1919, 250 U.S. 616, 624, 40 S.Ct. 17, 20, 63 L.Ed. 1173, which abandons Blackstone's dichotomy.

32. For these phrases, see Lasswell, Censorship, 3 Ency. of Soc. Sc. (1930) 290, 291.

33. Unites States v. Dennett, 2 Cir., 39 F. 2d 564, 568, 76 A.L.R. 1092.

34. United States v. Levine, 2 Cir., 83 F.2d 156, 158.

35. Burstein v. United States, 2 Cir., 178 F.2d 665, 667.

36. American Civil Liberties Union v. City of Chicago, 3 Ill.2d 334, 121 N.E.2d 585, 592.

37. Cf. the opinion of Mr. Justice Codd in Integrated Press v. The Postmaster General, as reported in Herbert, Codd's Last Case (1952) 14, 16: "Nor is the Court much impressed by the contention that the frequent contemplation of young ladies in bathing dresses must tend to the moral corruption of the community. On the contrary, these ubiquitous exhibitions have so diminished what was left of the mystery of womanhood that they might easily be condemned upon another ground of public policy, in that they tended to destroy the natural fascination of the female, so that the attention of the male population was diverted from thoughts of marriage to cricket, darts, motor-bicycling and other occupations which do nothing to arrest the decline of the population."

38. Such a statute was long ago suggested. See Ernst and Seagle, To the Pure (1928) 277.

39. Cf. United States v. Dennett, 2 Cir., 39 F.2d 564, 568, 76 A.L.R. 1092.

Alpert (loc. cit. at 74) writes of the American Youth Commission study of the conditions and attitudes of young people in Maryland between the ages of sixteen and twenty-four, as reported in 1938: "For this study Maryland was deliberately picked as a 'typical' state, and, according to the Commission, the 13,528 young people personally interviewed in Maryland can speak for the two hundred and fifty thousand young people in Maryland and the twenty millions in the United States. 'The chief source of sex "education" for the youth of all ages and all religious groups was found to be the youth's contemporaries.' Sixty-six percent of the boys and forty percent of the girls reported that what they knew about sex was more or less limited to what their friends of their own age had told them. After 'contemporaries' and the youth's home, the source that is next in importance is the school, from which about 8 percent of the young people reported they had received most of their sex information. A few, about 4 percent, reported they owed most to books, while less than 1 percent asserted that they had acquired most of their information from movies. Exactly the same proportion specified the church as the chief source of their sex information. These statistical results are not offered as conclusive; but that they do more than cast doubt upon the assertion that 'immoral' books, corrupt and deprave must be admitted. These statistical results placed in the scale against the weight of the dogma upon which the law is founded lift the counterpane high. Add this: the 'evil manners' are as easily acquired without books as with books; that crowded slums, machine labor, barren lives, starved emotions, and unreasoning minds are far more dangerous to morals than any so-called obscene literature. True, this attack is tangential, but a social problem is here involved, and the weight of this approach should be felt." Id. at 74.

40. For such a report, slightly expurgated for adult readers, see Cleckley, The Mask of Sanity (1950) 135-137.

41. Cf. Larrabee, The Cultural Context of Sex Censorship, 20 L. & Contemp.Prob. (1955) 672, 684.

42. Myerson, Speaking of Man (1950) 92. See also the well known chapter on clothes in Anatole France's Penguin Island. . . .

43. See United States v. Levine, 2 Cir., 83 F.2d 156, 157 to the effect that "what counts is its effect, not upon any particular class, but upon all those whom it is likely to reach."

44. Cf. United States v. Rumely, 345 U.S. 41, 44, 73 S.Ct. 543, 97 L.Ed. 770.

45. See, e. g., United States v. Levine, 2 Cir., 83 F.2d 156, 157; United States v. One Book Entitled Ulysses, 2 Cir., 72 F.2d 705; Roth v. Goldman, 2 Cir., 172 F.2d 788.

46. See Roth v. Goldman, 2 Cir., 172 F.2d 788. . . .

47. See discussion in Roth v. Goldman, 2 Cir., 172 F.2d at page 797.

48. The importation statute relating to obscenity, 19 U.S.C.A. § 1305, does make an explicit exception of the "so-called classics or books of recognized and established literary * * * merit," but only if they are "imported for noncommercial purposes"; if so, the Secretary of the Treasury has discretion to admit them.

49. See infra, point 9, for further discussion of that vagueness.

50. As to interstate transportation, see 18 U.S.C. § 1462 which contains substantially the same provisions as 18 U.S.C. § 1461.

51. One court, at the suit of a publisher, enjoined a chief of police—who went beyond threat of prosecution and ordered booksellers not to sell certain books—on the ground that the officer had exceeded his powers; New American Library of World Literature v. Allen, D.C. Ohio, 114 F.Supp. 823. In another similar case, where a prosecutor was enjoined, the injunction order was much modified on appeal; Bantam Books, Inc., v. Melko, 25 N.J.Super. 292, 96 A.2d 47, modified 14 N.J. 524, 103 A.2d 256.

If, however, the prosecutor confines himself to a mere threat of prosecution, the traditional reluctance to restrain criminal prosecutions will very probably make it difficult to obtain such an injunction. Sunshine Book Co. v. McCaffrey, Sup., 112 N.Y.S.2d 476; see also 22 U. of Chicago L.Rev. (1954) 216; 68 Harv. L.Rev. (1955) 489.

This may be particularly true with respect to a federal prosecutor. See Mr. Justice Jackson, The Federal Prosecutor, 24 J. of Am.Jud.Soc. (1940) 18: "The (federal) prosecutor has more control over life, liberty, and reputation than any other person in America. His discretion is tremendous. He can have citizens investigated and, if he is that kind of person, he can have this done to the tune of public statements and veiled or unveiled intimations. Or the prosecutor may choose a more subtle course and simply have a citizen's friends interviewed. The prosecutor can order arrests, present cases to the grand jury in secret session, and on the basis of his one-sided presentation of the facts, can cause the citizen to be indicted and held for trial. He may dismiss the case before trial, in which case the defense never has a chance to be heard."

52. See, e. g., Joseph Burstyn, Inc., v. Wilson, 343 U.S. 495, 72 S.Ct. 777, 96 L.Ed. 1098.

53. It is, therefore, doubtful whether, as suggested by Emerson (loc. cit. at 656-660), a statute calling for punishment involves very much less arbitrary conduct and very much less censorship than one calling for prior restraint. In actual fact, by his threats of prosecution, the prosecutor does exercise prior restraint. Much, therefore, that Emerson says of prior restraint authorized by statute applies as well as to censorship through a prosecutor's threats of prosecution: The "procedural safeguards built around criminal prosecution" (the stronger burden of proof, the stricter rules of evidence, the tighter procedure) are likewise absent. The "decision rests with a single functionary," an official, rather than with the courts. The prosecutor, by threats of prosecution, accomplishes prior restraint "behind a screen of informality and partial concealment that seriously curtails opportunity for public appraisal" and entailing the "chance of discrimination and other abuse." The "policies and actions" of the prosecutor, in his censorship by threats of prosecution, are not "likely to be known or publicly debated; material and study and criticism" are not "readily available."

54. For startling instances of "prosecutor censorship" see Blanshard, The Right to Read (1955) 184-186, 190; 22 U. of Chicago L.Rev. (1954) 216.

55. United States v. Levine, 2 Cir., 83 F. 2d 156, 157.

56. Plato furnished "an ideal blueprint for a totalitarian society"; Chroust, Book Rev., 1 Natural Law Forum (1956) 135, 141. . . .

57. See Frank, Self Guardianship and Democracy, 16 Am.Scholar (1947) 265.

58. Becker, Freedom and Responsibility in the American Way of Life (1945) 42.

59. Chafee, Government and Mass Communication (1947) 53.

60. Message at dedicating exercises of the New York Museum of Modern Art, May 8, 1939.

61. Frank, Fate and Freedom (1945) 194-202.

62. Milton remarked that "not to count him fit to print his mind without a tutor or examiner, lest he should drop * * * something of corruption, is the greatest * * * indignity to a free and knowing spirit that can be put upon him."

63. Cf. Chafee, The Blessings of Liberty (1956) 113.

Milton said that the "sense" of a great man may "to all posterity be lost for the fearfulness, or the presumptuous rashness of a perfunctory licenser."

64. Rosen v. United States, 161 U.S. 29, 41-42, 16 S.Ct. 434, 480, 40 L.Ed. 606.

65. United States v. Levine, 2 Cir., 83 F.2d 156; Parmelee v. United States, 72 App. D.C. 203, 113 F.2d 729.

66. According to Judge Bok, an obscenity statute may be validly enforced when there is proof of a causal relation between a particular book and undesirable conduct. Almost surely, such proof cannot ever be adduced. In the instant case, the government did not offer such proof.

67. Nash v. United States, 229 U.S. 373, 377, 33 S.Ct. 780, 57 L.Ed. 1232; United States v. Wurzbach, 280 U.S. 396, 399, 50 S.Ct. 167, 74 L.Ed. 508; United States v. Ragen, 314 U.S. 513, 523, 62 S.Ct. 374, 86 L.Ed. 383.

Marvin Miller v. State of California

United States Supreme Court

413 U.S. 15 (1973)

[Editors' Note: Marvin Miller was convicted of mailing unsolicited obscene materials in violation of a California statute. The conviction was affirmed on appeal. In this decision the Supreme Court specifies a new test for the constitutional validity of state statutes which are "designed to regulate obscene materials." We have included sections of Mr. Chief Justice Burger's opinion. Footnotes have been renumbered as necessary.]

Mr. Chief Justice BURGER delivered the opinion of the Court. . . .

I

This case involves the application of a State's criminal obscenity statute to a situation in which sexually explicit materials have been thrust by aggressive sales action upon unwilling recipients who had in no way indicated any desire to receive such materials. This Court has recognized that the States have a legitimate interest in prohibiting dissemination or exhibition of obscene material[1] when the mode of dissemination carries with it a significant danger of offending the sensibilities of unwilling recipients or of exposure to juveniles. . . . It is in this context that we are called on to define the standards which must be used to identify obscene material that a State may regulate without infringing on the First Amendment as applicable to the States through the Fourteenth Amendment.

The dissent of Mr. Justice BRENNAN reviews the background of the obscenity problem, but since the Court now undertakes to formulate standards more concrete than those in the past, it is useful for us to focus on two of the landmark cases in the somewhat tortured history of the Court's obscenity decisions. In Roth v. United States, 354 U.S. 476, 77 S.Ct. 1304, 1 L.Ed.2d 1498 (1957), the Court sustained a conviction under a federal statute punishing the mailing of "obscene, lewd, lascivious or filthy * * *" materials. The key to that holding was the Court's rejection of the claim that obscene materials were protected by the First Amendment. Five Justices joined in the opinion stating:

> "All ideas having even the slightest redeeming social importance—unorthodox ideas, controversial ideas, even ideas hateful to the prevailing climate of opinion—have the full protection of the [First Amendment] guaranties, unless excludable because they encroach upon the limited area of more important interests. But implicit in the history of the First Amendment is the rejection of obscenity as utterly without redeeming social importance * * *. This is the same judgment expressed by this Court in Chaplinsky v. New Hampshire, 315 U.S. 568, 571-572, 62 S.Ct. 766, 768-769, 86 L.Ed. 1031:
> " '* * * There are certain well-defined and narrowly limited classes of speech, the prevention and punishment of which have never been thought to raise any Constitutional problem. *These include the lewd and obscene * * *. It has been well observed that such utterances are no essential part of any exposition of ideas, and are of such slight social value as a step to truth that any benefit that may be derived from them is clearly outweighed by the social interest in order and morality. * * *'* [Emphasis by Court in *Roth* opinion.]
> "We hold that obscenity is not within the area of constitutionally protected speech or press." 354 U.S., at 484-485, 77 S.Ct., at 1309 (footnotes omitted).

Nine years later, in Memoirs v. Massachusetts, 383 U.S. 413, 86 S.Ct. 975, 16 L.Ed.2d 1 (1966), the Court veered sharply away from the *Roth* concept and, with only three Justices in the plurality opinion, articulated a new test of obscenity. The plurality held that under the *Roth* definition

> "as elaborated in subsequent cases, three elements must coalesce: it must be established that (a) the dominant theme of the material taken as a whole appeals to a prurient interest in sex; (b) the material is patently offensive because it

affronts contemporary community standards relating to the description or representation of sexual matters; and (c) the material is utterly without redeeming social value." *Id.,* at 418, 86 S.Ct., at 977.

The sharpness of the break with *Roth,* represented by the third element of the *Memoirs* test and emphasized by Mr. Justice White's dissent, . . . was further underscored when the *Memoirs* plurality went on to state:

> "The Supreme Judicial Court erred in holding that a book need not be 'unqualifiedly worthless before it can be deemed obscene.' A book cannot be proscribed unless it is found to be *utterly* without redeeming social value." *Id.,* at 419, 86 S.Ct., at 978 (emphasis in original).

While *Roth* presumed "obscenity" to be "utterly without redeeming social importance," *Memoirs* required that to prove obscenity it must be affirmatively established that the material is *"utterly* without redeeming social value." Thus, even as they repeated the words of *Roth,* the *Memoirs* plurality produced a drastically altered test that called on the prosecution to prove a negative, *i. e.,* that the material was *"utterly* without redeeming social value"—a burden virtually impossible to discharge under our criminal standards of proof. Such considerations caused Mr. Justice Harlan to wonder if the *"utterly* without redeeming social value" test had any meaning at all. See Memoirs v. Massachusetts, *id.,* at 459, 86 S.Ct., at 998 (Harlan, J., dissenting). . . .

[1] Apart from the initial formulation in the *Roth* case, no majority of the Court has at any given time been able to agree on a standard to determine what constitutes obscene, pornographic material subject to regulation under the States' police power. . . . This is not remarkable, for in the area of freedom of speech and press the courts must always remain sensitive to any infringement on genuinely serious literary, artistic, political, or scientific expression. This is an area in which there are few eternal verities.

The case we now review was tried on the theory that the California Penal Code § 311 approximately incorporates the three-stage *Memoirs* test, *supra.* But now the *Memoirs* test has been abandoned as unworkable by its author,[2] and no Member of the Court today supports the *Memoirs* formulation.

II

[2-5] This much has been categorically settled by the Court, that obscene material is unprotected by the First Amendment.[3] . . . We acknowledge,

however, the inherent dangers of undertaking to regulate any form of expression. State statutes designed to regulate obscene materials must be carefully limited. See Interstate Circuit, Inc. v. Dallas, *supra,* 390 U.S., at 682-685, 88 S.Ct., at 1302-1305. As a result, we now confine the permissible scope of such regulation to works which depict or describe sexual conduct. That conduct must be specifically defined by the applicable state law, as written or authoritatively construed.† A state offense must also be limited to works which, taken as a whole, appeal to the prurient interest in sex, which portray sexual conduct in a patently offensive way, and which, taken as a whole, do not have serious literary, artistic, political, or scientific value.

[6-8] The basic guidelines for the trier of fact must be (a) whether "the average person, applying contemporary community standards" would find that the work, taken as a whole, appeals to the prurient interest, . . . (b) whether the work depicts or describes, in a patently offensive way, sexual conduct specifically defined by the applicable state law; and (c) whether the work, taken as a whole, lacks serious literary, artistic, political, or scientific value. We do not adopt as a constitutional standard the *"utterly* without redeeming social value" test of Memoirs v. Massachusetts, 383 U.S., at 419. 86 S.Ct., at 977;[4] . . .

[9, 10] We emphasize that it is not our function to propose regulatory schemes for the States. That must await their concrete legislative efforts. It is possible, however, to give a few plain examples of what a state statute could define for regulation under part (b) of the standard announced in this opinion, *supra:*

(a) Patently offensive representations or descriptions of ultimate sexual acts, normal or perverted, actual or simulated.

(b) Patently offensive representation or descriptions of masturbation, excretory functions, and lewd exhibition of the genitals.

[11-13] Sex and nudity may not be exploited without limit by films or pictures exhibited or sold in places of public accommodation any more than live sex and nudity can be exhibited or sold without limit in such public places.[5] At a minimum, prurient, patently offensive depiction or description of sexual conduct must have serious literary, artistic, political, or scientific value to merit First Amendment protection. . . . For example, medical books for the education of physicians and related personnel necessarily use graphic illustrations and descriptions of human anatomy. In resolving the inevitably sensitive questions of fact and law, we must continue to rely on the jury system, accompanied by the safeguards that judges, rules of evidence, presumption of innocence, and other protective features provide, as we do with rape, murder, and a host of other offenses against society and its individual members.[6]

Mr. Justice BRENNAN, author of the opinions of the Court, or the

†Footnote omitted.

plurality opinions, in Roth v. United States, *supra;* Jacobellis v. Ohio, *supra;* . . . and Memoirs v. Massachusetts, *supra,* has abandoned his former position and now maintains that no formulation of this Court, the Congress, or the States can adequately distinguish obscene material unprotected by the First Amendment from protected expression, Paris Adult Theatre I v. Slaton, 413 U.S. 49, 73, 93 S.Ct. 2628, 2642, 37 L.Ed.2d 446 (Brennan, J., dissenting). Paradoxically, Mr. Justice BRENNAN indicates that suppression of unprotected obscene material is permissible to avoid exposure to unconsenting adults, as in this case, and to juveniles, although he gives no indication of how the division between protected and nonprotected materials may be drawn with greater precision for these purposes than for regulation of commercial exposure to consenting adults only. Nor does he indicate where in the Constitution he finds the authority to distinguish between a willing "adult" one month past the state law age of majority and a willing "juvenile" one month younger.

[14] Under the holdings announced today, no one will be subject to prosecution for the sale or exposure of obscene materials unless these materials depict or describe patently offensive "hard core" sexual conduct specifically defined by the regulating state law, as written or construed. We are satisfied that these specific prerequisites will provide fair notice to a dealer in such materials that his public and commercial activities may bring prosecution.[7] . . . If the inability to define regulated materials with ultimate, god-like precision altogether removes the power of the States or the Congress to regulate, then "hard core" pornography may be exposed without limit to the juvenile, the passerby, and the consenting adult alike, as, indeed, Mr. Justice Douglas contends. . . .

III

[15] Under a National Constitution, fundamental First Amendment limitations on the powers of the States do not vary from community to community, but this does not mean that there are, or should or can be, fixed, uniform national standards of precisely what appeals to the "prurient interest" or is "patently offensive." These are essentially questions of fact, and our Nation is simply too big and too diverse for this Court to reasonably expect that such standards could be articulated for all 50 States in a single formulation, even assuming the prerequisite consensus exists. When triers of fact are asked to decide whether "the average person, applying contemporary community standards" would consider certain materials "prurient," it would be unrealistic to require that the answer be based on some abstract formulation. The adversary system, with lay jurors as the

usual ultimate fact-finders in criminal prosecutions, has historically permitted triers of fact to draw on the standards of their community, guided always by limiting instructions on the law. To require a State to structure obscenity proceedings around evidence of a *national* "community standard" would be an exercise in futility.

As noted before, this case was tried on the theory that the California obscenity statute sought to incorporate the tripartite test of *Memoirs*. This, a "national" standard of First Amendment protection enumerated by a plurality of this Court, was correctly regarded at the time of trial as limiting state prosecution under the controlling case law. The jury, however, was explicitly instructed that, in determining whether the "dominant theme of the material as a whole * * * appeals to the prurient interest" and in determining whether the material "goes substantially beyond customary limits of candor and affronts contemporary community standards of decency," it was to apply "contemporary community standards of the State of California." . . .

[17] . . . Nothing in the First Amendment requires that a jury must consider hypothetical and unascertainable "national standards" when attempting to determine whether certain materials are obscene as a matter of fact. Mr. Chief Justice Warren pointedly commented in his dissent in Jacobellis v. Ohio, *supra,* at 200, 84 S.Ct., at 1685:

> "It is my belief that when the Court said in *Roth* that obscenity is to be defined by reference to 'community standards,' it meant community standards —not a national standard, as is sometimes argued. I believe that there is no provable 'national standard' * * *. At all events, this Court has not been able to enunciate one, and it would be unreasonable to expect local courts to divine one."

[18-22] It is neither realistic nor constitutionally sound to read the First Amendment as requiring that the people of Maine or Mississippi accept public depiction of conduct found tolerable in Las Vegas, or New York City.[8] . . . As the Court made clear in Mishkin v. New York, 383 U.S., at 508-509, 86 S.Ct., at 963, the primary concern with requiring a jury to apply the standard of "the average person, applying contemporary community standards" is to be certain that, so far as material is not aimed at a deviant group, it will be judged by its impact on an average person, rather than a particularly susceptible or sensitive person—or indeed a totally insensitive one. . . . We hold that the requirement that the jury evaluate the materials with reference to "contemporary standards of the State of California" serves this protective purpose and is constitutionally adequate.†

---

†Footnote omitted.

IV

The dissenting Justices sound the alarm of repression. But, in our view, to equate the free and robust exchange of ideas and political debate with commercial exploitation of obscene material demeans the grand conception of the First Amendment and its high purposes in the historic struggle for freedom. It is a "misuse of the great guarantees of free speech and free press * * *." Breard v. Alexandria, 341 U.S., at 645, 71 S.Ct., at 934. The First Amendment protects works which, taken as a whole, have serious literary, artistic, political, or scientific value, regardless of whether the government or a majority of the people approve of the ideas these works represent. "The protection given speech and press was fashioned to assure unfettered interchange of *ideas* for the bringing about of political and social changes desired by the people," Roth v. United States, *supra,* 354 U.S., at 484, 77 S.Ct., at 1308 (emphasis added). See Kois v. Wisconsin, 408 U.S., at 230-232, 92 S.Ct., at 2246-2247; Thornhill v. Alabama, 310 U.S., at 101-102, 60 S.Ct., at 743-744. But the public portrayal of hard-core sexual conduct for its own sake, and for the ensuing commercial gain, is a different matter.[9]

There is no evidence, empirical or historical, that the stern 19th century American censorship of public distribution and display of material relating to sex, see Roth v. United States, *supra,* 354 U.S., at 482-485, 77 S.Ct., at 1307-1309, in any way limited or affected expression of serious literary, artistic, political, or scientific ideas. On the contrary, it is beyond any question that the era following Thomas Jefferson to Theodore Roosevelt was an "extraordinarily vigorous period," not just in economics and politics, but in *belles lettres* and in "the outlying fields of social and political philosophies."[10] We do not see the harsh hand of censorship of ideas— good or bad, sound or unsound—and "repression" of political liberty lurking in every state regulation of commercial exploitation of human interest in sex.

Mr. Justice Brennan finds "it is hard to see how state-ordered regimentation of our minds can ever be forestalled." Paris Adult Theatre I v. Slaton, 413 U.S., at 110, 93 S.Ct., at 2661 (Brennan, J., dissenting). These doleful anticipations assume that courts cannot distinguish commerce in ideas, protected by the First Amendment, from commercial exploitation of obscene material. Moreover, state regulation of hard-core pornography so as to make it unavailable to nonadults, a regulation which Mr. Justice Brennan finds constitutionally permissible, has all the elements of "censorship" for adults; indeed even more rigid enforcement techniques may be called for with such dichotomy of regulation. See Interstate Circuit, Inc. v. Dallas, 390 U.S., at 690, 88 S.Ct., at 1306.[11] One can concede that the "sexual revolution" of recent years may have had useful byproducts in striking layers of prudery from a subject long irrationally kept from needed ventilation. But it does not follow that no regulation of patently offensive "hard core" materials is needed or permissible; civilized people do not allow unregulated access to heroin because it is a derivative of medicinal morphine.

In sum, we (a) reaffirm the *Roth* holding that obscene material is not protected by the First Amendment; (b) hold that such material can be regulated by the States, subject to the specific safeguards enunciated above, without a showing that the material is *"utterly* without redeeming social value"; and (c) hold that obscenity is to be determined by applying "contemporary community standards,". . . .

NOTES

1. This Court has defined "obscene material" as "material which deals with sex in a manner appealing to prurient interest." Roth v. United States, *supra,* 354 U.S., at 487, 77 S.Ct., at 1310, but the *Roth* definition does not reflect the precise meaning of "obscene" as traditionally used in the English language. Derived from the Latin *obscaenus, ob,* to, plus *caenum,* filth, "obscene" is defined in the Webster's Third New International Dictionary (Unabridged 1969) as "1a: disgusting to the senses * * * b: grossly repugnant to the generally accepted notions of what is appropriate * * * 2: offensive or revolting as countering or violating some ideal or principle." The Oxford English Dictionary (1933 ed.) gives a similar definition, "[o]ffensive to the senses, or to taste or refinement, disgusting, repulsive, filthy, foul, abominable, loathsome."

The material we are discussing in this case is more accurately defined as "pornography" or "pornographic material." "Pornography" derives from the Greek (*porne,* harlot, and *graphos,* writing). The word now means "1: a description of prostitutes or prostitution 2: a depiction (as in writing or painting) of licentiousness or lewdness: a portrayal of erotic behavior designed to cause sexual excitement." Webster's Third New International Dictionary, *supra.* Pornographic material which is obscene forms a subgroup of all "obscene" expression, but not the whole, at least as the word "obscene" is now used in our language. We note, therefore, that the words "obscene material," as used in this case, have a specific judicial meaning which derives from the *Roth* case, *i. e.,* obscene material "which deals with sex." *Roth, supra,* at 487, 77 S.Ct., at 1310. See also ALI Model Penal Code § 251.4(*l*) "Obscene Defined." (Official Draft, 1962.)

2. See the dissenting opinion of Mr. Justice Brennan in Paris Adult Theatre I v. Slaton, 413 U.S. 49, 73, 93 S.Ct. 2628, 2642, 37 L.Ed.2d 446 (1973).

3. As Mr. Chief Justice Warren stated, dissenting in Jacobellis v. Ohio, 378 U.S. 184, 200, 84 S.Ct. 1676, 1684, 12 L.Ed. 2d 793 (1964):

"For all the sound and fury that the *Roth* test has generated, it has not been proved unsound, and I believe that we should try to live with it—at least until a more satisfactory definition is evolved. No government—be it federal, state, or local—should be forced to choose between repressing all material, including that within the realm of decency, and allowing unrestrained license to publish any material, no matter how vile. There must be a rule of reason in this as in other areas of the law, and we have attempted in the *Roth* case to provide such a rule."

4. "A quotation from Voltaire in the flyleaf of a book will not constitutionally redeem an otherwise obscene publication * * *" Kois v. Wisconsin, 408 U.S., 229, 231, 92 S.Ct. 2245, 2246, 33 L.Ed.2d 312 (1972). See Memoirs v. Massachusetts, 383 U.S. 413, 461, 86 S.Ct. 975,

999, 16 L.Ed.2d 1 (1966) (White, J., dissenting). We also reject, as a constitutional standard, the ambiguous concept of "social importance." See *id.,* at 462, 86 S.Ct., at 999 (White, J., dissenting).

5. Although we are not presented here with the problem of regulating lewd public conduct itself, the States have greater power to regulate nonverbal, physical conduct than to suppress depictions or descriptions of the same behavior. In United States v. O'Brien, 391 U.S. 367, 377, 88 S.Ct. 1673, 1679, 20 L.Ed.2d 672 (1968), a case not dealing with obscenity, the Court held a State regulation of conduct which itself embodied both speech and nonspeech elements to be "sufficiently justified if * * * it furthers an important or substantial governmental interest; if the governmental interest is unrelated to the suppression of free expression; and if the incidental restriction on alleged First Amendment freedoms is no greater than is essential to the furtherance of that interest." See California v. LaRue, 409 U.S. 109, 117-118, 93 S.Ct. 390, 396-397, 34 L.Ed.2d 342 (1972).

6. The mere fact juries may reach different conclusions as to the same material does not mean that constitutional rights are abridged. . . .

7. As Mr. Justice Brennan stated for the Court in Roth v. United States, *supra,* 354 U.S., at 491-492, 77 S.Ct., at 1312-1313:

"Many decisions have recognized that these terms of obscenity statutes are not precise. [Footnote omitted.] This Court, however, has consistently held that lack of precision is not itself offensive to the requirements of due process. '* * * [T]he Constitution does not require impossible standards'; all that is required is that the language 'conveys sufficiently definite warning as to the proscribed conduct when measured by common understanding and practices. * * *' United States v. Petrillo, 332 U.S. 1, 7-8, 67 S.Ct. 1538, 1542, 91 L.Ed. 1877. These words, applied according to the proper standard for judging obscenity, already discussed, give adequate warning of the conduct proscribed and mark '* * * boundaries sufficiently distinct for judges and juries to fairly administer the law * * *. That there may be marginal cases in which it is difficult to determine the side of the line on which a particular fact situation falls is no sufficient reason to hold the language too ambiguous to define a criminal offense. * * *' *Id.,* 332 U.S. at p.7, 67 S.Ct., at page 1542. . . .

8. In Jacobellis v. Ohio, 378 U.S. 184, 84 S.Ct. 1676, 12 L.Ed.2d 793 (1964), two Justices argued that application of "local" community standards would run the risk of preventing dissemination of materials in some places because sellers would be unwilling to risk criminal conviction by testing variations in standards from place to place. *Id.,* at 193-195, 84 S.Ct., at 1681-1682 (opinion of Brennan, J., joined by Goldberg, J.). The use of "national" standards, however, necessarily implies that materials found tolerable in some places, but not under the "national" criteria, will nevertheless be unavailable where they are acceptable. Thus, in terms of danger to free expression, the potential for suppression seems at least as great in the application of a single nationwide standard as in allowing distribution in accordance with local tastes, a point which Mr. Justice Harlan often emphasized. See Roth v. United States, 354 U.S., at 506, 77 S.Ct., at 1320. . . .

9. In the apt words of Mr. Chief Justice Warren, the appellant in this case was "plainly engaged in the commercial exploitation of the morbid and shameful craving for materials with prurient effect. I believe that the State and Federal Governments can constitutionally punish such conduct. That is all that these cases present to us, and that is all we need to decide." Roth v. United States, *supra,* 354 U.S., at 496, 77 S.Ct., at 1315 (concurring opinion).

10. See 2 V. Parrington, Main Currents in American Thought ix et seq. (1930). As to the latter part of the 19th century, Parrington observed "A new age had come and other dreams— the age and the dreams of a middle-class sovereignty * * *. From the crude and vast romanticisms of that vigorous sovereignty emerged eventually a spirit of realistic criticism, seeking to evalute the worth of this new America, and discover if possible other philosophies to take the place of those which had gone down in the fierce battles of the Civil War." *Id.,* at 474. Cf. 2 Morison, H. Commager & W. Leuchtenburg, The Growth of the American Republic 197-233 (6th ed. 1969); Paths of American Thought 123-166, 203-290 (A. Schlesinger & M. White

ed. 1963) (articles of Fleming, Lerner, Morton & Lucia White, E. Rostow, Samuelson, Kazin, Hofstadter); and H. Wish, Society and Thought in Modern America 337-386 (1952).

11. "[W]e have indicated * * * that because of its strong and abiding interest in youth, a State may regulate the dissemination to juveniles of, and their access to, material objectionable as to them, but which a State clearly could not regulate as to adults. Ginsberg v. New York, * * * [390 U.S. 629, 88 S.Ct. 1274, 20 L.Ed.2d 195 (1968)]." Interstate Circuit, Inc. v. Dallas, 390 U.S. 676, 690, 88 S.Ct. 1298, at 1306, 20 L.Ed.2d 255 (1968) (footnote omitted).

Paris Adult Theatre I et al. v. Lewis R. Slaton, District Attorney, Atlanta Judicial Circuit, et al.

United States Supreme Court

413 U.S. 49 (1973)

[Editors' Note: Civil complaints were filed in Atlanta in 1970 alleging that two Atlanta, Georgia movie theaters were each exhibiting an obscene film, asking that the films be declared obscene, and asking that the theaters be enjoined from showing them. The trial court dismissed the complaints, but, on appeal, the Georgia Supreme Court held that the showing of the films should have been enjoined. The United States Supreme Court upheld the latter decision. Mr. Chief Justice Burger here argues that "the States have a legitimate interest in regulating commerce in obscene material and in regulating exhibition of obscene material in places of public accommodation." Mr. Justice Brennan dissents. We have edited the judgements and renumbered footnotes as necessary.]

Mr. Chief Justice BURGER delivered the opinion of the Court. . . .

[5-7] We categorically disapprove the theory, apparently adopted by the trial judge, that obscene, pornographic films acquire constitutional immunity from state regulation simply because they are exhibited for consenting adults only. This holding was properly rejected by the Georgia

Supreme Court. Although we have often pointedly recognized the high importance of the state interest in regulating the exposure of obscene materials to juveniles and unconsenting adults, . . . this Court has never declared these to be the only legitimate state interests permitting regulation of obscene material. The States have a long-recognized legitimate interest in regulating the use of obscene material in local commerce and in all places of public accommodation, as long as these regulations do not run afoul of specific constitutional prohibitions. . . . "In an unbroken series of cases extending over a long stretch of this Court's history it has been accepted as a postulate that 'the primary requirements of decency may be enforced against obscene publications.' [Near v. Minnesota ex rel. Olson, 283 U.S. 697, 716, 51 S.Ct. 625, 631, 15 L. Ed. 1357 (1931)]." Kingsley Books, Inc. v. Brown, *supra,* 354 U.S., at 440, 77 S.Ct., at 1327.

[8] In particular, we hold that there are legitimate state interests at stake in stemming the tide of commercialized obscenity, even assuming it is feasible to enforce effective safeguards against exposure to juveniles and to passersby.[1] Rights and interests "other than those of the advocates are involved." Breard v. Alexandria, 341 U.S. 662, 642, 71 S.Ct. 920, 932, 95 L.Ed. 1233 (1951). These include the interest of the public in the quality of life and the total community environment, the tone of commerce in the great city centers, and, possibly, the public safety itself. The Hill-Link Minority Report of the Commission on Obscenity and Pornography indicates that there is at least an arguable correlation between obscene material and crime.[2] Quite apart from sex crimes, however, there remains one problem of large proportions aptly described by Professor Bickel:

> "It concerns the tone of the society, the mode, or to use terms that have perhaps greater currency, the style and quality of life, now and in the future. A man may be entitled to read an obscene book in his room, or expose himself indecently there * * *.We should protect his privacy. But if he demands a right to obtain the books and pictures he wants in the market, and to foregather in public places—discreet, if you will, but accessible to all—with others who share his tastes, *then to grant him his right is to affect the world about the rest of us, and to impinge on other privacies.* Even supposing that each of us can, if he wishes, effectively avert the eye and stop the ear (which, in truth, we cannot), what is commonly read and seen and heard and done intrudes upon us all, want it or not." 22 The Public Interest 25-26 (Winter 1971).[3] (Emphasis added.)

As Mr. Chief Justice Warren stated, there is a "right of the Nation and of the States to maintain a decent society * * *," Jacobellis v. Ohio, 378 U.S. 184, 199, 84 S.Ct. 1676, 1684, 12 L.Ed.2d 793 (1964) (dissenting opinion)†. . . .

[9, 10] But, it is argued, there are no scientific data which conclusively demonstrate that exposure to obscene material adversely affects men and women or their society. It is urged on behalf of the petitioners that, absent

†Footnote omitted.

such a demonstration, any kind of state regulation is "impermissible." We reject this argument. It is not for us to resolve empirical uncertainties underlying state legislation, save in the exceptional case where that legislation plainly impinges upon rights protected by the Constitution itself. . . . Although there is no conclusive proof of a connection between antisocial behavior and obscene material, the legislature of Georgia could quite reasonably determine that such a connection does or might exist. In deciding *Roth,* this Court implicitly accepted that a legislature could legitimately act on such a conclusion to protect *"the social interest in order and morality."* . . .[4]

[11] From the beginning of civilized societies, legislators and judges have acted on various unprovable assumptions. Such assumptions underlie much lawful state regulation of commercial and business affairs. . . . On the basis of these assumptions both Congress and state legislatures have, for example, drastically restricted associational rights by adopting antitrust laws, and have strictly regulated public expression by issuers of and dealers in securities, profit sharing "coupons," and "trading stamps," commanding what they must and must not publish and announce. . . . Understandably those who entertain an absolutist view of the First Amendment find it uncomfortable to explain why rights of association, speech, and press should be severely restrained in the marketplace of goods and money, but not in the marketplace of pornography.

Likewise, when legislatures and administrators act to protect the physical environment from pollution and to preserve our resources of forests, streams, and parks, they must act on such imponderables as the impact of a new highway near or through an existing park or wilderness area. . . . The fact that a congressional directive reflects unprovable assumptions about what is good for the people, including imponderable aesthetic assumptions, is not a sufficient reason to find that statute unconstitutional.

If we accept the unprovable assumption that a complete education requires the reading of certain books. . . . and the well nigh universal belief that good books, plays, and art lift the spirit, improve the mind, enrich the human personality, and develop character, can we then say that a state legislature may not act on the corollary assumption that commerce in obscene books, or public exhibitions focused on obscene conduct, have a tendency to exert a corrupting and debasing impact leading to antisocial behavior? "Many of these effects may be intangible and indistinct, but they are nonetheless real." American Power & Light Co. v. SEC, *supra,* 329 U.S., at 103, 67 S.Ct., at 141. Mr. Justice Cardozo said that all laws in Western civilization are "guided by a robust common sense * * *." Steward Machine Co. v. Davis, 301 U.S. 548, 590, 57 S.Ct. 883, 892, 81 L.Ed. 1279 (1937). The sum of experience, including that of the past two decades, affords an ample basis for legislatures to conclude that a sensitive, key relationship of human existence, central to family life, community welfare, and the development of human personality, can be debased and distorted by crass commercial exploitation of sex. Nothing in the Constitution prohibits a State from reaching such a conclusion and acting on it legislatively simply because there is no conclusive evidence or empirical data.

It is argued that individual "free will" must govern, even in activities beyond the protection of the First Amendment and other constitutional guarantees of privacy, and that government cannot legitimately impede an individual's desire to see or acquire obscene plays, movies, and books. We do indeed base our society on certain assumptions that people have the capacity for free choice. Most exercises of individual free choice—those in politics, religion, and expression of ideas—are explicitly protected by the Constitution. Totally unlimited play for free will, however, is not allowed in our or any other society. We have just noted, for example, that neither the First Amendment nor "free will" precludes States from having "blue sky" laws to regulate what sellers of securities may write or publish about their wares. See [preceding page]. Such laws are to protect the weak, the uninformed, the unsuspecting, and the gullible from the exercise of their own volition. Nor do modern societies leave disposal of garbage and sewage up to the individual "free will," but impose regulation to protect both public health and the appearance of public places. States are told by some that they must await a "laissez-faire" market solution to the obscenity-pornography problem, paradoxically "by people who have never otherwise had a kind word to say for laissez-faire," particularly in solving urban, commercial, and environmental pollution problems. See I. Kristol, On the Democratic Idea in America 37 (1972).

[12] The States, of course, may follow such a "laissez-faire" policy and drop all controls on commercialized obscenity, if that is what they prefer, just as they can ignore consumer protection in the marketplace, but nothing in the Constitution *compels* the States to do so with regard to matters falling within state jurisdiction. . . .

[13, 14] It is asserted, however, that standards for evaluating state commercial regulations are inapposite in the present context, as state regulation of access by consenting adults to obscene material violates the constitutionally protected right to privacy enjoyed by petitioners' customers. Even assuming that petitioners have vicarious standing to assert potential customers' rights, it is unavailing to compare a theater, open to the public for a fee, with the private home of Stanley v. Georgia, 394 U.S., at 568, 89 S.Ct., at 1249, and the marital bedroom of Griswold v. Connecticut, *supra,* 381 U.S., at 485-486, 85 S.Ct., at 1682-1683. This Court, has, on numerous occasions, refused to hold that commercial ventures such as a motion-picture house are "private" for the purpose of civil rights litigation and civil rights statutes. . . . The Civil Rights Act of 1964 specifically defines motion-picture houses and theaters as places of "public accommodation" covered by the Act as operations affecting commerce. 78 Stat. 243. 42 U.S.C. § 2000a (b) (3), (c).

[15, 16] Our prior decisions recognizing a right to privacy guaranteed by the Fourteenth Amendment included "only personal rights that can be deemed 'fundamental' or 'implicit in the concept of ordered liberty.' . . . This privacy right encompasses and protects the personal intimacies of the home, the family, marriage, motherhood, procreation, and child rearing. . . . Nothing, however, in this Court's decisions intimates that there is any "fundamental" privacy right "implicit in the concept of ordered liberty" to watch obscene movies in places of public accommodation.

[17-21] If obscene material unprotected by the First Amendment in itself carried with it a "penumbra" of constitutionally protected privacy, this Court would not have found it necessary to decide *Stanley* on the narrow basis of the "privacy of the home," which was hardly more than a reaffirmation that "a man's home is his castle." Cf. Stanley v. Georgia, *supra,* 394 U.S., at 564, 89 S.Ct., at 1247.[5] Moreover, we have declined to equate the privacy of the home relied on in *Stanley* with a "zone" of "privacy" that follows a distributor or a consumer of obscene materials wherever he goes. . . . The idea of a "privacy" right and a place of public accommodation are, in this context, mutually exclusive. Conduct or depictions of conduct that the state police power can prohibit on a public street do not become automatically protected by the Constitution merely because the conduct is moved to a bar or a "live" theater stage, any more than a "live" performance of a man and woman locked in a sexual embrace at high noon in Times Square is protected by the Constitution because they simultaneously engage in a valid political dialogue.

[22, 23] It is also argued that the State has no legitimate interest in "control [of] the moral content of a person's thoughts," Stanley v. Georgia, *supra,* 394 U.S., at 565, 89 S.Ct., at 1248 and we need not quarrel with this. But we reject the claim that the State of Georgia is here attempting to control the minds or thoughts of those who patronize theaters. Preventing unlimited display or distribution of obscene material, which by definition lacks any serious literary, artistic, political, or scientific value as communication, Miller v. California, *supra,* 413 U.S., at 24, 34, 93 S.Ct., at 2615, 2620, is distinct from a control of reason and the intellect. . . . Where communication of ideas, protected by the First Amendment, is not involved, or the particular privacy of the home protected by *Stanley,* or any of the other "areas or zones" of constitutionally protected privacy, the mere fact that, as a consequence, some human "utterances" or "thoughts" many be incidentally affected does not bar the State from acting to protect legitimate state interests. . . . The fantasies of a drug addict are his own and beyond the reach of government, but government regulation of drug sales is not prohibited by the Constitution. Cf. United States v. Reidel, *supra,* 402 U.S., at 359-360, 91 S.Ct., at 1414 (Harlan, J., concurring).

[24-26] Finally, petitioners argue that conduct which directly involves "consenting adults" only has, for that sole reason, a special claim to

constitutional protection. Our Constitution establishes a broad range of conditions on the exercise of power by the States, but for us to say that our Constitution incorporates the proposition that conduct involving consenting adults only is always beyond state regulation,[6] is a step we are unable to take.[7] Commercial exploitation of depictions, descriptions, or exhibitions of obscene conduct on commercial premises open to the adult public falls within a State's broad power to regulate commerce and protect the public environment. The issue in this context goes beyond whether someone, or even the majority, considers the conduct depicted as "wrong" or "sinful." The States have the power to make a morally neutral judgment that public exhibition of obscene material, or commerce in such material, has a tendency to injure the community as a whole, to endanger the public safety, or to jeopardize in Mr. Chief Justice Warren's words, the States' "right * * * to maintain a decent society." Jacobellis v. Ohio, 378 U.S., at 199, 84 S.Ct., at 1684 (dissenting opinion).

[27, 28] To summarize, we have today reaffirmed the basic holding of Roth v. United States, *supra,* that obscene material has no protection under the First Amendment. See Miller v. California, *supra,* and Kaplan v. California, 413 U.S. 115, 93 S.Ct. 2680, 37 L.Ed. 2d 492. We have directed our holdings, not at thoughts or speech, but at depiction and description of specifically defined sexual conduct that States may regulate within limits designed to prevent infringement of First Amendment rights. We have also reaffirmed the holdings of United States v. Reidel, *supra,* and United States v. Thirty-Seven Photographs, *supra,* that commerce in obscene material is unprotected by any constitutional doctrine of privacy. . . . In this case we hold that the States have a legitimate interest in regulating commerce in obscene material and in regulating exhibition of obscene material in places of public accommodation, including so-called "adult" theaters from which minors are excluded. In light of these holdings, nothing precludes the State of Georgia from the regulation of the allegedly obscene material exh bited in Paris Adult Theatre I or II, provided that the applicable Georgia law, as written or authoritatively interpreted by the Georgia courts, meets the First Amendment standards set forth in Miller v. California, *supra,* 413 U.S., at 23-25, 93 S.Ct., at 2614-2616 [this volume, p. 360]. The judgment is vacated and the case remanded to the Georgia Supreme Court for further proceedings not inconsistent with this opinion and Miller v. California, *supra.* . . .

Vacated and remanded.

Mr. Justice BRENNAN, with whom Mr. Justice STEWART and
Mr. Justice MARSHALL join, dissenting. . . .

II

. . . The essence of our problem in the obscenity area is that we have been
unable to provide "sensitive tools" to separate obscenity from other sexually oriented but constitutionally protected speech, so that efforts to suppress
the former do not spill over into the suppression of the latter. The attempt,
as the late Mr. Justice Harlan observed, has only "produced a variety of
views among the members of the Court unmatched in any other course of
constitutional adjudication." Interstate Circuit, Inc. v. Dallas, 390 U.S. 676,
704-705, 88 S.Ct. 1298, 1314, 20 L.Ed.2d 225 (1968) (separate opinion) * * *
     The view that, until today, enjoyed the most, but not majority, support
was an interpretation of *Roth* . . . adopted by Mr. Chief Justice Warren,
Mr. Justice Fortas, and the author of this opinion in Memoirs v.
Massachusetts, 383 U.S. 413, 86 S.Ct. 975, 16 L.Ed.2d 1 (1966). We expressed the view that Federal or State Governments could control the
distribution of material where "three elements * * * coalesce: it must be
established that (a) the dominant theme of the material taken as a whole appeals to a prurient interest in sex; (b) the material is patently offensive
because it affronts contemporary community standards relating to the
description or representation of sexual matters; and (c) the material is utterly without redeeming social value." *Id.,* at 418, 86 S.Ct., at 977. Even this
formulation, however, concealed differences of opinion. . . . Moreover, it
did not provide a definition covering all situations. . . . Nor, finally, did it
ever command a majority of the Court. . . .
     In the face of this divergence of opinion the Court began the practice in
Redrup v. New York, 386 U.S. 767, 87 S.Ct. 1414, 18 L.Ed.2d 515 (1967),
of *per curiam* reversals of convictions for the dissemination of materials
that at least five members of the Court, applying their separate tests,
deemed not to be obscene.[8] This approach capped the attempt in *Roth* to
separate all forms of sexually oriented expression into two categories—the
one subject to full governmental suppression and the other beyond the
reach of governmental regulation to the same extent as any other protected
form of speech or press. Today a majority of the Court offers a slightly
altered formulation of the basic *Roth* test, while leaving entirely unchanged
the underlying approach.

III

Our experience with the *Roth* approach has certainly taught us that the outright suppression of obscenity cannot be reconciled with the fundamental principles of the First and Fourteenth Amendments. For we have failed to formulate a standard that sharply distinguishes protected from unprotected speech, and out of necessity, we have resorted to the *Redrup* approach, which resolves cases as between the parties, but offers only the most obscure guidance to legislation, adjudication by other courts, and primary conduct. By disposing of cases through summary reversal or denial of certiorari we have deliberately and effectively obscured the rationale underlying the decisions. It comes as no surprise that judicial attempts to follow our lead conscientiously have often ended in hopeless confusion.

Of course, the vagueness problem would be largely of our own creation if it stemmed primarily from our failure to reach a consensus on any one standard. But after 16 years of experimentation and debate I am reluctantly forced to the conclusion that none of the available formulas, including the one announced today, can reduce the vagueness to a tolerable level while at the same time striking an acceptable balance between the protections of the First and Fourteenth Amendments, on the one hand, and on the other the asserted state interest in regulating the dissemination of certain sexually oriented materials. Any effort to draw a constitutionally acceptable boundary on state power must resort to such indefinite concepts as "prurient interest," "patent offensiveness," "serious literary value," and the like. The meaning of these concepts necessarily varies with the experience, outlook, and even idiosyncrasies of the person defining them. Although we have assumed that obscenity does exist and that we "know it when [we] see it," Jacobellis v. Ohio, *supra,* 378 U.S., at 197, 84 S.Ct., at 1683 (Stewart, J., concurring), we are manifestly unable to describe it in advance except by reference to concepts so elusive that they fail to distinguish clearly between protected and unprotected speech. . . .

. . . These considerations suggest that no one definition, no matter how precisely or narrowly drawn, can possibly suffice for all situations, or carve out fully suppressible expression from all media without also creating a substantial risk of encroachment upon the guarantees of the Due Process Clause and the First Amendment.†

The vagueness of the standards in the obscenity area produces a number of separate problems, and any improvement must rest on an understanding that the problems are to some extent distinct. First, a vague statute fails to provide adequate notice to persons who are engaged in the type of conduct that the statute could be thought to proscribe. The Due Process Clause of

†Footnote omitted.

the Fourteenth Amendment requires that all criminal laws provide fair notice of "what the State commands or forbids." . . . In the service of this general principle we have repeatedly held that the definition of obscenity must provide adequate notice of exactly what is prohibited from dissemination . . . While various tests have been upheld under the Due Process Clause, see Ginsberg v. New York, 390 U.S., at 643, 88 S.Ct., at 1282; Mishkin v. New York, 383 U.S., at 506-507, 86 S.Ct., at 962-963; Roth v. United States, 354 U.S., at 491-492, 77 S.Ct., at 1312-1313, I have grave doubts that any of those tests could be sustained today. For I know of no satisfactory answer to the assertion by Mr. Justice Black, "after the fourteen separate opinions handed down" in the t ilogy of cases decided in 1966, that "no person, not even the most learned judge much less a layman, is capable of knowing in advance of an ultimate decision in his particular case by this Court whether certain material comes within the area of 'obscenity' * * *." Ginzburg v. United States, 383 U.S., at 480-481, 86 S.Ct., at 952-953 (dissenting opinion). . . . As Mr. Chief Justice Warren pointed out, "[t]he constitutional requirement of definiteness is violated by a criminal statute that fails to give a person of ordinary intelligence fair notice that his contemplated conduct is forbidden by the statute. The underlying principle is that no man shall be held criminally responsible for conduct which he could not reasonably understand to be proscribed." United States v. Harriss, 347 U.S. 612, 617, 74 S.Ct. 808, 812, 98 L.Ed. 989 (1954). In this context, even the most painstaking efforts to determine in advance whether certain sexually oriented expression is obscene must inevitably prove unavailing. For the insufficiency of the notice compels persons to guess not only whether their conduct is covered by a criminal statute, but also whether their conduct falls within the constitutionally permissible reach of the statute. The resulting level of uncertainty is utterly intolerable, not alone because it makes "[b]ookselling * * * a hazardous profession," Ginsberg v. New York, *supra,* 390 U.S., at 674, 88 S.Ct., at 1298 (Fortas, J., dissenting), but as well because it invites arbitrary and erratic enforcement of the law. . . .

In addition to problems that arise when any criminal statute fails to afford fair notice of what it forbids, a vague statute in the areas of speech and press creates a second level of difficulty. We have indicated that "stricter standards of permissible statutory vagueness may be applied to a statute having a potentially inhibiting effect on speech; a man may the less be required to act at his peril here, because the free dissemination of ideas may be the loser."† Smith v. California, 361 U.S. 147, 151, 80 S.Ct., 215, 217, 4 L.Ed.2d 205 (1959). That proposition draws its strength from our recognition that

"[t]he fundamental freedoms of speech and press have contributed greatly to the development and well-being of our free society and are indispensable to its continued growth. Ceaseless vigilance is the watchword to prevent their erosion by Congress or by the States. The door barring federal and state intrusion into this area cannot be left ajar * * *." Roth, *supra,* 354 U.S., at 488, 77 S.Ct., at 1311.†

To implement this general principle, and recognizing the inherent vagueness of any definition of obscenity, we have held that the definition of obscenity must be drawn as narrowly as possible so as to minimize the interference with protected expression. Thus, in *Roth* we rejected the test of Regina v. Hicklin, [1868] L.R. 3 Q.B. 360, that "[judged] obscenity by the effect of isolated passages upon the most susceptible persons." 354 U.S., at 489, 77 S.Ct., at 1311. That test, we held in *Roth*, "might well encompass material legitimately treating with sex * * *." *Ibid.* Cf. Mishkin v. New York, *supra,* 383 U.S., at 509, 86 S.Ct., at 963. And we have supplemented the *Roth* standard with additional tests in an effort to hold in check the corrosive effect of vagueness on the guarantees of the First Amendment.† . . .

The problems of fair notice and chilling protected speech are very grave standing alone. But it does not detract from their importance to recognize that a vague statute in this area creates a third, although admittedly more subtle, set of problems. These problems concern the institutional stress that inevitably results where the line separating protected from unprotected speech is excessively vague. In *Roth* we conceded that "there may be marginal cases in which it is difficult to determine the side of the line on which a particular fact situation falls * * *." 354 U.S., at 491-492, 77 S.Ct., at 1313. Our subsequent experience demonstrates that almost every case is "marginal." And since the "margin" marks the point of separation between protected and unprotected speech, we are left with a system in which almost every obscenity case presents a constitutional question of exceptional difficulty. . . .

As a result of our failure to define standards with predictable application to any given piece of material, there is no probability of regularity in obscenity decisions by state and lower federal courts. That is not to say that these courts have performed badly in this area or paid insufficient attention to the principles we have established. The problem is, rather, that one cannot say with certainty that material is obscene until at least five members of this Court, applying inevitably obscure standards, have pronounced it so. The number of obscenity cases on our docket gives ample testimony to the burden that has been placed upon this Court. . . .

The severe problems arising from the lack of fair notice, from the chill on protected expression, and from the stress imposed on the state and federal judicial machinery persuade me that a significant change in direction is urgently required. I turn, therefore, to the alternatives that are now open.

†Footnotes omitted.

IV

1. The approach requiring the smallest deviation from our present course would be to draw a new line between protected and unprotected speech, still permitting the States to suppress all material on the unprotected side of the line. In my view, clarity cannot be obtained pursuant to this approach except by drawing a line that resolves all doubt in favor of state power and against the guarantees of the First Amendment. We could hold, for example, that any depiction or description of human sexual organs, irrespective of the manner or purpose of the portrayal, is outside the protection of the First Amendment and therefore open to suppression by the States. . . . But such a standard would be appallingly overbroad, permitting the suppression of a vast range of literary, scientific, and artistic masterpieces. Neither the First Amendment nor any free community could possibly tolerate such a standard. Yet short of that extreme it is hard to see how any choice of words could reduce the vagueness problem to tolerable proportions, so long as we remain committed to the view that some class of materials is subject to outright suppression by the State.

2. The alternative adopted by the Court today recognizes that a prohibition against any depiction or description of human sexual organs could not be reconciled with the guarantees of the First Amendment. But the court does retain the view that certain sexually oriented material can be considered obscene and therefore unprotected by the First and Fourteenth Amendments. To describe that unprotected class of expression, the Court adopts a restatement of the *Roth-Memoirs* definition of obscenity . . . Miller v. California, 413 U.S., at 24, 93 S.Ct., at 2615. . . .

The Court evidently recognizes that difficulties with the *Roth* approach necessitate a significant change of direction. But the Court does not describe its understanding of those difficulties, nor does it indicate how the restatement of the *Memoirs* test is in any way responsive to the problems that have arisen. In my view, the restatement leaves unresolved the very difficulties that compel our rejection of the underlying *Roth* approach, while at the same time contributing substantial difficulties of its own. The modification of the *Memoirs* test may prove sufficient to jeopardize the analytic underpinnings of the entire scheme. And today's restatement will likely have the effect, whether or not intended, of permitting far more sweeping suppression of sexually oriented expression, including expression that would almost surely be held protected under our current formulation. . . .

V

Our experience since *Roth* requires us not only to abandon the effort to pick out obscene materials on a case-by-case basis, but also to reconsider a fundamental postulate of *Roth:* that there exists a definable class of sexually oriented expression that may be totally suppressed by the Federal and State Governments. Assuming that such a class of expression does in fact exist,† I am forced to conclude that the concept of "obscenity" cannot be defined with sufficient specificity and clarity to provide fair notice to persons who create and distribute sexually oriented materials, to prevent substantial erosion of protected speech as a byproduct of the attempt to suppress unprotected speech, and to avoid very costly institutional harms. Given these inevitable side effects of state efforts to suppress what is assumed to be *unprotected* speech, we must scrutinize with care the state interest that is asserted to justify the suppression. For in the absence of some very substantial interest in suppressing such speech, we can hardly condone the ill effects that seem to flow inevitably from the effort.[9]

Obscenity laws have a long history in this country. Most of the States that had ratified the Constitution by 1792 punished the related crime of blasphemy or profanity despite the guarantees of free expression in their constitutions, and Massachusetts expressly prohibited the "Composing, Writing, Printing or Publishing, of any Filthy Obscene or Prophane Song, Pamphlet, Libel or Mock-Sermon, in Imitation or in Mimicking of Preaching, or any other part of Divine Worship." Acts and Laws of Massachusetts Bay Colony (1726), Acts of 1711-1712, c. 1, p. 218. In 1815 the first reported obscenity conviction was obtained under the common law of Pennsylvania. See Commonwealth v. Sharpless, 2 S. & R. 91. A conviction in Massachusetts under its common law and colonial statute followed six years later. See Commonwealth v. Holmes, 17 Mass. 336 (1821). In 1821 Vermont passed the first state law proscribing the publication or sale of "lewd or obscene" material, Laws of Vermont, 1824, c. XXXII, No. 1, § 23, and federal legislation barring the importation of similar matter appeared in 1842. See Tariff Act of 1842, § 28, 5 Stat. 566. Although the number of early obscenity laws was small and their enforcement exceedingly lax, the situation significantly changed after about 1870 when Federal and State Governments, mainly as a result of the efforts of Anthony Comstock, took an active interest in the suppression of obscenity. By the end of the 19th century at least 30 States had some type of general prohibition on the dissemination of obscene materials, and by the time of our decision in *Roth* no State was without some provision on the subject. The Federal Government meanwhile had enacted no fewer than 20 obscenity laws between 1842 and 1956. See Roth v. United States, 354 U.S., at 482-483, 485, 77 S.Ct., at

†Footnote omitted.

1307-1308, 1309; Report of the Commission on Obscenity and Pornography 300-301 (1970).

This history caused us to conclude in *Roth* "that the unconditional phrasing of the First Amendment [that 'Congress shall make no law * * * abridging the freedom of speech, or of the press . . .'] was not intended to protect every utterance." 354 U.S., at 483, 77 S.Ct., at 1308. It also caused us to hold, as numerous prior decisions of this Court had assumed, see *id.*, at 481, 77 S.Ct., at 1306, that obscenity could be denied the protection of the First Amendment and hence suppressed because it is a form of expression "utterly without redeeming social importance," *id.*, at 484, 77 S.Ct., at 1309, as "mirrored in the universal judgment that [it] should be restrained * * *." *Id.*, at 485, 77 S.Ct., at 1309.

Because we assumed—incorrectly, as experience has proved—that obscenity could be separated from other sexually oriented expression without significant costs either to the First Amendment or to the judi ial machinery charged with the task of safeguarding First Amendment freedoms, we had no occasion in *Roth* to probe the asserted state interest in curtailing unprotected, sexually oriented speech. Yet, as we have increasingly come to appreciate the vagueness of the concept of obscenity, we have begun to recognize and articulate the state interests at stake. . . .

The opinions in *Redrup* and *Stanley* reflected our emerging view that the state interests in protecting children and in protecting unconsenting adults may stand on a different footing from the other asserted state interests. It may well be, as one commentator has argued, that "exposure to [erotic material] is for some persons an intense emotional experience. A communication of this nature, imposed upon a person contrary to his wishes, has all the characteristics of a physical assault. * * * [And it] constitutes an invasion of his privacy * * *."[10] . . . Similarly, if children are "not possessed of that full capacity for individual choice which is the presupposition of the First Amendment guarantees," Ginsberg v. New York, 390 U.S., at 649-650, 88 S.Ct., at 1286 (Steward, J., concurring), then the State may have a substantial interest in precluding the flow of obscene materials even to consenting juveniles.[11] . . .

But, whatever the strength of the state interests in protecting juveniles and unconsenting adults from exposure to sexually oriented materials, those interests cannot be asserted in defense of the holding of the Georgia Supreme Court in this case. That court assumed for the purposes of its decision that the films in issue were exhibited only to persons over the age of 21 who viewed them willingly and with prior knowledge of the nature of their contents. And on that assumption the state court held that the films could still be suppressed. The justification for the suppression must be found, therefore, in some independent interest in regulating the reading and viewing habits of consenting adults. . . .

In *Stanley* we pointed out that "[t]here appears to be little empirical basis for" the assertion that "exposure to obscene materials may lead to deviant sexual behavior or crimes of sexual violence." *Id.,* at 566 and n. 9, 89 S.Ct., at 1249.[12] In any event, we added that "if the State is only concerned about printed or filmed materials inducing antisocial conduct, we believe that in the context of private consumption of ideas and information we should adhere to the view that '[a]mong free men, the deterrents ordinarily to be applied to prevent crime are education and punishment for violations of the law * * *.' Whitney v. California, 274 U.S. 357, 378 [, 47 S.Ct. 641, 649] 71 L.Ed. 1095 (1927) (Brandeis, J., concurring)." *Id.,* at 566-567, 89 S.Ct., at 1249.

Moreover, in *Stanley* we rejected as "wholly inconsistent with the philosophy of the First Amendment," *id.,* at 566, 89 S.Ct., at 1248, the notion that there is a legitimate state concern in the "control [of] the moral content of a person's thoughts," *id.,* at 565, 89 S.Ct., at 1248, . . . That is not to say, of course, that a State must remain utterly indifferent to—and take no action bearing on—the morality of the community. The traditional description of state police power does embrace the regulation of morals as well as the health, safety, and general welfare of the citizenry. . . . And much legislation—compulsory public education laws, civil rights laws, even the abolition of capital punishment—is grounded, at least in part, on a concern with the morality of the community. But the State's interest in regulating morality by suppressing obscenity, while often asserted, remains essentially unfocused and ill defined. And, since the attempt to curtail unprotected speech necessarily spills over into the area of protected speech, the effort to serve this speculative interest through the suppression of obscene material must tread heavily on rights protected by the First Amendment. . . .

If, as the Court today assumes, "a state legislature may * * * act on the * * * assumption that commerce in obscene books, or public exhibitions focused on obscene conduct, have a tendency to exert a corrupting and debasing impact leading to antisocial behavior," *ante,* at 2638, then it is hard to see how state-ordered regimentation of our minds can ever be forestalled. For if a State, in an effort to maintain or create a particular moral tone, may prescribe what its citizens cannot read or cannot see, then it would seem to follow that in pursuit of that same objective a State could decree that its citizens must read certain books or must view certain films. Cf. United States v. Roth, 237 F.2d 796, 823 (CA2 1956) (Frank, J., concurring). However laudable its goal—and that is obviously a question on which reasonable minds may differ—the State cannot proceed by means that violate the Constitution. . . .

Recognizing these principles, we have held that so-called thematic obscenity—obscenity which might persuade the viewer or reader to engage in "obscene" conduct—is not outside the protection of the First Amendment:

"It is contended that the State's action was justified because the motion picture attractively portrays a relationship which is contrary to the moral standards, the religious precepts, and the legal code of its citizenry. This argument misconceives what it is that the Constitution protects. Its guarantee is not confined to the expression of ideas that are conventional or shared by a majority. It protects advocacy of the opinion that adultery may sometimes be proper, no less than advocacy of socialism or the single tax. And in the realm of ideas it protects expression which is eloquent no less than that which is unconvincing." Kingsley Int'l Pictures Corp. v. Regents, 360 U.S. 684, 688-689, 79 S.Ct. 1362, 1365, 3 L.Ed.2d 1512 (1959).

Even a legitimate, sharply focused state concern for the morality of the community cannot, in other words, justify an assault on the protections of the First Amendment. . . . Where the state interest in regulation of morality is vague and ill defined, interference with the guarantees of the First Amendment is even more difficult to justify.[13]

In short, while I cannot say that the interests of the State—apart from the question of juveniles and unconsenting adults—are trivial or nonexistent, I am compelled to conclude that these interests cannot justify the substantial damage to constitutional rights and to this Nation's judicial machinery that inevitably results from state efforts to bar the distribution even of unprotected material to consenting adults. . . . I would hold, therefore, that at least in the absence of distribution to juveniles or obtrusive exposure to unconsenting adults, the First and Fourteenth Amendments prohibit the State and Federal Governments from attempting wholly to suppress sexually oriented materials on the basis of their allegedly "obscene" contents. Nothing in this approach precludes those governments from taking action to serve what may be strong and legitimate interests through regulation of the manner of distribution of sexually oriented material. . . .

NOTES

1. It is conceivable that an "adult" theater can—if it really insists—prevent the exposure of its obscene wares to juveniles. An "adult" bookstore, dealing in obscene books, magazines, and pictures, cannot realistically make this claim. The Hill-Link Minority Report of the Commission on Obscenity and Pornography emphasizes evidence (the Abelson National Survey of Youth and Adults) that, although most pornography may be bought by elders, "the heavy users and most highly exposed people to pornography are adolescent females (among women) and adolescent and young adult males (among men)." The Report of the Commission on Obscenity and Pornography 401 (1970). The legitimate interest in preventing exposure of juveniles to obscene materials cannot be fully served by simply barring juveniles from the immediate physical premises of "adult" book stores, when there is a flourishing "outside business" in these materials.

2. The Report of the Commission on Obscenity and Pornography 390-412 (1970). For a discussion of earlier studies indicating "a division of thought [among behavioral scientists] on the correlation between obscenity and socially deleterious behavior", Memoirs v. Massachusetts, *supra*, 383 U.S., at 451, 86 S.Ct., at 993, and references to expert opinions that obscene material may induce crime and antisocial conduct, see *id.,* at 451-453, 86 S.Ct., at 993-995 (Clark, J., dissenting). As Mr. Justice Clark emphasized: "While erotic stimulation caused by pornography may be legally insignificant in itself, there are medical experts who believe that such stimulation frequently manifests itself in criminal sexual behavior or other antisocial conduct. For example, Dr. George W. Henry of Cornell University has expressed the opinion that obscenity, with its exaggerated and morbid emphasis on sex, particularly abnormal and perverted practices, and its unrealistic presentation of sexual behavior and attitudes, may induce antisocial conduct by the average person. A number of sociologists think that this material may have adverse effects upon individual mental health, with potentially disruptive consequences for the community.

*   *   *   *   *

"Congress and the legislatures of every State have enacted measures to restrict the distribution of erotic and pornographic material, justify these controls by reference to evidence that antisocial behavior may result in part from reading obscenity." *Id.,* at 452-453, 86 S.Ct., at 994-995 (footnotes omitted).

3. See also Berns, Pornography vs. Democracy: The Case for Censorship, in 22 The Public Interest 3 (Winter 1971); van den Haag, in Censorship: For & Against 156-157 (H. Hart ed. 1971).

4. *"It has been well observed that such* [lewd and obscene] *utterances are no essential part of any exposition of ideas, and are of such slight social value as a step to truth that any benefit that may be derived from them is clearly outweighed by the social interest in order and morality."* Roth v. United States, 354 U.S. 476, 485, 77 S.Ct. 1304, 1309, 1 L.Ed.2d 1498 (1957), quoting Chaplinsky v. New Hampshire, 315 U.S. 568, 572, 62 S.Ct. 766, 769, 86 L.Ed. 1031 (1942) (emphasis added in *Roth*).

5. The protection afforded by Stanley v. Georgia, 394 U.S. 557, 89 S.Ct. 1243, 22 L.Ed.2d 542 (1969), is restricted to a place, the home. In contrast, the constitutionally protected privacy of family, marriage, motherhood, procreation, and child rearing is not just concerned with a particular place, but with a protected intimate relationship. Such protected privacy extends to the doctor's office, the hospital, the hotel room, or as otherwise required to safeguard the right to intimacy involved. . . . Obviously, there is no necessary or legitimate expectation of privacy which would extend to marital intercourse on a street corner or a theater stage.

6. Cf. J. Mill, On Liberty 13 (1955 ed.).

7. The state statute books are replete with constitutionally unchallenged laws against prostitution, suicide, voluntary self-mutilation, brutalizing "bare fist" prize fights, and duels, although these crimes may only directly involve "consenting adults." Statutes making bigamy a crime surely cut into an individual's freedom to associate, but few today seriously claim such statutes violate the First Amendment or any other constitutional provision. . . .

8. No fewer than 31 cases have been disposed of in this fashion. . . .

9. Cf. United States v. O'Brien, 391 U.S. 367, 376-377, 88 S.Ct. 1673, 1678-1679, 20 L.Ed.2d 672 (1968):

"This Court has held that when 'speech' and 'nonspeech' elements are combined in the same course of conduct, a sufficiently important governmental interest in regulating the nonspeech element can justify incidental limitations on First Amendment freedoms. To characterize the quality of the governmental interest which must appear, the Court has employed a variety of descriptive terms: compelling; substantial; subordinating; paramount; cogent; strong. Whatever imprecision inheres in these terms, we think it clear that a government regulation is sufficiently justified if it is within the constitutional power of the Government; if it furthers an important or substantial governmental interest; if the governmental interest is unrelated to the suppression of free expression; and if the incidental restriction on alleged First Amendment freedoms is no greater than is essential to the furtherance of that interest." (Footnotes omitted.)

See also Speiser v. Randall, 357 U.S. 513, 78 S.Ct. 1332, 2 L.Ed.2d 1460 (1958).

10. T. Emerson, The System of Freedom of Expression 496 (1970).

11. See *ibid.*

12. Indeed, since *Stanley* was decided, the President's Commission on Obscenity and Pornography has concluded:

"In sum, empirical research designed to clarify the question has found no evidence to date that exposure to explicit sexual materials plays a significant role in the causation of delinquent or criminal behavior among youth or adults. The Commission cannot conclude that exposure to erotic materials is a factor in the causation of sex crime or sex delinquency." Report of the Commission on Obscenity and Pornography 27 (1970) (footnote omitted).

To the contrary, the Commission found that "[o]n the positive side, explicit sexual materials are sought as a source of entertainment and information by substantial numbers of American adults. At times, these materials also appear to serve to increase and facilitate constructive communication about sexual matters within marriage." *Id.,* at 53.

13. "[I]n our system, undifferentiated fear or apprehension of disturbance is not enough to overcome the right to freedom of expression. Any departure from absolute regimentation may cause trouble. Any variation from the majority's opinion may inspire fear. Any word spoken, in class, in the lunchroom, or on the campus, that deviates from the views of another person may start an argument or cause a disturbance. But our Constitution says we must take this risk, Terminiello v. Chicago, 337 U.S. 1 [69 S.Ct. 894], 93 L.Ed. 1131 (1949); and our history says that it is this sort of hazardous freedom—this kind of openness—that is the basis of our national strength and of the independence and vigor of Americans who grow up and live in this relatively permissive, often disputatious, society." Tinker v. Des Moines Independent Community School District, 393 U.S. 503, 508-509, 89 S.Ct. 733, 737-738, 21 L.Ed.2d 731 (1969). See also Cohen v. California, 403 U.S. 15, 23, 91 S.Ct. 1780, 1787, 29 L.Ed.2d 284 (1971).

Regina v.
Pink Triangle Press et al.

Provincial Court
Judicial District of York, Ontario

(1979) 45 C.C.C. (2d) 385

[Editors' Note: The accused were charged with unlawfully making use of the mails for the purpose of transmitting indecent, immoral, or scurrilous matter, namely, an issue of "The Body Politic," in violation of s.164 of the Canadian Criminal Code. In dismissing the charge, the judge summarizes the evidence, describes the nature of the issue of "The Body Politic" that is in question, discusses the interpretation of the law, and applies the law to the case at hand. The judgement illustrates the issues that can arise in an obscenity trial at a court of first instance.

Judge Harris dismissed the charge against Pink Triangle Press, but the Ontario Attorney-General's office appealed the decision, and the appeal court ordered a new trial. At the second trial, held in 1982, Pink Triangle Press was again acquitted, but the prosecution has again appealed.]

HARRIS, PROV. CT. J.: . . .

Let me now say what, in my opinion, is *not* at issue herein. This is not a trial

Reprinted from *Canadian Criminal Cases,* Vol. 45, pp. 385-411, by permission of Canada Law Book Ltd., 240 Edward Street, Aurora, Ontario, Canada.

(a) of the criminality or otherwise, or of the morality, decency or scurrility of
　　(i) homosexual acts, homosexuality or homosexuals,
　　(ii) child abuse or child abusers,
　　(iii) pedophilic acts, pedophilia or pedophiles.
　　This is not a trial
(b) of obscenity, either
　　(i) in itself, or
　　(ii) as related to any of the matters in (a), or
　　(iii) as related to ex. 1 or of any or all of its contents, or
　　(iv) as a factor determinative of the charge before this Court, or in any other way concerned with that charge.
　　This is not a trial
(c) of freedom of the press.
　　This is not a trial
(d) of the right of the accused to continue to publish The Body Politic and to distribute it by mail or otherwise.
　　This is not a trial
(e) of any offence under s. 159 which reads as follows:

> 159(1) Every one commits an offence who
> 　*(a)* makes, prints, publishes, distributes, circulates, or has in his possession for the purpose of publication, distribution or circulation any obscene written matter, picture, model, phonograph record or other thing whatsoever, or
> 　*(b)* makes, prints, publishes, distributes, sells or has in his possession for the purpose of publication, distribution or circulation, a crime comic.
> 　(2) Every one commits an offence who knowingly, without lawful justification or excuse,
> 　*(a)* sells, exposes to public view or has in his possession for such a purpose any obscene written matter, picture, model, phonograph record or other thing whatsoever,
> 　*(b)* publicly exhibits a disgusting object or an indecent show,
> 　*(c)* offers to sell, advertises, publishes an advertisement of, or has for sale or disposal any means, instructions, medicine, drug or article intended or represented as a method of causing abortion or miscarriage, or
> 　*(d)* advertises or publishes an advertisement of any means, instructions, medicine, drug or article intended or represented as a method for restoring sexual virility or curing venereal diseases or diseases of the generative organs.
> 　(3) No person shall be convicted of an offence under this section if he establishes that the public good was served by the acts that are alleged to constitute the offence and that the acts alleged did not extend beyond what served the public good.

(4) For the purposes of this section it is a question of law whether an act served the public good and whether there is evidence that the act alleged went beyond what served the public good, but it is a question of fact whether the acts did or did not extend beyond what served the public good.

(5) For the purposes of this section the motives of an accused are irrelevant.

(6) Where an accused is charged with an offense under subsection (1) the fact that the accused was ignorant of the nature or presence of the matter, picture, model, phonograph record, crime comic or other thing by means of or in relation to which the offence was committed is not a defence to the charge.

(7) In this section "crime comic" means a magazine, periodical or book that exclusively or substantially comprises matter depicting pictorially.

(a) the commission of crimes, real or fictitious, or

(b) events connected with the commission of crimes, real or fictitious, whether occurring before or after the commission of the crime.

(8) For the purposes of this Act, any publication a dominant characteristic of which is the undue exploitation of sex, or of sex and any one or more of the following subjects, namely, crime, horror, cruelty and violence, shall be deemed to be obscene.

(f) this is not a trial of any offences under ss. 22 or 422 which read as follows:

22(1) Where a person counsels or procures another person to be a party to an offence and that other person is afterwards a party to that offence, the person who counselled or procured is a party to that offence, notwithstanding that the offence was committed in a way different from that which was counselled or procured.

(2) Every one who counsels or procures another person to be a party to an offence is a party to every offence that the other commits in consequence of the counselling or procuring that the person who counselled or procured knew or ought to have known was likely to be committed in consequence of the counselling or procuring.

. . . . .

422. Except where otherwise expressly provided by law, the following provisions apply in respect of persons who counsel, procure or incite other persons to commit offences, namely,

(a) every one who counsels, procures or incites another person to commit an indictable offence is, if the offence is not committed, guilty of an indictable offence and is liable to the same punishment to which a person who attempts to commit that offence is liable; and

(b) every one who counsels, procures or incites another person to commit an offence punishable on summary conviction is, if the offence is not committed, guilty of an offence punishable on summary conviction.

Having stated what it is not, it is important to restate the core question to be decided in this trial: Is ex. 1, the whole of the December, 1977—January, 1978, issue of "The Body Politic" either indecent, immoral or scurrilous within the meaning of s. 164 of the *Code,* which reads as follows:

> 164. Every one commits an offence who makes use of the mails for the purpose of transmitting or delivering anything that is obscene, indecent, immoral or scurrilous, but this section does not apply to a person who makes use of the mails for the purpose of transmitting or delivering anything mentioned in subsection 162(4).

Although in presenting its case the Crown concentrated almost exclusively on the article "Men Loving Boys Loving Men" and specifically on certain specific passages in that article, I am satisfied that since the charge relates to the whole of ex. 1, I must consider the whole issue and not just part of it. I have, therefore, read the entire issue. It contains general news of and comment on activities in the "gay" community and it states its theme to be, "at least in part, a review of 1977" (ex. 1 p. 2, col. 1). To this end, in addition to what appear to be regular features of other issues, none of which were before me, it contains what the editorial page describes as "three articles which we think serve especially well to focus some of the year's major themes" (ex. 1, p. 2, col. 1). One article deals with events in Dade County, Florida; one with "gay-produced community television programs"; and one is "the third in a series of articles on youth and sexuality by Gerald Hannon . . . 'Men Loving Boys Loving Men' has been a troublesome item for us, as we note in its introduction. Read with care" (ex. 1, p. 2, col. 1). This latter article is further described in the table of contents on p. 3 of ex. 1 as follows: "Three men who love boys talk about their lives. And in the process, destroy some of the myths about pedophilia that have been used against the whole gay community. As the Save Our Children people push the 'molestation tactic', this sane, provocative article makes for must reading."

I am satisfied (although this is far from determinative of the legal issue) that judging from ex. 1, "The Body Politic" is a serious journal of news and opinion, apparently directed to those who are members of and/or wish to read about and consider the views, opinions and problems of the so-called "gay" community. The issue in question, ex. 1, contains articles, drawings and photographs featuring events affecting and of apparent interest to that community. By no means are all of these depictive or descriptive of sexual activities, although some are. A review of the book "The Joy of Gay Sex" (ex. 1, p. 19) reproduces a photograph showing two partly clothed men in a sort of embrace and clearly showing the penis of one of them; it also reproduces a drawing depicting two men in what appears to be an act of anal intercourse. Also reviewed on the same page is "The

Biography of Alice B. Toklas" and a book of letters from Gertrude Stein and Alice B. Toklas, which is accompanied by a photograph of author Samuel Steward, a dog and Alice B. Toklas (I hasten to say there is no sexual content to this photograph).

In the course of reading ex. 1, one also finds reviews of films, T.V. shows, theatre, art and music which have or may have aspects of interest to homosexuals. One finds general advertisements of restaurants, bookstores, travel agencies and specialized advertisements specifically directed to homosexual tastes. Among the latter is one for a charitable foundation bearing an income tax registration number. One finds a number of the aged Anglo Saxon four-letter words. The language used is in many instances quite crude. Crudity is not necessarily indecent, immoral or scurrilous, though it may be any or all of these.

In short, in ex. 1, one finds what can be found in many magazines and novels and books dealing with sex and sexual problems (many with varying degrees of explicitness) on sale in most book stores and magazine and newspaper stands in any large Canadian city and certainly in Toronto. There is no evidence before me that ex. 1 can be so obtained, and in any event the charge here deals only with its transmission through the mails, not with its general availability.

The specific article "Men Loving Boys Loving Men" discusses pedophilia and pedophilic acts and persons; it is not written in a prurient style nor does it have the typical hallmarks of hard-core pornography—it is not lascivious, sexually stimulating nor titillating. It does not use gross explicit language calculated to cause sexual arousal or stimulation. It forcefully argues in favour of a particular attitude of non-condemnation of pedophiles. The article was, as appears from the preface on p. 29 (reproduced later in these reasons), deliberately published and circulated following a specific and considered decision of the "Collective", and was "the latest in a series on youth and sexuality" by the same author—the others of the series were not put before me.

From the evidence adduced, I make certain findings of fact:

1. In the context of this trial, as a scientific term, "pedophile" means a homosexual male who can only obtain full sexual satisfaction by means of sexual relations with pubertal or in rare instances pre-pubertal boys. However, some pedophiles do not "act out", *i.e.,* do not permit themselves to obtain this satisfaction. But the author of "Men Loving Boys Loving Men" does not use pedophile in this sense exclusively—in my opinion, he uses it ambiguously—his pedophiles are sometimes lovers of both boys and men, even though all homosexuals are not of this unusual "heterosexual" nature. Pedophile in the usual every day sense means simply a lover (not necessarily sexual) of young people.

2. One's sexual behaviour and orientation is not acquired from what one reads or sees.

3. Homosexuality and pedophilia are not contagious and one's sexual behaviour is determined by one's genetic endowment and environment, or as put by the witness Dr. Sommers, "by nature and nurture", these being the same factors that determine one's non-sexual behaviour.

4. Pedophilic acts are illegal and in many cases may involve a variety of what is commonly known as "child abuse"—thus several offences under the *Criminal Code* may be involved in a pedophilic sexual act: gross indecency and buggery are but two; others could be assault, indecent assault, assault causing bodily harm, to name but a few.

It will be convenient at this point to set forth in full the preface to the article:

1977 has been the Year of the Children.

The year of the children Anita Bryant wanted to "save," of the children lesbian mothers lost. The year of the one child who died in a body-rub parlour on Yonge Street.

We have been sensitized.

There is some irony in this. In the lives of most gay people, children are conspicuous only by their absence. But they are not unimportant to us. We have begun to realize, for one thing, that many gay men and lesbians are parents themselves. Their battles for custody of their children have given them new visibility.

These custody cases, though, are only one part of a much broader assault. Dark warning is being given: children are to be the last frontier of heterosexist bias. Hints have been dropped that our right to be free from discrimination—when and if that right is recognized—just might not include the freedom to be a teacher, a counsellor or a child-care worker. We have been told that our magazines can't fall before their eyes and that our television programs, if they are shown at all, can't be aired until they have gone to bed. Regardless of the nature of our real everyday contacts—or lack of them—with children, all of us have been branded as every child's potential "molester."

Which brings us to the article below, "Men Loving Boys Loving Men," the latest in a series on youth sexuality by Gerald Hannon.

The people you will meet in it are "child molesters," "chicken hawks," "dirty-old-men." They are these things just as all of us are "pansies," "lezzies" and "queers." The names are only the most visible part of an elaborate and vicious mythology. (In Toronto this summer we found that the myth includes us all as "child-killers," too.) We know how much these myths and these words have to do with our real lives.

We know about some of them, that is.

The real lives of men who love boys and boys who love men are mysterious even for most other gay people. We are not immune from the general paranoia about children and sexuality, and many of us are willing to accept *that* part of the straight world's homosexual mythology even when we know the rest of it for the lie that it is.

A small part of the reality is presented below.

"Men Loving Boys Loving Men" is not printed here without awareness of the potential consequences. The decision to run the article was not taken lightly nor without debate within the Collective. We have had it on hand, type-set and laid out, for nearly six months, but we have hesitated, sensitive to the feeling that "the climate was not right" after the anti-gay media barrage which followed Emanuel Jaques' death in August.

We know now that the "climate" will never be "right." The Jaques trial is yet to come, and when that is over there will undoubtedly be something else we could point to if we wanted an excuse to move with the tide. The tide must be resisted, the discussion must be opened up.

We know that people who are more concerned with "respectability" than with rights will groan at our "irresponsibility" are likely to react as though they had just found a delectably rotten plum in a Christmas cake from a bakery they've never much liked. The issue might well be splashed sensationally across the tabloids (especially on days when there isn't much real news), lines may be quoted out of context and juicy bits read over the air to satisfy prurient interest. Columnists like the Toronto Sun's Claire Hoy will be delirious. We know about these things because they have happened to us—to all of us—before.

We also know this because we are aware of how desperate the enemies of gay liberation are. They are willing to hurl the bodies and minds of the very children they are trying to "save" into the fray.

The Body Politic, for instance, recently received a curious series of telephone calls. The voice at the other end of the line was that of a young boy, perhaps nine or ten years old. He asked on one occasion to speak to the author of this article (who, as we noted, has written on youth sexuality before), asked where he might buy TBP, asked finally where he could go to have sex. At least once the prompting voice of an adult male was audible in the background. The sound of a tape recorder was not, but could be assumed: it is illegal even to advise people under the age of 18 (and gay people under 21) to have sex.

We can only speculate about the character of someone who would rather manipulate a child into an act of fraud than have him know anything real about the lives of men who love men and women who love women. But the characters of three people whom this man with the tape recorder must fear so much, three "child molesters," three men who love boys, are here to be examined.

We leave it to you.

The Collective

The article itself is too long to reproduce in full, but enough must be quoted to show its flavour, content, style and thesis; *i.e.,* to reveal its true quality: . . .

The article by the accused Hannon begins:

There's a painting in the foyer of my YMCA. It's a dedication portrait, the kind you still expect to see in banks over an "Our Founder" plaque, except that banks have pretty much surrendered to the famed fabric school of interior design. Not so trendy, the YMCA. The ones I know still rely heavily on dark wood veneer and respectable oil paintings like this one of C. J. Atkinson, "Leader in Boys' work." Or so the dedication reads. It continues: ". . . here he realized a dream of his young manhood in the building of a community in which boys learned to do by doing."

He worked with boys, did Mr. Atkinson. He cared about them, worried about their welfare, worried more about the ones society didn't seem to have much of a place for, and finally arranged for the construction of this building, a sanctuary—at least until recently—for boys, for young men, "a dream of his young manhood."

I think I know something about C. J. Atkinson. I think he was a pedophile.

I don't know for sure, of course. If I did—if anyone else had—there wouldn't be an oil painting of the man gracing the foyer of a building belonging to the Young Men Christian's Association.

But I *do* know what he did. I know, at least, why he was celebrated. He loved boys. He had dreams for them. He made them his life's work. If you are what you do, C. J. Atkinson, benefactor and 'leader in boys' work,' was very much a pedophile.

It's not a good word. The Greek origin, "lover of boys," is nice enough, but it's a clinician's word; it's like homosexual, only worse. "People use it as a label for a disease" says Simon, one of the men we shall meet in this article, one of the men who says "I'm gay, but I like to be called boy-lover. I like the word 'boy.' It's strange . . . whenever I even see the word boy . . .".

We'll meet Simon and others like him because what they *do* is important. Like C. J. Atkinson, if they are remembered at all, they will be remembered for what they do. Not for what they *are*, not because they are 'nice people'. Niceness is not enough. No, Simon and Barry and Peter and thousands of others like them will earn the esteem of their community for the work they do with boys; they will earn the affection of their associates and friends because they have lived honest and loving lives, have formed meaningful and responsible relationships.

If they don't get caught.

What *do* they do, then? What is it like—a loving, sexual relationship between a man and a boy? If you read the papers, this is one picture: a psychopath draws a circle of hapless boys to him and after months of wild, degrading sex he murders them—the Houston story. Another: a pathetic man incapable of forming meaningful relationships with adults finally turns to children for his social/sexual outlet—basically harmless, but pathetic and obviously in need of help. Another: a group of well-placed and usually wealthy citizens make clandestine use of a well-organized "boy bordello," one that recruits runaways and waifs and makes big money by selling their sexual favours to the well-to-do.

Those things happen. But they happen less often than wife beatings, or the battering of babies. Psychiatrists see far, far fewer young people from man/boy relationships than they see boys and girls unable to cope with the strains of their happy homes.

The media equates boy-love and child molestation. And they use that equation as a weapon against all gay people. Children are molested when they are physically or psychologically coerced into a sexual act, and that sort of thing is almost exclusively a heterosexual preoccupation. "Homosexual offenders against children almost never used force, but . . . heterosexual offenders against children often did,"—the admirably clear and succinct conclusion of one American study. The same study noted, "Abuse is the major killer of children under two, and (intentional) neglect occurs ten times as often as abuse." And Barbara Chisholm, project director of the Canadian Council on Children and Youth, has said that as many as fifty per cent of girls now in training school may have been subjected to initial rape by their own fathers.

Boy-love is not child molestation. Boy-love is C. J. Atkinson. Boy-love is Simon.

There follows identification of Simon as a 33-year-old primary school teacher, social service agency worker, and Big Brother. He found "sexual, loving relationships with boys in each of [the four schools in which he has taught] and in each of the service organizations of which he is a member, including Big Brothers." Simon describes his relationship with his pupil David, a 12-year-old, who writes poetry to him. Their mutual caresses are described in explicit detail, and although they are not specifically sexual, they are arousing for the participants. Simon says David and he "satisfy each other. He satisfies my needs, not my desires". The relationship is apparently more based on affection than on sex—but David fellated Simon and Simon kissed David on the lips (which David apparently did not like). Simon considers that his affairs with boys are a sort of wholesome sex education for them; Simon only goes to bed with boys for whom he has affection—he is not promiscuous nor does he seek boy prostitutes. The last two paragraphs of Simon's conversation with the author should be quoted:

> I can have as much fun with a kid running around in a field as I did when I was 15 or 16. We go camping, we go downtown, we go to the Arcade, to movies, for rides on our bikes, we buy records and come home and listen, we bowl, we watch TV, we fuck. Actually, I've only really bum-fucked two kids. One of them asked me to, and the other indicated that he wanted it. They didn't like it all that much, but it seemed an experiment that they wanted to try.

> "A lot of my relationships with boys have not been all that *sexually* satisfying to me. Especially with the pre-pubertal kids—there's never been anything really sexual. Mostly just affection, care. Anyway, I don't find pre-pubertal kids all that exciting—it's a physical pleasure of the hugging, cuddling kind. And it's an emotional pleasure too, I never felt any guilt about the fact that these were kids—I worried about being caught, that's all. And I've never wanted to be different than I am. I'm content. I just want to liberate my kids a little bit and help them find their own sexual direction. Help them realize their sexuality is nothing to be ashamed of.

The author considers Simon a "romantic".

His next subject is Peter, who he sees as "cool", rich, 48. Says Peter:

> With boys you have to impress them at first, you have to call attention to yourself. I do it with a big car, or a deep tan, or an ability. I used to be quite

skilled at diving and I would have all eyes on me all summer. It's not the only way, of course. I've picked up boys in theatres. You sit down beside them and start making comments about the movie and then you might say "here's a quarter"—now it would have to be a dollar—"why don't you get us both a coke." Then there's a long, long period of courtship, talking, driving around town, having a hamburger. And it might never happen. There were lots of boys that I would have loved to make advances to and never did. Or it might take several months. Relationships that were building in the summer would mature in the depths of winter in a car parked in a secluded spot in the snow.

Peter's relationships last, and he describes continuance of sexual relations with Buddy up to and including Buddy's heterosexual wedding night, and thereafter. Peter's favourites are disadvantaged boys, at least one of whom he encouraged to and through university and who is now a professor. Their sexual relationship started when the now professor was 12. Peter prefers masturbatory activity but fellation is occasional and intercourse less frequent. Peter once had a *fellatio* relationship with a seven-year-old boy who "loved sucking". Peter also has adult male sexual partners, including casual pick-ups.

Don met Peter when Peter was 19 and Don 11. Don was seduced by Peter and they have remained friends and sexual partners ever since, though Don is heterosexual, now 40, married and with a 19-year-old son. Don says:

"If it hadn't been for Peter, I wouldn't be at all surprised if I'd grown up to be an Anita Bryant supporter. But I just don't have any of those crazy ideas about homosexuals waiting in dark alleys with candy to tempt some kid into the dark so he can fuck him. I know what happens. You know, I think it could have been good if the same thing happened to my son . . . I think it might bring us closer together."

He can't take the final step though.

"No, I don't think I'd want my son to be gay. But I can't defend that. I guess it must be things in my upbringing . . . but if he came to me and said he was, and was sure of it—yes, I'd accept him."

The author then writes of a camp-out with Barry—or rather of his being, so to speak, odd-man out while Barry and Billy (age 12—Barry's age is not given) play and sleep together. The author's conclusion to the article is as follows:

So, I had trekked off to the country and found—a relationship. Seen what I'd been hearing about from Simon and Peter, seen two people drawing delight from each other's company, seen two criminals at work. Let's not forget that.

Let's not forget that C. J. Atkinson and associates are criminals—the way we were before 1969, the way we still are if we try anything other than the things you can do with one (and only one) other individual over 21 and very much in private.

Anita Bryant won't let us—or anyone else—forget it.

"Save Our Children, Inc." is the name of the game, although the organizers seem to be cynically aware of just what that means: "The molestation was the thing that particularly got the headlines. We now know how effectively it can be used," said Robert Brake, one of the top officials of that organization. Who *wouldn't* want to save our children, after all, save them from things like the Houston mass murder horrors, save them from being pawed by nasty old men. That's what molestation means to most people, it's what the media encourages them to believe, it's a belief "Save Our Children" does nothing to discourage.

They've added a refinement. Recruitment. Because homosexuals can't reproduce, they must recruit.

Anita should know. Because recruitment is what she is all about.

She wants our children. And, yes, they're *our* children too.

She's going to get some of them, and some of those are going to grow up gay, and some are going to grow up straight. If they're gay, they'll grow up miserable, hating themselves, their desires and their community; becoming mean, or robot-like, or blustering hypocrites because that's what happens to love that's taught to hate itself. And if they grow up straight, they'll grow up proud to be American, secretly proud to be white, a majority that's "quiet" because its soul is empty, in marriages that last and last because nothing is quite so binding as mutual distaste and suspicion.

Anita's recruits. They've been with us for a long time. They tried to save our children from witches, and turned the middle ages into a charnel house of burning and innocent flesh. They tried to save our children from Jews, and almost succeeded through twelve years of methodical and monstrous savagery. They tried to save our children from communists, and sat with Senator McCarthy in judgement upon heroic lives trying to salvage some dignity, some integrity from that degrading exercise. Now they want to save our children from homosexuals. They want to save our children from us.

Yes, we have *our* recruits, though they are not, as Bryant would have us believe, legions of hapless children diverted from the straight and narrow by the corrosive touch of some predatory homosexual.

Don is one of our recruits. He's *not* gay, but "when I'm with straight people and they say something derogatory or stupid about gays I always try to turn it around, make them see they're stupid. I can't go as far as I'd like sometimes . . . I'd be suspect myself and that would be hard to take. But I try."

Simon's students are recruits. If they grow up gay, they grow up remembering a loved role model, they grow up knowing sexual acts are not disgusting, they grow up with the possibility of coming out long before the early-to-mid twenties, that age when so many of us finally caved in, or came out.

If they grow up straight, they may not, like Don, do their best to defend gay people in the small ways he's chosen, but somewhere in the back of all that domestic bliss they fall heir to, they are going to know the Anita Bryants of this world are out-and-out fruitcakes. And maybe, just maybe, if they're presented someday with a ballot which asks them to say a simple yes or no to civil rights for homosexuals, and they're alone in a polling booth and no one can see what they mark, then, maybe, they'll remember what happened to them 20 years ago and vote the way they remember.

I have seen a photograph of Anita and family praying together before they go to bed—in pyjamas yet. Besides marvelling that anyone would consciously do anything quite so kitsch, I feel a real sense of sadness for those kids, down on their knees and huddled between momma and poppa Bryant. One or more of them could very easily be gay. And he or she would be the truly molested child.

Every homosexual has suffered that molestation. Every homosexual's sexuality has been interfered with—impeded, strangled, diverted, denounced, 'cured,' pitied, punished. That is molestation. And it has nothing to do with what Simon, Barry and Peter are doing.

They are the heirs of Mr. Atkinson, "Leader in Boys' Work," community workers who deserve our praise, our admiration and our support. □

During the trial the issue was to some extent clouded by the Crown's emphasis on an allegation that the article approved, counselled and encouraged the commission of pedophilic sexual acts which would be offences under the *Criminal Code* (such as gross indecency, buggery, assault, indecent assault or assault causing bodily harm) and that *by reason thereof* the article and ex. 1 were indecent, immoral or scurrilous. That is to say, according to this one of the Crown's theses, it would be indecent, immoral or scurrilous to counsel the commission of offences under the *Criminal Code.* If there was counselling, that in itself would be an offence under ss. 22 or 422. But that is not what is charged here. If the Crown relied on s. 22 or on s. 422 then it should have charged the accused under the appropriate section. It did not do so. I express no opinion on the merits of such a charge.

The following questions in my opinion require to be considered:

A. Is s. 164 aimed at acts such as those of the accused in using the mails?

B. Is ex. 1 beyond the community standard of permissibility by reason of either its indecency, its immorality or its scurrility?

C. Is ex. 1 indecent, immoral or scurrilous, in the ordinary sense of those words? . . .

B. THE COMMUNITY STANDARD APPROACH

In my opinion, this approach as a test for determining indecency, immorality or scurrility should be applied in the same manner as would be the case if obscenity was being tested: see *R. v. Brodie* (1962), 132 C.C.C. 161, 32 D.L.R. (2d) 507, [1962] S.C.R. 681; and *Dominion News & Gifts (1962) Ltd. v. The Queen,* [1963] 2 C.C.C. 103, 40 C.R. 109, 42 W.W.R. 65 [reversed [1964] 3 C.C.C. 1, [1964] S.C.R. 251, 42 C.R. 209]. It is true that in those cases the "undue exploitation" of sex aspect was being considered —but as Ritchie, J., said in *Brodie* (at p. 185 C.C.C., p. 708 S.C.R.) the undueness is " 'undue having regard to the existing standards of *decency* in the community' " [emphasis added]. Short of being required to apply a purely subjective test—*i.e.,* what is indecent, immoral or scurrilous *to me*—I cannot imagine a fairer or most just way to determine decency, morality or scurrility than the objective test of the community standard; that is to say, the fact-finding tribunal—in this case the trial Judge must determine *on the evidence* what is the community standard of acceptance of material that is or may be indecent, immoral or scurrilous. This is a criminal case—the onus of proof is on the Crown, and the Crown would have to satisfy me by evidence beyond a reasonable doubt, that on the community standard test ex. 1, as a whole, is either indecent or immoral or scurrilous. It is not sufficient, and would be improper, to leave it to me to say "I know what I like—or do not like" and let that be the test.

The Crown did not lead any evidence of consequence regarding the whole of ex. 1 but it did lead much evidence as to the article. One witness, John Houston, Detective Sergeant, O.P.P., in charge of project P, involving the supply, distribution and availability of obscene or pornographic material in Ontario, and qualified as an expert in criminology and probably on obscenity and pornography, read and examined the article in question—*i.e.,* "Men Loving Boys Loving Men"—and his testimony about it may be summed up by his word "distasteful". Matters of taste are not legislated against in s. 164—and I may say that I cannot conceive of taste as being a matter for the criminal law in any event.

Another Crown witness was the Reverend Kenneth Campbell, an evangelical Baptist minister who is concerned with obscenity and pornography and is active in a movement known as Renaissance which was involved in school board banishments of several well-known books—including "Catcher in the Rye" and "The Diviners". He had a visceral, negative reaction to the article—not the whole of ex. 1 to which his attention had not been directed—and was sickened by it. His personal opinion was that the article is "offensive" to the general public. In his view homosexuality frustrated divine intent and homosexuals should not be allowed even to talk in the schools. Although he had not read "The Diviners", a novel—he does not read novels—he considered it to be immoral. He has "perused" "Catcher in the Rye" and considers it to be second rate. He approved of the removal of these books from schools. Shakespeare (in his opinion) should be edited before being used as a school text. In view of his attitudes regarding Shakespeare and the two books I have mentioned, I was not impressed by his evidence, and in any event, he did not deal with the alleged immorality, indecency or scurrility of the article.

Doctor Jerry Cooper, a well-recognized psychiatric authority read the article—not the whole of ex. 1—and all he found in it were rationalizations. To *him* these were immoral. He was no help on the matter of the indecency, immorality or scurrility on a community standard basis.

Mr. Claire Hoy, a newspaper columnist employed by the Toronto Sun read the article, having received ex. 1 through the mail (when and from whom the evidence did not disclose). He considers the preface to the article to be immoral, assuming as well that there would not be a high degree of public acceptance thereof. He found the article outrageous and advocative of pedophilia and he personally holds and strongly expressed his antihomosexual views. He describes homosexuals as "creatures" and has a low opinion of them which he believes is shared by many of the public. He finds them to be disgusting people and he is not objective—indeed he says he cannot be objective. He wanted this charge laid. He believes homosexuals want to get into the schools to proseletize. By and large those of his readers who respond to him substantially agree with him—but about homosexuals and pedophiles, not about the article or ex. 1.

Father Raymond Cousineau, a Redemptorist priest and teacher of Christian ethics at the Toronto School of Theology says that in his opinion the article presents the pedophilic acts which it describes as good, moral, beautiful and human things to do; therefore, he concludes, the article is immoral in that it presents the homosexual genital sexual relationship in a light which is not sufficiently negative to accord with Christian morality and with his opinion as to society's view. He agrees that others may draw different inferences as to whether or not the article really is advocating something immoral.

The witnesses called for the accused all had read the article and a number of them had read ex. 1 as a whole. June Callwood, a journalist, writer, and active in movements concerned with social problems of children, battered children and wives, found sexual interference with children appalling and was glad to see it examined in this article. In her opinion, the article would not offend the average Canadian, but would cause some uneasiness because, in her opinion, the pedophiles were presented as being so "human". The article is unsettling to her but not revolting, nor does she find it prurient or obscene; in her opinion, it does not advocate, encourage, suggest or proseletyze. She says that the act of any adult seducing a child is appalling, unethical and immoral—but the article attempts to discuss that side of adult-child relationships and it is good to have that kind of discussion begin. Endorsing or promoting such acts would, to her, be immoral.

Reverend Eilert Frerichs, a United Church minister and family and sex counsellor, read the article and found it to be the beginning of an important public debate on an issue not heretofore widely discussed even among homosexuals. The language used, though vulgar, is, in his view, that commonly used by "gays" and is not inappropriate in the context. He did not find the article to be prurient, lustful, or erotic, nor exploitative of sexuality. He finds the acts written about to be immoral, even as atom bombs and killing are immoral, but feels that it is not immoral to write about these immoralities.

For Reverend Clifford Elliott, a United Church minister, the article provided a real understanding of the problem because it dealt with actual occurrences and was not an abstract discussion. He did not feel that it advocated, encouraged or proseletyzed for pedophilia, and found it neither prurient, lustful, erotic, immoral nor indecent. He found it offensive to the standards of the ordinary Canadian and felt the article endorsed the activities of Simon, Peter, *et al.*

Thelma McCormick, a professor of sociology at York University, felt the article corrected the stereotype that all homosexuals are child molesters and that all child molesters are monsters. She found it gave her as a parent an insight into what children might encounter and thus she could prepare them all the better to counter such moves. To her, it was "oral history", not erotic, and she found no lascivious lingering over details. In her view, bearing in mind the lyrics of current popular rock music heard on radio, television and on records for home consumption, and stories in the daily press and on current events, this article should not be unacceptable to the average Canadian.

Doctor Leonard Goldsmith, a neuropsychologist and professor of psychiatry at University of Toronto and psychology at York, found the article balanced, reasonable, ethical, not inflammatory, not salacious, not prurient and felt that to equate a description of pedophilic acts with the acts themselves was not intelligent. He felt the preface to be crucial and found social benefit in the demythification and demystification of adult-child sexual activities. In some cases he found the article to be satirical, as in its reference to the need to recruit because homosexuals do not engage in sex for reproductive purposes.

There were a number of other witnesses for both the Crown and the accused whose evidence bears comment at this point. I refer especially, though not exclusively, to Dr. Peter Rowsell, Professor Leslie Dewart and Dr. John Money. They and other witnesses were helpful primarily in the general education of the Court about homosexuality, pedophilia, theology, the craft of journalistic writing and to some extent the nature of literary criticism and the method of extracting an author's hidden—*i.e.,* implicit—meaning and intent from his explicit statements. But they were not helpful on the issue of the community standard.

I am of the opinion that all in all the evidence adduced from the majority of both Crown and Defence witnesses establishes nothing which really assists the Court in ascertaining the limits of community tolerance, that is, the community standard, in this area. It would have been more helpful to have had evidence of competently conducted public opinion surveys of community opinion. Such was not proferred, nor was even the evidence of what might have purported to be several or many persons making up a representative sample of the Canadian community demographically speaking.

Professors, journalists, a police officer, psychiatrists, psychologists and ministers of some religions are not representative of the community as a whole, and even so, they all differed in varying degrees and ways. Despite the most profound and impressive qualifications and experience of those who had counselled homosexuals and pedophiles, there was no general agreement as to the morality or the immorality, the decency or the indecency, the scurrility or otherwise of the article as a whole, including its preface, nor of ex. 1 as a whole.

A useful epitome of the nature of admissible public opinion surveys, and the requirements essential thereto, is to be found in the judgment of Dickson, J., in *R. v. Prairie Schooner News Ltd. and Powers* (1970), 1 C.C.C. (2d) at 251 at pp. 265-6, 75 W.W.R. 585, 12 Crim. L.Q. 462:

> Basic to the admissibility of such surveys has been the acceptance of the public opinion polling as a *science* when approved statistical methods, social research techniques, and interview procedures are employed.
>
> Essential to admissibility is the requirement that the witness testifying be possessed of expert knowledge. Essential also is selection of the proper "universe", *i.e.,* that segment of the population whose characteristics are relevant to the question being studied. In the case at bar, the "community" whose standards are being considered is all of Canada. The universe from which the "sample", *i.e.,* the individuals to be polled, is to be selected must be representative of Canada and not be drawn from a single city. If, and only if, the sample is correctly selected can it be said that the opinions found to exist in the sample are representative of the entire universe.
>
> Although it has been held on high authority—*Transport Publishing Co. Pty. Ltd. v. Literature Board of Review* (1956), 99 C.L.R. 111 at p. 119, a decision of the High Court of Australia that " . . . ordinary human nature, that of people at large, is not a subject of proof by evidence, whether supposedly expert or not", it would seem to me that when it becomes necessary to determine the true nature of community opinion and to find a single normative standard, the Court should not be denied the benefit of evidence, scientifically obtained in accordance with accepted sampling procedure, by those who are expert in the field of opinion research. Such evidence can properly be accorded the status of expert testimony. The state of mind or attitude of a community is as much a fact as the state of one's health; it would seem therefore as proper to admit the opinion of experts on the one subject as on the other. A word of warning. The findings of a poll can be deceptively simple and frequently misleading. This is repeatedly emphasized in the writings on this subject. Such evidence must, therefore, if it is to be admitted, be received with caution and carefully evaluated before weight is given to it.

Absent such evidence, and absent any suitable alternative I was left with no real assistance on this branch of the case. On the community standard test, then, the Crown has failed to satisfy me beyond a reasonable doubt that ex. 1 taken as a whole is indecent immoral or scurrilous.

May I add that it is clear that the article in ex. 1 is apparently the third of a series by the same author on child sexuality—see the preface quoted above and the editorial comments also quoted above. To choose one of a series, without considering the context of the others—and no evidence was provided as to the others of the series—makes it difficult to reach an informed decision on the nature of the one. Surely, it must be considered as part of the total picture, rather than in isolation.

All of this is rather esoteric from the layman's point of view—and although it may be unusual, I think this judgment on this point should be put into more everyday language. In my opinion, there is little doubt today that on a community standard test the actual acts which occurred during the Holocaust—the destruction by the Nazis of over 6,000,000 human beings—would be deemed indecent and immoral. The details of this dastardly event are almost beyond human comprehension and yet a number of authors have written about and analyzed them and described the techniques and methods used in great detail—that the events they describe were indecent and immoral is one thing; are the descriptions thereof themselves indecent and immoral by reason of their subject-matter? I cannot imagine that they are or could be so found by any juridical test.

Another example of indecent or immoral subject-matter is that of crime reporting both current and retrospective. Almost daily one can read the most detailed descriptions of criminal acts of rape, child abuse, murder and the like. The painstaking criminal can find how-to-do-it articles in almost every newspaper and magazine. Are these journals indecent or immoral because they write in explicit detail about indecent or immoral acts? I think not.

Of particular relevance to the present case is the nature of the media's coverage of the trial of those accused of the slaying of Emanuel Jaques. This tragic matter was disclosed in full detail, including specific descriptions of anal intercourse and sadistic sexual and other acts, which were not motivated by affection or love, but by brutal lustful passion, and which led to the deliberately-caused death of the boy concerned. *There* was a how-to-do-it manual spread for all to read; *there* was a writing which the Crown here would argue should be found to be indecent and immoral, even as the Crown contends are the descriptions of the acts, be they actual or fictional, presented by the accused Hannon in the specific article which forms a major issue herein.

I realize the Crown's position before me is that the article in ex. 1 at least implicitly expresses approval and endorsation of the acts detailed. I cannot find that the *policy* of the article determines its *quality* of lawfulness or unlawfulness. Intention does not determine decency: see *R. v. St. Claire* (1913), 21 C.C.C. 350, 12 D.L.R. 710, 28 O.L.R. 271, which held that the author's motive was irrelevant, since although addressed to clergymen to persuade them by detailed description that a certain performance was indecent, the writing might fall into the hands of more susceptible persons. I do not think that the same conclusion would be reached today, but the ruling as to motive is still valid, in my view.

In my respectful opinion, I am entitled to take judicial notice, as I have done, of the media's coverage of the Jaques' case, as being a fact notorious in the community and part of the common experience of people in this community. In my respectful opinion, further, such coverage helps the community to understand—not to condone or approve or endorse—but to understand, to realize, what some people can do in the throes of sexual maladjustment. The Jaques killers were not men such as the Simon, Peter or Don of the Hannon article, selfish and self-seeking as those characters in that article about pedophiles may be. But the Hannon article helps us to understand—not to condone or approve or endorse—but to understand Simon, Peter and Don, and their sexual problems and acts. The Hannon article is as much reportage as was the coverage of the Jacques trial—albeit Hannon may be writing history in the fictional form—as was Capote in "In Cold Blood" for example—a well-known and popular writing device.

If the Hannon article, or ex. 1 is indecent and immoral, what of the newspapers that published the accounts of the Jaques case? What of s. 162(1)(a) in regard to them? It is my opinion that the right of the public to be informed—that right which is the cornerstone of freedom of the press—includes the right to know about this type of behaviour, the better to understand it, the better to deal with it, the better to keep men like Simon, Peter and Don from becoming so repressed and suppressed and confined to the closet that their untreated sexual problems may lead to more Jaques cases. At least, after reading "Men Loving Boys Loving Men" we know what they are, and what they are not, we know that not all homosexuals are pedophiles, we know something of how pedophiles feel, think and act, we can learn how to protect our children, and how to deal with pedophiles in ways that will lessen the likelihood of their criminal behaviour, so that they may lead their sexual lives in accordance with what the law allows. Sexual assaults on children are as criminal when committed by heterosexual pedophiles as by homosexual pedophiles—and even by heterosexual and homosexual pedophobes. It is the offence that is heinous, not the offender. If we condemn ex. 1 we are in effect condemning the messenger who brings the bad news.

If the books and articles to which I have referred—the histories, the crime reports, the press coverage of sex offences—were written as spurs to imitative action, if their intent was truly that of a how-to-do-it manual, then they—and "Men Loving Boys Loving Men"—might well be caught by ss. 22 or 422. But if, as certainly is the fact in regard to the books about the Nazi atrocities, and the coverage of the Jaques case, they are written as honest reporting, or as commentary on the recent past, or as guides for thoughtful discussion of evil doings, how can they be criminal? How can they, the comments and the factual records, take on the character of the acts upon which they comment and deeds which they chronicle?

They cannot, no more than can ex. 1 in this trial. And even if ex. 1 *might* do so, that possibility invokes the wise counsel of Freedman, J., in *Dominion News* to which I refer a little later in this judgment, dealing with the impropriety of the suppression of the not so bad, or of the possibly good.

C. THE ORDINARY MEANING OF THE WORDS

Since I am satisfied that the law requires me, in the light of the wording of the information, to consider the whole of ex. 1, I must on this branch of the case determine in law the meaning of the words "indecent", "immoral" or "scurrilous" as applied to the whole of ex. 1.

1. IMMORAL

Since in matters of morality, different times bring different limits of tolerance, I find it impossible to determine as a matter of law what is moral or immoral—and I think that any attempted proscription based on immorality calls into play factors that cannot be determined with legal precision in the absence of a legislated definition of what Parliament intended. There is no definition or interpretation of the word "immoral" in the statute. I find the term so ambiguous and indefinite that were "immorality" the only offence alleged here I would dismiss the charge without hesitation, for no one can be expected to govern his conduct (particularly if the result may be criminal charges), according to such an imprecise standard: see *per* Freedman, J., quoted in *R. v. Brodie* (1962), 132 C.C.C. 161, 32 D.L.R. (2d) 507, [1962] S.C.R. 681 (the Lady Chatterley case)). Morality normally is not the subject-matter of legislation—it is the stuff of ethics, religion and philosophy; it could be legislated—but it has not been here.

Much of what is immoral is not criminal: failure to honour one's parents is immoral—it is not a crime (although failure to financially support one's parents may well be); abortion may be and is considered by many to be immoral under any circumstances—in the proper situation it is not a crime; failure to love one's neighbour is immoral—it is not a crime; failure to pay one's debts is immoral—it is not a crime; taking life (be it human or animal) is immoral in many circumstances—it is a crime in only a few.

On the other hand moral acts may well be crimes: many persons would consider euthanasia under certain circumstances to be a moral act—it would still be a crime; assassinations for political purposes are often considered moral acts—they would nevertheless most likely be crimes; Robin Hood's immortality is based on the morality of taking from the rich and giving to the poor—his acts were crimes none the less.

I conclude therefore that in so far as the contention that ex. 1 is immoral is concerned, Parliament has failed to provide the Court with a sufficiently precise guideline to enable the Court to come to any conclusion as to what would be guilty conduct. The immoralities of yesterday so frequently become the nobilities of conduct today that failing statutory definition this Court can find no legally enforceable meaning in the term immoral. Whatever else it may be, ex. 1 cannot be legally immoral.

2. INDECENT

As for indecency, I adopt with enthusiasm the words of Fullagar, J., in *R. v. Close,* [1948] V.L.R. 445 (Aust). as approved by Judson, J., in *R. v. Brodie, supra,* at p. 182 C.C.C., p. 705 S.C.R., while *Brodie* and *Close* were obscenity cases, these *obiter* comments are important as giving guidance as to the proper approach to cases involving proscribed communication.

Fullagar, J., said:

> . . . in considering whether any given matter is indecent or offensive or disgusting it must often be of vital importance to consider the character of the artistic or literary and scientific context in which that matter is found. There does exist in any community at all times—however the standard may vary from time to time—a general instinctive sense of what is decent and what is indecent, of what is clean and what is dirty . . . But the decency or the indecency, the cleanness or the dirtiness cannot depend on the nature of the subject-matter treated. Everything in human life is the object of legitimate human interest . . . the decency or indecency, the cleanness or dirtiness, must depend on the treatment, the handling of the subject-matter, on the general purport of the thing in question or the purpose which the thing itself discloses.

There is a vital importance in the nature of the *treatment,* as distinct from the nature of the *subject-matter* itself. "The question is a question less of the nature of the material than of the handling of the material."

Using this test, the Crown would be entitled to succeed on the issue of indecency if it has shown that ex. 1 as a whole handled its material in a manner that was indecent. The Crown expended much energy in this case in attempting to establish that portions of ex. 1 were indecent (or, for that matter, immoral or scurrilous), particularly portions of the article "Men Loving Boys Loving Men" and especially a few specific paragraphs thereof. (In my quotations from the article I endeavoured to include most if not all of the parts specified by the Crown.)

If obscenity was at issue, and if the test was that of *R. v. Hicklin* (1868), L.R. 3 Q.B. 360 at p. 371, the old common law obscenity test (which is no longer the law in Canada) of whether the matter complained of had a tendency to deprave and corrupt those whose minds were open to such influences and into whose hands the publication might fall—the result might have been different. But obscenity is not at issue and *Hicklin* is not the test. The test in my opinion is: how was the material handled?

To revert once again to the Supreme Court of Canada's philosophy in *Brodie* (the Lady Chatterley case)—the members of the majority of the Court, though reaching the conclusion each on slightly different grounds, each emphasized the writer's honesty of purpose and accepted the testimony of literary critics as to literary merit. That is to say, they looked at the total book and found that its total merit outweighed the eroticism of its explicit language. Taschereau, J., dissenting (see pp. 170-1 C.C.C., p. 692 S.C.R.), felt that the majority was concluding that it was the frame that made the picture. It appears to me that while I am by no means dealing with writing of the quality of "Lady Chatterley's Lover", nevertheless it is the total composition (of ex. 1) that does make the picture in this case. Great literature it may not be; artistic excellence it may not have—but the contents of ex. 1 (or, for that matter, simply of the article "Men Loving Boys Loving Men") have not been proved beyond a reasonable doubt to be indecent. Shocking and offensive to the community ex. 1 (and some of its contents) may be, disgusting and upsetting as well, even distasteful, sickening, unsettling, or appalling; but I find that indecent as a whole it is not.

3. SCURRILOUS

What, finally, of scurrility? The word in its modern sense appears to denote meanness or viciousness in attack and coarseness or foulness in language— i.e., using coarse or foul language to attack in a mean or vicious way. This would be abusive, insulting language. Synonyms of scurrilous as found in a modern day edition of Roget's Thesaurus include ridicule and derision, disrespect and disrepute, malediction and cursing, insulting and contemptuous, detraction, defamation, slander, calumny, libel, lampooning, invective. The language need not necessarily be low, coarse or vulgar: see Proceedings of Inquiry Special Board of Review, chaired by Wells, C.J.H.C. under the Post Office Regulations—*Re National States Rights Party et al.*— Ottawa 1964, unreported at pages 41-58 of the transcript of evidence of Professor George Johnston of Carelton University, a philologist.

It appears to me that there must be an object of the scurrility, if scurrility there be. "Scurrilous" is an adjective—it must modify something. Who or what would be the object in this case? C.J. Atkinson? I do not know who he is; no evidence of his identity, or of his past or present or actual existence was led. There is no more evidence of his existence as a person living or dead than there is of the existence as persons living or dead of Simon or Peter or their friends. For all the evidence disclosed, they may all be fictitious creations of the author Hannon. Language, to be abusive or insulting, must abuse or insult some one or some group or some entity. I do not think one can abuse or insult a fictitious person, and I do not think there can be scurrility in the air. In the absence of any evidence as to the actual existence of any person, group or entity allegedly abused or insulted, I cannot find ex. 1 scurrilous.

D. CONCLUSION

To a considerable extent tenable and credible arguments exist on both sides of each of the issues of community standards and the ordinary meanings of immorality, indecency or scurrility, and this case, if nothing else, is close to the border line. In reaching my conclusions, I have been guided by the comments of Freedman, J.A., in *Dominion News & Gifts (1962) Ltd. v. The Queen,* [1963] 2 C.C.C. 103, 40 C.R. 109, 42 W.W.R. 65 [at p. 117]:

> . . . in cases close to the border line, tolerance is to be preferred to proscription
> . . . To suppress the bad is one thing; to suppress the not so bad, or even the possibly good, is quite another.

As I have already indicated, evidence proferred by literary experts as to merit, or as was the case here by sociological experts as to the nature of the material and its acceptability to the average Canadian and by clerics as to their emotionally charged moral and religious convictions, is not of material assistance to the Court. It is for this reason that Freedman, J.A.'s thinking is important, for it puts a brake, as he implied, on the possibility that the trial Judge will erect his personal taste or prejudice into a legal principle. As a person, I am appalled and disgusted by the acts of Simon, Peter and the others—but my feelings are subjective—and as a Judge, I must judge with objectivity and with concern for the right of free discussion and dissemination of ideas unless there be a clear incitement to unlawful action.

Such clear incitement I cannot find in ex. 1—I find it rather to be a plea for understanding addressed to the willing and limited audience of subscribers to "The Body Politic", and I find the evidence adduced to be overwhelming in so far as the impossibility (by the written word or otherwise) of conversion to pedophilia of a non-pedophilic homosexual is concerned.

In the result, therefore, I, having found that s. 164 was not aimed at the distribution by mail of magazines or journals to subscribers, and that there is insufficient evidence to establish a community standard, and that the word "immoral" being undefined does not establish an acceptable area for lawful action, and that neither indecent nor scurrilous apply to either ex. 1 as a whole or the article therein primarily objected to by the Crown, it follows that each of the accused is not guilty of this charge and I so find. It is unnecessary to deal with the question of vicarious criminal liability of the officer directors for the acts of the corporation.

Charge dismissed.

Bonnelle Strickling,
with David Copp and Susan Wendell

Selected Bibliography of Legal Essays and Cases

A Book Named "John Cleland's Memoirs of a Woman of Pleasure," et al., v. Attorney General of Massachusetts, 383 U.S. 413 (1966).

Alpert, L. M. "Judicial Censorship and the Press." *Harvard Law Review* 52 (1938): 40-76.

American Civil Liberties Union. *American Civil Liberties Policy Guide.* Policy 4(f) (Supp. 1977).

Bates, F. "Pornography and the Expert Witness." *Criminal Law Quarterly* 20 (1978): 250-264.

Blasi. "The Checking Value in First Amendment Theory." *American Bar Foundation Research Journal* 521 (Samuel Pool Weaver Constitutional Law Essay) (1977).

Brodie, Dansky and Rubin v. R., [1962 S. C. R. 681; (1962) 32 D.L.R. (2d) 507].

Cahn, Edmond. "The Firstness of the First Amendment." *Yale Law Journal* 65 (1956): 464-481.

California v. La Rue, 409 U.S. 109 (1972).

Canada. House of Commons. *Report of the Standing Committee on Justice and Legal Affairs.* Including the Third Report to the House (Report on Pornography). Third Session of the Thirtieth Parliament, 1977-78.

Canada. Law Reform Commission. *Limits of Criminal Law: Obscenity, A Test Case.* Ottawa: Information Canada, 1975.

Canadian Association of University Teachers. "How About the Venus de Milo? A Brief on Obscenity and Pornography." 1979.

Caron, Yves. "The Legal Enforcement of Morality and the So-Called Hart-Devlin Controversy." *McGill Law Journal* 15 (1969): 9-47.

Clor, Harry. "Public Morality and Free Expression." *Hastings Law Journal* 28 (1977): 1305-1313.

Cohen v. California, 403 U.S. 15 (1971).

Davidow, Robert P., and O'Boyle, Michael. "Obscenity Laws in England and the United States: A Comparative Analysis." *Nebraska Law Review* 56 (1977): 249-87.

Director of Public Prosecutions v. Jordan, (1976) 3 All E.R. 775 F. Bates. *Criminal Law Quarterly* (1978): 250-64.

Drouin, J. *Rapport Preliminaire du Comite Interministeriel de Moralite Publique,* vol. 2: *Jurisprudence et difficultes d'application de la legislation Federale en materiere d'obscenite.* Ministere de la Justice, Gouvernment du Quebec, 1969.

Emerson, Thomas I. *The System of Freedom of Expression.* New York: Random House, 1970.

———. *Toward a General Theory of the First Amendment.* New York: Random House, 1966.

Erznoznik v. Jacksonville, 422 U.S. 205 (1975).

Federal Communications Commission v. Pacifica Foundation, 438 U.S. 726, (1978).

Fox, R.G. "Obscenity." *Alberta Law Review* 12 (1974): 172-235.

———. "Criminal Law-Survey Evidence of Community Standards in Obscenity Prosecutions." *Canadian Bar Review* 50 (1972): 315-330.

Frank. "Self Guardianship and Democracy." *The American Scholar* 16 (1947).

Frankel, Charles. "The Moral Environment of the Law." *Minnesota Law Review* 61 (1977): 921.

Friedman, Jane. "Zoning 'Adult' Movies." *Hastings Law Journal* 28 (1977): 1293-1304.

Ginzburg v. United States, 383 U.S. 463 (1966), 86 S. Ct. 942, 969 (1966).

Great Britain. *Committee on Obscenity and Film Censorship.* The Report. Chairman: Bernard Williams. London: Her Majesty's Stationery Office, 1979; Cambridge: Cambridge University Press.

Grey, Thomas. "Eros, Civilization and the Burger Court." *Law and Contemporary Problems* 43, 3 (1980): 83-100.

Griswold v. Connecticut, 381 U.S. 479 (1965).

Haward, L. "Admissibility of Psychological Evidence in Obscenity Cases." *Bull. British Psychological Society* 28 (1975).

Herbert v. Lando, 99 S. Ct. 1635 (1979).

The Hill-Link Minority Report of the Commission on Obscenity and Pornography. Washington, D.C.: Government Printing Office, 1970.

Hlookoff et al. v. City of Vancouver et al. (1976) 65 D.L.R. (2d) 71 (B.C.S.Ct.).

Jacobellis v. Ohio, 378 U.S. 184 (1964).

Kalven, Harry, Jr. "The Law of Defamation and the First Amendment." In *University of Chicago Conference on the Arts, Publishing and the Law (1952).*

———. "The Metaphysics of the Law of Obscenity." In *The Supreme Court Review, 1959,* edited by Philip P. Kurland. Chicago: University of Chicago Press, 1960.

Kaplan, A. "Obscenity as an Esthetic Category." *Law and Contemporary Problems* 20 (1955): 554-559.

Kaplan v. California;, 93 S. Ct. 2680 (1973).

Knuller v. Director of Public Prosecutions, [1972] 2 All E.R. 898.

Lasswell. "Censorship." *Encyclopedia of Social Science,* vol. 3. (1930).

Lockhart, W. B., and McClure, R. C. "Literature, the Law of Obscenity and the Constitution." *Minnesota Law Review* 38 (1954): 295-395.

―――. "Obscenity and the Courts." *Law and Contemporary Problems* 20 (1955): 587-607.

Loewy, Arnold. "A Better Test for Obscenity." *Hastings Law Review 28 (1977): 1315-1323.*

Lutes, Robert E. "Obscenity Laws in Canada." *University of New Brunswick Law Journal* 23 (1974): 30-52.

Meiklejohn, Alexander. "The First Amendment Is An Absolute." In *The Supreme Court Review, 1961,* edited by Philip B. Kurland. Chicago: University of Chicago Press, 1962, pp. 245-66.

Mishkin v. New York, 383 U.S. 502 (1966), 86 S. Ct. 958, 961 (1966).

Model Penal Code #207.10 (Official Draft, 1962).

Murphy, Earl F. "The Value of Pornography." *Wayne Law Review* 10 (1964): 655-680.

Nawy, Harold. "Obscenity." *Journal of Criminal Law, Criminology and Police Science* 62 (1971): 520-525.

―――. "Obscenity and the Arts," Special Issue. *Law and Contemporary Problems* 20 (1955): 531-688.

Paul, James C. N., and Schwartz, Murray L. *Federal Censorship: Obscenity in the Mail.* New York: The Free Press, 1961.

Price, David G. "The Role of Choice in a Definition of Obscenity." *The Canadian Bar Review* 57 (1979): 301-324.

Provincial News Co. et al. v. The Queen, [1976 1 S.C.R. 89, (1975) 53 D. L. R. (3d) 402.

R. v. Anderson and others, [1971 3 W. L. R. 939, [1971 3 All E. R. 1152 (C. A.) R. v. Ariadne Devel. Ltd. et al., (1974) 19 C.C.C. (2d) 49.

R. v. Cameron, (1966) 58 D. L. R. (2d) 486.

R. v. Coles Co. Ltd., (1965) 49 D. L. R. (2d) 34 (Ont.C.A.).

R. v. Dominion News and Gifts Ltd. [1963 2 C. C. C. 103, [1964 S. C. R. 251.

R. v. Graham and Hewitt, (1977) 45 C. C. C. (2d) 245 (Alb S.Ct.).

R. v. Knuller, [1971 3 All E.R. 314 (C.A.), [1972 2 All E.R. 898 (H.L.).

R. v. The MacMillan Co. of Canada Ltd., (1976) 31 C.C.C. (2d) 286, 72 D.L.R. (3d) 33 (Ont. Co. Ct.).

R. v. Neville, [1971 3 W.L.R. 939; under name R. v. Anderson and others, [1971 3 All E.R. 1152 (C.A.).

R. v. Oz Publications, under name R. v. Anderson and others.

R. v. Penguin Books Ltd., [1961 Crim. Law Review, 176.

R. v. Penthouse International Ltd. et al., (1979) 96 D. L. R. (3d) 735 (Ont. CA).

R. v. Pink Triangle Press et al., (1979) 45 C. C. C. (2d) 385 (Ont. Prov. Ct.); (1980) 51 C. C. C. (2d) 485 (Ont. Co. Ct.); under name R. v. Popert et al., (1981) 58 C. C. C. (2d) 505 (Ont. C. A.).

R. v. Pipeline News, (1972) 5 C. C. C. (2d) 71.

R. v. Popert et al., see R. v. Pink Triangle Press.

R. v. Prairie Schooner News Ltd. and Powers, (1971) 1 C. C. C. (2d) 251.

R. v. St. Clair, (1913) 21 C.C.C. 350 (Ont. C.A.).

R. v. Times Square Cinema Ltd., (1971) 4 C. C. C. (2d) 229.

Robertson, G. *Obscenity. An Account of Censorship Laws and Enforcement in England and Wales*. London: Weidenfeld and Nicolson, 1979.

Roe v. Wade, 410 U.S. 113 (1973).

Roth v. United States, 354 U.S. 476 (1957).

Schauer, F. F. *The Law of Obscenity*. Washington, D.C.: Bureau of National Affairs, 1976.

———. "The Return of Variable Obscenity?" *The Hastings Law Journal* 28 (1977): 1275-1291.

Schwartz, Louis B. "Morals Offenses and the Model Penal Code." *Columbia Law Review* 63 (1963): 669-686.

Shapiro, Martin. *Freedom of Speech: The Supreme Court and Judicial Review*. Englewood Cliffs, N.J.: Prentice-Hall, 1966.

Sharp, F. L. "Obscenity: Prurient Interests and the Law." *University of Toronto, Faculty of Law Review* 34 (1976): 244-254.

Southeastern Promotions Ltd. v. Conrad 420 U.S. 546 (1975).

Stanley v. Georgia, 394 U.S. 557 (1969).

State of Ohio v. Flynt, B-761618 (Com. Plea Hamilton County, Ohio 1976).

Tadman, Martin. "Obscenity, Civil Liberty and the Law." *Chitty's Law Journal* 21 (1973): 226-233.

United States. *Commission on Obscenity and Pornography*. The Report. Chairman: William B. Lockhart. Washington, D.C.: U.S. Government Printing Office, 1970; New York: Bantam Books, 1970.

United States v. Ginzberg, 224 F. Supp. 129 (E.D. Pa. 1963); aff'd, 338 F 2d, 12 (3rd Cir. 1964); aff'd, 383 U.S. 463 (1966).

United States v. One Book Called "Ulysses," 5 F. Supp. 182 (S.D.N.Y. 1933), aff'd. 72 F. 2d, 705 (2d Cir. 1934).

University of Chicago Law Review. "Comment: Censorship of Obscene Literature by Informal Government Action." 22 (1954-5): 216-233.

Wellington, H. "On Freedom of Expression." *Yale Law Journal* 88 (1979): 1105-1142.

Wessling, J. J. "Constitutional Law: A New Test for Determining Obscenity." *Glendale Law Review*.

Young v. American Mini-Theatres, Inc., 427 U.S. 50 (1976).

Abbreviations used:

All E. R.	—All England Law Reports
C. C. C.	—Canadian Criminal Cases
D. L. R.	—Dominion Law Reports (Can.)
F. Supp.	—Federal Supplement (U. S.)
F. 2d	—Federal Reporter, 2d Series (U. S.)
L. R.-Q. B.	—Law Reports — Court of Queen's Bench (U. K.)
S. Ct.	—Supreme Court Reporter (U. S.)
S. C. R.	—Supreme Court Reports (Can.)
U. S.	—United States Reports (U. S. Supreme Court)
W. L. R.	—Weekly Law Reports (U. K.)

Notes on the Contributors

FRED BERGER is Professor of Philosophy at the University of California, Davis. He has published in the area of social and political philosophy and on the philosophy of John Stuart Mill. He is editor of *Freedom of Expression*.

LORENNE M. G. CLARK formerly Professor of Philosophy and Criminology at the University of Toronto, co-authored *Rape: The Price of Coercive Sexuality*. She has written many articles on feminist philosophy. She is currently practicing law in Digby, Nova Scotia.

EDWARD DONNERSTEIN is Professor of Psychology at the University of Wisconsin. He is the author of numerous articles on pornography and aggression.

JOEL FEINBERG is Professor of Philosophy at the University of Arizona. His books include *Social Philosophy, Rights, Justice and the Bounds of Liberty,* and *Doing and Deserving.*

ANN GARRY is Professor of Philosophy at California State University, Los Angeles. She is the author of several articles on the philosophy of mind and feminist philosophy.

BERL KUTCHINSKY is Senior Lecturer at the Institute of Criminal Science, University of Copenhagen. He has authored many articles on the European experience with pornography and crime. He was a researcher for the 1971 U.S. Presidential Commission on Pornography and Obscenity.

NEIL M. MALAMUTH is Professor of Psychology at the University of Manitoba. His research is mainly on the relationship among pornography, aggression, and rape.

DIANA RUSSELL is Professor of Sociology at Mills College in Oakland, California. She is author of *The Politics of Rape.*

T. M. SCANLON is Professor of Philosophy at Princeton University and the author of articles in social and political philosophy.

DOLF ZILLMAN is Professor of Communications and Psychology at the Institute for Communication Research in Bloomington, Indiana. He is author of *Hostility and Aggression,* and numerous articles on factors influencing aggression.

COMMITTEE ON OBSCENITY AND FILM CENSORSHIP
CHAIRMAN: Bernard Williams has been Knightbridge Professor of Philosophy at the University of Cambridge and is Provost of King's College. His books include *Morality: An Introduction to Ethics, Moral Luck, Morality and the Emotions,* and *Utilitarianism: for and against* (with J. J. C. Smart).

OTHER MEMBERS:
B. Hooberman, esq.
His Honour Judge John Leonard, Q.C.
Richard Matthews, esq., CBE, QPM
David Robinson, esq.
Ms. Sheila Rothwell
Professor A. W. B. Simpson
Dr. Anthony Storr
Mrs. M. J. Taylor
The Right Reverend John Tinsley
Miss Polly Toynbee
Professor J. G. Weightman
V. A. White, esq., MBE

PAPERBACKS AVAILABLE FROM PROMETHEUS BOOKS

SCIENCE AND THE PARANORMAL

____ESP & Parapsychology: A Critical Re-evaluation   *C.E.M. Hansel* $9.95

____Extra-Terrestrial Intelligence   *James L. Christian, editor*   7.95

____Flim-Flam!   *James Randi*   9.95

____The Fringe of the Unknown   *L. Sprague de Camp*   8.95

____Objections to Astrology   *L. Jerome & B. Bok*   4.95

____The Psychology of the Psychic   *D. Marks & R. Kammann*   9.95

____Philosophy & Parapsychology   *j. Ludwig, editor.*   10.95

____Paranormal Borderlands of Science   *Kendrick Frazier, editor*   13.95

____Superstition and the Press   *Curtis D. MacDougall*   12.95

____The Truth About Uri Geller   *James Randi*   8.95

HUMANISM

____Ethics Without God   *K. Nielsen*   6.95

____Humanist Alternative   *Paul Kurtz, editor*   5.95

____Humanist Ethics   *Morris Storer, editor*   9.95

____Humanist Funeral Service   *Corliss Lamont*   4.95

____Humanist Manifestos I & II   1.95

____Humanist Wedding Service   *Corliss Lamont*   2.95

____Humanistic Psychology   *Welch, Tate, Richards, editors*   10.95

____Moral Problems in Contemporary Society   *Paul Kurtz, editor*   7.95

____Secular Humanist Declaration   1.95

____Voice in the Wilderness   *Corliss Lamont*   5.95

____Rabbi and Minister   *Carl Hermann Voss*   7.95

LIBRARY OF LIBERAL RELIGION

____Facing Death and Grief   *George N. Marshall*   7.95

____Living Religions of the World   *Carl Hermann Voss*   4.95

PHILOSOPHY & ETHICS

____Animal Rights and Human Morality   *Bernard Rollin*   9.95

____Art of Deception   *Nicholas Capaldi*   6.95

____Beneficent Euthanasia   *M. Kohl, editor*   9.95

____Contemporary Analytic and Linguistic Philosophies   *E. D. Klemke*   13.95

____Esthetics Contemporary   *Richard Kostelanetz, editor*   12.95

____Ethics and the Search for Values   *L. Navia and E. Kelly, editors*   14.95

____Freedom, Anarchy, and the Law   *Richard Taylor*   8.95

____Freedom of Choice Affirmed   *Corliss Lamont*   4.95

____Fullness of Life   *Paul Kurtz*   6.95

____Having Love Affairs   *Richard Taylor*   8.95

____Humanhood: Essays in Biomedical Ethics   *Joseph Fletcher*   9.95

____Infanticide and the Value of Life   *Marvin Kohl, editor*   9.95

____Introductory Readings in the Philosophy of Science   *Klemke, Hollinger, Kline, editors*   13.95

____Invitation of Philosophy   *Capaldi, Kelly, Navia, editors*   13.95

____Journeys Through Philosophy (Revised)   *N. Capaldi & L. Navia, editors*   14.95

____Philosophy: An Introduction   *Antony Flew*   7.95

____Problem of God   *Peter A. Angeles*   9.95

____Psychiatry and Ethics   *Rem B. Edwards, editor*   12.95

____Responsibilities to Future Generations   *Ernest Partridge, editor*   9.95

____Reverse Discrimination   *Barry Gross, editor*   9.95

____Thinking Straight   *Antony Flew*   5.95

____Thomas Szasz: Primary Values and Major Contentions   *Vatz & Weinberg, editors*   9.95